ATHENA

ZODIAC

lovers

HarperCollins*Publishers*

HarperCollins*Publishers*

First published in Australia in 2003
by HarperCollins*Publishers* Pty Limited
ABN 36 009 913 517
A member of the HarperCollins*Publishers* (Australia) Pty Limited Group
www.harpercollins.com.au

Copyright © International Celebrities Pty Limited 2003
Illustrations Copyright © Stella Danalis 2003

HarperCollins*Publishers*
25 Ryde Road, Pymble, Sydney NSW 2073, Australia
31 View Road, Glenfield, Auckland 10, New Zealand
77–85 Fulham Palace Road, London W6 8JB, United Kingdom
Hazelton Lanes, 55 Avenue Road, Suite 2900, Toronto, Ontario M5R 3L2
and 1995 Markham Road, Scarborough, Ontario M1B 5M8 Canada
10 East 53rd Street, New York NY 10022, USA

National Library of Australia Cataloguing-in-Publication data:

Starwoman, Athena.
   Zodiac lovers.
   ISBN 0 7322 7475 3.
   1. Astrology. 2. Love – Miscallanea. 3. mate selection – Miscellanea
   I. Title
133.5864677

Illustrations by Stella Danalis
Back cover photograph by Bruce Cratsley; internal photograph by Robert Butcher
Cover design by Christa Edmonds, HarperCollins Design Studio
Internal design by Judi Rowe, HarperCollins Design Studio
Typeset by HarperCollins in 45 Helvetica Light 9.5/14
Printed and bound in Australia by Griffin Press on 79gsm Bulky Paperback White

6 5 4 3 2 1   03 04 05 06

To Venus,
the Goddess of Love

Credits and Thanks

A huge thank you to my wonderful, sexy soul mate John Demartini. You've taught me what unconditional love is all about (and a whole lot more). I am blessed to have you as my luscious Sagittarian star-mate!

To Elizabeth Helmore and Kylie Rothero, my two creative Gemini assistants. You are the best! Thank you for those wonderful times we shared at Main Beach. Those were magic moments in time. Those walks on the beach, copious cups of tea and bickies, and best of all, the hilarious and most informative 'master-mind' chitchats. It was fun sharing secrets about our personal and intimate love lives, all in the name of astro-research!

To Helen Littleton, my Taurus publishing goddess at HarperCollins. Thank you Helen for being in my life and playing such a profound role in it. This book would not exist without you. You are definitely its fairy-publishing godmother.

Last but definitely not least, a big thank you to Sandra Davies, my Scorpio editor at HarperCollins who magnificently put the bits and pieces of this book together so that it became a complete product. Whew!

Dear Starlovers

'What's love got to do with it?' Everything — I believe! For me, love is the most magnificent and intoxicating of all feelings. Falling in love, and out of love, has shaped my life, my actions, and my highs and lows more than anything else. And what befalls all of us in our love lives plays a huge part in developing who we are and what becomes of us!

Love is a topic close to my emotional Cancerian heart and it is such a paramount driving force, which is why I've written *Zodiac Lovers*. What follows is my personal view on the relationship forged between each zodiac couple. You'll find that some write-ups run for longer than others. This arises because certain couplings of zodiac signs are more complicated to explain and so demand a greater coverage.

This book uses the principles of astrology to glimpse the celestial love realms, but every relationship has its own uniqueness. While astrology provides wonderful insights into others and ourselves, exceptions apply to every zodiac rule, especially when it comes to love. So what works for one star couple may not work for the next.

Whoever you are and whoever you're in love with, I hope you enjoy the relationship insights offered in *Zodiac Lovers*.

May the force of love be with you,

Athena

Star Sign Couplings

aries aries aries aries aries aries aries
aries aries aries aries aries aries aries
aries aries aries aries aries aries aries
aries aries aries aries aries aries aries
aries aries aries aries aries aries aries
aries aries aries aries aries aries aries
aries aries aries aries aries aries aries
aries aries aries aries aries aries aries
aries aries aries aries aries aries aries

aries aries aries aries aries aries aries
aries aries aries aries aries aries aries
aries aries aries aries aries aries aries
aries aries aries aries aries aries aries
aries aries aries aries aries aries aries
aries aries aries aries aries aries aries
aries aries aries aries aries aries aries
aries aries aries aries aries aries aries
aries aries aries aries aries aries aries

ARIES

[21 march – 20 april]

romantic pursuit: the thrill of the moment

romantic vibration: headstrong and dramatic

secret love desire: to be the constant centre of their

lover's attention, even if they don't do the same themselves

element: fire

planetary ruler: mars

symbol: the ram

quality: cardinal (= activity)

colours: carmine, red, scarlet

gem: amethyst

best companions: leo and sagittarius

strongest virtues: resilience, loyalty and daring

traits to improve: impatience, over-

reactions and ability to create unnecessary dramas

deepest desire: to gain recognition and

approval from others

Aries celebrities

Alec Baldwin, Andrew Lloyd Webber, Aretha Franklin, Ashley Judd, Belinda Emmet, Celine Dion, Chaka Khan, Charlie Chaplin, Claire Danes, David Beckham, David Cassidy, Dennis Quaid, Diana Ross, Eddie Murphy, Elle MacPherson, Ellen Barkin, Elton John, Emma Thompson, Eric Clapton, Ewan McGregor, Francis Ford Coppola, Gary Oldman, George Benson, Gregory Peck, Harry Houdini, Heath Ledger, Jackie Chan, James Caan, James Woods, Jennifer Capriati, Joan Crawford, Julian Lennon, Kate Hudson, Leonardo da Vinci, Lucy Lawless, Magda Szubanski, Marcel Marceau, Mariah Carey, Mark Skaife, Marlon Brando, Marsha Mason, Matthew Broderick, Matthew Modine, Paloma Picasso, Peter O'Brien, Quentin Tarantino, Reese Witherspoon, Robin Wright-Penn, Robert Downey Jr, Rolf Harris, Rosie O'Donnell, Russell Crowe, Sarah Jessica Parker, Sarah Michelle Gellar, Steve McQueen, Steven Tyler, Timothy Dalton, Tommy Haas, Victoria Beckham, Warren Beatty

ARIES — ARIES relationship

The *'Struck by a love thunderbolt'* relationship

STAR ARIES–ARIES COUPLE
Sarah Jessica Parker and Matthew Broderick

Watch out! When these two star-mates get together and the love bug bites them, cosmic sparks start flying! You can bet that this will turn into a dramatic, romantic relationship exchange. Why do two Aries together become so romantically volatile? Because this zodiac combination is destined to be explosive, passionate and dramatic. Love fires (the type that may burn right out of control) are automatically ignited when these two fiery, passionate lovers match up. The red-hot planet Mars is their ruling planet and it stirs up the cosmic wavelengths between them. Mars is the planet aligned with passion, lust and sex. So no wonder when two Aries fall in love, the love-thunderbolts they feel can hit the top of the Passion Richter Scale. But eek! Their ruling planet Mars not only contributes to their lust, sex and an overload of feelings of intense passion, but also stirs up tension too. That's why there can be heaps of yelling, competition, jealousy and otherwise 'warring' type energy operating between these two as well!

With planet Mars running their affairs, certainly the Aries–Aries relationship has everything cosmically to make it exciting, passionate, explosive, challenging and even dangerous. So, when this relationship is hot, it is *really* hot. But when it goes cold, it can be close to tragic. Consequently, this relationship could easily be one that is all about breaking up and making up. Sadly, there may even be times when violence erupts between them. Without sensitive handling and lots of compassion and patience, this relationship can easily fall into a massive heart-tugging, relationship tailspin. And when this relationship slips into a feisty fighting-fest, it may just as quickly crash and burn as it has burned sparkling and bright. Consequently, it can take a lotta love to keep this relationship operating harmoniously.

aries

Aries woman—Aries man

 The *'If you don't do things my way . . . watch out!'* relationship

This is the 'hit by a super-love thunderbolt' and 'can't wait to get you into the cot and kiss you all over and more' relationship of the zodiac. When either gender of the Aries zodiac sign falls in love, particularly with another Aries, rest assured this is not a relationship that is destined to go through a smooth-sailing, simple 'hello, how are you?' exchange. Quite the opposite! It is written in the stars that this exchange is meant to be a high octave, adrenaline thumping, super-charged confusing, emotional, psychological and intellectual energy exchange. This combined zodiac energy can be super-buzzy, but a relationship that eventually ends up becoming a major emotional blowout too. Because of the volatile forces astrologically in force between this couple, the occasion of their first meeting often has a powerful overwhelming effect on both (or one) of them. Their meeting (if the chemistry ignites between them rapidly) can turn into the type of thing that scrambles their minds, ruffles their emotions and spins their plans, scatters other relationships and general everyday reality all over the place. They often feel like they have truly been hit by a love-thunderbolt. They are *thunderstruck*!

But that's only at the beginning! There's a long way to go before they reach relationship heaven. And this couple often discovers that jumping passionately into this relationship and merging their lives together, also involves jumping headfirst into all kinds of unusual dramas. For example, they may each have current relationship entanglements, and because they are involved with other partners, that leads to unhappy side-effects around them. Or they may be caught up in some other obligations or problems they need to overcome to be together. My point is, this relationship is seldom a simple, easy-going one. Usually there are complications, but perhaps that's exactly what this couple enjoys somewhat about being together. Indeed, sometimes the fact that they may be tasting 'forbidden fruit' by being together, is the spark that can make this relationship 'sizzle' more intensely. As Aries naturally love risky business, their dalliances in forbidden areas of relationship can be what adds more passion when one or both of them are already 'spoken' for. For any Aries, there's something about the thrill of being out of line, breaking the rules or doing what they shouldn't that appeals hugely to the Arian 'I love to take a risk' soul. Even if both partners are free to be with whomever they want, there's usually something a little reckless or dangerous in the way this couple plays their romantic games. Possibly they live too fast, spend too much money when they are together, laugh in the face of their responsibilities, or get into some kind of dangerous pastime; but usually when an Aries woman mates up with an Aries man either upfront or behind the scenes, there's some continuous highs and lows or other forms of drama going down.

There is also a broad range of potential possibilities between them (more than most couples of the zodiac) for their relationship to turn into a power struggle. With the argumentative planet 'it's my way or the highway' Mars as their joint ruler, it is important for this couple to remind themselves that they are both naturally egocentric, 'what I want is what's important' types of individuals, who are impulsive, wilful and petulant. As I mentioned earlier, their ruling planet Mars rules aggression as well as passion, and consequently their playful sexual or other exchanges can often border on roughhouse exchanges. It is not unusual for an Aries man and woman to play tomboy-type games (silly games at times) like flick each other with towels as they walk by each other in the bathroom; or bump into each other, playfully, as they walk down the street. They like to have continuous physical exchanges taking place between them, and they like to stay in each other's consciousness so they'll pull pranks or do something startling to attract this attention. Naturally, these physical exchanges can backfire occasionally and get out of hand, and turn into dangerous exchanges where somebody ends up getting either their feelings hurt or even incurring a physical injury.

The Aries couple is not your usual couple in any way, shape or form. Certainly don't be fooled by their appearances either. Although she may look like Little Red Riding Hood, and he may seem to be her perfect Big Bad Wolf, the Aries woman is not a docile, passive, ready to be his ever-devoted-slave-type of female member of the zodiac. She's an alpha female of the zodiac because she's born under one of its cardinal signs. She's a leader and a very independent soul. Indeed, she may be childlike, and very cute and cuddly at times, but at her core she is a liberated, independent, action-oriented and self-willed woman. Even if she flutters her eyelashes and looks defenseless and vulnerable, she's acting! Usually she likes to play the role of leader, and holds a strong opinion about what she wants for herself, her mate and everything else that's happening around her.

aries

Similarly, the Aries man is very determined to be exactly who he wants to be and he doesn't take criticism, advice or other people's opinions too kindly. So this couple may spend a lot of time telling the other one what they think and not too keen to hear that their partner thinks differently to them! Certainly over time this couple often discover that there isn't much room to compromise, and work out joint ideas or meet in the middle. So unless they learn to be extremely flexible with each other, this couple often finds that they end up 'head-to-head' fighting or jostling over trivial issues (crazy stuff like who's turn it is to turn off the bedroom lights); and that the true affection they feel for each other becomes lost in the pent-up energies created from their frustrations when the other one won't budge. This can be the couple that, through foolish pride or wilfulness, tends to sulk or turn away from each other, at the very times they need to kiss and make up. Stubbornness can mar their romantic relationship very quickly if they allow their desire to do everything the way they want to do it, without sharing or giving into anybody else's wishes.

Neither one of these individuals likes to lose face or feel they aren't running the show. Being adaptable, compliant and patient doesn't come naturally to Aries, but given time — and because love can conquer all — these are traits this couple can teach each other; and they'll need to for their wonderful loving relationship to survive. If they stay together for a long time, they'll have to realise that on certain issues (big or small) one of them will have to 'give' ground to the other, because neither can continue to rule the roost or hold the ruling vote all the time. A fair share of 'who calls the shots' is required.

If they can drum up some patience and learn some lessons about diplomacy, they'll pass through the tempestuous passion years of their relationship and move onto a more serious married life. Now, when they have children this couple really starts to discover the rewards of their union. They generally love being with their kids (being kids at heart themselves), and have just as much fun as their children doing all the things that kids do — like playing sports or games, going camping, learning to Rollerblade, getting a pet and mastering windsurfing. While the Aries woman might sometimes not keep the most tidy home and the Aries man may have to be cajoled frequently to mow the lawn; with their family, the highly prized family cat and dog around them, this Aries–Aries family is often one of the most upbeat, young-at-heart and happening families in their neighbourhood.

ARIES — TAURUS relationship

The *'Hey! Are you for real?'* relationship

STAR ARIES–TAURUS COUPLE
Victoria Beckham and David Beckham

Like East meeting West (and sometimes never the twain will meet), there are many differences to work through when these two very different zodiac signs start up a relationship. They're from two very different worlds — although their star signs sit next to each other on the zodiac wheel — but nevertheless their differences in outlook, opinion and desire is similar to the blending of two very different cosmic, zodiac cultures. This gap or span between them can sometimes make the relationship work (because they intrigue each other) or other times break it! But whatever it turns out to be it will certainly be a full-on learning experience for both partners. Dynamic Aries is a fire sign. They thrive on adventure, passion and excitement. They love risks, danger and experimentation. However, 'take things slowly' is the motto for earth sign Taurus. They thrive on living the easy life, set their sights on creating peace and quiet, and will go out of their way to avoid drama. Add these two totally different zodiac signs together and effectively you get a green-light zodiac effect saying 'go, go, go', and a stop-signal zodiac effect saying 'stop immediately'. This stop–go energy is what will set this couple's pace through life, and this adds up to a bumpy ride, but a ride that will take them on many an unusual journey.

What effect does that stop–start energy have on their long-term relationship? Well it will both help and hinder this couple's progress, contentment and communication. When it hinders them, this relationship will sometimes take on that strange feeling you experience when trying to drive a car with the handbrake on. You know immediately that something isn't quite right because you're going on a very jerky and bumpy ride to nowhere. When it helps them however, this same energy will equilibriate and balance them, with Taurus providing Aries with some stabilising power, and Aries providing Taurus with extra vim, vigour and enthusiasm.

Aries woman — Taurus man

 The *'It's certainly not easy loving you'* relationship

Put a safety belt around your heart. You'll need it. When the Aries woman teams up with a Taurus man, two of the zodiac's mighty passion planets join forces. Venus, the love and romance planet, rules Taurus; and Mars, the passion, lust and libido planet, rules Aries. Consequently passion, love and sexual adventures seem to naturally become parts of the lives of this couple. Between them — if the chemistry is ignited with its fullest potential — the tingly intoxicating buzz of sexual adrenaline is often in the air. But having sexual sparks flying is no guarantee that this couple will hit it off in the longer term. In fact, many one-night stands occur between an Aries woman and a Taurus man, more than permanent, long-lasting relationships. They can often handle and enjoy each other much more over a shorter time span than a long-term one.

While they may find each other sexually attractive over the short term, the personality traits of these two star signs are very different. Ms Aries is a gal in a hurry. She believes that even immediate gratification takes too long, whilst Mr Taurus does all he can to live his life on step — one moment, one careful step at a time. So does this relationship have true staying power? Well that can turn out to be a tricky question; yet in many cases for this couple the answer is simple: this relationship will go the distance, only if this couple works (sometimes very hard) at helping it to go the distance. Expecting things to fall neatly into place when these two strong-willed, somewhat egocentric individuals are concerned would be based more on fantasy than reality.

Why will they need to be prepared to weather the stormy times as well as sunny ones together? Well, any brief observation of Ms Aries reveals that she is the super quick-moving woman of the zodiac. With Mars as her ruler (the passion, take-action planet) she leaps into things and takes enormous risks before she even considers the consequences. Even in relationships, she's likely to be the one who makes the first move on Mr Taurus and initiates this relationship. She is often the go-getter, aggressor in any situation (even if she hides this aspect of her personality behind a gentle veneer). At her core, this Ram gal isn't shy, she isn't insecure, in fact, she's an independent, powerful person and in many ways she's both secure and an extremely confident gal. She's also very complex, and what's more difficult often for her Taurus guy to deal with, she's highly self-sufficient!

At least when Cupid's arrow hits her in the mating–dating game, without qualms Ms Aries is often very straightforward. She may even wear her heart on her sleeve. She's also prepared to put herself, her pride, or possibly even her reputation on the line to capture the heart of someone who appeals to her. In fact, it is this go-getter approach that comes naturally to her that can sometimes work wonders in attracting or winning Mr Take-Your-Time Taurus. On the other hand, her gung-ho approach may frighten him away.

Ms Aries is also often super-smart and can play marvellous romantic games when she's tracking down her Mr Right. If she senses that Mr Taurus is her man, she also probably 'intuits' that he is a man who doesn't like to be hassled. If she wises up to this side of his character, she may decide to play the waiting game where he's concerned, and may even play hard to get. But that's a rare occasion in the dating and mating habits of the Aries female. Usually this impetuous gal runs out of romantic patience pretty quickly. So because she may really want this relationship to work out, Ms Aries may initially be on her best behaviour (remember this is at least, at first).

As an example, it is possible that before they become a couple, she may have already known him a long time. Possibly they work together or they go to the same places — but once they've met, he may be unaware of the chemistry between them. If he acts more of a friend than a lover, Ms Aries often intuitively knows that she needs to be courageous and make herself noticed. Sometimes she 'picks up' on his steadfast approach to life and she becomes acutely aware that if she waits for him to make the first move, chances are she'll be booking into the retirement village before he makes his play. So being an Aries gal with a fiery, feisty nature, she'll either ask him out, make sure she gets him into a position where he can't avoid contact with her, or she'll play a seductive game to get him interested. Wear the 'come to bed' shoes with the red dress, and make sure Mr Taurus has had a few glasses of vino before she flutters her eyes at him too noticeably.

As she's laying her trail of seduction, what's Mr Taurus doing while all this dating and mating manoeuvring is going on? Probably what he always does and that is, suit himself. Whether he's working, playing or dating, underneath it all Mr Taurus is quite self-sufficient and he is extremely self-serving too (usually). He has a sense of what is good and what isn't good in life; he knows his habits (the good, bad and ugly ones) and sticks to them (unless they are the kinds of habit that eventually could kill him, then he may make an effort to break them).

He maintains certain boundaries and regularities in his lifestyle because they provide him with structure. He has his favourite foods, pursuits and friends, and he lives in a comfort zone specifically designed to keep him happy and fulfil his needs. So what Mr Taurus doesn't want, is some gal coming along and messing things up, unless he's really ready for a true, long-term relationship with kids, dogs, garden and the rest. Then he can become quite a matchmaker and go out looking for Ms Right himself.

Now if he's looking for a partner, when he meets her he may be excited, inspired and enchanted by Ms Aries, as she's such a lively, wonderful, enchanting gal. But there's also a side to his nature that is wary of anything that is lively, wonderful and enchanting because (eek!) it could threaten his everyday calm world. However, if the libido energy between this couple is running red hot, he'll forget any feelings of fear or trepidation about getting involved with this bright lassie, and he'll go off to have a wild, outrageous, romantic adventure with her. Depending on how adventurous, passionate and illuminating their first meeting or encounter together is, this experience will make him decide:

> to date her again
> to avoid her like the plague
> to forget she ever existed.

Should he decide on the last choice then he's quite comfortable to do just that. Next time he sees Ms Aries, he truly may not even remember her name. But, if he does decide to continue the relationship, then you can almost bet on it that most likely, he is *extremely* interested. Unless it is for some obscure reason or a special occasion, Mr Taurus doesn't do things to keep other people happy. He doesn't see it as his role to be Mr Nice Guy who everybody likes, he'd much rather suit himself. After all, the most self-indulgent planet of the zodiac Venus rules him. So if Ms Aries and Mr Taurus actually do make it for a second date (and many Aries woman–Taurus men relationships don't make it that far), there's something special happening. But that doesn't mean the chase or romantic game is over. Expect some strange relationship games to be played, because whether in the short or long term of their relationship both Ms Aries and Mr Taurus are definitely likely to give each other an ongoing romantic run for their money.

During the initial courtship days of this relationship it will be Ms Aries who needs to be on her best behaviour because Mr Taurus will be scrutinising her carefully. It isn't wise for her to throw too many tantrums or make too many demands. Maybe further down the path of their relationship she'll be able to be more self-expressive, but at the beginning she may need to keep a 'lid on her explosive or expressive nature'. Given time, a lot of manoeuvring and lots of passionate and sensual love making (something that is probably a most important part of this dynamic coupling), this couple may work through any personality differences, other problems or lifestyle obstacles. If these two compromise a little on their normal self-centred approach to life and meet each other half-way, then they'll have a fulfilling life together. Best of all, they'll learn something wonderful from each other: the joy of settling down into marital bliss and sharing a unique time that will constantly keep them guessing what the other is truly capable of doing.

Aries man — Taurus woman

 The *'Lead me straight to the bedroom'* relationship

Cupid's mischievous love-arrows cause all kinds of crazy things to happen when they are targeted towards an Aries guy and a Taurus gal. But crazy or not, there's certain to be loads of attraction between them. The problem is that any relationship flaws that affect this duo's feelings towards each other are likely to be major ones, rather than quiet, subtle ones.

In their favour, this couple has loads in common with each other because their star signs are next-door neighbours on the zodiac wheel. This connection provides them with some flowover energy. Plus, they are both ruled by two of the most potent relationship forces of the zodiac — the two love and passion planets. Mr Aries is ruled by the zodiac's most virile, lusty, masculine planet Mars, and Ms Taurus is ruled by the zodiac's most seductive, alluring, feminine planet Venus. If these two meet and sexual sparks ignite, they'll probably go 'missing in action' in the bedroom for a long time. But passion between these two signs often burns out just as quickly as it erupted; and Mr Aries, who doesn't like to be bossed around, may get a bad dose of the wanderlust if Ms Taurus decides to get too bossy or clingy.

While there is a great chance that this Aries guy and Taurus gal relationship will become a real successful love story, there are also odds against their romantic interest in each other continuing beyond the first few dates. If things go wrong between them, this union could quickly turn into a romantic stressfest. To their stubborn credit, if these two decide to enter into a relationship with each other — even if it causes them both some dramas — one thing is certain, they'll give each other a fine old time of it and be powerfully affected by what occurs between them.

If these two can pass their initial dating and mating tests and other challenges or uncertainties, they will both discover that Mr Aries has a great deal to offer Ms Taurus, and vice versa. He is exciting; and she loves his enthusiasm. He livens up her existence, keeps her on her emotional toes and constantly surprises her, all special components of life that Ms Taurus desires and needs to keep her stimulated, learning and inspired. She, on the other hand, has many useful characteristics that will serve him well, too. She calms Mr Aries down (something he often needs). She gives him a solid, reliable base of affection, emotional support, home and social life and also keeps him just a little under her steady-handed control. If she plays her support role well, knows when to speak up or say nothing, she can prove to be a fantastic asset in his life (and vice versa).

Where this couple can really go wrong is their over-zealous expectations regarding control, trust and any jealousy issues. Being both ruled by the passion planets of Venus and Mars, all hell breaks loose if these two come to loggerheads about old lovers, new lovers, potential lovers, flirtations or even photos or letters from past romantic histories they may find hidden away. She, in particular, can be very miffed about any past relationships Mr Aries has had (and he's likely to have had quite a few). She may tear up old photographs of him with another gal, even if it was the girl next door holding hands with him when they were only three years old.

Mr Aries is definitely no easy-going, light-hearted guy to deal with himself if he thinks his Fair Lady Taurus may have given her heart to any other fella before him. The fact that she has had previous suitors messes with his huge ego. Mr Aries can be super-unrealistic and unbearable when it comes to what's OK for him to do, and what's not OK for her. He should have a busy romantic past; she should have nothing much to speak of or look back upon. He makes up his rules of the relationship as it goes along, and generally the rules that he wishes to set down for this relationship are all (unfairly) written in his favour (naturally)! He can be cantankerous, moody and very childish about her past associations; and even have a fight (with fisticuffs) with her old boyfriend if they meet each other under the wrong circumstances. And heaven help her if he catches her smiling at the wrong person at the wrong time. He can be very erratic about reality, fidelity and romantic connections. He can spin tales, make up excuses and jump to all the wrong conclusions, stirring up a relationship hornet's nest and creating all the wrong kind of energy to affect the outcome of a relationship exchange. And she can be a stubborn, unyielding individual as well, so expect this relationship to be a very volatile one. However, if real romance is there, this volatility (instead of causing trouble) will just make their romantic connection all the more passionate, exciting and alluring.

Another issue that may cause them grief is working through who calls the shots. With this volatile combination, it is important that both partners are prepared to compromise, and that's probably not something either will feel easily comfortable doing. So expect to go through some power struggles on both small or big issues if you are a couple born under these two headstrong, stubborn and wilful signs.

ARIES — GEMINI relationship

The *'Living life in the fast lane'* relationship

STAR ARIES–GEMINI COUPLE
Warren Beatty and Annette Bening

Get ready to hear wedding bells peal, throw the confetti, and attach the old shoes to the back of the honeymoon car. This zodiac pairing has high potential for walking down the aisle and saying 'I do'. Why are they so suited? It's because astrologically, the Aries and Gemini relationship has a great deal 'going for it'. They share heaps of things in common. Both are curious, enthusiastic and love to chitchat the day and night away. In fact, there are enough similarities in force between these two to enable them to merrily tune into each other's mental universe. Although they have things in common, it doesn't ensure they are a perfect match. Yet hopefully, even their imperfections or oppositions to each other will prompt and arouse their continuing curiosity in each other. As much as they make believe they 'know each other well', there'll be times when their responses or actions will come as a surprise to their partner. One of the main things going for this relationship is that there's sufficient difference between them to keep them both constantly entertained by each other and guessing what the other is likely to come up with next.

A big plus for them too is that they both enjoy living life in the fast lane. Usually they both function on one speed of thinking, operating and decision-making — and that's fast! And while their volatile ability to make quantum leaps might scare another less go-getter sign of the zodiac, in their zodiac combination, this fast-moving action station approach works in their favour. Aries and Gemini tend to be adventurous and excited about new things, whereas many other star signs place a greater value on the past or the security of established conditions. So, if the chemistry and timing is right, when Cupid fires his romantic arrows and projects them towards an Aries and Gemini couple, often a great team is formed.

Aries woman — Gemini man

 The *'I'm not quite sure exactly where this is all going'* relationship

Tread warily Gemini man and don't assume you are in control of the action between you and Ms Aries, even if you live with her for fifty years. Underneath her charming exterior, you've got one helluva woman! You'll need to keep your wits about you constantly to deal with her ebbs and tides of emotion, outlook and attitude. Upset her or make her angry and there will be a high price to be paid — and you're likely to be the one paying it.

This Ram gal of the zodiac has the powerful planet Mars as her ruler, so she's volatile, explosive and dramatic — all qualities with which 'take action and take no prisoners' Mars provides her. She is inconsistent as well (just as you are), so there are many occasions when the Aries woman is not an easy woman to understand. This ability to be misunderstood also applies to Ms Aries herself, as there'll definitely be times when she doesn't really understand herself to boot! Those who (sometimes anxiously) gravitate in the world around her usually wait pensively to see if she's in a good or bad mood before they bring up sensitive topics for discussion, or offer an opinion her way. She's a firebrand and she isn't afraid to say what's on her mind, even if what's on her mind should be carefully censored before being voiced.

Now she's a real starwoman on all kinds of levels but this side to her character is also complicated by astro-forces beyond her control. Being ruled by the masculine planet Mars creates conflicts when it comes to the way she expresses her feminine self. It also sometimes unbalances her more sensitive, intuitive, nurturing side because Mars is the aggressive, hunter (not gatherer) planet of the zodiac. Its energy needs to be expressed not repressed and that's why those born under its domain, act on impulse not so much on instinct. It is the planet Mars that gives Ms Aries much more chutzpah, independence and stronger will and desire than possibly any sweet little gal truly needs. Fortunately for Ms Aries she's been born with this 'sense of power', so she's used to it. She applies this dynamic male-oriented energy to her advantage (without even knowing it). She channels it to make herself more powerful, courageous and independent — and this ability gives her an edge over the other women of the zodiac, and sometimes also over her partner. Now when the Aries gal meets up with a Gemini guy — her innate Mars (masculine) energy, often serves both of them wonderfully well.

Why does it serve them both? Because where Ms Aries has a stronger planet than she possibly needs motivating her personality development, lifestyle and trends, Mr Gemini has the opposite. He has the more adaptable, easy-going planet, Mercury, helping him to carve out his destiny. Mercury is the planet of concepts, communication and dots and dashes rather than solid, bold lines. So compared to Ms Aries, he is in the lightweight planetary zone. Mr Gemini has a more cerebral planet than a physical one affecting his personality. His ruler, the androgynous planet Mercury, is one that is most happy to spin our mental wheels and encourages us to enjoy thinking about things rather than going out and actually doing them. Mercury isn't all that interested in making us sexy, aggressive, or driven by desires. Mr Gemini is still likely to be sexy, but sexy in an unusual creative or possibly kinky way.

What turns on his sexual radio is often that rush of energy that the enthusiastic, go-getter, bold and daring Ms Aries has to offer, not to mention her passionate sexual energy flow. Usually in courtship or dating times, Ms Aries is more direct, raunchy and adventurous in her love pursuits than Mr Gemini. She is often able to express in a relationship what Mr Gemini has only thought about expressing!

So Ms Aries has a definite role to play when she meets up with her perfect Gemini man. Usually, she not only changes his life, turns him onto new desires, instincts and passions, but she also inspires and encourages him to be more dynamic and (eek!) even more sexy, go-getting and masculine. It may be a surprise to hear that many a Gemini man is lacking in these go-getting departments because he may seem to be all man on the outside, but there's always the little boy, a pensive thinker (or dreamer) lurking underneath his façade. He often has insecurities or weaknesses that he skillfully hides from view, because he tends to analyse his brilliance, his sexual appeal and his mental mechanics much more than most. He can also think too much. There are times when he over-analyses his existence to the point that he creates angst over things that may not ever happen. He may even wonder about his ability to be a great partner to a woman, or his ability to live up to her high expectations. This may even affect his viewpoint about his own masculinity at times — and Ms Aries is likely to make or break his masculinity in one way or another. In fact, she's likely to be his ultimate 'masculinity' test! If he passes her test, he emerges as one of the most wonderful men of the zodiac. If he fails it, he often falls into depression and becomes a pill-popper, drinker or gambler — yes, he can really fall apart at the seams.

Now if he can't pass the masculinity test, and she'll test him on all kinds of levels about his ability to stand up to her, he'll discover that she will soon walk all over him; and eventually, she'll probably do something that causes their relationship to hit a brick wall and encourages them to separate. So to keep the relationship in merry flow, a great deal depends on Mr Gemini assuming some control over setting the relationship's boundaries. If he lets Ms Aries set all of them they'll be too intense or pressured for his liking anyway. So he has to manoeuvre his way into managing to solicit a great and fair exchange when it comes to 'who rules the roost' or 'who wears the pants' in the family.

If Mr Gemini doesn't set some strong relationship boundaries, Ms Aries could go out of her way to create drama and chaos. She may put him down in public or cause him to lose face on more than one occasion. Or she may put him through silly emotional or loyalty tests he cannot pass. And when it comes to jealousies and possessiveness, if this relationship goes through any tests of fidelity, it could turn into a battle zone, as neither of these two signs are able to forgive or forget easily. The Aries woman and the Gemini man are both born under signs that need to 'grow up' before they can have a great relationship.

In a relationship together they can either grow together, or grow apart. If they are wise and compassionate in their handling of any crises, this relationship will prosper. But if they are too quick to throw in the towel when trouble erupts they'll both be quickly back on the single's scene again. Though with a little bit of luck, love and good timing, they can actually turn out to be one of the happiest, most connected and fun-loving couples of them all!

Aries man — Gemini woman

 The *'Is this really happening or not?'* relationship

If any two signs can give each other a healthy (or unhealthy) run for their money it is the Aries man and the Gemini woman. These two have different outlooks on life, but their differences can actually provide breakthroughs or other wonderful benefits for each other, rather than create limitations. As much as they may 'think' and 'react' totally differently when it comes to relationships and dating and mating, these two actually are surprisingly similar.

When facing the prospect of finding their mate (and starting a family), the Aries guy and the Gemini gal have a great deal in common. They love to have a companion, a soul mate, a friend, or a partner to share their world — and this definitely makes them both relationship material! When they decide to settle down (especially together) one thing is certain, they both need to change — *radically* — to fit in with each other's needs and desires. Their single lives and their relationship lives are both going to be poles apart from each other. In their single days both the Aries guy and the Gemini gal have wandering hearts, curious minds and delicate egos. When they come together and form a relationship you can be sure that there are games about to be played: romantic games, intellectual games and financial games. They are both going to be put through some incredible highs and lows when they join forces, and they are going to have to face some tests to their relationship endurance. Tests that will either drive them nuts, shatter them into fragmented, insecure personalities, or make them grow up and get on with life, by developing their personalities and maturing to the responsibilities of being a complete person (rather than a disintegrated one), and thereby becoming a better person.

Now, that's once they settle down; once they have committed to each other. But before that can happen they have to first survive or triumph over their intense courtship phase. After all, he's not an easy man to conquer when it comes to the relationship stakes. He's the man of the zodiac born under the dynamic, masculine planet Mars. This gives him a sensitive but enormous ego and usually a huge libido to match. He loves to be a 'jack-the-lad' type and give the feminine sex a run for their money. He's often the guy who tends to play the field, enjoy the chase and like the Australian wombat 'eats roots and leaves' for which he is famous. He often leaves a trail of broken hearts behind him before he decides to stop chasing the female pack (like the Ram which is the symbol of his sign), and settle with his alpha female mate!

Ms Gemini, while not quite as outgoing or driven by her desire to be a hunter of sexual hearts as he, is quite happy to have men hanging off her coat-sleeve as well. She also finds it emotionally less threatening to be free and not necessarily enclosed in an exclusive relationship structure. Ms Gemini is the gal who claims she doesn't really like having a boyfriend because he wants to know where she is all the time; and even worse, he has the affront to want to know who she is dating as well!

Ms Gemini loves having a lot of male (and female) friends. She loves to flirt, play the social field and keep her relationship options wide open. That's why when Mr Aries and Ms Gemini team up, they make an extremely interesting zodiac combination. If these two really attempt to match up for a long-term relationship, they are certain to go through some enormously enlightening experiences together (ones that lift them up and bring them right down too). Because from the get-go it is likely that they will push each other's buttons, they turn out to be each other's greatest teachers as well.

They'll teach each other about boundaries, fidelity, commitment, responsibility and learning to be more connected to one person (rather than with the group), all aspects of life that they generally need to learn. Plus, they'll have one of the most wonderful 'relationship bonuses' that any relationship can have: they'll also be able to be each other's best friend and companion!

ARIES—CANCER relationship

The *'Why don't you head north and I'll go south'* relationship

STAR ARIES–CANCER COUPLE
Marsha Mason and Neil Simon

Thinking about combining an Aries with a Cancer! Eek! If this combination is written on your cosmic agenda, then you either like to live dangerously or believe in taking high risks. Though they often tend to enjoy each other's company (some of the time), for the longer term, here we have two signs that really do not hit it off too well. Relationships, particularly romantic ones, can test these two signs to their limit. They will need to deal with levels of sensitive emotions and it is their difference in emotional levels that will probably put them through their biggest challenges and tests. The way they deal with their emotions is where they both have very little in common — and emotions play a huge part of being in love.

That's why (although they may have strong attractions to each other), put to the harsh test of time, Aries and Cancer usually don't add up to a smooth-flowing connection at all. Why? Because it's a case of merging two individuals with two very different desires, needs and wishes. Aries only thinks about what works for them and how they can suit themselves, whereas Cancers expect whoever they are dealing with (most especially their romantic partners), to consider the Cancers' needs first. Cancers structure their existence so that the rest of the world revolves around fulfilling their desires, needs and insecurities. So if any two signs are likely to find themselves at constant loggerheads, these two are likely to be at it hammer-and-tongs before they reach any kind of harmonious, compassionate understanding. Having said that, if the Aries is prepared to be nurturing and the Cancer is prepared to be less sensitive and develop a sense of humour, these two can end up having a funny, adventurous time together — the like of which they would never find with any other star sign in the zodiac, except with each other!

Aries woman — Cancer man

The *'I can tell already this is definitely going to be a hard work kinda'* relationship

Who is 'wearing the pants' in this relationship — that's going to be a major deciding factor when the Aries woman joins forces romantically with her Cancer man. You see the Aries woman is the strongest, straightest-shooting, stargal of the zodiac; and underneath his masculine veneer the Cancer man is emotionally intense and vulnerable. So when it comes to portraying female and male roles in a relationship, subliminally (over the longer term at least) frequent role-reversals become played out if this couple becomes an item. Now that exchange of power may be all experienced on subliminal areas but because there's a tug-of-war going on beneath the surface of everyday affairs between these two individuals, there's not likely to be too much peace and harmony in this household. But this tug-of-war of energy sharing can have its pluses. If this volatility rebounds over into the bedroom, there may also be lots of sexual fun and games abounding, the kind which quickly make up for any lack of harmony. Many problems or disagreements between these two will be resolved between the sheets! If passion is a big part of their exchange, they can often enjoy making up after an argument much more than most lovers do!

Life between them is most unlikely to involve smooth-sailing because the most aggressive, insensitive, self-absorbed planet of all, fiery Mars, rules the Aries woman; and this Mars (masculine energy) rulership makes her an exceptional gal of the zodiac. Without even knowing it, she is naturally attracted to portraying the dominant person in any relationship structure. Ms Aries has a most unusual unique 'take' or 'attitude' on life. In many ways she's in a league of her own because she's the one woman of the zodiac who has such a strong connection with both her female and male self. This makes her much more go-getting and competitive than her other zodiac female counterparts.

In Mr Cancer she is meeting in many ways her cosmic match, because he's the one man of the zodiac, who has something special in common with her. The fact is, like her, he's ruled by the planet that goes against the grain of his manhood — he's ruled by the Moon and that zodiac energy is uniquely related to the feminine forces of existence. It is a small mind-twister but Ms Aries is ruled by masculine energy, while Mr Cancer is ruled by female energy. It all gets rather confusing, doesn't it? And that's what happens to this relationship as a result of their unique rulership (which creates certain cosmic genetic influences upon their outlooks) it often becomes confusing too. But, surprise, surprise, sometimes magically these two uniquely focused astrological partners work this out and their relationship turns out to be hugely successful — but I do want to emphasise the 'sometimes' element here because lots of disastrous relationships come under the Aries woman–Cancer man heading.

So there are certainly some major tests ahead for this couple. Sometimes role-swapping resolves all kinds of possible problems. For example, it may work well for Mr Cancer to be more of the nurturing, considerate one, or home-maker in the household; and for Ms Aries to be more of the hunter-gatherer, leader and controlling force in the relationship. Now this delicate exchange of responsibilities, trendsetting and decision-making energy could take all kinds of lesser or bigger forms, but she is likely to be the one who needs to be the more assertive person in the relationship, even if only in her selected areas. It may take a more dramatic twist where Mr Cancer assumes the role of Mr Mum and Ms Aries plays the breadwinner. However, unless they really make some radical adjustments to what society is likely to expect from them, there are often some huge pressures on their relationship when it comes to deciding who wears the pants.

Ms Aries is not likely to be thrilled by Mr Cancer's desire for operating his life within structured safety zones, because she is naturally an impetuous risk taker. For example, she will spend money today and worry about finances tomorrow; whereas Mr Cancer would prefer to save today and *not* worry about finances tomorrow. They are decidedly coming from two different places on many levels of life, but where they may make a wonderful heart connection is when it comes to family. She can be a person who has strong ties to family — although she may think she doesn't have strong ties to them at all; for her, however, the saying 'blood is thicker than water' holds true. The same strong family ties apply to him. If they start their own family, this powerful family connection can help them overcome other potential relationship shortfalls. But to keep the love fires burning will demand patience, perseverance and commitment.

Ms Aries is impetuous. If Mr Cancer doesn't live up to her expectations — even if she has children with him — she can still pack her bags and head for the hills if she wants to, leaving him very angry and even obsessively aggressive towards her. A disagreement or breakdown of communication between these two can truly lead to major disasters occurring. If troubled times hit this couple, Mr Cancer doesn't know how to either forgive or forget. Consequently, if Ms Aries pushes Mr Cancer's most sensitive, emotional buttons, they are sometimes pushed forever. If things go terribly wrong between them, the ego struggles or family law battles that these two get into are the kind that make any onlooker's hair stand on end.

So it is far better if Ms Aries and Mr Cancer look carefully before they leap into this relationship, and if they see any early warning signals of possible trouble looming ahead they should avoid this relationship altogether. If they choose to combine forces unwisely, the price they might pay (or the trouble they may face in the future) could turn out to be a huge one. An Aries woman and a Cancer man should not enter into this relationship without carefully considering all the consequences. Once they've done that and still want to explore the wonders of sharing a life together, it may take vigilance and discipline for them to live happily ever after. If their hearts are truly connected, they'll share marvellous adventures along the way and never find each other boring or predictable at all. In fact, if love lasts for them, this will be a relationship 'excellent'.

Aries man — Cancer woman

The *'Whatever happens, let's put it down to too many glasses of vino'* relationship

Want to get a glimpse of this relationship through the world of nature. Then think of that old ram: there he is out in the fields, having the time of his life impregnating all those eager lady rams, and what's more, amazingly, he's impregnating them with no effort at all. In the farmyard, if the job demands that Mr Ram come up with the necessary performance, he can comfortably take care of at least fifty Ram-ettes on a single night. Why bring this 'farm yard' virility point up here? Well, it is naturally a huge exaggeration but the Aries man (whose astrological symbol just happens to be the farmyard's most virile Ram), indirectly has a lot in common with this description of abundance of highly charged virility. If he is not committed to one particular woman, then often he's the type of guy who likes to roam and spread his charms around. And even when he is committed, this man of the zodiac often faces the greatest difficulties with fidelity. He just doesn't fit well with a monogamous 'same gal every morning, noon and night' type arrangement.

Now into this scenario, along comes Ms Cancer Crab. She's all female energy, bundled up in a most appealing eye-fluttering, seductive package. By nature she is vulnerable, cute, cuddly, mysterious and alluring; she is also one of the most jealous, possessive and insecure gals of the zodiac. She would fight for love, die for love and battle to keep love in her life. She doesn't want any shaking, rattling or rolling to happen in her happy family life. So if the Cancer gal matches up with an Aries guy (who holds such naturally different mating tendencies than she), she is usually heading for a relationship ride that is certain to see her spending time sooner or later attempting to dry her tears at Heartbreak Hotel.

He's a wonderful human being, and though underneath the surface Mr Aries loves to be in love, most times he is mainly in love with himself. Not that he isn't capable of loving a woman with his total heart and soul, but she'll usually have to give him a powerful jolt of fear of losing her, before he realises he had better toe the line and be on his best behaviour. Often a Cancer gal is too easily disturbed or too emotional to be the one to give him this jolt that wakes him up to his own vulnerability of losing the love of his life. It takes another more forceful gal of the zodiac to tame him and teach him the lesson of love he needs most of all, if he's to make his relationship work, and bring 'commitment'. At least in the early days of their relationship, Ms Cancer is often too vulnerable to survive his insensitive responses. He wears her sensitive nature down and his bright love-light burns down low in her eyes when he breaks her heart time and again. And he's not the one to blame, because she tends to lift him up and put him on a pedestal from where he has no choice but to fall off eventually — and he'll have many occasions to fall from his love pedestal if he remains true to himself.

Mr Aries is just a very different soul to Ms Cancer. He loves his freedom (at least until he meets his match who turns out to be 'Ms Right for Him'). Ms Cancer knows all about locking up a man's heart and throwing away the key, but Mr Aries isn't likely to want that done. Sure she wants to keep her Aries man all to herself and capture his heart, body and soul with one magical flick of her eyelashes, but usually he isn't quite so accommodating. He doesn't have the same resilient staying power that she has, and if she expects too much from him (too much romance, attention, reassurance), eventually he'll start to resent her and treat her mean!

So what happens if these two meet and passions are stirred and the relationship takes on a more serious hue? Plenty of emotional weather storms and other forms of relationship dramatics, and more of the same are predicted ahead! They'll certainly have some wild nights of passion, plenty of adventures and loads of emotional and temperamental highs and lows; and they may thrive on this hurdy gurdy ride, at least in the short term. They certainly won't be bored; they'll totally be on edge with a fine line in force, between succeeding or failing in the relationship. But no matter how things turn out, each of them will learn a great deal from the other.

If they decide to continue the relationship into the longer term, there are likely to be many difficulties that they will need to overcome. Unless they truly learn to compromise in a major fashion, this relationship usually can't withstand the pressures it is destined to face. Some of the most enduring relationships (and some endearing ones at that) between an Aries guy and a Cancer gal are created when this couple are not lovers, but friends. Once the possessiveness and jealousy factors are removed from the Aries man–Cancer woman relationship equation, this couple generally hit it off fantastically. But if any couple in a love relationship is likely to be 'at war' with each other, the Aries man–Cancer woman is definitely a high probability!

ARIES—LEO relationship

The *'This whole love thing is actually turning out far better than I expected'* relationship

STAR ARIES–LEO COUPLE
Robin Wright-Penn and Sean Penn

A little like Tarzan meeting Jane! When an Aries meets up with a Leo in the romantic realms there's definitely a rumble happening in the romantic jungle. This is one of the more sizzling romantic combinations of the zodiac because both combinations of the Aries–Leo relationship have a great deal of zodiac sexual power going in their favour. These two are both fire signs (which means that they are go-getters by nature, adventurous, free-spirited and enterprising). They are likely to have loads in common and share many interests. Their main problems, however, will stem from their highly competitive natures, jealousy or rivalry. Both Aries and Leos want to be leaders, and if both of them are busy giving the other instructions, life can get very complicated.

Unless they are carefully given realm and rulership over a specific area of their lives, that is, *she* the home, *he* the business and financial realms, the sharing of daily tasks and everyday roles in their relationship can be transformed from normal operations into more of a battlefield, because neither of them like to give an inch. To create a harmonious happy home, it will take a lot of understanding and compromise between them to make this exchange work. However, if true love exists between them, the high rewards this exchange can provide for them both will make it well worth the additional effort required to make it work. If these two fall in love and their relationship balances out their individual ego issues, this couple are likely to score a home run in the heady, wonderful game of love.

Aries woman—Leo man

The *'Forget about dinner, lead me straight into the boudoir'* relationship

This combination of partners adds up to a new form of astrological Hollywood material. You could probably easily make a movie or soap opera about what happens when these two fall in love. After all, the Leo man is in a league of his own and so is the Aries woman. In astrological terms, what are these two individuals like? Well, for an exaggerated example, imagine Mr Leo himself, Rolling Stone's Mick Jagger. He's the archetypal Leo — brimming with confidence, up on stage strutting his stuff, shaking his Leo mane and prancing around. He's probably one of the most typical Leo men on this planet today. But whether your particular Leo guy is a Mick Jagger type or not, most starmen born under the sign of Leo are the centre of their own Universe.

The marvellous, brilliant Sun rules his sign of Leo. So, as our Sun is the centre of our Universe, Mr Leo innately knows that the world revolves around him, and usually he's right! Whether he's a shy Leo or a bolder one, he has a knack of enthusing the atmosphere with his bold, electric personality. He exemplifies the Leo man's innate stature where he resonates with energy that says he's 'as good as it gets'. Sure, Mick may be a highly exaggerated version of the Leo man, but in many ways he is just doing what many Leo men would love to do if they could (even though their ego would probably never admit it). Mick is turning on his Leo charms and making a fortune out of it as well.

Mr Leo is the man with unique boy-next-door appeal, who has a concealed tiger (or in has case, a lion), lurking in his tank. He's a true pistol of a guy (and as an aside, it's interesting to note that the media even call tennis champion Pete Samprass, Pistol Pete — and yes, he's a Leo!)

Mr Leo naturally has a way with the ladies (and some say he has 'his way' with them too). He's a first-class seducer (look at Leo, Bill Clinton) and most times an uncontrollable force to be reckoned with (like sports supremo Magic Johnson). Now the Leos given above are definitely the more flamboyant males of the Leo sign, and of course Mr Leo doesn't have to be in showbiz (although he often is). But if he's a real Leo guy, whether he's mowing his lawn, walking the dog, or shopping in the mall, he is likely to be somebody you suddenly sit up and take notice of once he comes into your company.

To get a sense of what makes Ms Aries tick astrologically, consider one of the more 'out-there' Ms Aries, Mariah Carey. Her life has taken her through some extreme highs and lows. She's (overly) dramatic, whose star shines brightly and then explodes into splintered stardust at times. While these two (Mick and Mariah) may be extremely exaggerated versions of the Ms Aries and Mr Leo personalities, there's a little bit of Mick or Mariah in every Leo guy or Aries gal. They may just express it differently, but underneath their everyday life both the Leo man and the Aries woman love walking on the edge of drama — and their bright light can easily go through some dips or fade as life puts them through many a test (which it always does particularly when they team up as a romantic couple).

When the Aries gal meets up with the Leo guy, their meeting is likely to be quite an event; and usually at their first meeting, something memorable happens! They may be at a nightclub dancing the night away with friends where they end up lip-locked in each other's arms; at a party that they initially attended with other partners, then most indiscreetly disappear with each other; or at the work place where they begin an illicit (not too private) relationship that has the rest of the office abuzz. Sex is usually their initial powerful connecting attraction; and while the sex is hot, these two are hot to the extent that they sizzle for each other. But if and when their passion dies, frequently these two signs (like bright moths seeking an always burning sexual flame) look elsewhere for their next thrill.

But if there's more than sex between them, they are likely to elope or do something quite dramatic in the space of a short time. Expect them to shock those who know them well with their unbridled actions of passion. This couple is not made up of two people who are composed of patient or 'play it safe' type energy. They usually do not do anything half-heartedly. They tend to jump right into the thick of things, and this ability to leap in headfirst, works both for and against them, especially in their relationship. They can rush in too quickly and make all kinds of 'I'll love you forever and a day' type declarations, promises and commitments to each other, and then lose a great deal of face (and possibly sleep) when they wake up the next day, or a week or two later, or even a year or so later and they can't stand to spend another five minutes in their partner's company. Neither the Aries woman nor the Leo man are highly predictable in their emotions, everyday needs, desires, passions or love relationships. In fact, they are rather unsteady when it comes to what they'll want or feel next, and it takes a strong tie to another individual — something very magical — to really make them stay with one person (particularly each other) for long.

Now one thing that does seem to make a difference to their commitment is once they hear the patter of little lion paws. A home and family means a great deal to both of these individuals. But even children possibly won't keep them together forever, should one or both of them fall in love with someone new. The fire signs of Aries and Leo both love the whole concept of romance and love, and if they can't find love or romance at home, they're the kind of people who — even without consciously looking for it — will find their passion fulfilled elsewhere. It takes a lot of love to keep love alive when these two fall in love, but if they can conjure this love-forever energy up, they'll have the most exciting, brilliant and intoxicating romance on the planet.

Aries man — Leo woman

 The *'Eek! This could really turn into the real romantic deal'* relationship

Expect some high romantic drama to erupt between these two. Passions will run riot, and they can both be very over-reactive about the smallest and biggest relationship positives and negatives. However, there are certain to be plenty of kisses, tears, dancing, romancing and roses. When an Aries man and a Leo woman TRULY, MADLY AND DEEPLY fall in love, they are likely to take love and romance onto a whole new dimension of experience. Many a love affair to remember has featured these two signs because an Aries man and a Leo woman often just naturally 'click' and feel comfortable together. These two are born under the two most seductive, go-getter signs of the zodiac. So merge the two of them, and if the sexual chemistry ignites, they are like two passion-driven human magnets being drawn towards each other. If there's a real mind, body, spirit and heart connection as well as a sex connection taking place, and should Cupid's love magic set its intoxicating spell over an Aries Man and Leo woman, nothing or no one will stand in their way.

However, putting some effort into developing and continuing their love-heart connection is the big deciding issue as to whether this relationship continues or not. With so much sexual appeal pumping up this couple's libido barometers and being a main attraction for their attraction to each other; no wonder both these individuals frequently confuse lust and love, and get confused over their true heartfelt feelings. This 'strong lust attraction' can lead them into a sexual escapade that doesn't really fulfil their real needs when it comes to settling into a committed, ongoing long-term relationship. Their sexual desire levels can create such a bright, burning passion between them at the commencement of their love affair that once the dazzling intoxication of their first intense lust dissipates, they feel a sudden drop in the energy flow between them and imagine that they now feel drained, as if there's nothing left to offer each other. That's why, to put their lust and love into perspective, this couple often needs to balance out their high passion with a cold dose of reality. They need to do more than simply unleash their passion together; they need to go out and do everything they can do together, to widen their scope of the experience of sharing their time together from romantic to practical levels.

What happens when the initial passion experienced between them cools, quite frequently instead of waiting to see what happens next (or how their relationship unfolds onto a different level of operation), the Aries guy and the Leo gal will impetuously run from each other, instead of towards each other. This happens if they have had a wonderful love affair, but one that burned itself out after the first chapter. To avoid this, if these two can extricate themselves from bed long enough to make some new friends, have some hobbies, pay some bills, keep their jobs going and organise their daily responsibilities, they have a chance for longer-term success.

Now romance often continues with this couple, but not without some tests and trials along the bumpy road to love. There are many fantastic relationships that feature an Aries man with a Leo woman, but often these longer-lasting relationships are formed only after both the Aries man and the Leo woman have exhausted their passions and hit the relationship wall a couple of times. They need to have their lust tempered; and once it does not necessarily run or rule their relationship, then they have matured sufficiently to realise that having fun in the sack doesn't necessarily mean that you are both ideal, lifetime companions. Once they start to become more balanced in their relationship perspective, then they often become more balanced in their appraisal of each other as prospective partners and see each other not so much with lust-filled, rose-coloured glasses, but with the new reality of noticing other endearing qualities within each other too.

If this couple truly does make a heartfelt loving connection, they have immaculate zodiac credentials for finding true soul-love together. There's no doubt that the right Aries man and the right Leo woman are astrologically very suited. They have a tremendous amount in common and they also naturally fall into step with each other's personality traits, desires and time clocks.

Fortunately for both of them, Mr Aries and Ms Leo adore a good drama. You'll find that if there isn't a drama happening in their lives they'll create one; and that's why they understand each other so well. They usually like to 'get up and go' at the same time. If they were partnered with another less active or less dramatic sign they would wear them out pretty quickly. Yet when these two zodiac mates find each other, instead of it being an overwhelming experience for them, it is exciting and uplifting. As a Leo gal pal of mine who has an Aries guy in her life assured me, 'The truth is, nobody else but us, could put up with either of us for long'. Perhaps there is some truth in this statement — she seemed pretty sure about it herself anyway.

One thing this couple may need to watch out for is their natural desire to be the leader, or their innate desire to be the star of the show, whether at home, work, play or with friends and family. There can be a very competitive side to both these signs and this one-upmanship can occasionally get right out of hand. So if Mr Aries and Ms Leo do not burn each other out through the initial courting stage, and they move onto a more serious relationship level of existence, they then need to be able to share the limelight with each other.

Also, jealousy and possessiveness could turn this couple into boxing partners rather than loving partners. They need to be very aware that a lapse of faithfulness could create Relationship World War Three. Plus, if they don't sidestep carefully around anything or anyone that could pose a threat to their relationship there will be a huge price to pay for their indiscretion. If they act with consideration for each other, then they can survive the usual relationship dramas; however, whether this relationship will make it into old age is entirely in the hands of fate. Due to their joint fiery and intense nature, anything could happen in between the Aries man and Leo woman's first meeting, their falling in love and their continued journey down the romance highway. One thing is certain, whatever happens, this relationship will never be boring.

aries

ARIES—VIRGO relationship

The *'Oh no! I can't believe that I just went and told you that I love you'* relationship

STAR ARIES–VIRGO COUPLE
Claire Danes and Ben Lee

It's time for this couple to learn a whole new bag of tricks, especially 'to feel, think and react differently' — as that's what's required when the Aries and Virgo cross paths romantically. There's certain to be some fun and games taking place, as well as some migraines and hissy fits. The impetuous nature of a feisty Aries meets its match when it is emotionally connected to a cool, calm and collected ground-bound Virgo. Both of these signs are capable of getting under the other's skin and making a powerful impact on each other.

They are poles apart in personality traits too, but in love relationships this factor alone can be one of the greatest single attractions — because, as they say, 'opposites do attract'. Where any true Virgo values organisation, safety and communication; conversely the Aries values excitement, impetuosity and assertiveness. Put these two signs together in a love relationship and something remarkable happens. If the magic of love is strong, then they can really help each other tremendously and be each other's most accomplished teacher. If the relationship doesn't survive, yet has gone beyond a casual encounter, then sometimes the fact that it isn't going anywhere in the future can cause a whole lot of trouble.

There can be a myriad of unusual side effects emanating from this couple's dalliance with each other. But whether they hit it off or end up hitting each other, they can serve each other at the very least by setting some boundaries about what they as individuals do or don't want from a relationship. The Virgo can help their Aries kick back and release their pedal from the metal as they go about racing through life. The Aries help Virgo to liven up, and stop holding on so tightly to security. If this sharing of different energies occurs, true love can reign supreme and both partners are enriched from the experience.

Aries woman — Virgo man

 The *'You're nothing at all like I expected you to be'* relationship

'Appearances can be deceptive' is often a statement that is commonly made with respect to all kinds of relationships. And with the Ms Aries and Mr Virgo astro-combination, we have a very interesting zodiac pairing. Sometimes Ms Aries and Mr Virgo are a somewhat strange zodiac couple to behold, or may appear on outward levels of observation to have little in common with each other, yet this relationship often (possibly miraculously) seems to work. Although the fact that it does work goes against some of the most basic cosmic odds.

Both individuals have extremely different temperaments, outlooks and natures. Ms Aries is a dramatic, impetuous fiery gal, and Mr Virgo is organised, steadfast and understated. Fortunately for them if you add this blend of attributes together, with a little patience and commitment they can add up to a very complete and multi-faceted relationship package.

They do have many physical aspects in common too. They may find each other extremely physically attractive, which will naturally help them overcome other possible difficult areas. So while they may sometimes have conflicting opinions, plans or dreams, at least with their physical passions they'll usually enjoy their love-making sessions tremendously. Ms Aries will have her moments of high passion, but she'll also have times when she just wants to be allowed to go off with her friends or follow her own program or schedule. She can also be quite moody and self-involved and this will mean she has her 'I want to be alone' times, where she's so distracted by her thoughts that she becomes a mediocre lover, or disinterested in exchanging even everyday-type pleasantries. Fortunately for her, Mr Virgo has a little of the same energy about him as well, as he can have unpredictable mood swings too.

Being a very dramatic and generous-hearted woman of the zodiac, Ms Aries will do her best to anticipate his every need, and if she can, will spoil him rotten and under most conditions offer him her best attention. But not always! There will definitely be times when she is caught up in her own inner dialogue, angst or creative musing, or distracted by things happening in the world around her (or to others near and dear to her, like family or friends). Similarly, if Mr Virgo has something pressing on his mind, or something urgent to attend to, he often tends to keep to himself. During these phases one or both partners may withdraw from physical touch or be quite cold to each other, not because of any real negative reaction to their other half but merely because there's other things tugging at their minds, thoughts or heartstrings.

During any times of extreme inner turbulence, if both parties reach this same mood or point at the same time, surprisingly it can sometimes work to their advantage. They'll both be so busy dealing with their own 'stuff' they inadvertently allow each other the space to attend to whatever it is that is preying on their minds. But if they are out of sync with each other's need for privacy, then this can lead to problems. Should any partner feel neglected or insecure, these times of distraction, withdrawal or distance may create argument or breed deep-seated insecurities between them. Consequently, the timing of their mood swings, the responses they have to problems, their ability to have their own quality time and to share time with their partner, are the delicate fabrics that will hold the tenterhooks of their relationship together. They will either merge well together, or, over time, gradually drift apart. So there are many 'ifs and maybes' surrounding their union, and only the test of time will reveal the answer as to how they will measure up when merging their lives and attempting to become a complete couple.

One thing that he has to offer that she will adore, is that Mr Virgo can be her Rock of Gibraltar. And if she plays her cosmic cards well, he'll take excellent care of most of her needs and also spend a great deal of time worshipping at her sexual altar. He will fulfil many roles in her life — and he'll do it in style — because he loves her excitement for life and the way she lights up his life. He'll be her play-mate, her love slave, her best friend, her brother, father and boy child, all rolled up in one, as the various phases and stages of life pass over them. Likewise, she has the capacity and the mercurial nature too, to fulfil similar feminine roles in his life.

Naturally, having stated the above, putting these two extremely different star-people together is not necessarily a recipe for happy-ever-after. Life won't always be a walk in perpetual sunshine for them; in fact, there'll be moments when their relationship journey will seem more like a climb up an emotional volcano. To their credit, however, if this couple falls in love they'll both go to powerful lengths to make it work, simply because they'll realise that they have met someone extremely wonderful. So this can truly turn out to be a 'through thick and thin' union if this couple realise their connection is a valuable and worthy one.

Although Ms Aries may be flamboyant and volatile, Mr Virgo is quite prepared to sit back and be her number one fan. His patience will teach her a lot about unconditional love too and he'll play many different roles in her life, possibly even that of her therapist. There will be times when he perfectly portrays the role of her father and comforts her like a child. Then there will be times he brings out her maternal instincts or has her fussing over him. They'll both thrive if they are blessed with a family; if not, they'll probably have pets or nieces or nephews to fuss over. If they have children she'll probably hope, before they are born, that they are boys, mini versions of him; while he'll probably hope they are girls, like her.

If this couple clicks, then their mutual admiration can run deep — BUT that's only if their hearts are truly locked in love. A frivolous or less dedicated connection between these two can lead to major disasters occurring, even domestic violence or verbal abuse. The wrong Ms Aries with the wrong Mr Virgo is a relationship accident waiting to happen. There's something in the Aries gal that does love to stir the relationship pot, and Mr Virgo has his limits of patience — limits that she is a professional at putting to many a test.

Also, her ability to create dramas (if over-done) may drain his enthusiasm for her company. If this occurs, he may occasionally be found looking extremely dismal or disenchanted. An unhappy Virgo man isn't hard to recognise; he's also likely to become ill as his body quickly reveals signs of stress.

Even if they go through some tough love, times when true love runs deep between them, any hurts or disillusionments will quickly mend and be forgotten rather quickly. One thing in Ms Aries favour is that as much as she lashes out or gets cranky with others if she's upset, she isn't necessarily the kind of person who holds a grudge for long.

With some endearing patience and perseverance, these two can work things out, *usually*. Ms Aries needs to respect that Mr Virgo wants peace and harmony, so sometimes she must tone down her full-on attitude or opinions. If she beguiles him with her charms — even if it means following her to the ends of the earth — then he's likely to go along with her plans, dreams and wishes and enjoy himself in the bargain. But these two will need to keep careful watch that they don't rock the relationship boat or do anything intentionally to put down, criticise or emotionally wound the other. It may take a whole lot of love to keep this relationship going, but it will be well worth the effort.

Aries man — Virgo woman

 The *'Now tell me truthfully, can I really trust you with my love'* relationship

Aries and Virgo together is quite a bizarre and unusual combination of astrological forces. That's why you possibly won't find an Aries man and a Virgo woman merging their hearts and other resources in life together too often. Clearly and simply, this combination frequently doesn't have too much in common. However, if by chance the magic elixir of love does brush against their sensual lips, this relationship is certainly going to be a magic carpet ride to cloud nine for these two star signs with no stops along the way.

No matter how it starts, finishes or manages to exist in between, their relationship is certain to be a strange journey, a unique learning experience for both of them, and a test involving trial and error. There's going to be some intense exchanges taking place between them, as these two aren't even opposites — they are more than opposites. In many ways this couple is coming from two different zodiac galaxies. However, it is this very absence of real earthly connection that can manage to glue them together at the heartstrings. They are likely to be each other's greatest mysteries, as well as being a fascinating study for each other. And who doesn't love a good mystery and a fascinating study? Not many.

Now there can be some strong attractions (physically) formed between these two signs. The Aries man is ruled by the fiery planet Mars, so he is very much the boy, man or masculine figure in astrology. It is important to note that Mars is the place that rules 'ego' and all the masculine characteristics. It promotes and endorses his ability to be a trailblazing adventurer and encourages him to flex his muscles and exhibit his more masculine energy. He's the kind of guy who really enjoys being the man of the house, the star of any show; and he often delights and with somewhat natural ease, falls into the role of playing the stud. In many ways he's also adept at playing the role of the Knight in Shining Armour too, because if there's a fair maiden who needs rescuing, then he's the man for the job, if she has captured his heart and his imagination!

Now enter the demure, understated but often most beguiling Ms Virgo! Ruled by the planet of communication, Mercury, this planet is one that has a more genteel approach than the feisty planet Mars that rules the Aries man. It is a very lightweight planet that tends to bring about an almost childlike quality to surround all it rules — and it rules the signs of Virgo and Gemini jointly. Because of her connection to the delicate zodiac force of Mercury, Ms Virgo is something like the dainty fairy-tale princess from an olde-worlde fairy tale, who has somehow mistakenly landed *kerplop!* in the modern world. The words 'sugar and spice and all things nice' resonate well with her, as she's indeed what little girls are made of, and more!

She is vulnerable, slightly overly sensitive and usually extremely feminine — sometimes her overt femininity makes her even more vulnerable than other gals of the zodiac who are also feminine. She's something of a whiz kid, too. It is likely that she's well read, great at crosswords, an expert on photography or some other hobby and usually a truly wonderful mother. She's also multi-talented — the kind of gal who can cook, garden, work a computer, organise the holidays, plan a financial budget and still have time to do extra work for charities.

So here we have Mr Aries and Ms Virgo, attractive opposites, being attracted to each other, and wondering 'what on earth' they are feeling if their hearts are suddenly hit by Cupid's sometimes wayward arrow. Will they ever truly understand each other's deepest desires, emotions and depths? Probably not. But if the chemistry and love connection between them is powerful, they are likely to have plenty of fun times trying. How can they ever really know where the other is coming from mentally, emotionally and intellectually? Not too easily. But this can all be swept away by their sheer delight of each other's uniqueness. After all, he's all man; she's all woman, and that fact is probably their biggest attraction draw card of the zodiac pack; and it is a mighty one to have in your romantic bag of tricks. They may have little else in common but this one fact alone makes them almost like Adam and Eve in certain respects. And it can overshadow any shortfalls they may have in other areas of their communication, desires or dreams. It can keep these two connected at the heart (and help them to survive and triumph over some major relationship dramas together) for years, and maybe even manage to live happily ever after — sometimes!

But they are likely to have their supreme ups-and-downs. Before they settle into ongoing harmony (especially during the early days of their relationship), Mr Aries is likely to give Ms Virgo a huge runaround — and possibly in their courting days he may break her heart time and again. But she's extremely patient and persevering. Indeed, she's the one gal of the zodiac who is capable of forgiving and forgetting. Even if he's done her wrong (and *eek!* he's likely to), if he's her man, she'll still come back for more, time and again to be his woman.

As he can be quite a cad at times, it may mean that a few bust-ups or detours on the highway to true love need to occur before (Eureka!) Mr Aries suddenly realises what a gem of a stargal he has scored with Ms Virgo. (Hopefully this realisation occurs before he has well and truly lost her love completely.) When he does realise what a prize he has, he'll be filled with remorse, and he'll be sorry he put her through so many love tests. If ever 'her value' or what his relationship with her offers him in the way of enlightenment strikes him (and he sees what a prize life has put before him in Ms Virgo), he will actually settle down and become a very devoted family man. When he does (and children come along) he can be one of the happiest men on the planet. In the meantime though, little Ms Virgo may have to go through hell and high water before this man of Mars makes up his mind to commit. The good news is that once Mr Aries has settled into the relationship, Ms Virgo is likely to get all the rewards she deserves for her patience and perseverance. And guess what! After experiencing some initial relationship stormy weather, this couple may even find something very rare together — the secret for living happily ever after!

ARIES — LIBRA relationship

The *'Excuse me . . . but . . . haven't we met before?'* relationship

STAR ARIES–LIBRA COUPLE
Heath Ledger and Naomi Watts

Uh-oh! These two signs oppose each other on the zodiac wheel and that's usually a powerful indication in astrology that this couple will be magnetically drawn towards each other (for both better and worse results). If they are attracted and Cupid's arrow hits its target they are likely to discover that they have entered uncharted emotional, psychological and relationship waters, and should be prepared for a rocky romantic ride. Both of them are likely to discover also that they are somewhat out of their depth; in some cases, delightfully so, in others, painfully.

One thing is definite, if these two signs match up, someone is going to have to do a lot of compromising to fit in with the other's needs and desires. And when it comes to compromising, if the one doing all the compromising is the Aries, they probably won't stay around for long! If it is the Libran, they may eventually end up finding someone else more accommodating to their desires. And having said all that, these influences do not mean that Aries and Libras cannot have a wonderful, enduring love match, because they often do! Yet, according to astrology, to achieve this harmonious union, this couple will need to be prepared to be very patient, compassionate and understanding with each other, especially over the longer term.

Aries woman — Libra man

 The *'You've definitely got a special way about you'* relationship

Like a moth to the romantic flame, fiery Ms Aries is frequently most powerfully attracted by the heady appeal that a seductive, charming and very attractive Libran man naturally exudes. If he fits her perception of the perfect man he can 'turn her on like a radio'. Bedazzled by his many charms, she will become lost in her thoughts and fantasies about him, position herself in places where she might cross his path, incessantly discuss his many (adorable) qualities with her friends, and if she desires to, may even succeed in marrying him.

Now Mr Libra is not entirely impervious to Ms Aries own special sexual web of attraction. If their physical allure is mutual to both of them, he probably has strong feelings towards her as well, or he may simply want to lure her into his boudoir, but in most cases, he's possibly not quite so dramatically attracted as she. Where she is impetuous about her feelings, he's a little more reticent with his. As he tends to shift his focus in many different directions (being one of the air signs), his attention span when it comes to matters of relationships can mean he often views Ms Aries with a more fleeting or transient romantic vision, than she holds of him. Unless he's ready to settle down and build his nest, Ms Aries, in her pursuit to make him her soul mate, could be about to go through more lows than highs on the pathway to romantic bliss (and have her emotions tied into knots). But if Mr Libra is indeed ready to commit (and Libran men do eventually get to a turning point in their bachelor lives where they want to have home, family and all the relationship trappings), then Ms Aries (if she's the one located in his romantic world at that time) is likely to be an ideal gal for him.

However, the success rate for an Aries woman with a Libran man when it comes to winning the happy-ever-after relationship stakes is often nowhere near as high as Ms Aries or Mr Libra hopes. They are likely to face a few stumbling blocks along the way to which both of them contribute. Ms Aries likes to make things happen overnight, and Mr Libra doesn't like to be pushed too quickly to take action. Especially when he is younger, Mr Libra finds it tough to commit to anything — and when it comes to a relationship, he likes life to be easy-going. Consequently Ms Aries' feisty, dramatic and impatient nature often makes Mr Libra feel threatened or pulls him out of his cherished comfort zone. Even if they have fallen in love very deeply, so often these two 'once crazy about each other' people gradually drift away from each other. Or they may have a major dramatic showdown bust-up, and when that occurs, it is usually Ms Aries who is left nursing a wounded or even broken heart.

Although Mr Libra may painfully miss his Ms Aries after this bust-up, he is the man of the zodiac who is naturally a master at 'relationship replacement'. If he moves away from one gal, or things don't work out as expected between them and the sizzle goes out of the relationship — often it's an amazingly short time span before he finds another stargal to fill the place in his heart (or bed). Sometimes he has overlapping relationships too, where he is still interlocked with one partner but also dating someone else on the side (usually in a slightly underhand way — for example, perhaps it's his current girlfriend's best friend). Until he is totally committed, many a Libran guy can be a 'flake' when it comes to relationships where often he gets into trouble because he likes to 'have his romantic cake and eat it too!'

He's a free spirit in many ways with the way he dilly-dallies around romantically and has a unique zodiac ability to attach his heartstrings to another with regularity rather than exclusivity. This casual approach and happy tendency of his, to keep his romantic or sexual options open can naturally make Ms Aries decidedly jealous and possessive. It is also one of the things that most attracts her. She is, after all, a go-getter individual, and she likes to go get things that are not so easy to acquire, so the Libran guy is often highly prized on her 'must win' list. Even if he has no intention of arousing jealousy in her, somehow Mr Libra manages to leave a trail or hint of his casual emotional connections, his secret infidelities or other indiscretions drifting behind him! However, he's not always guilty of all her charges.

He often has friendships with other gals that could be misconstrued as romantic ones when they're not. He innately enjoys the company of women, so he can flirt with the young teenage gal in the dry-cleaners, he can bedazzle the local barmaid with his banter, or he may tell jokes to old Mrs Murphy on the corner, until she almost splits her sides. Whether he is cavorting with old or young female admirers, Ms Aries takes it sorely to heart. She can tend to get dramatically carried away — tends to think him too frivolous and that he should be paying more attention to her (when he is simply being his usual charming self), and sometimes Mr Libra is wrongly accused of being an audacious flirt. Even if he does his best to persuade her otherwise, often she won't budge in her suspicions. If she keeps suspecting him and levels accusations or starts to ask questions about his whereabouts, then he can sometimes go out and 'give her something to accuse him of'.

She will probably never fence him in (although she'll try), but she can share his world with him when he goes out and wanders around, talking to his many devoted fans or hanging out with his male friends. As much as he loves his home and family, the Libran man does like to be a social mover and shaker — he enjoys the company and camaraderie of others. With the pleasure planet Venus ruling his zodiac sign, he usually likes to party and enjoy the best that life has to offer. However, if he plays too many relationship games, Ms Aries can become a formidable opponent. She may even turn into a super-sleuth as she sets about attempting to keep track of his movements, phone calls, or decode his secret thoughts. If Ms Aries suspects something is going on behind her back, she can become over wrought with the desire to get to the bottom of it. This can make her forget her friends, her responsibilities, or even her good intentions not to allow any man to cause her grief for long. Her ability to be sensitive to his popularity can also be a test for both of them.

Naturally not all Ms Aries–Mr Libra relationships head off in the emotionally tumultuous direction set out above, but many do! There are certainly many successful Aries–Libra relationships, but usually these involve those Aries gals and Libra guys who truly want to settle down and build a stable existence. This is something both Aries and Libras eventually crave, but they both still need to be 'good and ready' for it. When they are both ready to settle down and be a partnership many Aries gals and Libra guys actually turn out to have the best romantic lives together of all the signs of the zodiac! All it takes for them to achieve this is to be prepared to be adaptable, have faith in each other, and look forward to the future with confidence that their relationship will succeed. If they put doubts, fears or jealousies aside, united they will stand and they will discover that romantic heaven does exist on earth.

Aries man — Libra woman

 The *'Don't mess around with me'* relationship

Mr Aries is the epitome of the Marlboro Man of the zodiac but even with his macho approach to life, this guy still has many romantic and emotional soft spots. One of his softest will be found when he gets around to dating and mating (a topic and pastime close to his masculine heart), and the object of his desires is an alluring female born under the sign of Libra. For some reason this particular zodiac gal can get under his rugged skin, fill his dreams, take away his usually healthy appetite and cause him romantic angst more than just about any other stargal.

Naturally Ms Libra has some help from above when it comes to turning Mr Aries' heart, emotions and life in general, upside down. She has the rulership of the love planet Venus helping her to cast a cosmic spell around him, and no gal can do much better than that when it comes to winning hearts and keeping them. On top of this help from above, Ms Libra has incredible persuasive powers, and just as well. When she's dealing with Mr Aries she's likely to need to summon up all the charm and diplomacy she can muster. Perhaps that's why she has 'seductive charm' as a natural component of her personality; it is given to her to help her deal with Mr Aries. He's not an easy man to keep happy, content or faithful, as he's the man of the zodiac who is frequently tempted by the call of romantic or sexual greener pastures.

Mr Aries can be very self-righteous about what is right for him, and what is right for others. Although he's super-sensitive and extremely vulnerable when it comes to matters relating to him, Mr Aries can be a trifle less sensitive when it comes to the way he deals with and handles his relationships with other people. Whether he is operating in his nice guy or tough guy mode, underneath his outer behaviour, he's somehow suiting himself in one way or another. Mr Aries is a man with a big ego, so he is very self-nurturing whether he means to be or not.

Now when he's dealing with Ms Libra he may have met his match in this capacity because she has an amazing ability to suit herself too, and at the same time, stroke Mr Aries' ego. She manages to somehow make this relationship a win-win for both of them, and this is an amazing ability on her part and something very few other zodiac gals can offer him. Not only is she innately an adept pleasure to men, in her favour she is often very seductive and sometimes highly successful as a business gal as well. With this heady and wonderful combination of sensual body and business mind, plus abundant charm and diplomacy, these components can set Mr Aries' heart, mind and body into a spin. And she'll keep him on his toes (like no other gal can), because she's a master at sending out mixed messages. Every time Mr Aries thinks he has her figured out, she'll do or say something exactly the opposite of what he is expecting.

Ms Libra is one of the few femme fatales of the zodiac who can lead Mr Aries by his Ram's nose (actually, she probably leads him by another part of his masculine anatomy too delicate to mention here) on a somewhat merry dance. And she needs to be able to play these games to conquer his heart. Mr Aries is one of the more forward, pushy mating partners of the zodiac. His libido is strong. Therefore it's not surprising that 'faithfulness' is frequently not one of his most prized goals in life. Before he finds his 'Ms Right' this man of the zodiac usually manages to give any gal a great run for her money. But with Ms Libra he sometimes finds he does a lot more running after her than she does him, at least in the initial stages of their courtship. She keeps him wondering, lusting and dangling, rather than vice versa.

Now that doesn't mean this relationship is destined to last forever. Sometimes these two signs come together and drift apart several times before they decide to make a 'go' of a permanent relationship. The fact that Mr Aries is not naturally attracted towards settling down with one individual, and that Ms Libra has great problems making up her mind, often keeps these two on a dating treadmill for many years. Often it is the desire to start a family that actually gets them to commit to each other but even then, there's likely to be a few relationship power struggles along the way. However, Ms Libra usually wins any power struggles. As much as Ms Libra is a charmer, she is also very strong willed if she's (amazingly) made up her mind about something, she generally figures out a way to get it.

If she has 'decided' Mr Aries is the man she wants to keep as a permanent player in her life, she can be a formidable competitor when it comes to winning his heart. Her ruling planet Venus endows her with amazing feminine wiles and she can bedazzle this evasive man and make him forget his resolve not to get himself tied down to one filly, with just a couple of demure flutters of her eyelashes. Whether she can keep him 'charmed' indefinitely, well that's the kind of stuff you read about in Mills and Boon novels and you need to wait until the last page of their relationship saga to find out!

ARIES — SCORPIO relationship

The *'Hey, are you a heartbreaker too?'* relationship

STAR ARIES–SCORPIO COUPLE
Russell Crowe and Meg Ryan

Ouch! Love can really hurt with this zodiac combination! Put any Aries with any Scorpio in a relationship, and whether they are mild mannered or confrontational, the power-punching personalities of both these volatile and very powerful signs have the makings of a 'Star Wars' couple. Now let's not beat around the bush. Sex is usually their major initial attraction and bond, but any kind of tryst between an Aries and a Scorpio is 'awesome', because their combination makes up one of the most powerful formations of the zodiac. Together they are a force to be reckoned with — either healthy or destructive — depending on the way that they utilise their combined energy.

This couple creates a merging of two significant planetary rulers. Mars rules Aries (the planet of passion, adventure and war); and the most powerful planet of all, Pluto (the planet of rebirth, the underworld and sexuality) rules Scorpio. Naturally when these two astro-forces find each other they'll go through an incredible experience that is likely to change their lives and alter their future destiny. From this experience of being together or affecting each other's heartstrings, either both will be reborn and move onto a different level of awareness and operation; or they'll both go through some kind of personality meltdown or breakthrough. Or, suffer one of the worst cases of achy-breaky heart they'll ever have in their earthly existence.

Aries woman — Scorpio man

The *'I think we're heading towards possible romantic trouble'* relationship

This combination of Aries woman and Scorpio man is the kind of relationship story that Mills and Boon hail from. There's going to be everything happening with this zodiac mix of identities — things like previous partners emerging from their past to shake up this relationship, fateful meetings in surprising and mysterious places, and many different happy and tragic endings. This is not a relationship for the light-hearted. It is much more appropriate for a heavy-weighted-heart type individual who can withstand an abundance of ups and downs, because they know at the end of the day they are going to experience the most emotional and romantic ride of their life.

When the right Aries woman connects with the right Scorpio man, passions explode, jealousy and possessiveness is ignited, and everyday common sense and good logic fly straight out the window. In some cases, if these partners are already committed to someone else when they meet, in an instant, their long-standing marriages or other relationship connections are likely to be forgotten and overnight, their unions with others may suddenly find themselves heading for the relationship rocks. Because of the extremely volatile nature of both these individuals, this isn't likely to be a smooth-sailing kind of relationship. In fact, from the moment this couple fall in love or lust, what occurs is likely to be more like a soap opera than a symphony. One way or another, some kind of drama erupts.

If they are having an illicit affair (and many couples of this zodiac combination often meet under illicit circumstances), even if they try to keep their extra-marital activities under wraps, somehow there will be an electric sexual sizzle in the air around them that almost gives their secret away to others. Those who know them well will sense this aura of electricity. Usually there're other invisible ripples created from their alliance and their union spreads waves of consequences elsewhere. This doesn't only occur because they may be married to other partners; even if they are both single and free to be together without anyone else being affected, dramas will occur because of the dramatic nature of their personalities.

However, if Ms Aries and Mr Scorpio fall into each other's passionate arms, usually someone is upset by their involvement, somewhere (whether they be parents, friends or their peer group). But if the power of love is strong between them, even if it does mean having the whole world turn against them, nothing can or will stop them. They will have their way at any cost. That's just the way it goes when these two dynamic, determined people find each other and romantic magic rushes through their hearts, bodies, minds and spirits.

Fate often plays a role in the way that their relationship, passions and romance unfold. In some cases because of the strange things they feel, this couple may feel like they are victims of a love-spell or some other sorcery. They may sense that they almost have no control over what is taking place. Even if they attempt to avoid each other and never see each other again, unexpected serendipitous meetings may arise throwing them together again. It's as though the invisible components that make up our conscious universe weave together and create strong bonds of mutual attraction between them that cannot be broken until they've experienced whatever it is they are destined to experience together. In their case, when Ms Aries and Mr Scorpio really know how to push each other's love buttons, then it's a strong possibility that not only their lives but even the world at large may be affected by their meeting as well.

However, this extreme force of magnetic attraction can work both for and against them. It can overload their minds and stop them from dealing with everyday life responsibilities. They may become overly jealous and possessive and feel out of their emotional depth. But those Aries gals and Scorpio guys that survive the love surges that come hand in hand with their intense first attraction, often have very connected ongoing relationships. Some even make it into longer-term relationships and have wonderful family and home lives together. But often this union becomes a quest that pushes them both to choose constantly between the power of love and their individual love for power. Ms Aries and Mr Scorpio are very independent forceful people. That's why they are likely to go through many power struggles as they navigate their way through the gamut of experiences that being in a relationship entails. But if they manage to share the power equally, then they have one of the best chances of the zodiac to have a passionate, romantic, exciting partnership — a love match created in heaven (and sometimes created in hell).

Aries man — Scorpio woman

 The *'Whatever you're doing, don't stop'* relationship

Watch out Mr Aries. If you are a true free spirit of an Aries guy, who loves being foctloose and fancy-free; if you don't like to explain yourself to anyone and you have a rebellious spirit; if you're falling or have fallen in love with a Scorpio stargal — guess what? You may have to change your wild-at-heart ways. If you have set your romantic sights on a Scorpio siren you are going to have to watch your romantic p's and q's and be on your best behaviour — or else! Even if she's all things nice and sugar and spice on the outside, don't be fooled. Ms Scorpio isn't a lightweight contender when it comes to dealing with others in the relationship realms, she's much more of a heavyweight. Where you like to play the field, run the emotional female gauntlet and kick up your Ram's heels, Ms Scorpio is the opposite and won't take well to your frivolous behaviour. Of course, if she really truly gets you 'into her blood' she may hand over her power to you (and be the power behind your success) but she probably will only suffer any bad behaviour from you (or any shortfalls in your character) for the short-term, rather than the long-term if she's any true-blue Scorpio gal. In fact, give her the runaround, show weakness or be a heartbreaker, and she probably won't find it amusing at all. So, if you aren't prepared to settle down, play the game of life by her rules and generally behave yourself and be true to her, you are certainly messing with the wrong gal of the zodiac.

Especially in his younger years, it is Mr Aries' nature to have fun, take life lightly and only really care about what truly matters to him. Fair enough in most cases, but once he has aligned himself with a powerful Scorpio woman he is about to find his life alters dramatically. Ms Scorpio is ruled by the most powerful planet of the zodiac, Pluto, and that means she is no little, delicate rose. She's more like a rare black orchid. She may appear to be as cute as a button, soft as velvet and as alluring as any mythical siren, but underneath her cuddly exterior Ms Scorpio is a gal with sufficient power in her little finger to turn the tides or bring any powerful man to heel. And if she wants to conquer and change an Aries man and convert him to her way of living, loving and planning the future (if he is truly in love with her), this is something she can do with one hand tied behind her back.

As Ms Scorpio is so powerful on the inside, rather than exposing it on the outside, Mr Aries can be quite innocent and not be aware of 'who he is dealing with' when it comes to her. In their courting days, they may have some ego-battles and he'll often think he wins. But he doesn't! Ms Scorpio is a patient, resilient gal, who is prepared to bide her time and is capable of winning over him royally and getting what she wants eventually — without him even knowing it. Now if their relationship fails and they both go in different directions he may even imagine that she and he are still 'good mates'. Maybe they are 'friends' on certain levels, but when it comes to trust and loyalty, Ms Scorpio holds these highly on her list of values. If Mr Aries sells these high values of hers short and lets her down badly (something he often has a tendency to do), she won't have a short memory about this fact. In fact, she'll have a super-long one regarding his indiscretions or shortfalls. She doesn't take upsets lightly, so he shouldn't mess with her heartstrings unless he's prepared to pay the consequences of his actions for a long time to come.

If they do have a romance and it doesn't work out, over time they may drift back together again. He may even suggest or propose that they have a fresh start, and consider that if they do 'try again to patch things up', any indiscretions or problems he may have had with Ms Scorpio in the past are over and forgotten and start their relationship on a new page. WRONG! Ms Scorpio has the most brilliant memory in the zodiac for any romantic slights or hurts, and she isn't likely to take a chance on the wrong guy again.

That's why Mr Aries, if he truly loves his Scorpio gal, has to be extremely aware of the sensitive power, integrity and fair-play balance that exists in their relationship. As long as he plays fair, and is loyal and responsible in the relationship, he will have some of the most wonderful times of his life with his Scorpio gal. But if he isn't, he had better be prepared to face the wrath of the Goddess, as Ms Scorpio is closely aligned with the Goddess and she totally subscribes to the romantic theory — that 'hell hath no fury as a (Scorpio) woman scorned'. I'll finish this off as I started: WATCH OUT MR ARIES. Don't mess with the sensitive soul of the Scorpio woman, or you'll be sorry — and you can't say you haven't been warned.

ARIES — SAGITTARIUS relationship

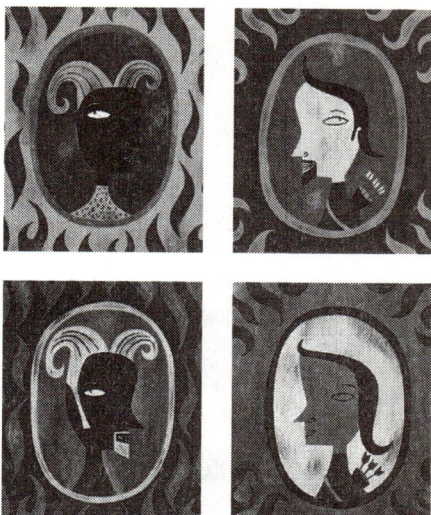

The *'Let's party!'* relationship

STAR ARIES–SAGITTARIUS COUPLE
Alec Baldwin and Kim Basinger

Hooray for love! Here we have some very special, magical zodiac matchmaking. Many kindred spirits are to be found born under the signs of Aries and Sagittarius. And because their powerful zodiac connection is so strongly in their favour, some great relationships and romances are forged when these two fire signs of the zodiac fall in love and become a romantic match. With the same gung-ho approach to life, and born with an optimistic outlook and generous nature, both Aries and Sagittarius are naturally like-minded. That's why they often become best friends and even high-suited lovers. Astrologically, they have strong links and share the same energy flow of fiery, enthusiastic energy. They naturally seem to be comfortable and at ease in each other's company because they share many common goals, personality traits and desires.

As they see life from the same 'fire-sign viewing window' astrologically, the greatest attribute that Aries and Sagittarius have to offer each other is 'understanding'. The fact that they are forged from similar astrological genetics gives them an abundance of similar tendencies, outlooks and life choices to call upon and share. When the right Sagittarius and Aries unite and become a loving couple, often their union transforms their lives into something like a lifetime party — a party for two (or when children come around) for three, four or even more! And don't forget the pets too, and the variety of friends, neighbours, family and long list of other hobbies and pastimes that generally play a big role in making their combined lives complete!

Aries woman—Sagittarius man

 The *'Eek! You might actually really be the right one'* relationship

This could be the 'real' thing if Venus (the planet of love, romance and poetry) decides to smile upon the Aries woman and the Sagittarian man. Certainly it won't be a run-of-the-mill humdrum relationship, whether it works or fails. As drama, excitement, passion and adventure is automatically written in the stars when the Aries woman and the Sagittarian man get together romantically. Their mutual flair for the overly dramatic, the desire to pursue their passion at all costs, ensures this union will generate a love story suitable for making into a motion picture. Their meeting will possibly happen in a most fateful way; and if there's a real attunement to each other and the timing is right, their love affair will be an intense one where passions run wild. If their attraction, desire and interest in each other are continued after the initial 'honeymoon', and their sexual intoxication phases of infatuation have run their course, they will have passed their first love test. Infatuation can blind both of these people to reality, so often they tend to fall in love with the idea of 'love' itself, rather than the person they believe they do adore!

Now falling in love and following their passions often seems to involve drama for these two. Often they face complications when they fall in love, because it is naturally a part of both of their natures to stir up dramas, no matter what they are doing. When these two are 'right' for each other they'll probably have to move certain pieces of their lives around to make space and room to be together. This may mean that they need to make a few major moves (change location, school, or job); or go through some kind of dealing with an ex-partner, getting themselves free from past entanglements etc, and game-playing situations.

Possibly Mr Sagittarius will have to let his current wife, fiancée or girlfriend know that his affections have moved elsewhere; and he'll have a tough time doing that because he doesn't like confrontation or dealing with disharmony with others. Or Ms Aries will be in a similar position where her heart is supposed to be promised to another. She may be engaged or even married, which leaves her with plenty of explaining to do. But if their meeting is a powerful one and they make a big impact on each other, overcoming all obstacles or hurdles placed before them, sooner or later they'll break old ties and move on to a new life together. Because when the love bug bites these two special zodiac lovers, it usually bites deeply! And they'll go to great lengths (or through enormous emotional turmoil) to be together.

They usually feel strongly connected because fate often plays a major role in bringing them together — in a way that would make them believe 'they were meant for each other'. There are many times when these two appear to be magnetically drawn towards each other, as destiny seems intent to propel them into each other's arms. For example, sometimes these two were next-door neighbours who grew up together, lost contact later in life and then met up again through a chance encounter. Their lives may cross paths in many unusual or very expected ways. They may even go to school together and have teenage crushes on each other. Or maybe they meet at a social gathering, at work, at a sports meeting or at a party. No matter where or how they may meet, should they 'hit it off', not only are they likely to be wonderfully suited as sexual partners but they are also likely to really enjoy each other's entertaining company. They may even get a thrill from the odd argument or from the excitement of the overly-dramatic, emotional storms that sometimes erupt between them (naturally as long as any disruptive times don't get out of control, otherwise they can turn into relationship World War Three). So the Aries woman and the Sagittarian man often have heaps of common interests and behavioural traits that bind them. They truly can feel that they are genuine soul mates and have a higher purpose to fulfil by being together too.

Although they do have excellent zodiac credentials for forming a winning romantic team together, naturally this couple (like all couples) will face many relationship highs and lows. They both have volatile natures and that means they are both short on patience and perseverance. If they do hit a rough patch in life and experience disillusionment, they can have some stormy moments and say some unwise things to each other. Fortunately both Ms Aries and Mr Sagittarius are born with naturally high spirits, and this combination of positive outlook is a tremendous blessing for them. It helps them to recover quickly from any setbacks. Plus, the great thing that the Aries woman and Sagittarian man have in common is that they love to kiss and make up. And they love to have fun much more than they enjoy bad times, so they'll go out of their way to make friends with each other again after a disagreement.

They also share mutual interests, which will help them build stronger foundations under the love structure. They may play sport together, go camping, travel in a campervan, buy properties and renovate them, have a big family, start a business together; but whatever they do they are both likely to have fun doing it. And if having fun with each other is a lifetime possibility they are offered by being together, combine this with their romantic attachment for each other; then these two are set on a pathway towards having the best times in each other's company. This is so important to both of them — to have a love-mate and playmate all in one. They will usually be highly successful socially too, because they both love expanding their lives through making friends and being around others. Over the course of their time together they both know that they have places to go, people to meet, adventures to seek, and this common interest is what often binds them to each other.

If they have a falling out with each other, another thing that 'gets them over any relationship disagreement or hurdle' is their ability to see the funny side to situations. They can usually enjoy a good laugh together. Now this laughter can stop abruptly and things may not appear to be so funny when serious problems erupt between them. Ms Aries and Mr Sagittarius can easily break each other's heart, just as much as they can make each other happy. So they need to be cautious, particularly when it comes to dealing with problems relating to the two most sensitive areas of their combined lives, 'faithfulness' and the way they 'spend' money (especially their joint money).

If these two signs aren't dedicated to each other enough to be honest, loyal, committed, and (particularly) realistic about the way they handle money and go about their spending sprees, stormy clouds may soon be blotting out the relationship sunshine over their lives. Both these areas of 'faithfulness' and 'over-spending' can become their relationship Waterloo. Ms Aries and Mr Sagittarius can be foolish when dealing with fidelity issues and money can quickly burn a hole in both their pockets if they aren't careful. Any breakdown in these two areas of life frequently leads them into the divorce or bankruptcy court, or both. But if they carefully sidestep around flirtatious temptations and set themselves a wise financial budget (or get a professional adviser), then this couple often find that they begin to live a wonderful lifestyle together. When this occurs, they will love each other even more (and become extremely devoted) because they realise that they have both helped to create this 'fantastic' lifestyle and they are grateful for the chance and the thrill of sharing it together. Have a good one!

Aries man—Sagittarius woman

 The *'I think I might be falling madly in love with you'* relationship

The omens are positive when these two very passionate zodiac signs align their hearts, minds and bodies in a love relationship. In fact, many happy marriages are forged between these two star signs! When Mr Aries and Ms Sagittarius fall in love, they do so with a special blessing from heaven above. And this union may even be a match made in heaven, because Mr Aries and Ms Sagittarius have the high-rated zodiac potential to create a wonderful partnership together.

Though while on astro-levels Mr Aries and Ms Sagittarius are so well suited, naturally as this world is filled with tests and trials (especially when relating to matters of romance and passion), there's still many things that can and might go wrong between them. And it often does! (Look at Aries, Alec Baldwin and Sagittarian, Kim Basinger as examples).

As they are aligned together as fire signs of the zodiac, sure, their first meeting can take their breath away; and their first kiss can do much more — it can set their hearts and souls on fire. Great passion, intoxicating desires and intense longings often overwhelm them. Once the relationship has passed beyond its first infatuation phase, before long the tough reality of living life in everyday terms (without all the romantic trappings) hits home very quickly. What they initially found so attractive in each other can sometimes become irritating or annoying. Instead of driving each other wild with desire, they can simply drive each other wild! If this occurs, one of their biggest problems is dealing with each other!

One of the most difficult things they have to deal with is the fact that they can both be very stubborn, independent people. As both of them are high on ego; low on tolerance, they sometimes argue or tend to disagree on everything and anything, rather than attempt to reach a compromise. So after the honeymoon is over, and the time arrives to navigate their love boat through the swirling ocean of everyday pressures and emotions that face any relationship, their wonderful connection often ends up being rocked by jealousy, anger or control issues.

Mr Aries is also the one man of the zodiac who doesn't naturally adapt easily to monogamy. Being one of the most appealing and sexually attractive guys in the zodiac male line-up, Mr Aries is very much a rebel and he's one man of the zodiac who can be extremely intolerant, too. He doesn't like anybody telling him what to do; even the one he loves. He doesn't take criticism kindly (even if it's well-intentioned). When problems erupt around him, he has a tendency to place the blame elsewhere, rather than look into his own role-playing or contribution to the problem.

He can also tend to operate his life under the heading 'do as I say, not as I do', and as Ms Sagittarius is a gal that will call 'a spade a spade' at any time; or 'a hypocrite a hypocrite' — he sometimes doesn't like the way Ms Sagittarius is so constantly aware of his shortfalls, and how she is just as happy to tell him about them. Or, if she doesn't say anything about his ego-quirks or other shortfalls; he may dislike the fact that she can constantly mirror his shortfalls of character or behaviour back to him, with just a look in her eye. He can feel as if she disapproves of him or is picking on him (when in fact it is sometimes his own guilt he is reacting to, not her attitude to him at all).

Being one of the most independently-minded and free-spirited stargals of the zodiac, Ms Sagittarius isn't likely to be an easy gal for Mr Aries to handle. And, even if she is totally in love with him (and consequently prepared to compromise as much as she can to keep him happy), Ms Sagittarius isn't a gal any man can walk all over indefinitely. She's smart too and it won't work for him to attempt to pull the wool over her eyes for long. If ever there was a gal who liked to be free to express herself and hates to be corralled, it is Ms Sagittarius. After all, the symbol for her sign is half man–half horse; and she's indeed a proud filly, one that doesn't like to be roped in by anyone, unless he is worthy of her heart's truest form of worship.

Mr Aries will need to win her respect to maintain and sustain her love for him, and often he can disappoint her (especially over the longer term). Mr Aries can be the type of guy who tends to throw his opinions, values and weight around; and at first Ms Sagittarius may like that 'outspoken' quality about him, but later on she won't appreciate his often over-dramatic opinions or responses. Particularly, she won't enjoy being told what to think, what to do, or how to live her life by him. She hates to be bullied or controlled, so Mr Aries is going to need to curb his natural tendency to shout out orders or get his own way at any price. Considering both their personalities are highly charged on ego, there are definitely facets of both the Aries man and Sagittarius woman's characters that cry out for a good dose of diplomacy. The fact that they have big egos and small amounts of diplomacy can definitely lead to problems in this match over the longer term.

Although they are linked so merrily and positively in the zodiac romantic lineup, this couple still has to work at being well suited, otherwise they will fail to meet the 'long-term' relationship test. This can truly be a relationship that falls into the category of 'I can't live with you, but I can't live without you' variety. If they battle against each other's strong will, they can have real battles with each other, and if they get out of hand, this relationship often hits the relationship wall. If it does, it hits it in a resounding and sometimes most ungraceful fashion. So if these two do not learn to treat each other kindly, develop patience and be prepared to compromise, they often just can't make their relationship past the test of time. Although they may love each other a great deal, the invisible magic spell that once bound them tightly becomes broken; it is often 'sayonara' for this duo.

Because of the intensity that can exist between them, it is no surprise that they can frequently be found seeking marriage counselling, trying to work out their differences. They know they truly love each other but sometimes they feel they just can't live together — and that realisation hurts. Plus of course, the fact that these two signs (especially if they are in love and developing their relationship over time), are so powerfully connected that they truly can be mirrors of each other's soul. Sometimes both of them are not always going to like what they see reflected back at them about themselves as they can get too close to each other for comfort. Nevertheless, if they can deal with the entire intensity that engulfs them at times, they can certainly complete each other's existence in a way that no other sign of the zodiac possibly can. And if they manage to overcome any obstacles, this relationship can be the most blessed one of the zodiac.

ARIES—CAPRICORN relationship

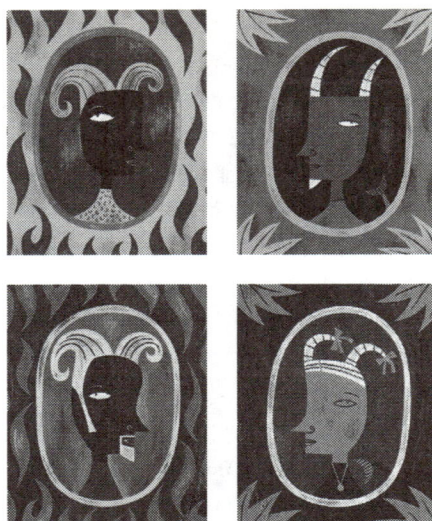

The *'all or nothing'* relationship

STAR ARIES–CAPRICORN COUPLE
Kate Hudson and Chris Robinson

Stirring up the relationship pot! That's what happens when you align an Aries and a Capricorn in the romantic stakes. The blending of these two signs often creates an intoxicating relationship mix or a horrible mess. Coming from different elements of astrology, fire (Aries) and earth (Capricorn) are not particularly suited, but that doesn't mean they can't develop their relationship into an ideal one. Occasionally the very difference in their natures is an asset more than a liability. As both of them are powerful individuals in their own right, if they decide to have a power struggle to see who wields the greater control over the other, they can turn a relationship into an 'all or nothing' affair. Consequently, this relationship often shows whether it will succeed or not within a short period of time. However, there are occasions when they somehow know they aren't right together, but they will stubbornly soldier on regardless, as there's a strong determination factor in force between them.

Also, there can be a fatefully strong, physical attraction in operation between them. This sexual attraction may make it difficult for either of them to acknowledge that all is not necessarily as compatible between the two of them as it perhaps could be, or should be. Both these signs rank amongst those placed highest on the sexually driven list of people in the zodiac — their sex drives often over-rule their common sense. They are likely to have some work to do to really find peace of mind with each other, but their endeavours can be well rewarded. And where the romance magic is strongly in force between them many times these two can fall madly in love and make a devoted couple who can also build up an excellent business, companionship team or family dynasty together.

Aries woman — Capricorn man

 The *'I don't know how or why but I think you're driving me crazy!'* relationship

'It's either my way or the highway' is often the catch-cry that flows between these two very stubborn and sometimes highly independent signs of the zodiac. As both are strong-willed, this zodiac combination can find it a major problem to operate on middle ground. That is why their relationship is either going straight forward, straight back or nowhere at all. No matter what happens or how fate plays its hand throughout their meeting, dating and romancing phases, the merging of the Aries gal with the Capricorn guy is unlikely to be smooth sailing. However, whether it sails along smoothly or not, whatever occurs between them is certain to be interesting, passionate and very educational!

When the Ram gal meets up with the Goat guy they have plenty in common and plenty that's not. One thing they do share is a highly developed sexual nature. If they are attuned to each other physically, often this couple can experience an almost instant attraction — the kind that stops their breath for a moment. Yet sometimes this instant attraction doesn't hang around for long. However, if they pass the initial relationship infatuation stage, they need to be ready to face some argumentative moments in their relationship. Being the Ram and the Goat signs of the zodiac, it is only natural that they will butt heads occasionally and often need to jostle each other to work out who is going to control the various areas of their relationship. (Some power games are likely to arise because neither of these two people like to give an inch!)

However, if they can overcome their initial differences the benefits they can derive from each other are boundless. Miss Ram brings adventure into Mr Goat's life and encourages him to dare to do things he would normally never consider possible. She opens up all kinds of unusual windows of opportunity for him that would otherwise remain tightly closed. What he provides for her is a sense of security and belonging that practically no other man of the zodiac can duplicate. He loves her, is dependable and steadfast, and most importantly, he brings stability into her life, something that she craves. She is rather spontaneous and headstrong and he is more practical and logical; together they can create a strong and supportive team that grows in strength because they manage to teach each other wonderful lessons as they go through life.

Once they get to truly know each other, sometimes (if they've managed to temper their stubborn one-eyed natures) they can even develop a genuinely wonderful and unique understanding and true friendship between themselves. So they become not only lovers but best friends, too. They may laugh at different things, but if they overcome their miscommunications, at least they will begin to laugh together. They have a great deal of strengths and weaknesses operating between them; but where he is strong, she is weak and vice versa — this balances their relationship exchange and makes them stronger all round. And while they can tend to live their lives at a very different pace from each other, that difference of pace can be good for them too, because it provides some excitement and variety to their routine.

A danger area for them is their ability to be temperamental and sulky at times. As long as they don't become constantly critical or cranky over trivial issues, they can usually sort through their differences of opinion. But if they get to loggerheads and their stubbornness won't let them forgive and forget, they can turn into enemies. Saying 'sorry' isn't likely to be a word either of them love to use. In fact, it possibly isn't featured in either one of their vocabularies. If this couple ever does start to get on each other's nerves, they will get on each other's nerves *big* time. Because both of them have a tendency to be hypercritical, they may also need to allow their partner to feel comfortable being themselves, and not try to change them to more the person they want them to be. Though generally their problems are workable ones if handled diplomatically; and often they are wise enough to see the values they offer each other, outweigh the disadvantages. Counselling is important for this couple when marriage difficulties erupt, as a third person can usually guide them through relationship troubled waters far better than if they attempt to negotiate their way through them alone.

In behaviour, Ms Ram is likely to be the outgoing one, while Mr Goat is more the introvert. This often means that she stirs him up and he quietens her down. Fortunately, most of the time he's her biggest fan and she is his, too! Although they may view life from very different perspectives, they enjoy learning to share each other's different world. They are often very social (playing the role of excellent hosts), trendsetters, successful in business (they may even work together, or have a company business), and they make great parents. In fact on many levels, particularly in the area of parenting, they make a terrific team.

On emotional levels, Ms Aries may at times be 'high maintenance' as far as Mr Capricorn is concerned because she has a dramatic, demanding nature. She can keep him on his toes and demand a great deal from him because she loves to be the centre of attention. If he is busy and otherwise occupied and she isn't receiving his attention, she'll attract a calamity or do or say something to get his full focus. Sometimes he finds her childlike and this appeals to him; other times he finds that she is childish in her behaviour and this can annoy him. She can be contrary and changeable and he likes to have more predictable energy flows surrounding him, rather than someone who is constantly creating dramas. This aspect of her character will either endear her to him, or wear him out — depending on his tolerance levels (and often Mr Capricorn is one of the most tolerant of all the zodiac men, so this can work well in her favour).

In everyday life, Ms Aries is likely to be a go-getter. While Mr Capricorn is not necessarily a couch potato or slouch, he is likely to be more laid-back than she. While she is anxious to travel, meet up with friends, organise family reunions or other get-togethers, Mr Capricorn can be content doing his work, organising the home and garden and watching his sport on TV, or playing a sport himself. He doesn't need to be so constantly on the 'go', but sometimes her desire to fill up their social calendar, works well for him. She can be a superb networker and often he benefits from the opportunities she conjures up where he is able to meet the right people, at the right time, to make the right deal (and have fun while he's doing it, too).

As mentioned earlier, one area where they will naturally fit together well is when the pitter-patter of little feet resound within their home. They delight in the family structure and the entertainment and satisfaction their children provide. Because of their love of the family unit, this couple often decides to have several or many children. If they are childless they are likely to explore IVF programs, adopt or become excellent aunts and uncles because they usually have a strong desire to raise a family.

If their sexual chemistry and passion is strong, even after a quarrel they will quickly kiss and make up. Plenty of their arguments are joyfully resolved in the bedroom and the boudoir, or wherever else they fancy making love. These are sometimes the best times in their relationships because Ms Aries and Mr Capricorn can be in a league of their own when their lusty, sexual passions are aroused (especially by each other). Naturally these same passions if unleashed outside the relationship can mean that infidelities (of either of them) eventually create tremendous strains upon their union.

Aries man — Capricorn woman

 The *'Watch out! I'm not just one of your toys'* relationship

The big issue that this couple is going to face is 'Exactly who is on top in this relationship?' When the Aries man and Capricorn woman team up it can be a case of either 'making love or war', because both of these individuals are going to be very strong-willed and want to have a controlling vote in whatever is happening between them. One thing will be certain, strong opinions will run hot in this relationship. These two have something to say about most things in life. Unfortunately, the impetuous Aries Mars man — who has a habit of just saying what is on his mind — can cause some problems because he says things that upset his Capricorn maiden, and when she's mad at him she's likely to make him suffer (one way or another). The Aries forthright man does not edit what he is going to say to anyone (even his true love). So if he feels like his partner should be doing something a little (or a lot) differently to please him, then he will come right out and say it.

If anyone can 'get under her goat' it's Mr Aries. The Goat girl, who is not usually over-sensitive, can all of a sudden go into one of those Saturnian black moods, after being hurt by his outburst. So much so that hours later her gloomy mood has really settled in, and there is nothing he can do to get her out of it. In fact, being a person who lives more for the moment than she does, Mr Aries often has no idea why she is even in that mood, as he has well and truly moved on and forgotten about his outburst precisely one and a half minutes after it happened. A major difference in personality traits exists between them and they'll discover this difference early on in their relationship. He acts and then forgets his action; she remembers everything. If he acts poorly or unwisely, she holds his behaviour close to her heart and broods over it! This can naturally cause tensions and in the longer term of this relationship, it does!

So the energies of these two can be, let's say, unsettling, and not always in sync with each other. Especially as the Mars man wants to be the boss and Ms Goat girl is definitely not one to be bossed around. But if Ms Goat girl is clever (and most of them are very clever indeed), and she really loves her assertive Man of Mars she will use her charm to get her own way. She learns early in their relationship that an over reaction to the Aries man's outbursts is definitely not the way to win his affections. Instead, she learns to play the feminine role by putting on her prettiest dress, spraying on the perfume he gave her for her birthday, smiling sweetly, getting his slippers, making a cup of tea and then settling him down for a night of sexual pampering (something he adores). Ms Capricorn is smart enough to soon have him eating out of her hand in no time (if that's her true desire).

But sometimes she gets cranky at him because he demands so much perfection from her and this can tire her out and burn up any passion she feels for him like wildfire. The Mars man loves femininity and he likes to stay in shape, eat well, look good and this is also how he sees his ideal mate. He will count her calories, insist she skips desserts and constantly remind her if she puts on an additional inch around the waistline. He wants to feel proud when he takes her out to dinner or to visit his family and friends. But keep in mind that he doesn't want to see how Ms Capricorn can benefit otherwise from looking beautiful. He wants to have her beautiful for him, and not attract attention from other men — jealousy lurks close to his heart, so that too can create problems.

The areas where this couple can be extremely successful are in business and finances. These two together can build up a substantial financial nest egg, but if the Mars man prefers his Goat girl to stay home and look after the family and house she may as well forget about going to work. She'll need to follow his wishes and be a loyal and loving support to him. She is just the right gal to entertain his business colleagues, organise social outings, so that he meets the right people and project the perfect image of a happy, healthy and successful family — all of which is very important to her Aries mate. If she supports him and they complement each other in their daily ways he will be a good provider; and she and the family will not want for much in life.

One of the main issues these two need to decide is 'who is in control?', and once this is sorted out, then there is hardly a couple who are happier. The concern for the Goat girl, if she's not strong enough, is that she can feel she has lost herself and is living vicariously through him. This is generally not a good thing for the Goat girl's soul, and it's only a matter of time till she breaks out and regains her personal control, which could very well mean fireworks in the relationship. On the other hand, our Mars man thinks he is doing his Goat girl a favour by trying to mould her and change her into what he believes is a better and more productive person — one who is more suitable for him and his lifestyle. Big mistake! Ms Capricorn is not about to be changed, moulded or coerced into doing anything, unless she can see a definite benefit to herself, so Mr Aries better quickly acquire a good dose of tactfulness, which is not one of his better traits.

But if these two can get past the control issue and find a healthy balance in their life, then they'll soon find their patience and tolerance of each other is well rewarded on sexual levels. Their bedroom antics are well worth being written up in the karma sutra. In fact, they can be extremely imaginative lovers and their bedroom frolicking won't stop at the bedroom. When the Aries Ram wants to make love, then the lounge, the kitchen table, the car or anywhere else for that matter is just perfect with him. If you are a Capricorn gal or an Aries guy who wants to keep this relationship thriving and desire to keep your partner home by your side, then make sure you keep the passion flowing. Romance each other, purchase a few of those sex books which show you 1001 ways to make love; make sure you both keep an open mind and you'll be forever in each other's heart! Also be fair with each other and avoid being unrealistic in your expectations of what a relationship is meant to be. When the Aries man and the Capricorn woman truly want to make this relationship work, they need to remember to try a little tenderness, be patient and allow the other person in the relationship the space and opportunity to be themselves. It is vital that each partner be allowed to express their unique personality and identity without criticism from the other. So if you're a Capricorn woman or an Aries man, remember it isn't wise to try to change each other too much. The secret to your successful relationship is to love each other as you truly are, because you are truly different but divinely different!

ARIES — AQUARIUS relationship

The *'Relax. You've got nothing to worry about. Ha ha!'* relationship

STAR ARIES–AQUARIUS COUPLE
Heath Ledger and Heather Graham

Hooray for romance! It often provides both the Aries and Aquarian with a new lease (or take) on life if they meet their perfect match and they become an Aries–Aquarius coupling. While this couple may sometimes be viewed as 'an odd or ill-suited couple', they still seem to sometimes have the right ingredients to set the world on fire. Aries and Aquarius together generate innovative, creative energy. And on everyday levels, the Aries and Aquarius share a great deal of common interests. They both love to look into the future and see something tantalising waiting for them. And they easily become bored with anything, or anyone, that isn't cutting edge. There's a strong desire within these two signs, to view life as an experiment or experience and not to live it as though it was a dress rehearsal.

And they can help each other evolve and grow too. Sometimes Aquarius however, being a fixed sign of the zodiac, becomes unhappily stuck in a rut. That's the ideal moment for Aries to arrive in their life and blast them out of that rut in an instant. Conversely, bold Aries often wanders too close to the cutting edge of life. When they do, Aquarius seems to have a natural ability to bring them back from the brink of getting too far out of the depth for comfort. So there's a great natural flow and adaptability between the subliminal and more obvious tugs, flows and exchanges between these two. If this link works in their romantic favour, their time together can be adventurous, enterprising and also extremely romantic and super sexy.

Aries woman—Aquarius man

 The *'I think, but I still don't really know, but maybe – yikes – I've got a crush on you'* relationship

If they are interested in each other as individuals, then when this pair doesn't make it as lovers, they can easily be friends. Because this couple (under the surface if not on apparent levels) seems to have a lot of mutual goals, aims and interests even if some of these shared involvements are strange ones. In fact, there's a great astro-flow in force between Ms Aries and Mr Aquarius. They seem to fit well together but, like all couples, only if the chemistry between them is 'right'. He's often the guy who reminds her somehow of her father; or reminds her of someone she knew in the past (possibly even a case of déjà vu of someone she feels she knew from a previous life). And what really keeps Ms Aries curious about Mr Aquarius is that he's mysterious, detached and unique as well. The Aquarian man of the zodiac is no open book. He's an under-the-surface kinda guy. He's not a flash Romeo type who flatters women, enjoys the chase and reels them in either. He doesn't need to prove that he can assert his charms over the opposite sex, but he does it anyway. He's more the strong, silent type, and this ability of his to be a trifle distant and aloof, makes him especially attractive to the much more flirtatious or go-getting Ms Aries — although this aloof and distant characteristic of his may not be so attractive to her later in the relationship.

When they meet Mr Aquarius may be standing apart from the crowd, gazing out the window or glancing at the book titles in a bookcase. Ms Aries (being the feisty 'take action' gal of the zodiac) may make the first move by introducing herself, asking him to dance or doing something outrageous to attract his attention. If she doesn't take the initiative they may not even end up meeting, so her ability to kick down barriers and seize the moment often portrays a pivotal role in the way these two get their relationship rolling forward.

Once Ms Aries has got his attention it won't take long (if the chemistry ignites) for him to become totally enchanted with her. She has 'oomph' and she easily entertains him, because she's the Ms Personality of the Zodiac; whereas he's Mr Cool, Distant and Detached. Where some gals just can't seem to get through Mr Aquarius' distant barriers, she's *sooo* comfortable at teasing him. She's also merrily flirtatious, making certain in her words, actions or behaviour that she's giving him something a little sexual to think about. Amazingly, she manages to make this sometimes sombre, serious man of the zodiac, chuckle at her antics. He likes the way she laughs, jokes and tells stories (and possibly wishes he was as easy-going at conversing with others, but he isn't). She likes the way he listens intently and seems very pleased to allow her to hold court or keep the focus of attention upon her. In fact, they put on a great show for each other, although she's mainly doing the show and he's often playing the role of audience — but what does it matter, it's still a good show. All in all, they can have a fine time together (so long as Ms Aries doesn't become bored and Mr Aquarius doesn't become tired of her antics). What may happen (if the chemistry and love bug isn't strong enough to keep the magic alive) is that she may burn him out and she may bore him — eventually. In the meantime though they are likely to have a lot of fun and loads of laughs, and lots of heart-to-heart discussions.

Although they may have a few obstacles to overcome when approaching the responsibilities and commitment involved in a long-term relationship, at least for a flirtation, a love affair or a magical tryst or close encounter, these two usually find each other fascinating and alluring. And there's definitely some unusual sexual psychic energy between them. This couple can experience electric shocks when their hands touch or their knees brush under the table. They make love gazing deeply into each other's eyes and have the power to create psychic electricity between them when their hearts and souls open up to each other.

Now what happens after the initial courtship? After their initial red-hot passion phase passes, she may find his sexual ardour cools more rapidly than hers, but still they maintain a closeness in their lovemaking that satisfies most of her highly charged sexual needs. In everyday life, he may be preoccupied and busier than she expected and not quite as attentive. To his credit, although distracted, he somehow still remembers to buy the chocolates or the flowers when the moment is right, so she doesn't feel left out. But there are times when she needs extra attention that he cannot provide, and this may encourage her to have outside interests (that don't include him), or get involved in situations that keep her busy at work or home so that she isn't bored. When children come along this couple truly shines. He makes a fantastic dad (even if he does expect the children to be quiet all the time). He teaches them to read and count and enjoys seeing their comprehension expand. He is patient but also a firm father and the children adore him; and they also usually behave better when he's at home than when he isn't. Ms Aries turns out to be queen of the kids once she's playing the role of mum. She holds sleepovers for the neighbourhood children, throws wonderful birthday parties, and even makes the 'dress-up' clothes for fancy dress. She loves joining in their games and sharing their dreams.

Although these two are very different as people, if they compromise and work through these differences they can have a wonderful time together. But there will be definite phases of their relationship when they'll need time apart, or to enjoy the company of other people outside of each other. Too much of each other could end up burning this relationship out. So a dash of independence, plenty of trust and lots of mutual freedom could prove to be just what this relationship needs to keep it sizzling and fresh.

Aries man — Aquarius woman

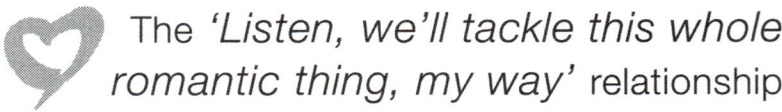 The *'Listen, we'll tackle this whole romantic thing, my way'* relationship

Uh-oh! Here's a combination that could turn out to be a wild one — the type where Murphy's Law seems to run their exchanges as much as fate and fortune too. There's high intensity operating between them and some romantic rivers to cross over as well, before they are successfully heading for happy-ever-after land. After all, you're dealing with two powerful individuals here. This zodiac man is born under the self-aware sign of Aries. He knows only one way of dealing with life, and that's 'his way'. He's independent, ego-driven and quite insensitive (not that he thinks he is), but he's also extremely attractive and adorable as well. Ms Aquarius is born under the detached sign of Aquarius. Even if she is cute, appealing and sometimes rather outrageous, she's always an intense thinker and she definitely has opinions of her own (fixed opinions most of the time). Her mental universe is the real world or solar system she lives in. And because her mind spins a million orbits a minute, she often is distracted by her inner dialogue or musings. In her exchanges with everyday life she usually misses a great deal, because she is thinking of something else when it happens and doesn't even notice.

As Mr Aries has a 'me-first consciousness' and is so tuned into himself (most of the time), and Ms Aquarius is tuned into everything around her; this can complicate their exchange of energy, communication and feeling. Where he's likely to be expecting (and wanting) to receive lots of attention from the Aquarian woman in his life, she's likely to be so busy thinking or preoccupied with everything else, that she may occasionally forget to give the attention to him! Horrors! How will he handle that? He'll probably get very miffed. So, sometimes there are going to be definite lulls in the communication flow or the emotional flow between them, but that doesn't necessarily need to create a major problem. As these two are very independent signs, sometimes these mental–emotional lapses or gaps between them works in their favour, allowing them room to grow, together and as individuals. If two people on this planet have what it takes to give each other 'space' these two have it, but they'll need to be secure within themselves to make this ability work for them.

As their relationship moves onto a more permanent level, Mr Aries will need to learn to be patient with his gorgeous Ms Aquarius. After all, she's the gal of the zodiac who always has 'plenty' or even 'too much' on her mind. As he is impulsive, impetuous and restless (and the man who believes that 'even immediate gratification takes too long'), he could become rather impatient with her at times because she just doesn't instantly see things his way. In fact she might frustrate him and he might even get cranky because she has opinions that don't always coincide with or match his. If he wants the relationship to work, Mr Aries is probably going to have to change. He'll need to learn to consider her desires, rather than simply leap to conclusions or take action on his own account. She teaches him that there is often more than one way to approach something or deal with life. If he is wise, he'll learn from what she has to offer, rather than battle wills against her. Sometimes she is his greatest mentor and he is hers, and when this occurs they are very ideally suited.

However, if they choose to battle wills (and both of them have very strong wills), this tugging and pulling at each other's heart and mind strings will cause ongoing arguments and conflicts. They need to appreciate and value each other's different ways of thinking and assimilating information and meet somewhere in the middle in their judgments. It is in working through differences and reaching compromises that this relationship will reach its true balance and power. But that won't come naturally. After all Mr Aries doesn't like to give an inch, and neither does Ms Aquarius, so frequently their frustrations with each other tear their relationship apart. Learning to give an inch won't come easily, but it is a magic healing tonic where these two are concerned and without it they create ripples or rifts that otherwise could have been avoided.

As they are both so one-eyed and strong-willed, it is likely that they'll have to put effort into being together and on occasions may need to go through the experience of breaking up and making up. When it is all said and done though, they'll find great comfort in each other's arms. When they are in tune and open to each other this combination of star lovers can be a very rewarding romance–relationship combination indeed.

But even with love magic helping their union blossom and grow, this relationship is destined to be challenging because both of these signs only have one way of approaching life — that's 'their way'. Stubborn, willful and determined, that union is not likely to simply be a love or lust match, but also a match of wills.

If they put in the time and effort necessary to achieve it, they can spend a lifetime of love together, though this isn't going to occur magically. They'll have to work at it because Ms Aquarius comes from a different mind-space and astrological zone from Mr Aries. And like foreigners who visit other countries, and need to adapt to new languages, food or customs they will need to do the same with each other in order to share their worlds. No matter how much love exists between them they constantly need to remember that she's an air (thinking) sign; he's a fire (action) sign, and that makes them look at life through very different zodiac eyes. Once they realise that and appreciate how this difference can open up new worlds to them, they can become cosmic travellers together, exploring new dimensions of living, loving and experiencing life that would not be available to them, if they weren't together.

ARIES—PISCES relationship

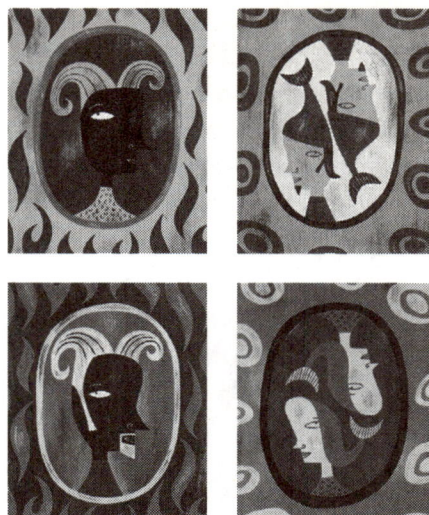

The '*Hello – goodbye,
I think I love you*' relationship

STAR ARIES–PISCES COUPLE
Sarah Michelle Gellar and Freddie Prinze Jr

Talk about taking a fish out of water! That's often what happens when you put a Ram with a Fish — and there is likely to be some confusion concerning exactly what is going on. These two signs manage to send many mixed messages to each other. But if real hot passion is the message they're sending, naturally this particular message is usually decoded very quickly. Both of these signs love to feel passion flowing through their veins. Aries is extremely passionate in nature, outlook and behaviour. They love a drama and deal with life and love in a dynamic, entrepreneurial and independent way. Pisces is also passionate, but softer in their expression of passion. In their outlook and behaviour they are also more flexible and less driven than Aries and prepared to go with the flow. Therefore, although this couple is frequently powerfully attracted to each other, often they'll have to learn to adapt to each other's very different perspective or take on life.

Not that their very different 'take' on life is bad for them. Sometimes they actually learn a great deal from each other and merge well together because they provide new dimensions of life to explore. The Aries will enjoy the Pisces sentimentality and beguiling (almost fantasy) outlook on life. And the Pisces will admire the brave, bold and bouncy way that the Aries goes about their everyday affairs or business. Where these two will really find a helpful common ground is in their passions. Both Pisces and Aries experience strong, sexual urges, and whatever sexual fantasies Pisces has in their dreams, Aries is likely to be the one sign of the zodiac that can make these sexual fantasies a reality.

Aries woman — Pisces man

 The *'This is some very weird love magic'* relationship

This is like 'the genie in the bottle' romantic relationship. Both of them feel as if there's some incredible love magic going on, but there'll be times they may ask themselves is this good or bad love magic. They may even feel that they have had a romantic wish come true by meeting each other. Unfortunately that feeling of fateful togetherness usually occurs at the beginning of the romance, not necessarily at the end of it. When these two meet and have a romantic connection — watch out! Reality is likely to be forgotten and total irrational fantasy will take over. And because their zodiac boundaries are expanded *waaay* beyond the romantic boundaries that most couples operate within, this couple is quite capable of just about anything and everything (for both better or worse) if their stars are romantically aligned. Ms Aries is likely to assume the role as leader in this relationship and be the one who calls the next move, but not always. Although Ms Aries is a powerful, strong-willed stargal, if she meets the right Pisces man and she loses her heart to him, he has the same effect on her as kryptonite has on Superman. In an instant, she loses her cosmic power and sometimes hands it over to him. Therefore, strange control issues or ego games are often played between this couple until they sort out who is going to be doing what to whom. Sometimes this imbalance affects them badly because this is one relationship that can often get off to a crazy, messed up start.

Their first meeting may occur under unusual or weird conditions. At first meeting Ms Aries may feel that her head has somehow gone into orbit and she just can't think straight. This 'sense of losing her mind' occurs quickly if Mr Pisces (who is something like the sailor of the zodiac) casts his psychic love-net out over her. When he begins to psychically pull her towards him she is unlikely to even guess that she's being caught 'hook, line and sinker'. He can conquer her heart without looking like he's up to anything — throwing out this invisible love-net is something Mr Pisces is an expert at doing. If he is one of the more slippery fish Pisces guys of the zodiac, he can be quite a player in the romantic stakes and often has many different relationships going on at once. Therefore there are many males born under this 'fishy' sign that break hearts and hate to be restricted where romance is concerned. That's why just casting the love-net isn't any guarantee that he is in love with any particular stargal, because sometimes this sexy man of the zodiac can be extremely indiscriminate about who he casts his attentions towards. In fact, part of the fun for him can be just throwing out his net and seeing what he catches!

However, being so flighty and experimental in his romantic notions may not last long once the right Ms Aries comes along. As these two signs are next-door neighbours on the zodiac wheel, there's something of a boy-gal, next-door association between them. This means they have the ability to create a relationship, which gives them the scope to be romantic lovers, kindred spirits, as well as best friends. Ms Aries is not a gal who takes her affections lightly. She is very dramatic and knows what she wants; so she isn't likely to take any shortfalls of behaviour from Mr Pisces too calmly. She isn't one of those coy gals of the zodiac who plays the love game like it's chess, or bides her time. She acts on her impulses and instincts, she is headstrong and she falls in love quickly. So if Mr Pisces isn't really serious about her but just having some fun and intends to make love and then move on elsewhere, then she'll pick up on it faster than most other zodiac gals, and she'll be gone in a puff of smoke before he even realises his cover has been blown.

Although they are very different from each other, if there's a genuine love connection taking place between them, this couple can settle into a very successful romantic relationship. Naturally they'll probably go through their stormy seasons and there could even be some bust-ups or separations before they settle into a long-term, committed relationship. However if their love is true, they generally seem to manage to work through their differences and continue on with their romance possibly suffering a few bruises or dents through what occurred, but not actually encountering a relationship train wreck as yet.

If this couple is sufficiently attracted to each other to want to make this relationship endure; and they move beyond the initial dating phase and begin a serious, long-term relationship, fate will play a huge role in how their relationship unfolds. Life will take them through many unusual twists and turns during their combined journey through life and there is likely to be some strong karma between them. Destiny will play many roles in what occurs between them and their children or friends may figure in this karmic connection as well. One thing is definite — this is no ordinary relationship, so extraordinary events, circumstances and experiences are certain to arise when these two share their life together.

Aries man — Pisces woman

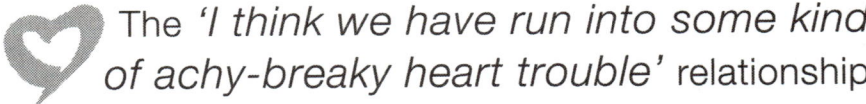 The *'I think we have run into some kind of achy-breaky heart trouble'* relationship

Mr Aries had better firmly strap on an invisible parachute around his heart because he'll need it to help him float gently down from cloud nine some time in the future. This is one zodiac romance that will take both parties on a bumpy and exciting, but also an extremely unusual romantic ride. That's because the experience of falling in love takes on a whole new dimension when these very different star signs are combined. Invisible love-bolts may even race through the air when the Aries Ram meets up with his special Pisces siren. The strange feelings he suddenly experiences churning over in the middle of his stomach may momentarily have him thinking his last meal isn't sitting well in his tummy. What he is experiencing, however, is swirling depths of emotions that he has possibly never felt before. This man of the zodiac is not generally vulnerable to coming down with serious, long-lasting bouts of the love bug. In fact, he can be quite self-sufficient and unsentimental, so any heart-felt shifts that ruffle up his emotions can make him feel extremely confused. Consequently, if he meets the Pisces gal who sweeps him off his usually steadfast hooves, she often succeeds in not just simply getting him to fall in love, but getting him to dive headfirst through all of his well-structured 'love barriers' into the swimming pool of love.

When he makes his play to win her heart he moves swiftly (and usually successfully). While many men of the zodiac find the Pisces Mermaid attractive (and she's likely to have many beaus), any other contenders who are attempting to win her affections are likely to be swept aside very quickly. Mr Aries generally has little problem stomping on any opposition or competition if he is set to win her heart. He's a go-getter and when it comes to playing a winning hand against competitors in the mating–dating arena, Mr Aries usually has a pile of well-rehearsed and well-practised tricks to call upon. If Ms Pisces is similarly attracted to him, then once he puts on his mating ritual (where he does his own form of mating dance or leaves some kind of love trail around him), he will find she easily flows into his eagerly opened arms. If she isn't attracted to him (and sometimes he does find that Ms Pisces doesn't somehow 'get' his kind of special love appeal), she'll flick her Mermaid's tail and swim off elsewhere without a backward glance.

Generally, these two star lovers seem to click and if they like each other, Mr Aries isn't likely to take long before he gets himself straight into her loving arms. If these two truly 'fancy each other' they are the kind that hook up together quickly and the relationship zings along as if it had been a feature in their lives for a long time, even after a short space of time. Now this applies mainly if Mr Aries is the one smitten first by his desire for Ms Pisces. If the reverse applies and Ms Pisces is smitten first and she is the one languishing after Mr Aries' attentions, sometimes he will give her a powerful run for her romantic money and can be highly capable of breaking her heart as well. Mr Aries truly likes to be the pursuer, the hunter — and if Ms Pisces lets him know she is doing the pursuing, he is likely to lose interest or use the fact that she is 'smitten' by him to unfair advantage. He may keep her on his baited hook for a while until he tires of her and then go look elsewhere for a chase. Fortunately most Pisces gals are shy and have the ability to naturally know how to play the flirting game successfully. And being a Fish gal, she is also an expert at baiting a hook and reeling in the men she wants.

If the relationship proceeds into something more permanent than an intense love encounter, certainly these two can become each other's teachers when it comes to learning about life, love and the meaning of existence. If real love exists between them they'll learn to eventually develop some wonderful traits that they didn't have before simply because they'll *need* to learn these traits, in order to cope with and learn about each other. Their love will put them both through many a test, but each test they face in learning to understand and grow closer will have a great reward at its end. They'll have expanded as individuals and have secured the bonds that they wanted, as a couple. In fact, Mr Aries joining up with Ms Pisces is similar to both of them signing up to attend a personal development seminar on breaking through relationship or romantic boundaries. Their togetherness is certain to open up both their minds and get them to look at life, each other and themselves with a new and better perspective.

Of course, during their initial passion-driven dating phase, they probably won't see the differences that surround them. They'll be too busy making love to notice. On the physical levels of expression they have an ability to really connect, so their love making will be intense and passionate. Their physical passion for each other will be the first stepping-stone to opening their hearts and loving each other unconditionally. However, once the initial passion is fulfilled, they'll then face the harsher realities of everyday living. That's when they'll have their work to do and need to treat each other respectfully and compromise on certain issues. However, as Mr Aries is not such a great compromiser, it is likely that Ms Pisces will be doing most of the bending to his will, to keep everything moving along in their union. However, this role of being the more subservient one in the relationship, where he is man and she is woman, can sometimes fulfil many of her fantasies. She loves a real man, someone who knows his own mind and has a masculine attitude to life and wants to be the boss, and in her Aries man that's exactly what she's found!

taurus   taurus   taurus   taurus   taurus
taurus   taurus   taurus   taurus   taurus   taurus
    taurus   taurus   taurus   taurus   taurus
taurus   taurus   taurus   taurus   taurus   taurus
    taurus   taurus   taurus   taurus   taurus
taurus   taurus   taurus   taurus   taurus   taurus
    taurus   taurus   taurus   taurus   taurus
taurus   taurus   taurus   taurus   taurus   taurus
    taurus   taurus   taurus   taurus   taurus

    taurus   taurus   taurus   taurus   taurus
taurus   taurus   taurus   taurus   taurus   taurus
    taurus   taurus   taurus   taurus   taurus
taurus   taurus   taurus   taurus   taurus   taurus
    taurus   taurus   taurus   taurus   taurus
taurus   taurus   taurus   taurus   taurus   taurus
    taurus   taurus   taurus   taurus   taurus
taurus   taurus   taurus   taurus   taurus   taurus
    taurus   taurus   taurus   taurus   taurus

TAURUS

[21 april – 21 may]

romantic pursuit: seeking someone they can trust

romantic vibration: determined

secret love desire: to be catered for sexually,

emotionally and in every other way possible by their lover,

but never hassled

element: earth

planetary ruler: venus

symbol: the bull

quality: fixed (= stability)

colours: earth tones, orange and yellow

gem: coral, emerald

best companions: virgo and capricorn

strongest virtues: strength, commitment

and determination

traits to improve: over-indulgences, lack of

flexibility and stubborn temperament

deepest desire: to be respected

for who you really are

Taurus celebrities

Aaron Spelling, Al Pacino, Andie McDowell, Andre Agassi, Audrey Hepburn, Barbra Streisand, Bianca Jagger, Bill Crosby, Billy Joel, Burt Bacharach, Candice Bergen, Cate Blanchett, Cher, Claudia Karvan, Daniel Day-Lewis, Darren Hayes, David Reyne, Debra Winger, Dennis Hopper, Dennis Rodman, Ella Fitzgerald, Emilio Estevez, Enrique Iglesias, Eva Peron, George Clooney, George Lucas, Grace Jones, Harvey Keitel, Jack Nicholson, James Brown, Jana Wendt, Janet Jackson, Jerry Seinfeld, Jessica Lange, Jet Li, Jimmy Barnes, Joe Cocker, Judy Davis, Katherine Hepburn, Kirsten Dunst, Lee Majors, Michelle Pfeiffer, Natasha Richardson, Orson Welles, Paula Yates, Penelope Cruz, Pierce Brosnan, Queen Elizabeth II, Renée Zellweger, Rudolph Valentino, Salvador Dali, Shannon Doherty, Shirley MacLaine, Shirley Temple, Sigmund Freud, Stevie Wonder, Tony Blair, Tony Danza, Tori Spelling, Uma Thurman, William Shakespeare, Willie Nelson

TAURUS—TAURUS relationship

The *'Let's hope we never disagree about anything, otherwise it may get very messy'* relationship

STAR TAURUS–TAURUS COUPLE
Adolf Hitler and Eva Braun

Ruled by the love planet Venus, this relationship has the benefit of having help from above — and what's more they'll probably need it! Putting two Taureans together will create a great relationship or one of the worst. After all, any couple has to find middle ground and compromise on some things, however 'middle ground' and 'compromise' aren't usually in any Taurean's vocabulary.

Most of us are familiar with the saying, 'as stubborn as a bull' — well the bull is the Taurus zodiac symbol. What happens when you put two bulls together? They usually butt heads. Naturally this head-butting intensity can be turned into wonderful fun and games when it is applied in the bedroom and released in a passionate fashion. But imagine the relationship intensity when *two* nose-snorting, foot-stomping, mad bull-type Taureans disagree over a glass of red at their local wine bar; not see eye to eye over politics; discuss in what religion to bring up their newborn child; work out whose turn it is to take out the garbage; or decide how to spend their annual holidays. Eek!

And as their ruling planet Venus is rather flighty and easily distracted, her support cannot be relied upon over the relationship long haul. That's why this relationship often doesn't always turn out the way one expects. It can start off all loving and passionate and end up miserable. Putting two strong-willed people into a relationship (especially a romantic relationship) means that they'll either work together or work against each other. After some initial power struggles — which lead to headaches and heartaches — they usually realise that it is much better to say sorry and be sweet and forgiving than build up a brick wall of resentment or anger between them. So if you're a Taurus matching up with another Taurus, remember, be sweet, loving and considerate; if necessary, give more than an inch give a 'love' mile to the person you love, 'cos if you love them, they're worth it!

Taurus woman—Taurus man

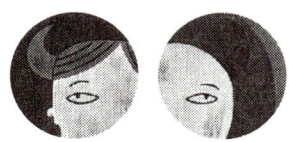

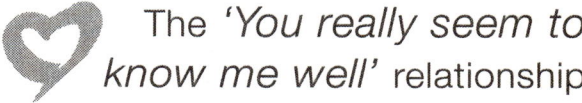

The *'You really seem to know me well'* relationship

Talk about these two zodiac romantic partners having heaps in common — they've got plenty. And they both have traits or characteristics that provide a great combination of energies to develop a steady, balanced and successful relationship. Deliberate. Persistent. Focused. Multiply those traits (and numerous others) by two and you've got one heck of a *powerful* couple. Not that either Mr or Ms Taurus actively seek (necessarily) to have authority and control — mind you (fame possibly; fortune, *most definitely*) — it's just that no one else seems to be as *responsible* or *thorough* as the two of them.

And because of their Venus rulership, they are often very attractive, seductive individuals as well (and are quickly adept at charming those around them and getting exactly what they want). When it comes to knowing what they want, from the time she is a babe-in-arms, the Taurus woman usually knows exactly what she wants. What's more, she knows just how to get it. Forget about feminine wiles, she uses her feminine appeal just as naturally as any other gal of the zodiac and probably more efficiently. But being a siren who can lure in anyone she fancies is not her only natural talent — though being Venus-ruled, she could quite easily charm the pants off anybody — this gal is also a staunch believer in laying out a ground plan, being organised and her personality is based upon rock-solid determination. And as she gets older, she's not afraid of putting in some good old hard work at getting what she wants and keeping it.

Now here comes her somewhat perfect match, but the question is — is he a match enough for her strong, silent will. Usually Mr Taurus is equally determined, possessing strength of purpose that carries him silently over any stumbling block that should appear in his way. He does not give in, he will not give up. His resolve is legendary, and there are few who could equal his courage, or iron will. And Mr Taurus is no stranger to hardship and adversity, either. But where others would resign themselves to defeat, Mr Taurus turns into a bulldozer. He puts his head down, rump up, and continues along his chosen path. He can truly be a force to be reckoned with. Now this force can be super nice in business, everyday success, sporting activities etc, but he has to handle this attitude more charismatically when it comes to wooing his Taurus ladylove, and keeping her happy after the initial honeymoon period.

He and she may not always see eye to eye on everything (in fact it is possibly unlikely that they will see eye to eye on too many things at all). That includes all manner of issues — marriage, children, career, and yes, love. Life (and love) wasn't meant to be easy, just ask any Bull. But, even if they have views that are poles apart, that won't stop him (or her) nonetheless from slogging it out to make it *work*. And as Mr and Ms Taurus are so obviously alike, they understand perfectly what makes the other tick; especially if love is strong enough to make them prepare to bend with the breeze and fit in with each other's plans or point of view. If they can overcome a natural tendency to be too demanding on each other, then being together is like *coming home* to a warm, safe and secure place. This can be a major relationship–romantic bonus for both of them because emotional safety and security are two of their favourite things. Both of them enjoy financial security as well, and that's often something that they share together — a desire to get ahead financially. That's why you'll so often see a Taurus (man or woman) madly saving for a rainy day (even the ones who live in the Sahara). To them, one of the greatest joys in life is knowing they won't have to scrape the bottom of the cookie jar, should some unexpected financial setback befall them. Money is power and power is, well *powerful*.

You would think then, as these two have *sooo* much in common, their lives together should be a merry sexual and passionate frolic through the fields, complete with dandelions and butterflies, *right*? Not precisely. No matter what any Bull would have you think, there is still that teensy-weensy issue of inflexibility that I mentioned earlier to sort through. It isn't an easy thing to resolve and it needs to be constantly addressed if this couple decide to make a 'go' of their relationship. When a Taurean makes up his or her mind to do something (or not to do something), nothing — and I mean *nothing* — is going to change their mind. When Taurus man and Taurus woman clash wills and lock horns, you can almost feel the earth rumbling beneath your feet.

Ms Taurus is more likely to be the gal who gives in to her Taurus mate and lets him have his way. Nevertheless most proud Bull gals (who are more susceptible to the feminine influences of their ruling planet, Venus) will have some vastly different ideas to her Taurus mate about certain issues, not the least of which concerns the home. If you've ever seen some of the lavishly decorated houses in those fancy designer magazines, you can bet that Taurus women own a good number of them. Aesthetics are all important. If the mood takes her, and she decides her home doesn't look *nice*, Ms Taurus will either have a pink fit (refusing to go home, *ever again*), or she'll head straight for her nearest, most exclusive home furnishings store, credit card in hand. Following hot on her tail is Mr Taurus, who demands she hand over her Visa and leave the store *immediately*. Well, now he's gone and done it. She pretends she doesn't even *know* him and proceeds to purchase the most expensive item in the store.

Once home, Bull man insists she return the one-off *original* Ming vase — or else. Ms Taurus, fluttery eyelashes in readiness, charms and canoodles until she realises she's getting nowhere, and fast. No matter how hard she tries, he won't budge. So, she refuses to back down. Without any outside assistance, hell will freeze over before these two find any sort of middle ground (and you can bet even that's going to have its conditions and provisos before either will agree to anything).

There could be other issues, certainly, that cause *disagreement* in the dual Taurus relationship. Children can be another hot topic for this couple, and it could take years before they decide (grudgingly) to compromise. It's not that one usually wants kids while the other does not. Sometimes it's more a question of how many; who's going to give up work to stay at home; and are they financially equipped to handle the new addition(s)? Once the formalities are out of the way though, Mr and Ms Taurus will set about making babies in the same fashion they do everything else — thoughtfully, slowly and with a minimum of fuss. *There's nothing to get excited about,* they tell delighted family and friends (in the eighth month of the pregnancy), *it's just a baby.* And that all but sums it up. The unhurried Taurean approach to life extends all the way to starting a family. No wonder some of them are well into their forties, before they realise they'd best get cracking.

n the scheme of things, the Taurus–Taurus combination has plenty of pluses, not the least of which include a huge serving of patience, practical thinking and a wonderfully easy-going attitude. It's very hard to ruffle the Taurus Bull's calm demeanour and stately manner. Many have tried and failed — often giving up in frustration and exasperation from the limited response they receive. And the Taurean couple are no different to anyone else in that respect either. Quite often, one will unwittingly choose to face-off against the other, leading to all manner of upset, ranging from slight annoyance, all the way to blind fury. (Think of a charging bull!) But, when all is said and done, this couple's tender, gentler characteristics usually win out over any long-term bitterness or disharmony. It seems this love match is destined for permanence. But then, what else *would* a Bull be interested in?

TAURUS — GEMINI relationship

The *'I think I'm stuck to you like glue'* relationship

STAR TAURUS–GEMINI COUPLE
Andre Agassi and Steffi Graf

When love comes in and takes you for a spin, the whole world turns in a crazy, mind-churning fashion. Well, when you get a Taurus together with a Gemini — and the love magic stirs up the romantic pot — this is the kind of relationship in which that type of giddy feeling occurs. You can almost see the surprised look on both their faces. Why are they surprised? Because they feel like they have had their feet swept out from under them. Especially for the Taurus, because you can bet your average rock-solid Bull is somewhat out of their depth, when he or she hooks up with a flighty, unpredictable Twin.

Think of it this way: Taureans hate to be caught unawares (the motto 'Be Prepared' was probably written by a Bull, while drama-loving, excitement-craving Geminis shy away from anything resembling *routine*). And though opposites do attract, remember too, that oil and water don't mix. The oil (Taurus) kind of keeps to itself, trying hard not to blend in with the water (Gemini). But even though the two never quite 'get it together', there are those rare moments when someone 'shakes' the bottle and the two are momentarily combined.

Taurus woman—Gemini man

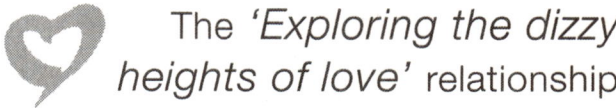

The *'Exploring the dizzy heights of love'* relationship

They say love can cross any divide, but there are some chasms that need more than l-o-v-e to make it safely to the other side. The Taurus woman and her Twin mate must delicately walk the dizzy heights of love, balanced precariously on the edge of relationship ruin, before they can truly and honestly call themselves a couple.

When Ms Taurus sets her sights (and her heart) upon a Mercury man, there's no turning back (not for her, at any rate). She'll blissfully ignore all the warning signs, advice from friends and family, and the clear ringing of her own intuitive alarm bells when it comes to her Gemini mate. Bulls are stubborn by nature, and there is no one as resolute or unwavering as a Taurean woman. Once her matter-of-fact mind is made up, that's it. There are few people who can put a dent in the iron will of a Taurus maiden, however I'm sure plenty have spent a (wasted) lifetime trying! Once she has decided she really does love her Gemini companion, she will try everything in her power to persuade this footloose and fancy-free man into living the kind of earth-bound, secure existence she is accustomed to.

Mr Twin though, has other ideas altogether. His notion of fun is definitely not sitting at home baking cookies or sewing new cushions for the lounge (and after all why should it be). To him, life is a carnival ride — fast, exhilarating and at times, a little scary. There are places to go, people to meet and things to do — why would anyone want to stay in all the time? While his adaptive abilities make the

Gemini man quite comfortable in any situation, his staying power is something of a missing link. Hanging around the house with his Taurus sweetheart might be exciting initially (hey! It's new and unlike anything he's tried before), but sooner rather than later, his fascination with the remote control and microwave oven will wane, and he'll head off (alone) to circumnavigate the world single-handedly.

This leaves Ms Taurus in a curious predicament. She loves her carefree Gemini man with all her heart, yet when he insists on being his own person (regardless of how many home-cooked meals, bottles of good wine and soothing massages she provides), she remains deeply hurt by his outwardly selfish *indifference*. But, true to her 'beast of burden' karmic destiny, the Taurus woman will suffer in silence, all the while convincing herself that things will only get better. Unfortunately, in this instance, it's a case of 'get in, while the going is good'. When the Taurus gal finds herself besotted with a Twin man, it's important to make hay while the sun shines, because tomorrow there may be storm clouds brewing on the horizon.

Change and spontaneity are like an addictive drug to any Twin, and in his hurry to seek new experiences or to rationalise the fears of his more *thorough* Taurus gal, Mr Gemini inevitably seals the fate for them both. Without a little patience from him, and a little impulsiveness from her, this is not a relationship likely to make it smoothly to the church on time.

Taurus man — Gemini woman

 The *'Road to love can take you on many a strange journey'* relationship

He is her Rock of Gibraltar, her Knight in Shining Armour and her dream lover. She is his fantasy girl, the stealer of the keys to his usually firmly locked heart and his sexy siren. They can also be each other's one-way ticket to a lunatic asylum. Sure, they can love each other to death; swear to love, cherish and obey, but when the Taurus guy and the Gemini gal cross paths, life is never straightforward. There's going to be lots of relationship zigs and zags ahead. Plus there are bound to be plenty of hurt feelings (him), impatience (her) and frustrating moments (both). That's not to say though, that this is a love affair designed to either fly high on the wings of the love dove or doomed to fall deeply into the abyss of relationship hell. This combination of earth and air has the potential to go either way, but don't be fooled for a moment that life in this Taurus guy and Gemini gal household will be 'normal', especially if Ms Twin has her way (which, in case you were wondering — she usually does).

Fortunately — most fortunately — this earth man's patience is both legendary and extraordinary. There are a select few who have the ability to push this gentle giant's buttons, but then he never quite met anyone like his Gemini gal. Rightly or wrongly, intentional (yes, sometimes!) or otherwise, the Gemini Ms can be as punishing as a prison warder and as cutting as a razor blade. Then, five seconds later she's all light and airy, wondering, 'What on earth could be wrong with him? Why is he upset with me?' Oblivion is a game she likes to play (and invented, for that matter); and for the record, she's good. If you've ever heard a saint swear chances are, he's just encountered his own Twin Diva.

Ms Gemini's 'here today, gone tomorrow' attitude is unsettling for the earth nature of her Bull partner; and the fact that she throws caution to the wind (a terrifying thought for most Taureans), means life with a Twin woman can be a draining, worrying existence for her Taurus mate. This is a man who likes to do things properly; slowly wins the race as far as this guy is concerned. What then, can he do, when the object of his affection acts first and thinks later? If he's serious about holding onto her, he'll give her his blessings and hang around to pick up the pieces when her plans (and sometimes, not surprisingly, her life) fall apart. If you love something, set it free. Locking Ms Gemini away in an ivory tower is a sure-fire way to send her running as far, and as fast, in the opposite direction (quite often checking out her prospects as she goes) leaving her dumbfounded ex-partner choking on a cloud of Mercury dust.

If Mr Taurus does prove to have the staying power to keep up with his erratic, sometimes fickle companion, he'll experience a multitude of moods, personalities and character traits that may leave him foaming at the mouth. She'll spend money as quickly and easily as her Taurus honey tries to save it, and change jobs more often and with as little effort as anyone he's ever met before. And this Twin gal will flirt outrageously, too! Not because she can't take commitment seriously, but because everyone else is just so darned interesting (and anyway, why limit yourself to meeting only a few people, when there's six billion of them out there somewhere?) Just when Mr Taurus thinks he's got Ms Gemini all worked out, he realises that was only a 'passing phase' and it's back to the drawing board again.

Yes — it takes Superman strength and nerves of steel to withstand the forces of Ms Gorgeous Gemini (and her other naughty and sometimes most destructive Twin half). To his credit, the Taurus man is in many respects just the guy for doing the job. His sturdy, stable, earth character makes him grounded and capable of enduring even the most tempestuous of storms his Gemini lover may wittingly or unwittingly hurl at him! Throw in a dash of commitment, loyalty, smouldering passion and undying love, and there is definite wonderful, miraculous potential for an intense, if not completely drama-free, relationship.

TAURUS — CANCER relationship

The *'Home is wherever you are'* relationship

STAR TAURUS–CANCER COUPLE
Penelope Cruz and Tom Cruise

When a Taurus Bull and a Cancer Crab decide to click their ruby heels together, and follow their own form of romantic yellow brick road, there really is *no place like home*. It's their sanctuary of love and their temple of romantic indulgence. Security-seeking Taurus and home-loving Cancer are perfectly suited to spending hours indoors, cooking lavish meals (Cancer) and then eating them (Taurus). Both include money high on their list of priorities, along with making babies and visiting their mothers (neither of whom live very far away).

This mutual desire for a harmonious and stable domestic existence is often the main ingredient in the Taurus–Cancer relationship. It's only when the subject of emotion (or lack of it) comes up, that this shining partnership may begin to tarnish.

Taurus woman — Cancer man

 The *'You better treat me right'* relationship

If you've ever seen a grown man crying for his *mummy* you can almost bet he's going to be a Crab. Cancer is the sign ruled by the moon (emotions) and astrologically symbolises 'motherhood'. Not surprisingly then, this combination of feelings and femininity in Mr Crab can lead to some rather unfortunate hang-ups if he's not careful to cut the apron-strings at an early age. Cancer man has mother issues that the rest of us couldn't even begin to imagine! He's quite comfortable being waited on hand and foot (there'll be no sharing of household chores when Ms Taurus invites this little nipper home). In fact, most Crab men expect their women to fuss and fawn over them the way their mothers did when they were still tiny, squawking babies. It seems as though some things never change. In adulthood, Mr Cancer is still a squawking baby — only larger.

Secretly (*secretly?*), Ms Bull's crabby beau wants to be pampered — that much is clear. But how well does that concept sit with this sensible, practical earth maiden? Well thankfully, this gal loves to spoil her men, but that doesn't mean she expects nothing in return from her lover. Just as most Crabs don't rush headfirst into anything, particularly romance, Ms Taurus is just as cautious and thorough before handing her heart out to anyone. The Venus-ruled Taurean woman has exquisite taste, a love of the finer things in life and a sensual appetite to rival any other (and that's just what she expects for dinner!) When love is on the menu this zodiac *connoisseur* will always leave room for dessert (and perhaps even an after-dinner mint!)

Taurus girl will dote on her Cancer boy, and he, in return, will teach her to trust her emotions, rather than attempting to 'plough' through them as though they were fields of corn waiting for harvest. This is easier said than done for Ms Taurus. To her, emotions are nothing more than a waste of time and common sense. Best to get on with the job, than worry about what was, what might have been and whether his mother can make it for Sunday night dinner.

Taurean women seldom let feelings get in the way of a good time, but when the mood takes them, they can mope around for months. Cancer man, on the other hand, changes moods faster than most people change socks, though none last longer than a couple of days at most. He can go from happy to sad, rational to neurotic, in the space of a few seconds, then disbelievingly wonder what's wrong with everybody *else* (who are at a loss as to what they've said or done *this time* to upset their moody friend).

Fortunately, for all their apparent differences on an emotional level, there are other factors that make this union of souls a positive one. If you look at two of the major causes for separation in many relationships — children (whether to have them, or not) and money (he/she spends too much and I can never pay the bills) — then Ms Taurus and Mr Crab are perfectly suited to a lifetime of financially stable, child-rearing moments together.

Taurus man — Cancer woman

 The *'I'm counting on you, so don't disappoint me'* relationship

When you're talking *true love* it's hard to find any man more capable of the *real love thing* than a Taurus man. It may not happen easily, 'cos he doesn't surrender his heart without a great deal of caution. In fact, you might not pick him for being a romantic guy at all. But don't let his lack of obvious emotion or indifferent attitude fool you. It's all an act to ensure his softer side (and he does have one) isn't yanked out into the open for everybody else to see (and poke fun at). When this guy falls in love, he falls hard. Heaven and earth won't move this bovine Romeo when his sights are set on the woman of his dreams.

So now that heaven and earth are taken care of, what about that enigmatic, emotional Moon maiden, Ms Cancer? When this lunar lady swoons, sways and floats her feminine way into his life and captures his heart, the Taurus man will never be quite the same again. His rock-solid façade has been penetrated and he's suddenly charging through uncharted territory, complete with an alien landscape of new experiences and emotions. Yes — *emotions.* For Mr Taurus, this is like visiting a strange and foreign land (far away from the safety of home), where nobody speaks his language, the food tastes different and he completely forgot his travel insurance. What's worse, *Señor* Bull's tour guide turns out to be this crazy, but enchanting, woman, who seems to cry an awful lot. For the most part, however, he will remain impartial to her emotional performances — preferring to plod along at his own pace without too many distractions to intrude upon his plans. Remember, this is a guy who likes to take his time (just watch him eating dinner, and you'll see what I mean. Everyone else has moved onto coffee and cake, while he's still munching through the first course.) 'When I'm good and ready' is a favourite saying of this unhurried zodiac *plodder,* and true to his namesake, the only way to get this Bull moving is to wave a red flag in front of his face. Even then, there are no guarantees. He's just as likely to change direction and pretend he didn't even notice.

So, when Cancer woman crawls by with her 'sideways' approach to life and cloak-and-dagger attitude toward love (Ms Cancer is not prone to *advertising* her attraction), more often than not her Taurus flame remains absolutely clueless of her intentions. It's not until she's standing at his front door, suitcase (and a photo of her mother) in hand that the light switch in his Bullish head comes on. When this Moon maiden decides to come out of her shell (with plans of moving into the warmth and protection of her Taurean mate's *safehouse*) you can bet one of them will be in for a surprise (and it won't be Madam Crab!)

There are no prizes either, for guessing your average Bull man is a tad slow on the uptake when it comes to romance and all things *love.* The potential for a Mills-and-Boon type encounter is promising however, and once committed, this guy is there for the long haul. And if his Cancer sweetie can learn to curb her sometimes jealous nature and lunar moodiness, she too will have the very thing she seeks most — eternal love and permanence in her emotionally unpredictable life.

When Taurus man gives his heart and soul to Ms Cancer, there is no turning back. He'll weather the stormy tides of her emotions with all the patience and virtue he can muster, protecting her delicate nature from the cold, harsh realities of life. But Crab gal must remember that beneath this seemingly impenetrable exterior lies a delicate heart, easily bruised. Taurus boy loves to love, and Cancer girl *loves* to be loved. Together, they can provide each other the sense of worth and belonging they both so desperately need for a lifetime and beyond.

TAURUS—LEO relationship

The *'Love sure is a funny thing'* relationship

STAR TAURUS–LEO COUPLE
Bianca Jagger and Mick Jagger

Ego is not a dirty word, that's according to a Leo at any rate. These proud, majestic creatures bask unashamedly in anything that somehow reflects back a wonderful image of who they are. They seek praise, love, admiration and adoration. But love sure is a funny thing. It attracts the weirdest, but often most perfect people towards each other. Take Taurus guy or gal for example. The Taurus Bull doesn't like flashy, showy things and they often even blanch white when someone gives them a compliment or alternatively blush bright red. This is a sign that *must* warily tread the *like-to-get-to-know-you* trail before he or she feels comfortable giving their heart away (everything's about comfort for a Bull). They need to feel loved and appreciated, requiring truckloads of warmth and devotion from their significant other. When two such *needy* signs pair up, and neither receives the attention they seek, it's not uncommon to find Taurus sulking silently in frustration, while Leo roars loudly in regal fury.

Taurus woman — Leo man

 The *'Don't mess with me'* relationship

When the Lion King sends his bright, shining brand of love out into the world beyond and smack bang into the heart of a Lady Bull, it's often a case of too much of a good thing. *Can you ever have too much of a good thing?* you're all wondering. Well, I guess that depends on whom you ask. If you want a totally unbiased, straight-shooting answer though, might I suggest you abandon your idea of discussing the matter with a Leo man, and raise your concerns with a less theatrical individual.

Put the same question to the Taurus earth maiden for example, and she'll answer you with all the serious contemplation and thoughtful deliberation she can muster. Her response will be as honest, straightforward and truthful as any you'll ever have the good fortune to receive, and she won't even expect a cheque in the mail for her efforts.

The *good thing* she's referring to though, may be slightly different to the one her Leonine mate is talking about (himself, of course). You see, in the Lion King's world everything revolves around the Sun, and as he is the chosen sign of the zodiac — being Sun-ruled and all — it makes perfectly good sense that any reference to matters good, great, fantastic, bright or wonderful (you get the picture), must relate to the one, the only, *him*. If the world is a stage (which it is) and Sir Leo is the leading actor, then surely his Taurus love must feel honoured to be his number one *fan*.

And that of course, is where it all (usually) comes unstuck. Any man silly enough to think a Taurus woman is going to follow him around like a *lap dog* should seriously consider checking into rehab. She is her own woman. Not yours, not mine and certainly not Mr Leo's. He may have royal blood, but she's got molten steel running through her veins. In fact, give her enough time and this Venus-ruled gal will be the leading lady in her own show, complete with superstar dressing room, bottled water and a nice Leo man to attend to her every need.

Don't think she won't like it either. Secretly, many Bulls like to be in control, and having somebody worship the ground you walk on (even if they're being paid to do it), isn't so bad either. But in all honesty, her Leo mate is not cut out for the job. He's far too busy assessing his own star appeal and whether his new Calvin Klein jeans make him look *fat*. Then, once he tears himself away from his full-length mirror (no, not the one in the bathroom, the portable version in his Jeep Cherokee), he's got at *least* a hundred friends to catch up with (ninety-eight of them women), and could Ms Taurus please make an appointment to see him later?

Oh dear. That just *won't do* at all. Taurus gal likes stability, security, home-cooked meals and a partner who pays attention (not *needs* attention). She will patiently endure his flamboyant antics, pompous attitude and distinct lack of punctuality, even sometimes feigning interest in his affairs. But when she can no longer tolerate her Leo man's outlandish behaviour, she won't be backwards in coming forward. Should he pass the point of no return, Sir Leo could run to the other side of the planet and still feel the threatening *stomp* of his ladylove's feet.

At this point in the performance, Leo man is advised to exit stage-left, apologising profusely as he goes, promising to spend more time at home and less time acting the part of egotistical maniac. If — and only *if* — she chooses to hear his wretched cries for mercy, there's a chance she'll reconsider her position and graciously offer her forgiveness. Then, twenty years later, she will (for no *apparent* reason) run him through with her sharply honed horns, leaving his pride (and his buttocks) severely scarred.

Forgiveness is one thing — who ever mentioned *forgetfulness*?

Taurus man — Leo woman

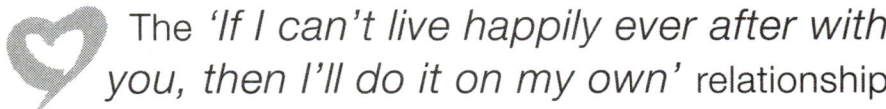 The *'If I can't live happily ever after with you, then I'll do it on my own'* relationship

Once upon a time, there was a Taurus guy who waited ever so patiently for his Leo gal to come home, prepare his dinner, fetch his slippers and rub his shoulders with a long, soothing, sensual massage. He waited and he waited. Eventually, she did come home, though still she did not attend to his needs. Instead, she ran herself a bubble bath, then after soaking for hours, proceeded to apply all manner of moisturisers and sweet-smelling scents to her perfectly smooth skin. But being the tolerant man he was, Mr Taurus waited some more. He waited — and he waited. Twenty years later, he was still waiting. By that time his Lion Queen was long gone. Taurus man on the other hand was still hungry, his feet were cold and his shoulders hurt like hell.

Ms Leo lived happily ever after.

The moral of the story? *Ms Leo waits on (or for) no man*. She is the queen of the zodiac and expects to be treated as such. In her home (or castle), this lady wears the pants (and the crown) as she regally issues a multitude of orders to her loyal and devoted subjects (usually, Mr Taurus). *But* — the Lion princess is not all *look-at-me-when-I'm-speaking-to-you* or *click-of-the-fingers-I-wanted-it-yesterday* attitude (*nearly*, but not all). She is Sun-ruled and therefore a generous, magnanimous soul, capable of lavishing oodles of warm, heartfelt affection on her Bull mate.

And let's face it — he *likes* it that way. All Taureans are sensual creatures, relying on a close physical relationship to make them feel wanted. They may not be terribly *exciting* in the sack (that's because their earthy nature makes them simple lovers), but they have a tenderness and gentleness about them that makes up for any lack of imagination. Leo gal finds this quality rather *endearing*, and so she's quite content smothering *her* man with all the touchy-feely love he can handle.

That though, ladies and gentlemen, is where the harmonious qualities of this particular fire and earth combination end. It takes a lot of time and effort catering to the Leo woman's every whim and desire and quite frankly, that is *wasted* time and effort in the Taurus man's mind, which could be better spent increasing one's wealth (or resting comfortably on one's sofa in front of the television on a Sunday afternoon).

She likes to shine, bringing attention to herself (and anyone who happens to be with her). He prefers to plod silently around in the background, accepting his applause in quiet, humble dignity. She wants caviar and those dainty little crackers for hors d'oeuvres, while he is determined to have pretzels as his pre-dinner snack. Ms Leo orders a limo to deliver her to the airport (where she is clearly flying first class); Mr Taurus catches a bus and take's his seat in economy. Now of course this is an exaggeration and maybe the roles are reversed, but often the values between these two are poles apart — and that can create all kinds of misunderstandings, arguments and disagreements of the type that gradually wear away at the love power and grind it to dust.

The list of possible complications between them goes on, but what it boils down to, is this: Leo girl is searching for a mate who recognises her claim to the throne and will treat her with all the stately manner her regal bearing deserves. Taurus boy, on the other hand, is looking for a partner who will, quite simply, *be there* when he gets home from work, footy or a beer with the boys on a Friday night. He doesn't want bossing around (and this is an exercise in futility anyway); he isn't interested in fancy meals and expensive clothes (that's a *complete* waste of money); and he sure as eggs won't be caught bowing and scraping to anyone.

But maybe — just maybe — if Leo woman thinks with her head rather than her ego, Bull man might surprise her. He is perfectly capable of meeting at least *some* of the requirements she desires in a mate, but like all good things, they come to those who wait. Although *waiting* is not a favourite pastime of any Lioness, she will do well to remember that just as Rome wasn't built in a day, neither will her Bull mate be conquered on the first date.

TAURUS — VIRGO relationship

The *'We could quickly become a habit'* relationship

STAR TAURUS–VIRGO COUPLE
Audrey Hepburn and Mel Ferrer

This is a zodiac combination that seems to have a pretty good romantic track record (at least this couple often stay together and don't get divorced). But then one could query — do the Taurus and Virgo couple remain together because of habit, commitment or because it can be too much trouble to start afresh with someone new? I prefer to think they stay together because they somehow fit together quite nicely in all kinds of ways. Yes, there's often more to the relationship tale than one realises with this couple, and quite often they live under false pretensions to the outer world or to each other — because underneath their very normal outer appearance these two are very complex and intense individuals. But somehow they seem very able to work out their differences, and manage very well at doing it too — thank you!

They are also both perfectionists on all kinds of levels (some that work for them, some that work against their relationship). And they are both quite scared of change, risk or misfortune. They like a relationship that can be summed up by: Safe. Secure. Reliable. Trustworthy. And even if they date for many years they may still be afraid of making a mistake or a commitment. I've known a Taurus and Virgo couple that have been engaged for six years now, and still haven't set the date. Whenever they get close to setting a date for their marital nuptials to take place, someone says, 'Oh, but hang on a minute, aren't we *rushing* things a little? And what about *details?* Who's got the details?' No wonder they haven't got things worked out between them yet — there's always some confusion arising somewhere to keep them hesitating about taking the next step (not just in their relationship but in other areas too).

If they are a couple, even in an unhappy relationship, then they usually don't cheat on each other (if they do they usually leave their relationship very quickly as this couple isn't into relationship dishonesty unless there's no way around it). No Taurus man or woman is very likely to run off into the arms of anyone else, even if they are another earth sign. They don't like impetuous behaviour too much. But the same thing applies to them, they can be super hesitant with each other, too. They don't like to rush into anything (because that's what less *informed* people do). Even when Virgo guy or gal has collected the necessary data, sorted the wheat from the chaff and ensured their calculations are precise, there's still every chance he or she won't be easily convinced that love is the one great thing missing from their life. Many people born under Taurus or Virgo often find their happiest times are when they live on their own or with a pet, than when they set up their lives within the structures or boundaries of someone else's rules or regulations. But they often don't discover this side to their character until later in life, so in their early years they can be looking for love — of the romantic kind — most determinedly.

Taurus woman—Virgo man

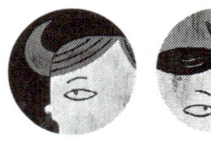

 The *'Let's give it a good old-fashioned try'* relationship

Ms Taurus and Mr Virgo can fall in love and live happily ever after, but it often isn't quite as simple as that. They have some working out to do before they can settle into romantic bliss indefinitely.

Certainly he can appear to be Mr Cool (just look at Keanu Reeves, Hugh Grant, Richard Gere — all super Mr-Cool-Himself Virgos, as examples). This is one man of the zodiac who seems to have his act together — but does he? He has a knack of exuding a sense that he is complete, composed and organised, nevertheless he is often much more complex and confused than he appears. What's more, he doesn't want anyone to find this out! Ms Taurus has a lot in common with him because in her own fashion she is Ms Cool too — she's savvy, smart and organised, but in a totally different manner from him. She's much more in touch with the outside world than he is (he's more attuned to his inner world). This difference between them can mean that she sometimes has to play a role or put on an ongoing act to please Mr Virgo (or vice versa). Or, she may have to change to please him — and sometimes changing doesn't come easily to either of them.

After the initial 'kissy-kissy, I love you my honey bunny' part of this love affair is over and both partners are seeing each other with not quite such love-struck eyes, things can sometimes go a trifle haywire. After all, it is natural for Ms Taurus to take the practical stand and for Mr Virgo to take the more intense neurotic stand. This kind of difference in outlook can lead to something like this:

MS TAURUS: Stop worrying.

MR VIRGO: Okay, but hurry up! We're going to miss the 9.48 bus, and there's an eighteen-minute wait for the next one at 10.06. And if we have to take that bus, we'll miss the connecting train at 10.19, and have to hang around that dirty station for ages. Oh, I think I need to go to the bathroom, my tummy doesn't feel so good.

MS TAURUS: No. Come on, I'm ready. We're going NOW.

MR VIRGO: Don't know if I can wait. What if there's no toilet paper at the train station?

Sounds a little *ridiculous*, doesn't it? And to you and me, it probably is, but catching buses, missing trains and dealing with empty toilet rolls are all *very* important matters to Mr Virgo. How can he live a stress-free life for goodness sake, when all these stressful things keep happening to *him*? If only he'd been born luckier (without that awful allergy to peanuts that makes his face go all puffy); with parents who loved him more, and a dog named Shep. It's not his fault. Really.

Just like it's not really any oversight on Ms Taurus' behalf that she's so decidedly *slow*. Some things just take a little longer to do, especially if you plan on getting it right the first time. Anyhow, before you even *begin* doing something, you have to meticulously plan the entire process and proceed at a cautious pace until the desired outcome is achieved.

Re-enter Virgo man.

Did somebody mention *meticulous planning*? Well, here's the perfect (oh, how he *loves* that word!) man for the job. Mr Virgo is the King of Fuss, the Champion of Detail. And don't worry, if there's something out of place with whatever it is he's overseeing, then you're sure to know about it. It's all very comforting, really, knowing that nothing will escape the eagle-sharp eyes and lightening-quick mind of this thorough Mercury man. That goes for his love affairs too. Yep — though he may not be endowed with an obvious ability to make the earth move for his partner on a *romantic level*, he'll sure tell her when she uses the wrong toothbrush.

But Ms Taurus can often warm up more than Mr Virgo's heart once she gets him into the bedroom. And it's often in the love-making areas of their home where this relationship really finds out about — perfection! When these two hit the right passion and sexual spots with each other, this collision of passionate forces can be a healing force for both of them. Sex can be the love drug that keeps these two 'happy ever after', and naturally for any romantic relationship this is a terrific bonus to have working on your side in the longer term. Sure he tells her that it's unhygienic to use a toothbrush longer than three months, describing in painstakingly researched detail what each bacteria is called, looks like and whether it can make you sick, but that's just the foreplay. When Ms Taurus leads him to bed and gives him a full body massage and caresses his stressed-out brow and rubs his tired feet, he forgets his toothbrush, the bacteria, and all the other issues that have been worrying him recently, and just lets her guide him into her sexual altar and leave him happily spending many hours worshipping at it.

There will be times when they drive each other slightly mad, but even with this kind of run-around going on between them she's not angry, and neither is he. This pair have an *understanding,* which comes from their natural earth–earth zodiac compatibility. It would take a lot more than a simple tête-à-tête over personal hygiene and bad spending habits to raise this couple's temperature. The mere fact Ms Taurus has even *reached* that level of comfort with a Virgo man is a remarkable effort in itself, suggesting he's both secure with and somewhat dependent upon, his good, solid Taurus gal.

And she likes to be depended upon, too. It makes her feel complete and *appreciated.* She'll happily cook, sew and clean (cleanliness is next to Godliness for most Virgos) — all without complaint. Mr Virgo can be difficult to please, but this Venus-born Taurus gal has the touch of the goddess about her. She is capable of soothing the most cynical heart with her selfless dedication and unrestrained affection.

For that, he will cherish her like no-one else before, even if she is a trifle dismissive of his anxiety attacks and heart palpitations.

Taurus man — Virgo woman

 The *'I truly think that we can make this love thing work'* relationship

When Ms Virgo and Mr Taurus first meet each other and their love stars are shining brightly they are likely to know it immediately, even if they don't consciously acknowledge it to themselves. Something just *feels* right. It may not be a sudden thunderbolt of passion and it's probably not something they would classify as a case of love at first sight — but there *is* a special love buzz or electricity in the air around them, a unique form of zodiac romantic connection or affinity. Always a lover of beautiful women, Mr Taurus will smile his languid smile at the demure and lovely Virgo gal in front of him. Ruled by sensuous Venus, the Taurean man is led by his senses and he just *feels* instinctively that she could change his world. Meanwhile, her agile Mercury-ruled mind is working overtime, and images of the proposal, marriage ceremony and honeymoon flash before her eyes! Yep, these two are on the same track (albeit Ms Virgo is a few paces ahead of slow-moving Taurus!)

Like two peas in a pod, earth-ruled Virgo and Taurus are a good match because their goals and aspirations are in sync. Both tend to seek long-term relationships based on trust, loyalty and commitment. Of course, there are always exceptions and young Bull males in particular, often wield their powers of sensual seduction on many an unsuspecting female! Even though he finds himself attracted to the charms of the Virgo woman, Mr Taurus can be slow to act. You see, the Bull makes decisions (in life and love) only after very careful consideration. He won't discuss a situation until he is ready to make up his mind. So, while Ms Virgo is worrying about whether he will *actually* call her, he is quietly pondering whether she is *actually* the girl of his dreams! Waiting for Mr Taurus to come to a conclusion can drive Ms Virgo mad with frustration. Ruled by the lightning-quick planet of Mercury (governing the mind and communication), she is super speedy when it comes to making decisions (though she'll worry afterwards if she made the right choice!) Thankfully, when Mr Taurus finally decides that he *feels* good about the prospective relationship, he will pursue her with a passion. To his credit, he is patient when it comes to love and romance and he won't stop until he wins the object of his desire.

To understand the Taurean man just pause for a minute and check out his symbol, the sexy, jostling and tempestuous Bull. Masculine and physically commanding, most Taurean men are heavily built, strong and have a tendency to put on weight (if their sweet-tooth gets out of control!) Taurean men are actually quite peaceful specimens. They don't go *looking* for trouble but when they are incited into action by a bullfighter — or a seductive, alluring and mysterious Virgo woman — let's just say they're quick to anger. So if you are a Virgo woman currently involved with a Taurean man, try to avoid waving a red cape in front of him, which would disturb his grass-munching.

Stubborn Mr Taurus may sometimes try to push his demure Virgo gal around. But he will soon learn that looks can be deceiving. Yes, she's quietly spoken. Yes, she's modest. But no, she's *not* a pushover. The funny thing about Virgo women is that people think she is quiet; if only they could hear what's going on in her head — she'd lose her Ms Discretion crown title. The Virgo woman is brainy as well as beguiling and her IQ normally runs rings around her Taurus. That's not to say he isn't intelligent. But the Virgo gal has an exceptionally analytical mind. She will breeze in and in less than five minutes give him a solution to a problem that's had him stumped for a week!

She's attractive, natural and poised, and many top models such as Kate Moss and Claudia Schiffer or screen legends like Sophia Loren and Lauren Bacall possess the elegant Virgo bearing. The Virgo woman has style and she's compulsive with neatness. It's no wonder that she'll tell her Taurus guy to tuck in his shirt (or throw it out altogether), straighten his tie or advise him to skip second helpings of food. He is often elegant in a comfortable, unkempt sort of way. He appreciates beauty and luxury — and often has a streak of vanity — but the Taurean man prefers not to waste time on being perfect. He favours comfortable clothes and a comfortable house where he can kick off his shoes and fall down on a comfortable sofa. His Virgo gal is meticulous about grooming and neatness and she is typically a perennial lint-picker. She'll catch his shoes before they fall on the floor and smooth down the sofa cushions when he's finished his nap! Her love of order spills into all areas of her life. Thankfully, petty differences between Ms Neatness and Mr Sloppy aren't big enough to drive a major wedge between them.

What *is* more likely to cause problems between them is his stubbornness and her harsh criticism. Cool Ms Virgo can be a hard-to-please partner, girlfriend, wife and lover. She calls a spade a spade — and she's not into pampering her Taurus guy's ego with false compliments. He appreciates her honesty (most of the time) and he is also pleased to discover that his Virgo gal is really *not* such a cool customer. Though she might not express her feelings in public showering him with hugs and kisses, she is a tender lover in private. Earthy Mr Taurus is naturally 'comfortable' with his body and sex. He encourages her to lose her inhibitions and she'll stop worrying so much about 'getting it right'. Taureans are very sensitive to smell and touch, and a sure-fire way for Ms Virgo to get him in the right mood is to give him an erotic massage with sweet-smelling oils.

For all her reasonableness and discrimination, Ms Virgo can be highly critical of her man (and interestingly she's even *tougher* on herself!). She strives for perfection in the world and this sometimes blinds her to the fact that it's normal for human beings to make mistakes. To her credit, she forces her Taurean guy to go outside his comfort zone and stretch himself. Deep down, he would hate to disappoint her. When push comes to shove, Mr Taurus and Ms Virgo admire each other and that creates a solid basis for a relationship. She respects his determination and strength of purpose. He is affectionate, tender and gentle and a solid rock of calmness that anchors her when she starts to worry about everything from their children's school marks to whether the dog has been vaccinated on time. Ms Virgo feels safe in his arms and gives him loyalty in return. His approach to romance is like his attitude to life — he's either one hundred per cent in the relationship or, he 'wants out'. It would take something pretty dramatic to make him leave her, but if she did let him down in a big way he is not the kind to forgive and forget.

Thankfully, Mr Taurus is loyal and she's devoted to him. If they do walk down the aisle (and earth signs tend to prefer marriage to living in a de facto relationship), it's likely to be a long-lasting and strong marriage. They both love children and their home will be big and comfortable. Ms Virgo will be firm about an ordered and minimalist décor and Mr Taurus will insist on room to house his various 'collections'. His collections may include expensive objects d'art or simply his stamps or coins amassed since childhood. Differences aside, this relationship has big-time potential. And when he starts to pick lint off her suit and she begins to sleep in now and again, they'll know that they have found the secret ingredient to life-long love.

TAURUS — LIBRA relationship

The *'If you let me in your heart, I'll be everything you need'* relationship

STAR TAURUS–LIBRA COUPLE
Judy Davis and Colin Friels

Pleasure with a CAPITAL 'P' defines this relationship. Co-ruled by Venus, the planet of beauty, romance, harmony, love and pleasure, Libra and Taurus both believe that love is the most important thing in the world. True romantics, they both inherently know what turns the other on forever! So, will the relationship between earthy, practical Taurus and breezy, ethereal Libra be an affair to remember or a lifetime of love? That depends on the individuals, but these two have the 'zodiac goods' to make it a fairy tale romance.

They also have a great deal to learn from each other on all kinds of levels, and even though their love is true and their romance binds them, Taurus and Libra are like chalk and cheese in many respects. Stubborn earth-sign Taurus is slow to make changes in life but when he does, not even heaven, earth and the stars combined will make the Bull change his or her mind. Air-ruled Libra will agonise over what decision to make and then — in a spontaneous fashion — is just as likely to go back to base one. Though they should simply just agree to disagree. Born under the gracious rulership of the planet Venus, they adore the finer things in life and will shower each other with lavish gifts and gestures.

Where Taurus is incredibly patient and loyal, Libra can be flighty, changeable and occasionally quite unreliable. Taurus often has to provide the relationship anchor while the Libran goes out and explores the world or does *'their own thang'*! But to Taurus great credit, they are patient, understanding (some of the time) and prepared to provide the stable force in the relationship, 'cos the Libran gives them so much entertainment, devotion, beauty and fun in return.

Taurus woman — Libra man

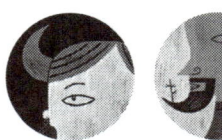

 The *'I'm ready to fulfil all your secret desires'* relationship

Venus, the gentle planet of love, relationships, beauty and harmony, rules both Ms Taurus and Mr Libra and this planet's positive energy is a great romantic force to have on your side. No wonder these two lovers of romance discover an instant bond when they meet. Both thrive on falling in love, courtship, romance and pampering their partner. Although Mr Libra pursues his Taurean starmaid with a passion, she may initially be cautious about getting involved with him. Her heart beats faster when he moves in close and she knows she could easily be swept off her feet by his amorous overtures. But Ms Taurus is not a reckless kind of gal. Her tender heart has been broken before and when it falls into itty bitty pieces it takes a *long* time for it to mend itself. She wants to know the rules of the game before getting involved with the zodiac's Casanova. Yes, attractive Mr Libra can be a flirtatious ladies man. However much his reputation precedes him, lover boy Libra *really* is seeking his soul mate; a partner-in-crime with whom to share his life and love. Perhaps due to his famous indecisiveness, he's let good relationships slip through his fingers before. He's also chosen incompatible partners because of his love of getting swept up in the game of romance. Still, ever the optimist, Mr Libra is forever hopeful that the Venusian goddess of his dreams will appear before his very eyes.

So, when the Libran guy meets the Taurean gal he is often lost for words (an unusual occurrence for the talkative Libra male!) Ms Taurus is natural, sensual and very sexy. The feminine Taurean woman is confident and sure of her own attractiveness. She very often has a voluptuous Venusian figure, beautiful skin and a deep-honeyed voice. Many Taurean women (just think of singers Janet Jackson, Barbra Streisand and Cher) have beautiful singing voices and she is likely to entrance him from the moment she speaks. But whether it's her sexy voice or ample curves that first attract his attention, it won't take long for Mr Libra to pursue her with unbridled passion.

Interestingly, Ms Taurus' strength, determination and patience quite often make her Libra guy feel like a flake! He is enormously intelligent but sometimes ends up being the 'Jack of all trades and the Master of none', simply because he can't decide what it is he wants to do with his life. The Taurean woman is a practical gal (like all earth-sign women) and she knows that a soothing cup of herbal tea, a hot bubble bath or watching a romantic 1940s movie under a cosy blanket on the sofa will fix any problem! She has the uncanny ability to peacefully sleep right through the night — never kept awake by insomnia due to mental overload, unlike her Libra beau whose mind tends to work 24/7! He admires how she stays so calm under pressure!

Both approach life in completely different ways and this can cause tension between them. For example, when Ms Taurus needs to make an important decision she is typically *very* quiet about it. She spends time alone thinking things over and then decides based on what *feels* right. She's the kind of girl who will stick resolutely to her choice even if she discovers she's made a mistake. This explains why many Taurean gals find themselves stuck in going-nowhere relationships, jobs or other situations. Like her zodiac sign, the Bull, she can be extremely bullish at times and *nothing* or *no-one* will budge her.

Whereas Mr Libra — like his zodiac symbol the Scales — is constantly balancing up evidence, information and other data in order to make the 'perfect' decision. As he has the ability to see both sides of an issue (Librans make great judges, lawyers and mediators), he'll contemplate (out loud!) all sides to his dilemma until he completely exhausts himself and others. Even so, he *still* might not make up his mind. Though Mr Libra may feel dazed and confused at times because of his own quick-thinking, ever-changing mind, his general attitude in life is happy-go-lucky. He's able to bounce back quickly with a bright smile when things go wrong *and* he is the King of Positive Affirmations! When his Taurean gal falls into her occasional dismal spell of inertia and gloominess he'll be the one to pull her back out.

The Taurean woman is incredibly practical and her ten-year plan usually includes marriage and family and 'building' a future. She can also be very ambitious and enjoy a successful career. As opposed to her Libra man — who often gets ahead because of his personality and his ability to network — Ms Taurus is pure and solid determination and hard work. She is a 'plodder'. Like the other earth signs (Capricorn and Virgo) she is also quite attached to her earthly possessions, and *that* includes her man! When Ms Taurus and Mr Libra first meet, they eat out at the most happening restaurants (both adore good food and wine and she, in particular, has a tendency to put on weight!), parties and art exhibitions in town. Before too long, her idea of a perfect night will be to stay at home and enjoy a home-cooked meal and a good bottle of red wine in front of the fireplace. But outgoing Mr Libra is not really a happy home-body. He's gregarious and socially active and he loves to entertain. And, like all air signs, he needs to communicate with lots of people in order to feel self-realised. So what is Ms Taurus supposed to do, you ask? Either join him once a week on a night on the town, or simply give him the freedom to go out and do what Libras do best — meet people. If their relationship is based on trust, she needs to let him be himself. After all, as much as birds need to fly, they also need time to rest and snuggle down in the comfort of their nest with their lovebird by their side.

Taurus man — Libra woman

 The *'Every time you walk in the room my heart skips a beat'* relationship

When Mr Taurus falls for the beguiling, 'sugar, spice and all feminine things nice' seductive charms of Ms Libra, he had better be warned that she is no flighty feminine pushover! In fact, the dimpled and beautiful gal standing before him — delighting him with her feminine wiles and entertaining stories — is actually very adept, even an expert, at getting what she wants. She may seem pliable, easy-going and soft-spoken but Ms Libra is not the kind of girl to be bullied into submission by any man, even her true love. Hmmm. So by the time Mr Taurus actually discovers that his Libra gal isn't a 'yes' girl who does everything he desires or expects, she will have worked her charm on him to such an extent that he finds he can't live without her even if he now realises he is heading into some kind of uncharted territory!

Ya see, Mr Taurus likes things to go his way; he doesn't like to have to bend or change at all to suit anyone else — even his ladylove. But let's get one thing straight. Mr Taurus adores women and has great respect for them but — deep down — the typical Taurean male doesn't really, truly believe that men and women are equal in all ways. Men are men, and women are women in his logical form of thinking. He's an old-fashioned guy when it comes to the role-playing of the sexes, and Ms Libra is a modern-thinking gal on exactly the same subject. Like all other areas of his life, in his love relationship he likes to be in control. But he may as well wave a white flag and surrender, because when it comes to the home, romance and matters of the heart, Ms Libra is the boss, whether he realises it or not. And a smart Libra gal actually 'manages' her gorgeous Bull man in such a subtle, diplomatic way that unless he's very wily, he truly has no idea that it is *she* who is running the show! She is an expert at wrapping him around her little finger and leading him to places he would never go with anyone else but her — in his heart, emotionally, financially and commitment wise. She rewards him greatly for his special treatment, especially in the bedroom where he quickly becomes her love slave.

This gal can certainly hold the keys to this gentleman's heart. With her intelligence and a smile that makes him feel all warm and fuzzy inside, Ms Libra leaves her Taurus guy completely and utterly smitten! Yep — the Libra woman knows how to coerce Mr Taurus into surrender armed with her secret weapons of charm, tact and intelligence. Nevertheless, this isn't just a one-way romantic street. Ms Libra is also enraptured with the charisma of sexy Mr Taurus, and he can get her to do all kinds of things on his behalf that she might baulk at doing for any other zodiac guy. His planetary ruler, Venus, was the ancient goddess of love. He innately knows all the tricks in the book to win over his Libra gal. A man of few words, he will offer her understated compliments that thrill her and mean more than any gushing compliment ever could. It is often what this man doesn't say that impresses her the most. He will also give her flowers, chocolates, jewellery or a romantic candlelit dinner may come under his 'standard' romantic repertoire. But he also has the ability to leave her speechless with his recital of a beautifully penned love poem, the song he strums on his old guitar, drawing or some other artistic touch to express his love. Mr Sensuality also has a way with touch. As an earth sign, he adores giving and receiving hugs, caresses, massages and he'll constantly have his arm draped around her or his fingers will be entwined in hers as they walk down the street.

There is certainly a very magnetic attraction when Mr Taurus and Ms Libra meet. The Taurean male is deeply affectionate, very sentimental and quietly romantic. For him sex is a sensual and erotic experience and though he can be a little on the unimaginative side, he makes up for this with technique! He's a highly skilled lover devoted to the pleasures of the flesh and when he matches up with sexy Ms Libra sparks are going to fly.

His arms are a safe haven for the Libra gal who (being 'in love with being in love') has had her fair share of broken hearts. The interesting thing is, though Ms Libra may have had her heart broken more times than he, she has the amazing ability to 'bounce back' more quickly. The Taurean man, who feels things very, *very* deeply, recuperates slowly from a broken love affair. In many cases it can take him years before he is ready to trust a woman again.

If they decide to get married, and they are mature enough emotionally it's likely to be long-lasting and happy. The Libra woman is well-suited to marriage and her wish list often includes a husband, comfortable house, several children, good friendship and a luxury life. Mr Taurus seeks security, and that includes emotional *and* material security. Being in a serious committed relationship suits stable Mr Taurus down to the ground. Some astrologers joke that the way to a Taurean man's heart is through is stomach, and that's not far from the truth! Mr Taurus adores fine wine and food, and if she isn't already a culinary whiz Ms Libra had better learn to whip up some gourmet meals if she plans to win her Taurus man!

No matter how much he protests at times, the Taurean man is really just a big softie, particularly where his own children are concerned — he is a tender, loving father. On the whole, they can be a very compatible couple as both love family, friends, good food, nice décor, the Arts and luxury holidays! Both are very sociable by nature. If they do argue, it's likely to be about her penchant for extravagance (when feeling down, there is nothing like a shopping spree to lift her spirits) or his restrained spending (earth signs tend to 'hold on' to their possessions and money). Thankfully, they do seem to balance each other out. Her natural 'tomorrow is another day' attitude takes the edge off his natural pessimism. If *anyone* can cheer up Mr Taurus when he's stuck in a rut or down in the dumps, it's his bright and breezy Libra gal. In return, he gives her the sense of stability she needs. His rock-solid presence soothes her nerves when, in typical Libran fashion, she has her moments of agonising indecision! Mr Dependability is just what the zodiac love doctor prescribes for the restless Libra gal.

TAURUS—SCORPIO relationship

The *'opposites attract'* relationship

STAR TAURUS–SCORPIO COUPLE
Uma Thurman and Ethan Hawke

Situated on opposed sides of the horoscope wheel, there is a major 'opposites attract' energy between earth-ruled Taurus and water-governed Scorpio. Being opposites, they have a strong chemical, magnetic attraction and it's often a case of lust at first sight that brings them together. Not long after exploring the physical side of their relationship, Taurus and Scorpio discover a *different* kind of appeal.

Born with polar opposite personality traits, they find themselves attracted to the character qualities that they themselves lack. This balancing act might be why the fascination exists. For example, intense Scorpio admires the way Taurus controls emotions and keeps them on an even keel; whereas Taurus would love to have Scorpio's ability to probe powerfully into people's very thoughts, minds and souls! Even though Taurus is an open book and Scorpio an endless mystery, this relationship can be a mutual admiration society full of love, respect and a healthy dose of passion. Once they do commit to each other, their union can become a steady, stable powerhouse. Sadly, in many cases this relationship becomes a test of wills with neither party being prepared to be pushed, pulled or pressured. Only time will tell if Taurus and Scorpio end up being soul mates or cell mates.

Taurus woman — Scorpio man

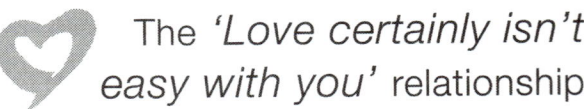 The *'Love certainly isn't easy with you'* relationship

When Ms Taurus and Mr Scorpio first gaze at each other across a crowded room, train, supermarket queue, bar etc etc, there is *definitely* a big attraction. Sensual Ms Taurus is an attractive woman with an earthy appeal and Mr Scorpio has to be one of the most intensely sexy men of the zodiac with his magnetic 'come to bed' eyes. Yes sireee! Opposites attract and that is definitely what happens when the Bull and Scorpion meet. Once they get to know each other better, the attraction runs deeper than the purely *physical*. They actually sense in each other the qualities that *they* themselves lack. So in a way, being together makes them feel whole and complete. Actors Uma Thurman and her Scorpio husband, Ethan

Hawke, symbolise the attraction between the Taurus woman and the Scorpio man. Their intense relationship is full of love, passion and mutual respect. However, like all Taurus–Scorpio couples they have had to work harder than most to make it work.

The Taurean woman is often tall, voluptuous and/or physically strong. She also has a heavy step and some Taurean women battle constantly with their weight. But her solid physicality says a lot about her character. Ms Taurus lives on terra firma with her feet solidly planted. She has strong ideas and opinions and she is not afraid to call a spade a spade. Her directness can get her into trouble sometimes (and it *can* leave Mr Scorpio shocked at times), but her virtues are her honesty and openness. What you see is what you get with Ms Taurus and she is generally not into playing emotional games with her guy. The Scorpio man adores her honesty and inner calm. She's dependable (a character trait he admires), patient and determined. She generally doesn't hide her emotions — and even if she *does* try to cover them, she won't do a very good job! You see, though Ms Taurus goes about life guided by how she *feels* about things, she's not a highly emotional gal.

So how does Mr Scorpio differ from his strong-willed, fixed opinioned and sometimes outspoken Taurus gal? Well, the Scorpio man is a master of disguises — and you never quite know what's going on in that handsome head of his! Like all water signs, Mr Scorpio is emotional and sensitive. Although he might appear coolly detached on the outside, that's not to say there isn't an emotional storm brewing within him! He's a puzzling combination of cool rationale and searing emotion. Presenting different masks to people is simply Scorpio's self-protective mechanism and Ms Taurus will soon learn that her guy is a survivor from way back! While he guards his own secrets well, Mr Scorpio has an uncanny ability to probe other people's deep and dark secrets. When she first meets him, Ms Taurus gets the feeling that he can read her thoughts just by gazing hypnotically into her eyes. It can make her feel uneasy at first. But the fact is, she envies his ability to *know* what people are thinking and feeling. The Taurus gal doesn't typically get ruffled, but her Scorpio guy has the ability to leave her lost for words or make butterflies dance in her stomach. He's from Pluto, the planet of explosive passion and mystery and she's from Venus, the planet of love and peace.

Sex is steamy for this astro-couple and they will suddenly find themselves turned on and ready for romance in the strangest places and at the oddest hours. It might happen when he suddenly gazes into her eyes or when she gives him a sensual rub on the shoulders; but they will find themselves (especially early in their relationship) unable to take their hands off each other! When in love, she is completely devoted and can border on possessiveness. Even though the Scorpio man has a reputation for being the zodiac's sex symbol, he is extremely loyal when he's with the right partner. Sex is an intense experience for him (almost bordering on a religion!) and happily, earthy Ms Taurus matches his powerful desires.

She admires her Scorpio guy's dedication and intensity to goals in life. If you listen to a Scorpio talk you begin to understand that their life has been a roller coaster ride made up of ecstatic highs and bleak lows. He is wise beyond his years. Although the Taurean gal is swept away by the romance of being with such a mysterious and powerful man, his occasional bouts of the 'silent treatment' and his Scorpion 'stings' can frustrate her. That's when she stamps her feet, snorts through her nose and charges in the fashion of her astrological symbol, the Bull! When angry or upset, Mr Scorpio tends to let fly a comment aimed to sting or, his Machiavellian actions speak for themselves. He can be fairly devious when he wants to be, and she'll know straight away that's she's in the bad books. Ms Taurus, on the other hand, will simply tell her guy straight up that she's a) angry, b) upset, or c) going to leave him.

Yep, if she loves him and wants to be with him Ms Taurus needs to understand that her Scorp guy is a very complicated and very intense man. He is interested in the esoteric and the world that can't be 'seen'; whereas she is the most practical woman in the zodiac! If earth-bound Ms Taurus can't *see* it or *touch* it, then it doesn't exist. Though at times she might make fun of his psychic feelings or interests in the supernatural, she does respect his otherworldly 'powers'. Funny thing is, as different as they are, the Taurus woman and Scorpio man do have things in common. Both tend to see life in a 'black' or 'white' kind of way. They don't spend too much time studying the shades of grey. Both of them are also 'fixed' signs — which basically means that they are stubborn and wilful in their ideas and actions. They have passionate views — and whether they are discussing politics, child-rearing techniques or the ozone layer it is sure to be a lively conversation!

If they ever decide to harness their positive character traits they can create amazing things together (such as starting a business or other projects). So what lies in the future for Ms Taurus and Mr Scorpio? That depends on each of them and how far they are willing to stretch themselves to meet each other half way. Both are people who believe in giving ALL or NOTHING. If they give all, the Bull and Scorpion can be the most devoted and loyal couple of the zodiac.

Taurus man—Scorpio woman

 The *'You and me forever or never'* relationship

To caution the unsuspecting Taurean male, the Scorpio woman should come with a government warning that reads: 'A relationship with Scorpio women may lead to serious romantic complications. Become involved at your own risk.'

In most cases, the easy-going Bull has no idea of what he is getting into when he becomes involved with powerful Ms Scorpio. And how could he possibly know? When they first meet, her intensely seductive gaze mystifies him, making his testosterone start to surge. You see, the Taurean man is very masculine (just think of his astrological sign, the Bull), and he's an easy target for a sexy and mysterious woman like Ms Scorpio. She has her own brand of deep, seductive beauty that is intriguing and distracting (just think of actresses Demi Moore, Julia Roberts and Lauren Hutton). She has the ability to have almost any man she chooses wrapped around her little finger.

She too, is greatly attracted to Mr Taurus. Taurean men are very masculine looking. He often has a powerful body with a strong chest and muscular legs and his earthy good looks tend to get better with age (just look at heart-throb actor George Clooney and tennis player Andre Agassi). Ruled by Venus, the planet of beauty, relationships and love, Mr Taurus is charismatic and he has natural sex appeal. He's a romantic in a sweet, homespun kind of way. He much prefers cosy home-cooked meals sitting in front of the fireplace with his gal, than painting the town red on a Saturday night. His ideal companion is classy, polite, attractive and preferably a good cook! Of course if he falls under the spell of a gal like Ms Scorpio — who has enormous sex appeal to boot — then he won't care whether she slaves over a hot stove or simply orders takeaway every night!

Mr Taurus is incredibly affectionate and gentle, and he's at his best with a woman who loves and adores him. It can take him a lifetime to find the right gal (he is incredibly patient!) but when he finds her he wants it to last a lifetime. Mr Taurus wants stability in his love life and he makes a devoted husband when he's with the right woman. (Of course if Ms Scorpio is not 'The One' for him he should tell her straight out, as she is a natural detective with a nose for discovering people's secrets!) The Scorpio woman is also looking for a deep commitment. She can't stand superficial people or relationships and she's not a love 'em and leave 'em kind of gal. In this way, they find in each other someone willing to make a serious commitment.

The Scorpio woman is strong-willed, a good friend, a formidable enemy, and prone to intense likes and dislikes. She tends to live in the world of 'black' and 'white' and she doesn't suffer fools gladly. Though her Taurean guy admires her discipline and inner strength he doesn't envy her strong emotions. He's an uncomplicated kind of guy and he prefers direct, open communication. 'Why does she have to keep so many secrets? She knows everything about me!' he'll ponder to himself. But what irks Mr Taurus more than anything else about his Scorpio gal, is the underhand way she lets him know that he's in the bad books. Her techniques include letting loose spiteful comments or giving him the cold treatment for days on end. Upfront Mr Taurus can't understand why he's on the receiving end of such stinging remarks or conniving actions.

Ms Scorpio, on the other hand, gets frustrated by his cautious outlook and unwillingness to take a chance. She lives life to the fullest, but Mr Taurus often holds back his impulsive instincts until he knows the outcome is a sure-fire thing. And he thinks that she is too rash at times. It also annoys Ms Scorpio that her guy is so attached to his material possessions. Ruled by the element earth, Mr Taurus is possessive — and that includes his woman, house, car and other material goods. He likes to touch nice things, wear nice things, eat nice things and own nice things. The physical world gives him comfort. Though his life 'lesson' this time around is to acquire some mastery over the physical, practical and earthly world; he does also need to learn to 'let go' of possessions. To the contrary, Ms Scorpio loves to throw old things away, and liberating herself of unwanted 'stuff' rejuvenates her in more ways than one. She sees life, as more than the material world and most Scorpio women are interested in topics such as religion, life-after-death, personal growth or the occult.

For each of them, the force of habit is strong and both are determined and purposeful. In fact, both are so persistent that it takes them years to get out of a love relationship that's going nowhere. Each stands firm on their beliefs and this is where they encounter problems in their relationship. Neither likes to be bullied. So where does this leave them? Well, often they'll find themselves sitting stubbornly on the sofa, arms crossed and with their backs to each other. Ms Scorpio and Mr Taurus need to work on compromising and meeting each other half way, otherwise their obstinacy will get in the way of their happiness. Both of them have trouble forgiving and forgetting and this can make their relationship very, very challenging.

Though the Scorpio gal and Taurean guy will have to cope with their fair share of frustrations together, they can learn a great deal from each other. He brings stability and meaning to her life and she can help him surmount his fears and inertia. If *anyone* can encourage the Scorpio woman to share her deepest feelings, it will be Mr Taurus (he's one of the best listeners in the zodiac). And if anyone can encourage the Taurean man to cast aside possessions for a moment — to see the unseen — then it's Ms Scorpio. So the good news is, if both are willing to make adjustments, this can be a union bound for relationship bliss.

TAURUS — SAGITTARIUS relationship

The *'You're delightful, but can I put up with you, that's the question'* relationship

STAR TAURUS–SAGITTARIUS COUPLE
Diane Keaton and Woody Allen

The Taurus–Sagittarius relationship is often akin to those ad lib recipes you conjure up when you haven't gone shopping and you just grab everything out of the fridge and cupboards, throw it in the pan, heat it up and hope it will work out. Sometimes experiments like this *do* work out and are so fantastic you wish you could re-create them again, but most times the result ends up tasting a little strange. You see, trying to mix Sagittarian liveliness with Taurean serenity isn't such an easy recipe for ongoing relationship success. Taurus is from the planet Venus, a place where beauty, tranquillity, peace and love rule the day. Sagittarius, on the other hand, hails from the over-the-top planet Jupiter, where excitement, risk, freedom and vitality are valued. Let's face it, both planets have their pros and cons but for this couple to live happily ever after they'd better find a neutral territory to live in together (often this turns out to be the bedroom where passion makes up for any lack of connection elsewhere). On most levels of operation in everyday life, compromise is the key to any relationship and this compromise angle applies even more so for Taurus and Sagittarius. If they don't learn to give and take (and both can be quite stubborn), then their romance is destined to fizzle rather than sizzle.

Taurus woman—Sagittarius man

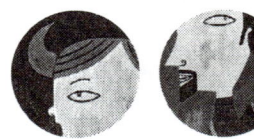

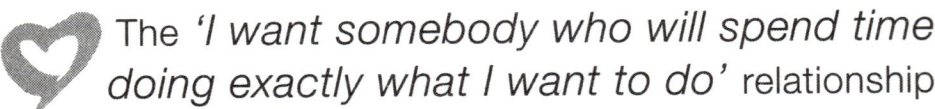 The *'I want somebody who will spend time doing exactly what I want to do'* relationship

It's been said that laughter is a powerful aphrodisiac, and Mr Sagittarius and Ms Taurus prove just how true that statement is when they first meet each other. Mr Sagittarius's antics and funny stories will soon have Ms Taurus doubled over and laughing that deep, throaty, sexy laugh of hers. Many Sagittarian men (like Archer comedians Woody Allen, Ben Stiller and Brendan Fraser) have a sexy charisma that's aligned closely to their sense of humour. He loves to laugh at his own failures and shortcomings and that is very attractive to Ms Taurus. Fortunately, she also has the ability to hold the Archer spellbound with her funny one-liners, amusing jokes and hearty laugh. She is expressive and often has a wonderful slapstick sense of humour.

Though their first date might be a big success, it's sometimes left up to fate as to whether they become 'buddies' or 'lovers'. Neither Taurus nor Sagittarius innately jump into relationships, it usually isn't their style. He might have a reputation for being a heartbreaker but the truth is, the Sag male is rarely in a hurry to make a romantic commitment. Ms Taurus, on the other hand, is simply a slow-mover who rarely dives in without first testing the romantic waters for depth, warmth and stability. Inevitably it will either be the Archer's love of taking a risk OR the Bull's infamous determination that is responsible for setting the second date! Naturally if the sexual chemistry is super hot you can forget their slow approach when it comes to commitment. But the sex-vibe attraction will need to be highly charged to overcome both of these signs' natural tendencies to avoid losing control of their need to keep a cool head and loads of independence.

In any case, Mr Sagittarius is a passionate fire sign that makes the most of every opportunity in life. At times his risk-taking can turn into recklessness but thankfully he tends to have incredible luck wherever he goes and whatever he does. There always seems to be a guardian 'angel' looking after the Sagittarian man. His symbol is the Centaur, a creature from Greek mythology that was half-man and half-beast. The Archer encourages Mr Sag to aim high but he often has a tendency to shooting arrows all over the place, falling short of his true mark. He can be more comfortable playing the role of playboy or 'jack of all trades, master of none', rather than settling on one specific target; and this can often drain his resources and keep him unsettled. In this way, Ms Taurus is a wonderful influence on her Archer. She's patient and focused and will encourage him to shoot for one target at a time until he gets the bull's-eye!

Ms Taurus admires Mr Sag's adventuresome spirit, cheerful nature and his intelligence, but there is also something of a 'little boy lost' in him that tugs at her heartstrings. Of course, there are times she thinks he has gone too far and her penchant for convention clashes with his love of raging against the establishment. If she isn't careful she might smother her independent Sagittarian man. She needs to understand that having freedom doesn't mean he won't be faithful to her. When he's with a woman he loves, it's rare that he will stray. What he *does* require in his love life is variety and excitement. Fire-ruled Sagittarius is passionate and fiery and his libido is high! In bed they are a good match and her erotic, passionate and extremely sensual side gets a most appreciative audience when Mr Sag is her love-making partner.

But it isn't because she has tremendous love-making appeal that gives her an edge over the other women he may be courting — many women please Mr Sag in the love-making department as he enjoys variety. He loves her also because she's smart, independent and a good listener. She is also extremely patient. One thing Mr Sag should bear in mind is that Ms Taurus is made for marriage. That's not to say *all* Taurus gals *must* marry, but her need for emotional security is best fulfilled when she's happily married. The downside is that most Sagittarian males break out in a rash at the very mention of marriage. If she loves him, her patient nature and determination to get what she wants will win out over his initial doubts! If they set up house together, Ms Taurus and Mr Sagittarius both need to keep an eye on their weight and their bank balance! Venus, the pleasure planet, rules her and she loves nothing more than rich culinary delights and spending sprees on beautiful things. Thankfully, she usually reaches a limit whereby the sensible little voice in the back of her head reminds her of the 'all things in moderation' motto. Unfortunately her Sagittarius guy doesn't have such a guilty conscience. Jupiter rules 'expansion' and by nature Mr Sagittarius is a man of extremes. Many Archer males love to eat, drink, gamble and basically take a risk in life wherever possible. Ms Taurus will probably find herself clamping down on his crazy adventures if he takes them to the extreme.

But for all his occasional failings or shortcomings, Ms Taurus adores him. He has a positive outlook on life that is contagious. He is almost always gregarious, enthusiastic and cheerful and he helps pull her out of her lethargy when all she wants to do is spend days in bed. Ms Taurus admires the thrilling life Mr Sagittarius leads. He visits exciting places, meets interesting people and does exhilarating things. But that doesn't necessarily mean she wants to join him in his adventures. That's because Ms Taurus wants a peaceful life and stability. Though she may have travelled (Europe is a favourite), the Taurean woman is an earth sign who likes to be 'grounded' in more ways than one. Security is important to her (emotional and financial), and she's much more comfortable working nine to five and coming back to her home sweet home every evening. She is also the kind of woman who prefers a cosy dinner for two with her Archer man, rather than 'sharing' him with his friends at the pub on a Friday night.

Though initially he might like her possessiveness (it can be a sexy turn-on for Mr Sag), it will soon grow cold on him. It's not that she doesn't trust him, because Ms Taurus is not the jealous type. It's simply that she wants him all to herself! Sooner or later, the Taurus gal is going to learn that to keep her Sag guy she needs to give him freedom. Ruled by Jupiter, he is made to be out in the world surrounded by interesting and unusual people.

Their pace in life will sometimes be a barrier as they 'view' life at different speeds. Ms Taurus takes her time in everything she does and tends to stay in situations that's she's long outgrown. Earth sign Taurus is slow-moving and she tends to think about things very slowly before deciding on a change.

MR SAGITTARIUS: Honey, I don't understand why you stick it out at your job. You've been telling me for years you don't like it.

MS TAURUS: Yeah, I know. But I don't want to leave until I'm sure I have something else lined up. I can't leave myself out on a limb.

MR SAGITTARIUS: But how will you find something better if you're not out there looking for something else? Just take a chance. Quit your job and then concentrate on looking for something else.

MS TAURUS: Sweetie, that's easy for you to say. These things take time you know. I'm just going to wait until the time is right.

MR SAGITTARIUS: If you understood the basic laws of the Universe, you'd realise that when a void is created it will be filled with something else. Take my advice and resign tomorrow. I bet you twenty dollars that within a week, you'll find something else!

MS TAURUS: Get serious. And how would you expect me to pay the bills if I didn't find something straight away. I'm not rash like you — it doesn't work for me!

And so it goes around and around. You see, whereas Ms Taurus is a realist, and borderline pessimist, Mr Sagittarius is an optimist who could also be accused of being a dreamer. So who is right? Well, there's no right or wrong here. It's simply the way they each view the world. So the question is: though they adore each other, can they live together?

Taurus man—Sagittarius woman

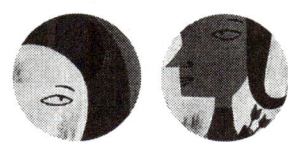

 The *'You're a little strange, but I like your kind of strange'* relationship

In some cases, well-travelled, outgoing and educated Ms Sagittarius is just a little too sophisticated for the more reticent Taurean man. She often speaks another language, has a degree or two, climbs mountains for a hobby and mingles with her friends from the United Nations. The Taurean guy could be a little too bland for her. Now before you Bulls start blowing smoke through your nostrils in outrage, just listen for a moment (and I know you are excellent listeners!) I'm not saying that Taureans are dull. What I am saying is that Ms Sagittarius is probably the most independent, bold, restless, philosophical, footloose and fancy-free, annoyingly arrogant and passionate woman of the zodiac. She thrives on challenge, excitement and adventure and often runs from routine, responsibility and commitment (the three pillars of a Taurus belief system!) The Sagittarian gal can be a handful and men are often scared of her.

So, along comes Mr Taurus into her life. He's stable, dependable, kind-hearted, stubborn, determined, affectionate and sensible. Whether she runs a mile OR feels strangely attracted to him depends a lot on her maturity and 'where she's at' in life. If Ms Sag has already been there and done that (and had her heart broken in the process), dependable Mr Taurus is truly a Godsend. He brings much-needed stability into her life. When it comes to the crunch, he's conservative and she's radical. He's calm and she's excitable. He's inclined to pessimism while she is an eternal optimist. He believes in responsibility and she does everything she can to avoid it. This relationship is pure 'chalk and cheese'. But even though their differences can pose a challenge, it doesn't mean that these two can't have a long and fulfilling relationship. In many ways, they balance each other out. And to be honest, what's the point of seeking a partner who is exactly the same as you? These two can learn from each other and grow in the process.

The physical attraction between the Taurean guy and Sagittarian gal is strong. She adores him because he's incredibly masculine (Bulls normally have a strong, imposing physique), yet his masculinity is softened by the feminine influence of his ruling planet, Venus. He relates to women very well and intuitively senses their needs. He's incredibly affectionate and he makes her feel totally loved and adored. When it comes to sex she's open, passionate and generous, and many fiery Sagittarian women are used to making the first move. Mr Taurus is likely to either love her initiative OR feel slightly uncomfortable about it. He's a slow mover where love and romance are concerned, and she may scare him away if she's too upfront. Once they become lovers, his sensuality matches her own. He likes to take his time romancing his gal and this includes a slow and steady build-up to a night of passion. He might cook her dinner, followed by stargazing with a glass of champagne, then he'll give her a back rub and then he'll . . . need I say more. The interesting thing is, where she is quick to jump into the physical side of the romance, he'll be the first to mention the words *serious, long term* and *marriage*.

When deeply in love, Mr Taurus naturally wants to 'formalise' things and that eventually means marriage.

Independent Ms Sagittarius isn't so eager to tie the knot! Highly independent, she often equates 'marriage' with a loss of freedom and she's more inclined to suggest they live together first to test the waters. If Mr Taurus has decided that she is 'The One' he's patient enough to wait until she is ready. Then, when she least expects it, he'll ask her to marry him. When she does say 'yes' it's usually because a) she answered impulsively, b) she's mature enough, or c) she's realised that he is just too good to let go.

The Taurean man is a gentle, understanding and loyal guy who is as solid as a rock. He'll never break a promise or forget an anniversary. In fact, Mr Taurus is more sensitive than she realises and she can easily insult his masculinity or damage his ego with her heavy-handed comments and lack of tact. She has a habit of firing her truthful (and sometimes hurtful) arrows at exactly the wrong moment. He's not an overly sensitive guy, but if she wounds him she'll have to suffer days of his sulking. He is not the kind of guy to forgive and forget quickly and her 'just get over it!' attitude will irk him even more.

He does, however, love her bright and sunny disposition and philosophical outlook on life. If life doesn't turn out as expected she shrugs her shoulders, gets into her Archer's stance and shoots off another arrow towards a new target. She tends to look at the bright side of life. Mr Taurus smiles at her optimism (he brushes it off as naiveté) but a part of him admires her idealism. Earth-bound Taurus, on the other hand, is a born realist. He's practical and uncomplicated and believes in doing things 'by the book'. And as much as she tries to convince him that 'life was meant to be easy' he stubbornly sticks to his view that the secret to life is hard work. She relies on street smarts and luck. In fact, the Sagittarian gal is one of the luckiest women he knows. Whether it's bingo, the horse races, magazine give-aways or landing the best job in town, Ms Sagittarius is very lucky. Ruled by Jupiter, the benevolent planet, she always seems to be in the right place at the right time.

She encourages him to take risks and stretch himself, whereas he injects some much needed realism into her life (especially when she starts shooting her arrows without aim). The Taurean man is a master at goal-setting. He understands that you need to walk before you can run and he opens up her eyes to 'long-term planning'. Particularly where her financial arena and career are concerned, he is a very good influence in her life.

But unless he's a truly liberated man (and many Taurean men can be a little on the chauvinistic side), he's never going to be comfortable with his Sag gal's fiery independence. She's not an easy person to live with and there is nothing more she loves than a good argument. She has a quick mind and she's skilled in debate. Her Taurean guy, on the other hand, isn't interested in arguing for the sake of arguing. He sees no point in wasting time on petty discussions and halfway through their debate he has a tendency to 'switch off'. That's when his gaze shifts from her animated, talking head to the sports program on television just over her left shoulder. To be honest, Mr Taurus is an easy-going guy who prefers leading a comfortable life to changing the world. In extreme cases, he can be apathetic and lazy, and these tendencies can drive his socially and physically active Sagittarian gal insane. Sometimes the passion in this relationship is smothered by his stubbornness and her self-righteousness (the two 'biggies' that cause tension between them). But if they learn to give and take, they'll discover that compromise (and long-lasting happiness) are beautiful things indeed.

TAURUS—CAPRICORN relationship

The *'There's a hole in my heart that can only be filled by you'* relationship

STAR TAURUS–CAPRICORN COUPLE
Renée Zellweger and Jim Carey

Why is it that so many Taureans and Capricorns breathe a karmic sigh of relief when they find themselves settling comfortably into each other's arms? Probably because it's the closest they've *ever* been (and will *ever* get) to finding that elusive 'Perfect Match'. There's a strong tie between these two earth signs, whose four feet are planted firmly and squarely on terra firma. Taurus and Capricorn are like two peas in a cosmic pod. They are both motivated by the same things in life, such as strong family values, emotional stability and financial security.

The Capricorn Goat is likely to wear the pants in their relationship, with the Taurus Bull placidly following behind. But bossy Capricorn shouldn't underestimate Taurus' ability to get fired up when his or her strong beliefs are challenged. Taurus is a fixed sign prone to stubbornness. So what occurs when the Bull and Goat lock horns? Well, usually nothing more than bruised egos; but occasionally it's better for one of them to give an inch or a mile to keep things harmonious. Usually clever Capricorn and sensible Taurus are too smart to let petty bickering about the 'small stuff' in life get in the way of a rock-solid relationship. Theirs is often a once-in-a-lifetime romantic affair that's too valuable to mess up. But of course, no zodiac match is infallible. There are temptations, distractions and challenges that lay waiting on the pathway of every romantic journey. So, even the comfy and cosy Taurus–Capricorn match still has to pass the test of time, but usually this cosmic couple seem to pass it, better than most.

Taurus woman — Capricorn man

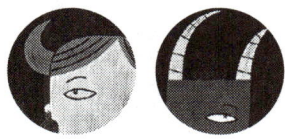

 The *'I think I feel safe when I'm with you, but I can't be certain'* relationship

'About time!' is what my Taurus friend said when she met the man of her dreams, a handsome and talented Capricorn (who was quite a good-looker, too!) I had heard her complain for years about non-committal, unpredictable boyfriends and *finally* she had met someone who wanted a stable, long-term relationship as much as she did! You see, it's hard to find a more perfectly matched couple in the zodiac than Ms Taurus and Mr Capricorn. Both are ruled by the element earth, which gives them a longing for a stable, secure, love relationship. Yes, marriage material they certainly are (and I'm happy to say that my Taurean friend and her Capricorn beau are now about to head down the aisle).

There is a certain feeling of 'destiny' in the air when Ms Taurus and Mr Capricorn first meet. They often meet through work, a social club or sports group or they are introduced by family or friends who have been bugging them forever with the line, 'You've got to meet my friend, you'll get on like a house on fire!' Actually, when they meet it's more a case of 'smouldering embers' than 'flaming fire', and their initial attraction keeps growing as they get to know each other more and their love builds up in strength and power over time.

The Taurean woman is knocked over by Mr Capricorn's elegance, confidence and good taste. Most Capricorn men are gentlemen and he'll open the door for her and help her take off her coat. She gets the idea that there's more to his refined exterior than first meets the eye. There's a twinkle in his eye (just think of sexy Capricorn actors Mel Gibson or Anthony Hopkins) that suggests he's not as serious as he appears. Although he is focused on work and life in general, he does have a dry sense of humour. And as he gets older he loosens up! In fact, it's *her* sense of humour that makes Mr Capricorn fall for the Taurean gal. She can be incredibly comical, and her funny one-liners appear at the least expected moments followed by a hearty, earthy (but also very sexy) laugh (think Debra Winger and Cher). The fact that she makes him laugh is very attractive to him. Oh, that, and her sweet face and curvy body! The Taurean woman (ruled by Venus, the planet of beauty and femininity) normally has luminous skin and curves in all the right places! She's often got a magical glow around her (courtesy of Venus) that makes heads turn and men in particular (especially Mr Capricorn) take immediate notice.

Whatever occurs, success is on the cards in more ways than one for this couple. Capricorn men are high achievers (just think of his astro-symbol, the Goat, trekking up to the top of the mountain). He's ambitious and a strong leader and his mission to make it to the top will be stopped by no man (or woman for that matter). Many Capricorn men are found in top corporate jobs, running their own business or even running for President! Even if he's more of an artsy type, he'll be renovating old buildings or taking on landscape gardening to make his livelihood. He can work at unusual jobs, but he usually likes to be busy. Success in his career and home life is important to the Capricorn man, mainly because he is concerned about 'status' and what people think about him. Above all, the Goat guy wants to be accepted and admired by his family, friends and society at large.

Thankfully, Ms Taurus is the perfect companion to share his journey on the way to the top. Many Taurean women are successful in their own careers and others are excellent 'support' to their high-flying Capricorn men. As down-to-earth as she is, the Taurean woman has a strong attachment to the material world. She's often quite a brilliant business gal herself and has skills, talents and abilities that make her quite a go-getter in the material realms. However, the difference between her and Mr Capricorn is that she doesn't really care what people think about her or the way she lives her life. The Taurean gal is attracted to money because it gives her *security*. Things like a healthy bank balance and a stable relationship make her feel secure and that everything is OK in her world. And, of course, she simply loves beautiful things. Ruled by Venus — the planet of love, relationships, peace and beauty — she has an eye for art and design and she adores the 'feel' of quality clothes and jewellery.

As both of these signs are organised, dedicated and patient, they often build up their own form of relationship dynasty. Now, I'm not saying that *all* Capricorn males and Taurean females will construct a mini-empire full of lavish homes, opulent cars and luxury yachts! They are, however, more likely than most couples to work towards creating wealth and a comfortable lifestyle. Both are determined and dedicated to reaching their aspirations. Their goals are identical and this gives them a good chance of having a happy and satisfied relationship.

Speaking of satisfaction, it can sometimes take a while before Mr Capricorn and Ms Taurus get in total sync where sex is concerned. Both are earthy, sensual lovers but they also tend to 'hold back' on being totally abandoned in their expression of intimacy until they know and trust each other. Mr Capricorn can be very cautious when it comes to romance. He doesn't like to leave himself vulnerable. He'll take his time in wooing her but that won't mean he's not determined to win her heart (and possibly her hand in marriage). Patient Ms Taurus doesn't jump into love relationships either, she doesn't want to hand over the keys to her heart without being certain she is doing the right thing. So in terms of their romantic evolution, so often their 'timing' is perfectly matched. Once they trust each other, their sex life is wonderful, warm and intimate, and they lose any fears they may hold about trusting each other enough to step hand in hand into the love realms of life together. Once some initial barriers are removed, though Mr Capricorn *appears* to the outside world as being conservative and cautious, he does let his hair down now and again, and again, and again where sex is concerned. Actually he can be quite kinky, and she is a sensual, erotic lover who responds easily to touch, smell and taste. Together they can blaze quite a sexual trail into adventurous, erotic and inventive sex. However, their sexual flow always depends greatly upon their emotional love connection. Especially as Ms Taurus's senses are highly developed and love and sex are inseparable to her, so if there's any doubt about her man in her mind, her lessening interest in him sexually quickly reflects it.

But on most levels they understand each other well and can support and help each other grow and prosper. The Taurus woman is a down-to-earth, practical woman and she knows how to help her Capricorn guy wind down and relax (and he *is* prone to tension and stress). She'll give him gentle back massages, make him delicious home-made soup or put on classical music to ease his stress. She is a master at 'soothing the senses'. They both share a love of art and music and will enjoy visiting art exhibitions, going to concerts or simply spending quiet weekends at home. They also love travelling together and getting away on weekends to the country or the mountains. Ms Taurus is happy to go hiking or skiing with him (two of his favourite sports), as long as there is a comfortable bed and good food and wine at the end the of the day followed by a cosy snuggle up with her Capricorn Honey Bunny!

Yes, Mr Capricorn and Ms Taurus hit the romantic jackpot when they find themselves in each other's arms. And they prove that 'smouldering lasting romantic embers' win out over 'quick-burning sexually lit flames' any day. Happy romantic journeys.

Taurus man—Capricorn woman

 The *'We can't fight it, so we may as well just enjoy it'* relationship

From the moment they were born, if the right stars were in alignment, then Mr Taurus and Ms Capricorn were meant to be together. Due to their natural zodiac characteristics and magnetic fields, there's a cosmic plan that draws them together and there is no way — I repeat — no way that they can fight it, if their destinies are intertwined! Now I know there are lots of pragmatic earth-ruled Taureans and Capricorns out there who scoff at words like 'cosmic' or 'destiny' or 'higher force' but, it all boils down to the fact that there is a natural chemistry between them. Of course that's not to say they won't have disagreements like any other couple. Life won't always be a bowl of cherries for the Bull and the Goat. They have their fair share of problems, but it's going to take something major to cause them to split permanently. Once Mr Taurus and Ms Capricorn make a commitment, they are there for the long haul! In fact, more Taurus–Capricorn couples are likely to reach their Golden Wedding Anniversary than any other matches in the zodiac. Call it true love or call it habit, but there's no denying that Mr Taurus and Ms Capricorn are good for each other.

When they first meet, he is struck by her independence, discipline and classical feminine beauty (just think of model Christy Turlington and singer Sade). She is also as determined, if not more so, than he! He also gets the feeling that he's going to have to work hard to win her love. And thankfully, Mr Taurus has the patience to take on the challenge. You see, Ms Capricorn is discriminating when it comes to love and romance. She's been hurt before and underneath her aura of self-sufficiency is a woman who craves for love yet also fears it. Like Taurus, when her heart is broken she finds it hard to forgive or forget. This is because her loyalty is unmatched by any female in the zodiac. She'll stand by her man through thick and thin and if he betrays her, her world falls down around her.

Mr Taurus understands her sense of devotion in love (he too is very loyal) and he'll take his time in wooing her. But what is hard for him to understand is her Ice Queen attitude at times. It might help him to understand that stern Saturn, the planet of self-discipline and wisdom, rules her. She simply *can't* allow herself to follow her heart completely. Many times Ms Capricorn is ruled by her head not her heart, and she simply can't help it. She is also not willing for a man to dominate her. His patience will pay off. Once she 'decides' she wants to be with him he won't find a more loyal and tender gal in the zodiac. They share the virtue of patience and their relationship is based on trust, love and loyalty.

At first glance it appears that Mr Taurus is not brimming over with sentiment, but look carefully and you'll see that the Bull is kind, affectionate and loyal. His Capricorn gal is thrilled to discover that her physically imposing hunky Taurean guy (and Taurean men are usually strongly built) is really a big Teddy Bear! He's not the kind of guy, however, to shower his gal with hugs and kisses in public. He is conventional in that way, and prefers to express his feelings when they are alone. When he's with the right woman he is extremely romantic in tender and gentle ways. He'll make dinner for her (in fact, he's often a superb cook) and serve it with exceptional wines by a cosy fireplace. Or, he'll buy her perfume and flowers.

His good taste and love of beautiful objects and experiences is influenced by his planetary ruler, Venus (ruler of love, pleasure and beauty). He relates well to women and he learns from female friends and family members what it is that women want and need. In their sexual relationship, Mr Taurus is quite a lover! Earthy and sensual, he is a man connected to his 'senses'. He is highly sensitive to touch, taste, smell, sight and sound — because of this, he is highly attuned to his own sexual needs and to hers. He also has a deep, earthy voice that drives Ms Capricorn wild when he starts murmuring sweet nothings into her ear. His patience and leisurely love-making style helps bring out her unfulfilled sexual yearnings and she responds with tender love making. In both romance *and* sex they can be a perfect match.

If they get married (and if the time and place of when their romance starts to bloom is right — 99.9% will!), they truly set about 'building' a life together. A Bull and Goat married couple seek security and this includes financial stability. Investing in real estate and other low-risk investments is the preferred way to increase their wealth and very few of them will seek out high-risk options such as trading shares. Both are attached to material possessions and they are likely to have an interest in art, antiques or cars.

Both are devoted to their families and vacations are full of family and friends coming and going. Their house is always full of guests or if not, their own children. Starting their own family is a life goal for both of them — though Ms Capricorn might not be your 'garden variety' stay-at-home mum. Generally, the Capricorn woman is quite ambitious (even more so than her Bull partner), and she is likely to return to full-time or part-time work after her children are born. The Bull and Goat are both reserved and modest and 'everything in moderation' is their motto. He tends towards extravagance when it comes to buying beautiful things and he'll stubbornly insist on having the most stylish paintings, kitchen appliances, fabrics and furnishings (including his 'favourite' armchair) for his castle. She'll probably scold him for spending too much money. But it will take more than her admonishments or his stubbornness to get in the way of their happiness. The boat may rock occasionally, but thankfully Ms Capricorn and Mr Taurus are earth signs with steady a footing and a dislike of going overboard!

TAURUS — AQUARIUS relationship

The *'It's a bitter kinda love, but it's also sweet'* relationship

STAR TAURUS–AQUARIUS COUPLE
Ryan O'Neal and Farrah Fawcett

A short astro-science lesson of the zodiac elements helps to understand the relationship between an earth sign and an air sign. Ya see, Taurus is ruled by earth, a strong, durable element that is only moved by powerful outside forces, such as earthquakes, foods, famine or avalanche. Aquarius is governed by air, a free-moving element constantly travelling as it pleases, unattached to anything above the earth. So does this mean your Taurus–Aquarius relationship is going to work out or not, I hear you ask. Though the answer's not that easy, it's true that Taurus and Aquarius are opposites in outlook, feelings and desires — in other words, they have little in common. Their relationship is an undeniable case of 'opposites attract' and sometimes they are so different that the conflict and tension is too much between them. But sometimes their differences provide them with a buzzy new realm of romantic experience and sexual adventure to explore.

Only the really deep and meaningful Taurus–Aquarius relationships make it past first romantic base. In many cases the Bull and Water Bearer come into each other's lives — and then depart — and for reasons that are only seen later in hindsight. They often teach each other an important life-lesson, or fill a void that was previously empty. Those Taureans and Aquarians who manage to transform their affair into a life-long relationship are certainly evolved souls who understand what it means to love somebody unconditionally. These couples prove that understanding, respect and tolerance are the key to lifelong love, no matter how different they are from each other.

Taurus woman—Aquarius man

 The *'Let's just see how it goes before we make too many big plans'* relationship

Though there are exceptions to the rule, this relationship often begins with a sizzle and ends with a fizzle. Sixties super-couple, Cher and ex-husband Sonny Bono tested the waters and, like many Taurus woman–Aquarius man matches, discovered that when the novelty wore off they were left staring at a stranger. The Taurus woman and Aquarius man often find they eventually drain each other's creativity. That's why it often takes bags of patience, understanding, persistence and a load of luck for this combination to work. It's because Taurus and Aquarius sit smack-bang opposite each other on the horoscope wheel. Their differences can make for a big attraction between Ms Taurus and Mr Aquarius, and being with somebody who is so glaringly different can be fascinating, thrilling and a challenge.

This attraction was also apparent between Taurean Shirley Maclaine and her on-again-off-again love affair with Australian politician Andrew Peacock, a freethinking Aquarian. Sometimes their friends will look at the new couple, shaking their heads in wonder at how two such different human beings could have found their way into each other's arms (and they'll secretly wager bets on how long it will last).

When they first meet, the charismatic, intelligent and friendly Aquarian man dazzles Ms Taurus. He seems to be such a force of wisdom, insights and general street smarts — it almost makes her feel inferior. Plus, he's like nobody else she's ever met before. Those born under Aquarius are unique and innovative and she finds his detached sex appeal irresistible. The ruling planet of Aquarius is futuristic Uranus, the planet of the invention, the unexpected and the higher mind. Add to that the fact that he's an air sign, which means he's more comfortable living on a mental plane than dealing with his feelings. He's eccentric, often a creative genius and he marches to the beat of his own drum. Ms Taurus falls in love with his kindness and the way he treats everyone with the same friendliness, respect and curiosity.

Now, when Mr Aquarius meets Ms Taurus he is blown away by her style, sensuality, determination, thoughtfulness and down-to-earth nature. He will most likely consider her just a 'friend' for some time, as it takes a special woman for him to make the leap from friend to lover. He admires her calmness and the fact that her feet are securely planted on terra firma. She is also surprisingly patient with him (and he knows from experience that women consider him difficult 'boyfriend material' *let alone* 'husband material'). Ruled by Venus, the feminine planet of beauty, pleasure and love, Ms Taurus is 'all woman'. Tender, serene and earthy, she physically glows when she's loved and cherished. When she falls in love, she wants it to last forever and if she is with the right person it inevitably will. The question is: is eccentric Mr Aquarius the right guy for sensible Ms Taurus?

Though the Aquarian man is a true humanitarian with a deep desire to help people, he can be a bit of a loner. There are times when people overwhelm him, and he'll retreat into silence (perhaps staying home all weekend, attending a meditation retreat or a solo bushwalking trip). When it comes to one-on-one romantic relationships, he often feels out of his depth. He has the ability to turn his emotions on and off like a tap and this is something his Taurean gal just doesn't understand. When she is in a relationship she's loyal, devoted and gives one hundred per cent. Emotional security is important to her, and she needs an abundance of affection, attention and love. Problems arise when her Aquarian guy is sometimes not able to fill these needs. He can be very detached to his emotions *and* hers! Any woman involved with Mr Aquarius has to be willing to expect the unexpected — that is a big 'ask' of a Taurean gal. Being with him is an unusual and mysterious romantic experience, and at times she'll feel she's merely tagging along for the cosmic ride.

Though she prefers a 'conventional' type of love relationship, that doesn't mean she's a strictly conventional gal. Taurean women are individualists in their own way. Stars like Cher, Uma Thurman, Barbra Streisand and Andie McDowell have done things 'their way' and haven't changed themselves to suit their man (or if they do, they soon learn that it doesn't work). She won't flout convention for the sake of flouting convention. Mr Aquarius, on the other hand, can be a rebel without a cause. An Aquarian man with a solid cause or mission can be quite inspiring, but if Mr Water Bearer doesn't know where to channel his energy he more often than not winds up being a rebel without a cause. His life is about learning through experience. Ms Taurus, on the other hand, prefers not to put herself out on a limb. She normally won't act unless she is pretty sure of the outcome. In this way, they are very different.

The wonderful thing about his love for her is that he respects her for exactly *who* she is. He is also truly interested in what she has to say and that makes her feel secure. She, too, is supportive of his occasional bout of confusion. You see, Mr Aquarius often feels as though life pulls him in two directions. Finding the balance between chaos and order is a typical Aquarian dilemma, and at times he's wise and smart and at other times he's simply foolish.

It might take him a few years to talk about marriage, or even living together, and thankfully Ms Taurus is extremely patient. If they do decide to live together, their house will be a tranquil, serene place, combining her Venusian eye for beautiful tastes, sights and smells, and his love of avant-garde design. When they pick up their clothes off the bedroom floor (both can be a little disordered) their home might even have the finesse to appear in a home décor photo spread. They make great parents, as both are patient, tolerant and friendly.

Taurus man—Aquarius woman

 The *'When a man loves a woman life can really get weird'* relationship

There is something about the Aquarian woman's vague expression that both alarms and attracts Mr Taurus. Or maybe it's her dreamy eyes that sparkle with intelligence and mystery. Or perhaps the unique way she makes odd socks and mismatched colours look veritably cool. Whatever it is, he can't quite pinpoint it. What he does know is that she looks and acts in a unique manner. She's unpredictable, innovative and smart (often bordering on genius). Ms Aquarius dares to be different and her gift to the world is originality. And there is something about her slightly aloof manner that makes the Taurean man desire her even more. No wonder he finds it hard to understand her. You see, the Aquarian woman is constantly getting to know *herself.*

Yes, it takes nerves of steel to cope with an Aquarian woman, so the calm and tranquil Bull male may just be the perfect man to cope with Ms Aquarius. Patience is his middle name and if he has his heart set on conquering the Aquarian woman he is willing to wait. But he should realise that she is a woman who will never be truly 'conquered'.

Even when it comes to sex, the Aquarian woman will be slightly detached. Mr Taurus is a sensual, erotic and deeply passionate lover. He loves slow, languorous sex and her tendency to turn on and off like a light can confuse him. He wants to pull her back from the clouds and possess her mind, heart, body and soul. This ain't likely to happen! Aquarian women fear being 'possessed' and losing identity to a man perhaps more than any other females in the zodiac. Getting into sync where sex is concerned is a major achievement for Taurus and Aquarius. When he wants physical intimacy she's often more inclined to want a game of scrabble, and when she is hit with a sudden lightning bolt of desire, he might be in the middle of making his favourite soufflé, where timing is everything! But when they get it right, sex between the Bull and Water Bearer brings together imagination, passion, sensuality and complete abandon. Her 'out there' originality combined with his homespun earthy sensuality can create nights of passion to remember.

And remember he will. The Taurean male never forgets (or forgives for that matter!) and he will remember decades later a certain meal they shared in Paris, a particular night of making love under the stars or the time she bought him an outrageous Hawaiian shirt for his birthday. He's romantic and has a penchant for thoughtful details. Unfortunately, his sweet love offerings often go unnoticed by vague Ms Aquarius. Though her lack of detail and romance sometimes annoys him, it's *his* lack of interest in what is happening in the world that irks her. She's the kind of gal who belongs to humanitarian, environmental or animal rights groups. She's an activist who wants to change the world and the 'big picture' is more important to her than trivial day-to-day matters. You can imagine how his love of routine and systematic approach to life seems trifling to her at times. You see, Ms Aquarius has a flexible plan of action, and she might be here today and gone tomorrow. For this relationship to work, the Taurean man needs to be very sure of himself. If he is insecure (and some Taurean males do have an insecurity complex) a relationship with the Aquarian woman is going to be more pain than pleasure.

The Bull can, however, bring a much-needed sense of stability to his Aquarian gal's life. She has a colourful past and has experimented living in different places, doing different jobs and often falling in and out of unsuitable relationships.

Depending on what is occurring in her life at the time, he could just be the best thing that ever happened to her. Though he might not always approve of what she does, he'll stick up for her through thick and thin. He's charming, kind-hearted and dependable. He's the kind who can be 'totally devoted' and when he falls in love, he wants it to last forever. Some Taurean men will actually enjoy living out their 'wild side' vicariously through their Aquarian gal. He is not the kind of guy to openly challenge convention and challenge authority, though a part of him loves the fact that she does fight against and occasionally beat the system.

So will it ever work out in the long term for Mr Predictable and Ms Unpredictable? Well, sometimes the gap between them is too wide to bridge. The fact that they are both very stubborn also makes it difficult for them to compromise with each other. But that doesn't mean that it's never going to work between Mr Taurus and Ms Aquarius. If he treats her with respect and friendliness and doesn't demand too much of her attention and time, then she'll be a loyal partner. And if she cuts down on her parties, social events and political hunger strikes in order to enjoy cosy home-cooked meals with Mr Taurus, then the future looks just rosy! It may even lead to wedding bells, but Mr Taurus will patiently take his time convincing commitment-phobic Aquarian woman of the joys of marriage and children — but that's another story!

TAURUS—PISCES relationship

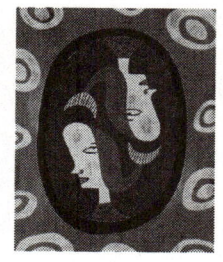

The *'I'm not quite certain, but we might turn out all right'* relationship

STAR TAURUS–PISCES COUPLE
Enrique Iglesias and Jennifer Love Hewitt

Though Pisces and Taurus are different in many ways, there is enough empathy between them that makes for a nice, cosy relationship. Ruled by Neptune — the planet of dreams, the unseen and spirituality — Pisces is an otherworldly being who swims through life in his or own unique style. Pisces aspire beyond the limits of earthy knowledge and they are highly intuitive, sensitive, otherworldly magicians. Taurus, on the other hand, is a rock solid, practical. sign. Emotional and financial security *matter* to Taurus, and the Bull has his (or her) feet firmly planted on the ground. There's no-one more responsible and sensible than Venus-ruled Taurus. And for that matter, Taurus doesn't believe in magicians!

Just like in nature, sometimes the Bull and the Fish need such different environments to survive, that living together is simply impossible. But there is a secret that happily married Taurus–Pisces lovers have discovered. If they focus on what they have in common (rather than what differentiates them), then long-term relationship success is possible. They are romantic, tolerant, affectionate, kind, gentle and understanding, and both are searching for a soul mate to share their cosmic journey.

Taurus woman—Pisces man

 The *'Will you be mean or nice? I've gotta know straight away'* relationship

Everybody loves a mystery, and that aspect of finding something or someone fascinating because you can't really fathom it out, can sometimes work well in this relationship's favour. After all, there's something most elusive about Mr Pisces that completely confounds the down-to-earth (I love everything under my control) Taurean woman. And whether she's been in a relationship with him for ten weeks or ten years, it's unlikely she'll ever truly know him. He is constantly contradicting himself and he is extremely changeable. He isn't a straight shooter, so dealing with him is like dealing with a riddle. Now, hopefully, that statement won't put you sensible Taurean gals off, because as his stars reveal Mr Pisces is one of the most intriguing men under the earth, sun, moon and stars! He's hot, he's cold, he's slippery and he's amazing — he's not a normal guy at all. And subliminally, many a Taurus starmaiden is seeking someone exciting; someone who can make her feel more intensely, make her love more totally, and make her heart pound when she's making love. He's definitely able to do all that; and what's more he's exciting, challenging and unpredictable as well.

His astrological symbol is the Fish, and Mr Pisces moves in the depths of another world that is very difficult for more earth-bound types like Ms Taurus to understand. It can sometimes infuriate her that he has no plans, no structures, no routine and no discipline in his life. He can also be a 'Drama King Fish' at times, and get sidetracked by people, places and projects instead of sticking to his goals. And dream he does. The Pisces man is clever, creative, intuitive and imaginative, and he loves to fantasise. The problem is, he often lacks the realism to make his dreams come true. He is a truly inspired man but the duality of his nature is very apparent. He is the sign that can sink to the depths of despair (some Piscean men escape with alcohol and drugs to mask their pain), or at the other end of the spectrum their sensitivity helps them achieve amazing things (like Pisces Albert Einstein).

Now because he flaps around in so many stormy seas within himself, usually Mr Pisces adores being with his Taurean gal. She makes him feel safe and loved and less of a 'fish out of water'. She is the kind of earthy woman who makes a house feel like a 'home'. She adores taking care of her lover in all sorts of thoughtful ways. He's an incurable romantic and will sweep Ms Taurus off her feet with his special brand of romance and fantasy. He loves to be in love and his sensitivity, gentleness and charisma are next to none. Ms Taurus responds well to his romantic gifts (she loves to receive flowers, chocolates etc) and his sensual and romantic love-making style matches her own. Because he is like 'one-hundred-men-in-one' and highly unpredictable, she won't know whether to expect gentle, tender lovemaking or a raunchy, highly-passionate night of sex. And to be honest, Mr Pisces probably won't know either! His actions depend on his 'mood' and that can change by the minute. Yep, there's a strong sexual attraction between the Pisces man and the Taurean woman. Both are very sensual beings, and they are comfortable communicating their sexual desires to each other. The combination of her earthy passion and his otherworldly fantasy and imagination make them a powerful match.

The Pisces man is easily seduced and she can make the most of this by setting the scene for passionate nights. He adores her sexy (but subdued) dresses that show off her feminine curves and the way she prepares him a sensual bath complete with oils, incense and the sound of Tibetan chanting in the background. Water-ruled Pisces is one of the few men in the zodiac who adore hot baths (plus he loves anything exotic!) He also loves the fine foods, the best massages and the great music she plays to turn him on, and he often does the same for her.

But all is usually not totally free-flowing between them. Their verbal communication is often at odds. Pisces can't stand a direct question and unfortunately Ms Taurus is the Queen of Direct Questions! The uncomplicated Taurean gal likes to know where she stands and his vague answers will sometimes drive her insane. She demands honesty and dependability and his 'wishy washy' answers frustrate her. Though some Piscean men can be very two-faced — more typically he avoids a straight answer because he doesn't like to be pinned down. His feelings, thoughts and desires are constantly changing. If she loves him and wants to be with him, the Taurean gal needs to trust and allow him to be himself. It's the nature of the Fish to glide in and out and up and down in his elusive way. If she tries to box him in the Piscean man is likely to quietly disappear from her life.

Problems may occur in their relationship if he is the kind of Fish who gets swept downstream into a world of fantasy where he shirks responsibility for his own actions or gets involved with the wrong people. Pisceans are trusting souls who are easily influenced by other people and they need to be careful about the company they keep. Ms Taurus is a no-nonsense woman who is probably the best thing that ever happened to him (and his friends will tell him this too). He, too, brings wonderful things into her life. She learns that being impulsive once in a while is highly satisfying and with her Merman by her side she discovers that her carefully structured life leaves no room for change. She gets to peek through the door into the spiritual, dreamy and unseen world of his planet Neptune.

The fact is, although Ms Reality and Mr Fantasy are different in many ways, they are magnetically attracted to each other. Each has traits that the other would like to have and they are fascinated by each other. There are similarities, too. They're tolerant, romantic, humorous and the Bull and the Fish both seek peace and tranquility in their lives. The downside is that both Ms Taurus and Mr Pisces are prone to periods of gloominess and negativity. The best thing they can do is coordinate their 'blue days' so they aren't both brooding at the same time! His depressions tend to be deeper than hers, but she has a way of cheering him up with her warm laugh, silly jokes, cups of tea and affectionate hugs. And that's love.

Taurus man — Pisces woman

 The *'Was it the kiss we shared, or was there a real earthquake?'* relationship

Mr Taurus loves beauty and so he's likely to have met his match when a Pisces stargal floats into his life, wrapped up in a dream and carrying the keys to his heart close to her beautiful breasts. Ms Pisces is the magical Mermaid of the zodiac with soft and dreamy eyes that can hypnotise the object of her affections. Typically, the Pisces gal is soft-spoken, dainty, gentle and feminine, and she is often *quite* aware of her seductive powers (or at least she is clever enough to give off that impression). In fact, Ms Pisces can unabashedly wear low necklines, flutter her eyelashes and laugh prettily if she wants her suitor to fall under her ethereal powers of seduction. Her ruling planet is Neptune, the God who rules the unseen depths of the ocean and she is one of the dreamiest women in astrology. She adores romance and she even has the ability to 'create' romance where it doesn't exist. This often sees her making unwise choices when it comes to love, sex, marriage and romance. Romantic Pisces, Elizabeth Taylor, is a prime example of the Pisces woman who is addicted to love (and marriage).

Ms Pisces is receptive and emotional, and matters of the heart mean a lot to her. So what happens when earthy Mr Taurus crosses her line of seductive fire? The Taurean man (being a lover of feminine and natural women) tends to fall head over heels in lust and/or love when he comes up against her mysterious and feminine wiles.

Whereas the Taurean man is an open book (and she adores that he is so charmingly uncomplicated), the Piscean woman is a mystery that will never be solved. At times it bothers Mr Taurus that he will never 'possess' her mind, body and soul. But he can live with that. After all, her feminine charm, humour and mystery never fail to arouse him. Ms Pisces understands him and although the typical Taurean man is not a chatterbox, he is seeking a partner who will truly listen to him. She is like a butterfly who enters his world, bringing light touches of joy, love, fun, imagination and her own special brand of magic. She also teaches him to trust his own intuition and that the world is not simply everything that we can see, touch and smell. Ms Pisces often helps him to find his own spiritual path, while he teaches her to keep one foot (at least!) on the ground.

Their attitude to money is markedly different and can cause trouble in their relationship. Ms Pisces has a love/hate relationship with money. Cash is a four-letter word to non-materialistic Pisces woman. She worries about it if she doesn't have enough of it, yet when she has it she resents having to manage it. Money tends to slip through her fingers, especially if she is feeling down. She's a compulsive shopper when she is depressed and can also resort to other compulsive habits (such as drinking, eating, smoking etc) to mask her sadness or frustration. She prefers having fewer material possessions and more money for spontaneous things like travelling, buying clothes, scuba diving gear, or giving money away to charity. Mr Taurus has interesting 'feelings' about money. He looks after it very, very carefully, as financial security makes him feel safe.

Interestingly, feeling 'safe and secure' in all areas of his life is what Mr Taurus seeks (and Ms Pisces will tease him no end about his materialistic streak!) He will spend money on beautiful things and experiences (he adores good food and wine and beautiful things in his home), but he believes in the sensible 'everything in moderation' rule. He thinks carefully before making big purchases (a house, car, boat etc), and with his patience and persistence he tends to secure the best price available. So it's no wonder the Taurean guy thinks his Piscean gal is flaky when it comes to money. If they live together or marry, she'll be the first to admit that he should manage their finances. She resents the power that money has to dictate how she lives her life. Ms Pisces can be unrealistic when it comes to her earning, saving and spending habits and she normally doesn't mind at all when practical Mr Taurus takes over the reins. She trusts him completely and besides, it gives her more time to be creative and dream.

Whereas Ms Pisces loves to dream and create, her Taurean guy prefers more down-to-earth endeavours. The wonderful thing is, each balances out the other. Taurus teaches his Piscean gal to accept responsibility for her actions. He also offers her practical and sensible ideas to turn her dreams into reality. She is highly talented, intuitive and creative, and her potential to reach the stars is enormous (just look at successful Piscean career women Cindy Crawford, Sharon Stone and Ivana Trump). However, many Piscean women lack the motivation and staying power for successfully maximising their talents and creative ideas. She can become resigned and scattered and give up too easily. When things get too difficult she also has a tendency to focus on other people (helping others makes her feel fulfilled), rather than concentrate on her own problems. Her Taurus guy is wonderful at encouraging her to be patient and 'hang in there' (he is the zodiac's King of Persistence). His rock-solid influence in her life is very often just what she needs to carry her over the stormy waters that often disrupt her delicate emotional and highly vulnerable life.

Even though the Pisces woman can be scattered and melancholy at times, it doesn't mean that she can't take care of herself. He can be blind at times to her sensitive feelings and act in a domineering way. But look out Mr Taurus. Though she may appear to be a timid, fragile girl waiting to cry on the shoulder of a big, strong man, she can — thank you very much — take good care of herself. In fact, Ms Pisces is quick and bright and she's more capable than people give her credit. If her Taurean guy tries to boss her around with the obstinacy of his astrological ruler, the Bull, she is likely to perform a disappearing act more quickly then he can say abracadabra! As in all relationships, give and take is the key for lasting love for Mr Taurus and Ms Pisces. When they learn to compromise the Bull and the Fish can live happily ever after.

gemini gemini gemini gemini gemini
gemini gemini gemini gemini gemini
gemini gemini gemini gemini gemini gemini
gemini gemini gemini gemini gemini
gemini gemini gemini gemini gemini
gemini gemini gemini gemini gemini gemini
gemini gemini gemini gemini gemini
gemini gemini gemini gemini gemini
gemini gemini gemini gemini gemini gemini

gemini gemini gemini gemini gemini
gemini gemini gemini gemini gemini
gemini gemini gemini gemini gemini gemini
gemini gemini gemini gemini gemini
gemini gemini gemini gemini gemini
gemini gemini gemini gemini gemini gemini
gemini gemini gemini gemini gemini
gemini gemini gemini gemini gemini
gemini gemini gemini gemini gemini gemini

GEMINI

[22 may – 21 june]

romantic pursuit: erratic and changeable

romantic vibration: easily bored

secret love desire: to find a lover who wants

to experiment sexually

element: air

planetary ruler: mercury

symbol: the twins

quality: mutable (= flexibility)

colours: yellow, blue

gem: agate, aquamarine

best companions: libra and aquarius

strongest virtues: creativity, curiosity, sharing

your dreams or visions with others

traits to improve: self-doubts,

fear of the future, mood inconsistencies

deepest desire: to be understood

for who you are

Gemini celebrities

Alanis Morissette, Angelina Jolie, Anna Kournikova, Anne Heche, Annette Bening, Bjorn Borg, Bob Dylan, Boy George, Brooke Shields, Clint Eastwood, Courtney Cox Arquette, Drew Carey, Elizabeth Hurley, Gary Sweet, Germaine Greer, Helen Hunt, Isabella Rossellini, Jason Donovan, Jewel, Joan Collins, Jo-Beth Taylor, John F. Kennedy, Johnny Depp, Joseph Fiennes, Juliette Lewis, Karl Urban, Kasey Chambers, Kathleen Turner, Kylie Minogue, Lauryn Hill, Lenny Kravitz, Liam Neeson, Lindsay Davenport, Marilyn Monroe, Mark Wahlberg, Michael J Fox, Mike Myers, Morgan Freeman, Naomi Campbell, Natalie Portman, Nicole Kidman, Noah Wyle, Pat Cash, Paul McCartney, Pia Miranda, Prince, Prince Philip, Prince Rainier of Monaco, Prince William, Priscilla Presley, Richard Wilkins, Salman Rushdie, Sarah O'Hare, Steffi Graf, Stevie Nicks, Tim Allen, Tom Jones, Venus Williams, Wynonna Judd

GEMINI—GEMINI relationship

The *'Just the two of us'* relationship

STAR GEMINI–GEMINI COUPLE
Kylie Minogue and Jason Donovan

Get ready for some crazy times, fun, games and other mental and emotional hijinks when these two same-sign people match up together. When I think of two Geminis dating, mating and building (or attempting to build) a loving relationship, I always recollect a statement made by psychologist Karl Jung, 'The meeting of two individuals is like the merging of two chemical substances. If there is any reaction, both are transformed.' I believe this statement offers great insight into the Gemini–Gemini romantic mix. When two Geminis get together, they operate on a high vibrational level and the zodiac chemistry is sizzling. If the romantic chemistry between them is strong enough, both their lives will be transformed. That doesn't mean, however, that if you're a Gemini mating up with another Gemini, you are destined to live happily ever after. Like all relationships you'll have your fair share of good and bad times — times four! That's because there are four of you to deal with: both of your twin selves plus each of you. The Gemini–Gemini union has plenty of angles, shapes and feelings all mirrored back to each other through their partner's eyes to make it a most entertaining exchange.

If you are one half of a Gemini–Gemini union, you're probably reading this in the hope that I will deliver to you easy answers to your puzzling Twin love match, and can immediately reveal how it's going to 'go'. Uh-oh, sorry! I don't know the answers to how you should handle or prepare for the many relationship highs and lows that await you. The truth is Gemini, if you're in love with another Gemini, in a cosmic sense, you're in for a rocky ride but a most enlightening one. In many ways you've made your bed and now have to sleep in it; and I hope it's king size, because remember there are two sets of Twins here. Whatever happens though, you've found someone who, in their deepest most intimate self, is so alike you that it's possibly scary. Expect equal measures of excitement, confusion, adventure, brilliance, frustration and elation. What you'll definitely *not* experience is boredom — but burnout, that's possibly on your relationship agenda.

Gemini woman—Gemini man

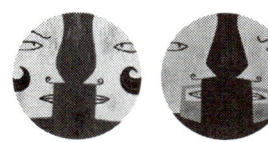

 The *'I'm looking at you in the mirror of love'* relationship

When a Gemini man and a Gemini woman meet and fall in love there is a very strong, all round cosmic connection. As you are both so attuned to each other, even your first meeting was probably a memorable occasion. It may have turned into a major 'gabfest' if the strong connection between you opened up the cosmic airwaves. Or perhaps the opposite applied 'cos feelings between you were *sooo* strong; you both were struck dumb and couldn't utter a word. However, usually you two tend to chat up a storm. In most Gemini–Gemini matches it seems that on meeting up you find each other most interesting: while one spoke, the other nodded and *didn't* look perplexed when his or her new Gemini pal jumped deftly from one topic to another, slipped in a double entendre or performed other verbal back flips. The fact that their communication wires are so well connected turned their conversation into a verbal party. And on all kinds of levels, being able to hit it off so well and without any real effort, was a big adventure. As one Gemini who had teamed up with another shared with me: 'When I met my Gemini true love — Hallelujah! It felt like coming home.'

That's why in many cases Geminis who are attracted to each other sense a soul mate, or a spiritual companion, or a wonderful connection flowing between them; it feels like heaven has finally delivered someone who'll love *and* understand them. Twin lovers provide a mirror image to each other, even if they physically *don't* look alike. The way they view the world, or their recognition has more to do with the quickness in their stride, the twinkle in their eye, and the flurry of hand movements when they speak.

But some Gemini couples *are* physically alike, and dangerously so. A Gemini friend told me her ex-Twin man looked *so* much like her that she felt as though she were making love to her brother (a side effect of the relationship she actually found rather kinky but also very scintillating!) She said they could be very close to each other and intimate but then they would go through periods when there were no passionate trysts in the bedroom. Instead, they curled up under the doona eating popcorn and watching movies, laughing and chatting away, more like friends or siblings than lovers. That's not to say that all Twin sexual liaisons will be a flop if they look similar to each other, although sometimes the friendship feelings overshadow the love and passion areas! Most Geminis are imaginative, sexy and understand that curiosity is the mother of sexual invention, so Geminis usually come up with something to keep the bedroom antics interesting. However, there's likely to be many times when they both decide to watch videos or read books and forget about lust and passion for a while.

Ruled by the communication and mind planet Mercury, speaking, writing and listening (though they're least adept at the latter!) are as essential to Geminis as the air they breathe. They can exhaust themselves with their banter; and if this Twin-match makes it into long-term territory they will need to find time to 'ground themselves'. As they spend abundant time exercising their mental muscles Gemini couples need to shut down the 'Monkey Mind' and learn to relax. Yoga, meditation or martial arts will work wonders and help them release the mental clutter that spells double trouble when they're together. On the positive side, their mental agility and imagination can create fabulous joint projects, especially if they ever decide to write a book or television series together!

The biggest challenge in this relationship is that Gemini negative tendencies are, naturally, twinned! Multiply two times confusion, superficiality, lack of focus, restlessness and irresponsibility, and it's easy to see that CHAOS reigns. Two Geminis together can tempt the other to scatter their energies to the four winds and neither one will provide the stability the other needs. If the Gemini love match is going to last, one Twin may need to play the role of stern parent and set ground rules, otherwise they're unlikely to get their relationship (or dreams) off the ground.

Always thinking that the grass is greener on the other side, Geminis are prone to infidelities. These two can't afford to get too casual and take each other for granted. The typical Twin is not a soppy romantic and never will be, but care should be taken that this union doesn't get too 'Buddy-Buddy'. Surprising each other with gifts (erotic poetry books, sexy weekends away), will work wonders in keeping their desire running high.

Travel will be a common theme for the Twins and their curiosity will take them to many far-flung corners of the globe. At least one Twin in the Gemini duo is likely to be studying at any given time. There's plenty of intellectual stimulation at home and their children will be bright, extroverted and well-travelled. If Geminis do set up house together, they are wise to hire an accountant or financial planner to handle their joint finances. Otherwise, bills won't be paid (they'll simply forget), and their earnings will be scattered, instead of being saved.

One cosmic plus in this Mercury-influenced partnership, is the innate understanding of the other's need for freedom, self-expression and light-heartedness. If Gemini guy and Gemini gal find a harmonious frequency together on the same love channel, they'll move heaven and earth in this cosmic love match to live happily ever after.

GEMINI — CANCER relationship

The *'Tell me your secrets, and I'll tell you mine'* relationship

STAR GEMINI–CANCER COUPLE
Nicole Kidman and Tom Cruise

It's a wonderful, head-spinning, romantic world that opens up to the love-struck Gemini and Cancer. Though their joint vision of their future together isn't likely to be part of a real world, it's likely to be more a fantasy than a reality and maintaining it could be tough over the long term. However, if love is truly the connection between these two star signs, expect this to be a thrill-a-minute or a crazy type of relationship. There won't be much practical energy surrounding them either. They may elope, run off with each other to Timbuktu or do something quite outrageous because of their desire to explore each other more completely. These two signs are both a little highly strung some of the time, and when fate propels them together in a love match, you get double highly strung results, which often leads to creating some equally strange behaviour from both of them.

On the downside, their zodiac combination also doubles the chances of them being jealous, possessive or upset with each other. However, the fact that they can be prone to over-reacting doesn't mean that this relationship can't be a terrific one. Mutual sexual attraction, abundant admiration and sometimes fascination are united when Geminis and Cancers collide in the love realms. Being next-door-neighbour zodiac signs, they often have enough crossover planetary influences to make the romantic match work like a dream (or become a living nightmare). Typically head-ruled Geminis and sensitive, easily hurt Cancers come from different zodiac galaxies — the *only* sure thing in this love match is a myriad of changing conditions, feelings and desires. Nowhere in the other zodiac couplings will you see so many and varied mood swings as you will here with this duo.

Gemini woman—Cancer man

 The *'Can't live with you, can't live without you'* relationship

Think of Nicole Kidman (Gemini) and Tom Cruise (Cancer) as your Gemini gal–Cancer guy relationship example. They seemed to have it all, and more, when it came to having a successful relationship — and they probably did have it all. But something went wrong, and when it did, it sunk their love boat in a matter of what seemed moments. That's often the story of the Gemini woman–Cancer man relationship: it all goes along hunky dory for a good time, and then suddenly, 'Hello, nobody's home; everybody's gone to live at the Heart Break Hotel'; or they've run off with someone else and gone missing!

But this relationship certainly has romantic wheels and seems to take both partners along for a hectic ride in one way or another. It often starts off with a speedy launch, a very impressive beginning. As it whirls along, Ms Gemini can usually learn a lot from her Cancer lover, as he can from her. She can learn a great deal about the romantic games and dating. Hailing from the zippy planet Mercury, independent Ms Gemini is not opposed to asking a guy out on a first date or paying for dinner. She's quite happy making the first moves or being the go-getter when it comes to go-getting someone's heart.

Where her Cancer suitor is concerned, however, she should step back and savour each moment of his sensual seduction techniques. After all, romance is his speciality and he's an expert when it comes to winning the heart of his chosen maid. Like a knight in shining armour, he'll sweep his Gemini gal off her feet with his chivalry. Ruled by the mystic Moon, he's intuitive, imaginative and attentive. He'll discover that sunflowers are her favourites, and then surprise her the next time they meet with an enormous bouquet. He's a man in touch with his feminine side, and in some cases even *more* attuned to the Venus love energy than Ms Gemini (who is often considered the tomboy of the zodiac).

There are, however, challenges for this cosmic couple and a prime example is how the fairy story of Gemini, Nicole Kidman, came to a crashing end with Cancer, Tom Cruise. When this couple falls apart, it falls apart big time. The Cancer man is one of the most possessive signs in the zodiac neighbourhood — a trait that is likely to clash with his freedom-loving Twin lover. They operate under very different romantic ideals, expectations and agendas. Ms Gemini is particularly two-sided when it comes to her feelings. 'I love him, I love him not' swings easily and frequently into her overactive, 'grass-may-be-greener-elsewhere' consciousness. She may not even know it, but there's a side to her romantic personality that is hard to please, especially over the longer term. Initially, the *idea* of her chivalrous Cancer knight is exciting and new for the Gemini gal. His romantic courting methods seem quaint. She thinks his deep attachment to his mother is cute. She adores the daily phone calls professing undying love and devotion. But she'll start to get that niggling feeling that there's something not quite right. All of a sudden, his quaint courting methods are suffocating; he's too much of a mummy's boy and the daily phone calls are, well — *intrusive*. You see, she's a busy girl with an agenda to match. Drinks with the girls on Friday night; Saturday morning yoga class, followed by lunch with old school friends; a movie with her brother later that night, and a writing workshop all day Sunday. The Gemini gal doesn't *need* a man in her life with which she has to share every single moment.

Her easy laugh, vivid imagination and whimsical 'I-can-do-anything' attitude are initially what wins him over. But when the Cancer guy discovers Ms Gemini's dual nature — she can 'be with him' or 'not be with him' — it can make him very hurt. He retreats, wounded, to the security of his Crab shell where he can remain silently sulking for days on end. And here's where the hilarity really begins. She'll coax him out of his shell with her love and light touch. Then, just when he's ready to join the party, her Mercury-ruled mood switches from sweet to sarcastic and she's making cutting comments about his family. She knows exactly where to push his buttons, because criticising a Cancer's family is a major no-no! Wounded, he retreats to his shell again and the pattern continues.

The Cancer guy–Gemini gal match has so many astro-challenges up against them that it's confusing. They need patience (from her) and adaptability (from him) and practice in getting their moods to match. But he's a tender, gentle guy, and when his Gemini gal has exhausted herself out in the big wide world and returns, tired and confused, he's there to comfort and love her again.

There is plenty of sexual chemistry between Crab–Twin lovers as they both live in the world of fantasy and imagination. She brings variety and invention into the bedroom, while he offers abundant affection and intuitive sensuality. One thing's for sure, their sex life will never be boring!

In home and money matters, this love match approach things very differently. She adores eating out, while he likes the cosiness of a home-cooked meal. He's cautious with cash, while she believes in living (and spending!) for the moment. They are best together when they realise what the other needs *and* gives it to them. When the Cancer man recognises her need for emotional freedom and she learns the gift of patience, there's no stopping their cosmic ride (albeit with detours) to Paradise Found.

Gemini man—Cancer woman

 The *'Hold on tight . . . we're heading for a bumpy ride'* relationship

If you are one half of a Mr Gemini–Ms Cancer love match get ready for an emotional roller coaster ride. He's a masculine air sign from Mercury, the planet of the mind. She's a feminine water sign who hails from the Moon, where emotions rule the day. In this love match, there's no easy guidebook, no road maps, no plan of easy action for visiting each other's territory. You just have to be prepared to go with the general flow of whatever is happening. Nevertheless, whether or not the visit into each other's hearts and hopes for love eternal is transient or permanent, there *are* ways to make the stay more pleasant and less stressful. The answer: be prepared to give and take, and be extremely easy-going and non-judgmental with each other. Huh! Guess it will be hard work at times as well.

Now Ms Cancer is no easy gal to settle into a long-term relationship with if you aren't prepared to go through some rocky, unsteady times. The changeable Moon governs Ms Cancer's moods, and like her cosmic ruler, her emotions are in constant ebb and flow. Even though most Cancer gals keep their feelings well hidden under a cool, calm and collected façade, she's a delicate flower when it comes to her feelings and emotions. Once bruised, she seldom forgets. A broken heart takes much longer to heal for her than for most zodiac stargals (apart from maybe her water-sign sister, Pisces). Humiliation and rejection are more than she can bear and her Gemini mate needs to learn to treat her with kid gloves. Although he might worship the ground she walks on, his astrological make-up doesn't know how to deal with her extremely sensitive heart.

Mr Gemini does his best and tries to be his most romantic when he's around her, but she isn't an easy gal to please, and she sometimes sets him romantic or emotional tests to see if he can pass them. He so badly wants to understand what it is that makes her tick. *'Why can't she just come out and say what she wants? How am I expected to read her mind!'* says a frustrated Twin male to his friends (or anyone else who will listen). It's simple: he needs to treat her like she's the *only* woman in the world. This is tough for Mr Gemini. A romantic candlelit dinner spent gazing into his lover's eyes is not really his style. It's not that he isn't crazy about her, it's just that there are *lots* of interesting people and things happening in the restaurant that cause his eyes to roam once in a while.

If the Cancer gal can't understand and accept his distractions, lack of focus and need for freedom, this relationship will spiral downward, and fast. Patience, affection and an abundance of love will help him enter (and stay in) the Moon maiden's heart. This dreamy and emotional water sign needs to hear, constantly, how much she's loved, cherished and adored. Giving his sweetie gifts of flowers, chocolates or jewellery (try moonstone) will win her over.

Ms Cancer though is also extremely clever and knows how to 'play the victim' at the flick of an emotional switch, a manipulative game that will have the Gemini's eyes rolling back into his head. He just doesn't buy it. Deep down she knows it, though it won't stop her from trying! He's a straight-talking kind of guy and game playing is not his style, but he is changeable. One day he's playful, extroverted and charming, and the next he's distant, restless and unavailable. These two will be kept on their toes trying to second-guess the other.

So what, you might ask, can Air boy and Water girl offer each other? Well, the truth is, not many of these love matches make it to the altar, but if they *do* weather the bumpy storm — and it might always be one of those 'on-again-off-again' relationships — they'll be companions for life. They appreciate each other's vivid imagination. They're good talkers and at their famed dinner parties expect interesting company, exciting repartee, creative table settings and divine food (prepared by her). The Moon maiden loves to tell a story: she has people hanging on her every word with her dreamy way of describing in detail even the most mundane of events. Meanwhile her Twin mate will be juggling plates, playing magic tricks and telling the wittiest jokes at the table. Her wacky, lunar sense of humour holds him spellbound, while she adores his wit and charm.

If they do marry and have children, she'll be a wonderful nurturing mother and her Gemini man, always a kid at heart, will adore teaching them to surf or learn alongside them the latest computer games. In her moments of insecurity, he'll be able to sweet-talk her out of her protective Crab's shell and she'll offer her Little Boy Lost a warm and tender home.

GEMINI — LEO relationship

The *'You spin my heart all over the place'* relationship

STAR GEMINI–LEO COUPLE
John F. Kennedy and Jacqueline Bouvier Kennedy

When Leo and Gemini fall in love and start to gaze at each other with loving eyes, it's fair to say that the Gods must be crazy. There's definitely a dash of love madness as well as love magic being unleashed. How does 'in-your-face' Leo cope with 'all-over-the-place' Gemini? And vice versa? Well, truth be known, there's often a very strong (almost magical) chemistry between the sons and daughters of Mercury and the Sun. Like Merlin, Gemini and Leo are both masters of magic. If they *believe* enough, then *anything* is possible. With a little give and take (and strong enough belief!) they can conjure up a magic romantic spell to last a lifetime. But it's going to take the combined and continuous power of both of them to keep the magic flowing.

Gemini woman—Leo man

 The *'You're a hard person to catch up with'* relationship

He probably spotted Ms Gemini in a bar or café, newspaper spread before her, playing at her breakfast as she chatted airily on her mobile phone. As she spoke — eyes flashing flirtatiously in his direction — the Lion King made his predatory plan of attack. Glancing at himself in the mirror, he strutted to her table, told her that using a mobile phone has been linked to brain damage, and said she'd be better off talking to *him* than taking such a careless health risk. The Gemini gal might have thought that his ego was *bigger* than her phone bill. After all, she's the Gossip Queen of the zodiac, but there was something about his powerful masculinity that made her heart pump faster and faster, and she was smitten by his confidence (she loves confidence in her man, and he has oodles of it; or at least he had oodles of it until she's through with him).

The Leo lover is loyal, generous and very affectionate. He spoils his Gemini lady with his time and money, and sweeps her off her feet. They have plenty in common; especially a love for socialising, dining out, travelling and playing and watching sport together. Their sex life is exciting and adventurous, and while she turns him on with her cleverness and Little Girl Lost charm, he's a warm-hearted, hot-blooded hero who'll change her outlook on sex forever. It won't take long before their cosmic union develops into a mutual admiration society both *in* and *out* of the bedroom.

Ms Gemini soon discovers that her Sun-ruled Leo guy needs to be the 'Star' in their love production. That's fine by her. Changeable Gemini likes to try out different roles, and she'll frequently run back stage to shimmy into yet *another* costume. The Gemini gal is an air sign who'll go wherever the wind may blow. Like a magician, she has the ability to be in two places at once in her very own 'now-you-see-me, now-you-don't' style. Being under the spotlight on centre stage is just not her *thang*.

Though Ms Gemini allows her lover to *be* the Star she won't necessarily *treat* him like one. If Mr Leo's career or social life gives him an outlet for directing and dominating (and quite often they do) she can consider herself very lucky. However, if he's an unfulfilled or frustrated 'leader of the pack' he'll simply turn to his partner to pamper his pride. This could spell trouble, as the Gemini gal is not the most patient of zodiac girls. If His Majesty threatens her personal freedom she'll simply wave him goodbye as she flies out the window upon Mercury's wings.

Typically though, a clever Mercury girl is wise enough to turn the other cheek. She's forgiving and understands that her King of the Jungle is merely a big cat who'll purr and roll over when she gives him her love and affection. He might have an exaggerated need for respect, but hey, this guy really *does* adore her. Even when he appears arrogant (advising her on her choice of clothes, car or career), he truly only wants to guide and help his Gemini love. If this relationship is going to last the distance, the Leo man must understand that his beloved knows how to stand on her own two feet. In fact, many Twin girls juggle jobs while still at school and are the first of the zodiac sisters to fly out of the family coop.

In the Leo man–Gemini woman household, expect abundant love, laughter and excitement. Flighty Gemini begins to enjoy the stability of living with a man who treats her like a queen, while he learns to give her the independence she needs. Having children will bring them great pleasure and both will be doting parents. One thing they will definitely need to do is hire a cleaner, as neither Ms Gemini nor Mr Leo are fond of housework! There should never be a dull moment and if there is, well, you can count on the Leo man to create a drama to fill any boring relationship void! Even if he does start a fire in his dramatic Leonine way, his Gemini partner will simply blow out the flames with her light and airy feminine touch.

Gemini man — Leo woman

 The *'I don't know whether to kiss you or hit you!'* relationship

Okay, let's get one thing *really* clear here. The Leo woman doesn't like to be ignored, taken for granted *or worse* — taken for a romantic fool. She has a ferocious pride and a big ego, and she's willing to travel any distance, pay any price, or go through hell and back to tame her man to make him hers. If she's gone through all that and she's got him, Ms Leo needs to have absolute faith in her guy forever after, 'cos she's earned it. And may God protect any man, Gemini or otherwise, who finds himself on the receiving end of Ms Leo's Leonine wrath, as he'll truly discover the meaning of *hell hath no fury like a woman scorned.*

So, is the Gemini man up to playing the Game of Love with the feisty Lioness Man Tamer, who knows exactly how to crack the relationship whip to keep him in his correct place in respect to her? Or, can the elusive slip-through-your-fingers Mr Gemini be tamed? As we *are* talking about the Twin here, the answer is yes *and* no. Sometimes, one Twin part of himself can be tamed, while other times, the other Twin part just disappears from his personality and what's left in its place suddenly refuses to be organised, controlled, fussed over or fenced in. Just think of the famous Gemini–Leo couple Jack Kennedy and Jacqueline Bouvier (eek!) There could be trouble brewing, especially if the Leo gal has a jealous streak and Mr Gemini has wandering tendencies.

Mr Gemini is an air sign and he's constantly on the move seeking change and variety. He likes quick bets and short investments. Consider how making long-term investments (whether it be a relationship, buying a house, studying for a degree etc) has him squirming, making a face and saying, *'I'm just not sure if I'm ready to commit to that'.* You see, what a Gemini man fears more than anything, especially in his love relationship, is boredom. Luckily, there's no chance of boredom with his Leo love. He's spellbound with her regal aura and amazed at how she always looks beautiful. No matter if she's pulling out weeds, attending a black-tie event or shopping at the local supermarket, the Leo woman is classy and poised.

Funnily enough, there are times when her Twin feels as though he's in over his head (or not in control at all) in this relationship. She may be a bit too much for him to comfortably handle. She's strong, and he knows it. This can intimidate him, and make him seek reassurance that he's a 'real man' from other gals outside of his relationship. Why does he need reassurance that he's a real man? It's simply that most Gemini men *act* and *feel* like little boys, even those who reside in retirement villages! His Leo woman ain't no 'girl' — she's a Lady! But what really wins him over is her heart of gold, generosity and warmth. The Leo woman is at her best when in love; just watch her transform magically from scowling lioness into purring pussycat.

He also loves the fact that she's constantly surprising him. It excites him to suddenly discover that she's a brilliant skier, talented painter or that she spent a year living in Madagascar. Wherever they go she turns heads. There's something about her that suggests she has royal, blue-blood running through her veins. Even if she doesn't encourage it, she'll always get the attention.

gemini

Fortunately, Mr Gemini is not the jealous type and her popularity doesn't usually faze him. He's usually busy coming up with some scheme, dream or project that stops him thinking about what she's up to all the time anyway. His ability to be caught up in a world that doesn't include her (and in which he sometimes manages so cleverly to hide or keep from her), can quite fascinate Ms Leo. What also attracts Ms Leo to her Twin lover is his clever mind, charm and wit. He's a great companion who won't be fazed when accompanying her to a formal family event; followed by dancing all night long (one of her favourite pastimes) at the hip club of the moment. He'll even visit her old school chums, her old maiden aunt, and the old boyfriend, who suddenly turns up from out of town and, seems to enjoy himself being there. She likes his easy-going social energy and the fact that he doesn't mind her taking centre stage.

Of course there's more than all that. When this astro-couple have a true cosmic connection, the sex is awesome. She likes a man to have finesse in bed and thankfully, Mr Gemini is a smooth lover who can read her mind, treating her to slow and sensual play one day and wild and passionate sex the next. Though sometimes she'll get the feeling that his body is present but his mind elsewhere, and she's probably right! Occasionally there's one Twin in the heart of the action, while the other looks on, sipping a cup of coffee. That's what you get with 'two-places-at-once' Mr Gemini. However, when he's focused and really 'with her' he can be a steamy bed partner and her combination of fiery passion and loving warmth will envelop his senses.

Many Gemini men–Leo women combinations end in happy marriages. They might live extravagantly but with a mutual love of travel, the arts and literature and healthy doses of love and excitement, it can hardly get much better than this!

GEMINI—VIRGO relationship

The *'Are we fooling each other, or is this a true love experience?'* relationship

STAR GEMINI–VIRGO COUPLE
Sarah O'Hare and Lachlan Murdoch

As Mercury, the zippy planet of communication and the mind, rule both of these star signs, Virgo and Gemini start off their relationship one step ahead of the rest of the zodiac romantic pack. Cerebral and curious, they are on the same mental 'tuned-in' wavelength and they communicate well. They have heaps in common and plenty of mutual agendas to share. Travel, activity and the pursuit of knowledge mark this relationship. But where Gemini likes to juggle new ideas and concepts, Virgo prefers pure, unadulterated fact. In this love match, steady Virgo helps ground scattered Gemini, while the Twin leads Virgo on an adventure of a lifetime. Whichever way they work out of the sum of their relationship it usually ends up on the plus side. They can offer each other something that no other signs of the zodiac can offer them — a kindred spirit to share time and space with. What's more, they aren't likely to be bored for a second. In fact they would be wise to hold on to their hearts and get ready for take off to a world of romantic adventure and experience that is sometimes quite extraordinary!

Gemini woman — Virgo man

 The *'I can't believe you are to me'* relationship

'Can't live with them, can't live without them' is what's often described by each partner (sooner or later down the relationship path), when the Gemini gal and the Virgo guy meet each other, fall in love, or have an affair. In fact, this couple often seem to be magnetically connected, even if they don't make it onto the full-time marriage circuit, or go beyond a first date. There's something special between them. Probably the best way to sum up the connection between the Gemini woman and Virgo man is the on-again-off-again relationship between British actors Liz Hurley (Gemini) and Hugh Grant (Virgo). Even when separated, these two remained good friends; and sometimes being 'the best of friends' is where the Gemini gal and the Virgo guy find themselves best suited of all.

Although there may be an occasional drama in this love match, the Gemini gal and Virgo guy usually get along well and seem to happily resonate on the same level. Thanks to their planetary ruler, cerebral Mercury, Ms Gemini and Mr Virgo enjoy each other's clever mind, fast wit and sense of humour. There is a sense of ease in their relationship and you can honestly say that they enjoy each other's company. They often also give each other a sense of 'here-is-where-I-belong' relationship security, which can be a rare thing to have in a relationship.

Though like any relationship, there are differences between them that present challenges to their love match, and this cosmic duo often have trouble understanding the world in which the other lives. She's outgoing and sociable; he's often reclusive and if he's a typical Virgo, he prefers to live alone. When she meets him, Ms Gemini is attracted to his sweet, unassuming and easy-going nature. He's often very attractive, in a laid-back understated way. But she soon realises that her earthy Virgo guy is more sensitive than meets the eye.

When the Twin girl and her Virgo lover argue she considers it a mere 'difference of opinion', while his hurt can run very deep. He's a believer in love, fairness and good old-fashioned truth, and if his Gemini maid wins the argument by cleverly twisting the truth (something she's very good at), he won't forgive and forget quickly. In less than an hour, she's ready to go out to dinner hand in hand. Not so for her Virgo lover. He'll spend the evening (if not the weekend) punishing his Twin for her offence by silently sulking.

Neither Gemini nor Virgo are normally the most highly-sexed signs of the zodiac (especially after that intensely passionate first sexual adrenaline rush has run its course), and their love making will be light and ethereal. They turn each other on with their sexy banter and they feel emotionally secure enough with the other to follow through in the bedroom. Self-controlled Mr Virgo is even likely to loosen up with his impulsive Gemini woman and start showing some affection and passion in public places, something he usually avoids.

There are many wonderful, practical things that Mr Virgo will offer Ms Gemini. Her relationship to money is haphazard to say the least. The typical Gemini woman has no 'formal' money management plan, and merely seems to materialise cash when she needs it: she plucks it out of thin air. Her Virgo guy will set her a budget, invest her money and may even manage it himself. She's likely to see her bank balance double through his efforts! In more mundane matters, her lack of punctuality will drive him to despair, while his insistence on neatness will be ever so 'boring' to laid-back Gemini.

Thankfully, a few harmless domestic irritations will do little to dampen their love. In fact, the Gemini gal is one of the better candidates for pulling Mr Virgo out of near-certain bachelorhood! Sensible and cautious Virgo is fond of making lists. Life's duties can weigh him down, and if he feels guilty about not fulfilling his obligations — and they're almost always self-enforced — he's likely to get sick. In fact, the Virgo man is the number one hypochondriac of the zodiac. Luckily, the Gemini gal adds lightness to his existence, and most likely adds years to his life! She'll poke faces at his duties, and take him to the fairground for the day. And he'll love it!

Gemini man — Virgo woman

The *'I love you just the way you are'* relationship

When Ms Virgo and Mr Gemini fall in love, they recognise a kindred spirit in each other's bright eyes. And it's no wonder, both are children of Mercury, the fast-moving planet of the mind, communication and travel. Good communication is what makes this love match work. Their minds are quick and so is the way they speak. The Gemini man and Virgo woman are the couple you see out at a restaurant chatting and laughing animatedly. No matter if they've been dating, for three months, or married for thirty years, they *always* have plenty of interesting things to talk about. There's loads of love, laughter and respect, and that's what makes the Virgo gal and Gemini guy click.

The Gemini man loves her quick mind, cheerful nature and femininity. He falls in love with her selflessness and her innate need to serve. She's the kind of girl who'll help out at Meals-On-Wheels or down at the local animal shelter. In fact, many Virgo girls spend their early years being caretakers of some kind (often looking after a parent, sibling or partner), and their need to be of 'use' is extremely high.

Ms Virgo is attracted to her Gemini guy's carefree, 'live-for-the moment' lifestyle and the way he can talk himself *into* or *out of* just about anything! Acquiring knowledge is important to them both. But while Mr Gemini gathers bits and pieces of knowledge for his own sake (this man *always* wins at Trivial Pursuit), Ms Virgo tends to collect and classify knowledge that's useful — she neatly files the instruction manuals to all her home's appliances!

The Virgo woman is very often beautiful and talented, but don't think that's enough to keep her happy. You see, Ms Virgo is a perfectionist with an innate need to excel. They are always trying to prove something, mainly to themselves! Worrying is her number one hobby and luckily her Gemini guy will tell her *'Hey, don't worry, everything will work out fine'*. Many marriage matches between Virgo women–Gemini men start businesses together and, more often than not, they are very successful. In fact, it's higy probable this love match will move together to another city, interstate or even overseas because of career or business commitments of one or both of them.

Though while it might be fascination that initially brings Ms Virgo and Mr Gemini together, it's very often frustration that causes them to part. Despite her razor-sharp mind, Ms Virgo is a gal who needs lots of love and appreciation. She might find her Gemini guy lacks the romantic gestures that make her feel womanly, cherished and adored. It's not that he doesn't respect her. The typical Gemini guy is simply not the kind to remember birthdays or anniversaries; yet celebrating important milestones is, *to her,* a big deal. His charm might blind her for a while, but serious Ms Virgo may start filing away errors and flaws in her Twin mate's personality. You see, she's a practical earth gal who lives in reality, while her

Gemini guy's airy outlook on life is steeped in fantasy. Similarly, once the honeymoon period for Mr Gemini starts to wane, he's probably going to have second thoughts too. All of a sudden, he'll complain that she worries too much; she's too neat, or too rigid in her thinking.

For this cosmic match to reach it's astro-potential, both Ms Virgo and Mr Gemini need patience and be willing to compromise. There are many Virgo man–Gemini woman couples who merely crash and burn through intolerance of each other. But there are others who, despite their differences, create fairy tale romances that last forever. His quirky habits, quiet charm, sense of humour, and love of animals and young children make her smile. The typical Virgo woman is reliable and caring. He's had his heart stomped on before (*and* done his fair share of heartbreaking), so her dependability shines like a beacon of light for his travel-weary soul.

GEMINI—LIBRA relationship

The *'It's all so perfect . . . at least it is for now'* relationship

STAR GEMINI–LIBRA COUPLE
Paul McCartney and Linda McCartney

Ruled by the element air, Gemini and Libra have plenty in shared interests, attitudes and desires in common. Airy, light and changeable, they are versatile, sociable and flexible, with a rare ability to be all things to all people. There's definitely a major chemical sexy vibe and other forms of mutual attraction when they find themselves in each other's arms. The downside is that their negative tendencies are glaringly highlighted when they're together, sometimes they just can't get their romantic acts together. After all, Librans have trouble *making up* their minds, while Geminis just keep *changing* their minds. If it doesn't work out, both Gemini and Libra will shrug their shoulders philosophically and move on. If destiny serves them the 'real thing', then their true love will jump obstacles and find a way. However, over the long term if both partners aren't careful, occasionally their true love might get lost on the pathway of everyday co-existence.

Gemini woman — Libra man

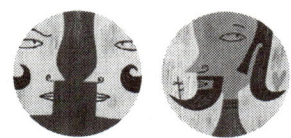

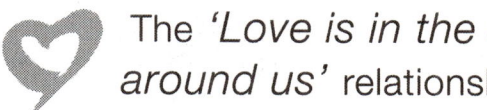

The *'Love is in the air around us'* relationship

Ms Gemini and Mr Libra are so alike. If the stars are right for them at their moment of meeting, there's no wonder they feel an instant karmic connection, and feel lust or love struck immediately. If Cupid has fired his arrows in their direction — even if they are with other partners at this time — love (or at the very least 'let's-go-immediately-to-bed' type electricity) is in the air. In fact, a Gemini girlfriend once told me she physically felt a scary buzz of electricity run through her veins like fire the first time she kissed her Libran husband. She was erotically energy-zapped by his lips! Maybe it's because air-ruled Gemini and Libra are operating on the same emotional, mental and psychic wavelengths. But there is an immediate sense of familiarity when Ms Gemini and Mr Libra meet each other. Both are changeable, colourful chameleons, and the knowledge that they've found a cosmic playmate willing to share life's roller coaster ride give them a powerful, ongoing, romantic aphrodisiac.

Ms Gemini feels safe, secure and understood in the arms of her understanding Libran guy. As a fellow air sign, he doesn't feel threatened or confused when she starts her mental juggling act, changing her mind several times in the hour. Meanwhile, he'll have trouble making up his mind at all. Like his astrological sign, the Scales, the Libran man will weigh up his feelings and thoughts and is a master at talking himself out or into just about anything. To stop going insane (because they can't make plans or decisions), this couple need to practise making mutual decisions, such as where they're going to eat dinner, what colour they'll paint the bedroom, and stick to them. Consistency, or a complete lack of, is their main challenge to their relationship's happiness and stability.

If Mr Libra and Ms Gemini decide to set up house together, these lovebirds will create a charming, tastefully decorated love nest. It will be full of flowers, books, peaceful music (the Libran man can't stand loud music), and interesting artefacts bought on their travels together. It probably won't be very neat (Ms Gemini rarely hangs up her clothes after wearing them), but will have a comfortable 'lived-in' appearance instead.

But not all is the hippy ideal of peace and love that harmony-loving Mr Libra would like. In fact, when the Twin gal and Libran guy argue, you can bet that she starts it and he finishes it! Geminis quite enjoy arguing, as it gives them a chance to exercise their mental muscles. After a bout of verbal gymnastics Ms Gemini rarely feels offended or holds a grudge. Her Libran lover, however, may not be so quick to forget. What offends him more than anything else in life is unfairness, ugliness and discord. He craves peace and tranquillity, balance and beauty. If his Twin lover gets bored and tries to rock the boat one time too many, she might find herself on the end of the Libra wrath, and this is not a pretty sight.

When a Gemini woman considers marriage she looks for an intellectual equal, which makes Mr Libra a prime candidate. He typically has a solid education, fine manners, refined tastes and a sparkling sense of humour. Together they'll be best buddies, doting parents and passionate lovers — there's no role they can't take on together.

Gemini man — Libra woman

 The *'I feel good when I'm with you and I knew that I would'* relationship

This couple just seems to be naturally attuned to each other. They fit the zodiac relationship groove so well that they could even be deemed 'groovy'! Now I know 'groovy' is a back-to-the-60s, old-fashioned word, but somehow it just sums up what this couple can look like to an outside observer. They frequently look right together (whereas often other couples have a physical appearance of being mismatched). When you check them out at a distance, it's hard to find a more charming couple in the zodiac than Mr Gemini and Ms Libra. In fact, watching a Gemini man and his Libran maid socialise at a party is quite scintillating, and you can probably learn a great deal about how to upgrade your own social graces or approaches by doing just that. These two have an amazing ability to 'work a room'. Just watch how they mingle and mix, glass of wine in hand, easily joining one conversation and then smoothly spinning around to join another. Air signs live very much on a mental plane and these two are sparkling conversationalists.

Usually they really like each other a great deal, even at first meeting, and much further down the pathway of life after that as well. The Gemini guy's cool poise, quick wit and ease with words can be irresistible to the Libran woman. If he turns her on visually and she feels magnetically drawn to him, once they talk she feels that she's finally found a guy who'll keep her mentally, physically and emotionally stimulated. Although the future he offers her might be fraught with uncertainties, a Libran female in love will overlook this slight problem if he fits into her idea of the right partner for her. After all, she'll have time to work her magic spell on her innocent Twin lover, and she probably feels because he's initially *sooo* charming and easy-going that she'll be able to modify any of his shortfalls to fit in with her way of thinking. In other words, if he needs changing or improving, she is likely to be the one for the job. Hold on, if this approach is her romantic plan, then she's likely to be in for one hell of a challenge. In the long term, there is one thing Mr Gemini isn't and that's changeable. He is what he is, so keep that in mind when you're dealing with him. He may change within his own boundaries of operation, but he won't change to operate within anyone elses, simply because he can't.

Now if any gal of the zodiac does have a better chance than most of beguiling him with her feminine charms and put him on his best behaviour (even if only temporarily), it's Ms Libra. With feminine Venus smiling down on her, the Libran woman is typically gracious, well-groomed and good looking. Just think of the feminine charms of screen sirens Catherine Zeta-Jones and Brigitte Bardot. Although the Gemini guy loves a pretty face and sexy body, he's been there probably already and done that. With Ms Libra what turns him on more than anything is her flawless, calming outlook, plus her creative, quick mind and her ability to be such an all-round accomplished kinda gal. She's got a touch of challenge to offer him too. Fortunately, his Libra gal gives him enough mental challenge to keep the excitement flowing. There's a little psychic energy between them too, which keeps them posted and updated on each other, even at a distance. And while they are busy circulating at a party, these two lovebirds may exchange knowing looks, pass on secret messages with the glint in their eyes, or discreetly slip each other sexy love notes when no-one is looking. They know how to turn the other on with just the right choice of action, expression, or unspoken or spoken words.

While these two air signs have plenty in common there are differences that can cause challenges in their love match. One of them is their attitude to marriage. Though Gemini needs and desires love, if his personal freedom is threatened this Mercury bird will flap his wings and prepare for his disappearing act before you can say abracadabra! Even if the Twin has found the Libran woman of his dreams, he's likely to put off saying the words *'Will you marry me?'* for as long as humanly possible. It's not that he doesn't worship the ground on which his sexy Libran gal walks, it's simply that the words *'until death do us part'* make him sweat profusely. The Gemini man wants to experience as much as possible during his time on planet Earth. But if any woman can convince the Twin that marriage doesn't spell 'the end', the Venus Goddess can.

You see, marriage suits Ms Libra down to the ground. This romantic woman of Venus has, since childhood, dreamt of being swept off her feet by a charming, handsome prince and her princess dream comes true when she arrives at the altar in her wedding dress. One sure thing that Mr Gemini will learn is that his Libran woman likes to have things her own way. She's a leader and she's always 'right'. Though she might have a coy smile that could melt icicles, the Libran woman is tougher than she looks. She knows how to use her beauty, grace *and* charm to get what she wants.

If marriage is on her mind — because she is much stronger in will than he is — then her Gemini guy will probably, sooner or later, walk down the aisle with her. Marriage, in fact, is really not such a bad thing for Mr Gemini. From the safe base of marriage, he'll feel comfortable to go out and explore the world before returning again, happy but weary, to her loving, open arms. In fact, many a Libran gal is subconsciously driven to either emulate her parents' marriage (if it was a happy one), or avoid making the mistakes her parent's made (if it was an unhappy marriage). Either way, this gal will fight tooth and nail to keep discord and upset out of the family home. With a little patience and discipline, Ms Libra and Mr Gemini have a great chance of creating their own fairy tale romance that lasts a lifetime!

GEMINI — SCORPIO relationship

The *'I think this romantic stuff is all a bit too much to handle'* relationship

STAR GEMINI–SCORPIO COUPLE
Lenny Kravitz and Lisa Bonet

If you are a Gemini heading into a love match with a Scorpio or vice versa, then watch out! You are about to play with a loaded emotional and volatile romantic gun. Don't think I want to pull the plug on the Gemini–Scorpio love party; however, I do feel it's my duty as an astrologer to warn you Twins and Scorpions before you accept a lift home, coffee invitation, dinner date, marriage proposal or any other kind of commitment, offer or deal from each other. The Scorpio–Gemini love match (or mismatch) is akin to trying to fit a square peg into a round role. But, as Gemini would cheerfully attest, 'There are always exceptions!', and Scorpio would deeply add, 'Our connection rises above all of that'. Miracles do occur in the astrological game of love, but just don't say I didn't warn you.

Gemini woman — Scorpio man

 The *'Ahhh . . . is this really good or really bad?'* relationship

These two don't score high on the zodiac's compatibility chart, but that certainly won't stop headstrong Mr Scorpio and challenge-loving Ms Gemini from trying and sometimes beating all kinds of 'this-relationship-just-won't-work' odds! Curious and cerebral Ms Gemini is fascinated by men that challenge her mentally *and* excite her sexually, so imagine her delight upon meeting the suave Scorpio Love God. Pondering the magnetic aura he exudes, she'll smile and nod as he talks in that deep, rich voice. Meanwhile her mind works overtime and she thinks: *'God he's so brainy!'*; and *'I wonder if he'd go trekking with me in Nepal?'*; and *'I knew I should have worn my new lacy bra and knickers tonight!'*

Ms Gemini has a tendency to jump ahead of herself, but she'd better know what she wants before getting involved with the Scorpio man. This guy doesn't suffer fools easily. He plays for keeps and believes in 'forever' and 'commitment'. But to Ms Gemini, those very words make her jump out of her skin with fear. Although he is sweet, gentle and sensitive, the Scorpio man has plenty of self-control and an abundance of 'attitude'. He's a fixed sign, so when he's decided to do something, it's hard to talk him out of it — and even Ms Gemini's clever verbal skills won't sway him.

His Gemini woman's absent-mindedness, restlessness and clever verbal gymnastics often test his patience threshold. The Gemini woman often *thinks* she knows 'what's best' for her Scorpio guy and she'll get very excited (eyes darting back and forth and arms flailing around as she speaks) as she tries to convince him of her grand plan. Often she'll push him too far, encountering the Scorpio wrath as a result and, believe me, it won't be a pretty sight. Here's an example: a Gemini girlfriend of mine continually encouraged her Scorpio husband to patch things up with his estranged sister (and no wonder, Geminis are very close to their siblings). He hadn't spoken to his sister in years because of a messy inheritance. Mr Scorpio finally accused my Gemini friend of interfering in his life, they divorced and shortly after he reunited with his sister!

So my point is, you just can't tell a Scorpio man what to do! And here's the deal. Though the typical Scorpio guy doesn't want his own affairs to be examined, he's quick to criticise his Gemini gal. He'll want to know where she's going, who she's going with, and what time she'll be home. Freedom-loving Gemini gals can't stand tabs being kept on them and his possessiveness may cause further rifts in their relationship.

There are plenty of wonderful cosmic lessons they can learn from each other and respecting and accepting the differences between each other will keep the magic flowing in their relationship. The truth is, neither one of them is going to change: she's the Queen of Trivia and he's the King of Depth. But the Scorpio man can benefit from his Gemini gal's impulsive 'seize-the-day' outlook on life and learn to be more impulsive. The Gemini woman, you see, is the kind of girl to take the day off and go skydiving instead! She, in turn, can learn some integrity from her Scorpio guy. He's honest, loyal, faithful *and* a man of his word. Ms Gemini, on the other hand, has a habit of overcommitting herself, and therefore has no choice but to backtrack on her promises. Alongside her Scorpio lover, she can learn how to 'walk her talk'. So whether the Ms Gemini–Mr Scorpio love match ends in tears, nuptials or the divorce courts, you can bet one thing: the karmic lessons they learn from their love connection will keep the astro-Gods smiling for aeons to come.

Gemini man — Scorpio woman

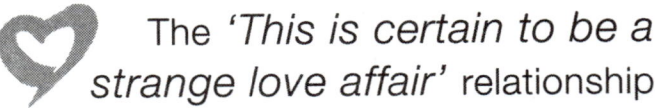

The *'This is certain to be a strange love affair'* relationship

The Scorpio gal is a high maintenance woman. In love, and in life, she's one of the most powerful women in the zodiac. Just watch the way she walks into a room, commanding attention with her sexy, magnetic intensity. This gal doesn't need to chase after men, they come running to her like moths to a flame. After an encounter with Ms Scorpio many men find themselves running (or limping) as far *away* from her as humanly possible. The Scorpio woman has a tendency to eat her man alive, *and* she'll spit out the remains afterwards. But don't let me intimidate you. After all, you Gemini guys surely knew what you were getting yourselves into when Ms Scorpio gave you that first sexy come-get-me gaze. Or did you?

Although Ms Scorpio sees things as either 'black' or 'white' (just listen to how she absolutely 'hates' or 'loves' a dress, restaurant or movie), *she* herself is not as straightforward. She's passionate, intelligent, tenacious, loyal and charming. The Gemini man loves these things about her. He'll even put up with (and laugh about) her need to be a control freak. Just think of complex Scorpio women such as Indira Gandhi, Julia Roberts, Winona Ryder and Roseanne Barr. The wonderful thing is that Mr Gemini loves variety (they get bored if they know the script ahead of time) and luckily, Ms Scorpio writes the script to her own life though she'll rarely give him a sneak preview!

Life is often a winding road for the Scorpio woman while the Gemini guy prefers the quick straight path. Both are survivors. She's experienced the depths of despair and the heights of ecstasy, making her an 'old soul' on the planet. She'll forgive but rarely forget. Her Gemini guy has more of a child's innocent spirit. He can bounce back quickly from heartache or upset — with trademark optimism and self-confidence — and rarely holds a grudge. Each, in their own way, instinctively knows how to pick up the pieces and start again. When they find true love together there's an instant recognition that together they can take on the world and fulfil their wildest dreams and desires.

Unfortunately, the Gemini man–Scorpio woman success stories are few and far between. These two players in the astro-game of life are just very different. While Gemini men will tune into the 'light-and-easy' channel, Ms Scorpio prefers the classical music station. She might accuse him of being flaky, flighty and flirty. He'll retort that she's judgmental, sceptical and critical. Both, of course, are right. It's when she starts to probe into his psyche 'looking for dirt', that the Gemini man begins to feel unnerved. Even if he's one hundred per cent innocent in the face of her accusations or insinuations, her penetrating gaze will make him squirm and he'll feel guilty anyway! Even though the truth-seeker Scorpio woman has the ability to 'get to the bottom of' almost anything, don't expect her to reveal any deep dark secrets of her own. This could drive Mr Gemini crazy, causing him to cry in indignation: *'Huh! Talk about double standards!'* Her words can be like daggers, but he's also a very clever verbal opponent.

The Gemini man is usually the first one to back down from a disagreement. Pride is not a big deal to him, so he will often concede that she was right after all (whether she was or not!) She'll then melt, saunter sexily into his arms and murmur that she wants to make love to him, right then and there. Sex is often what occurs after the Scorpio gal and Gemini guy have finished arguing and it's usually amazingly passionate. He's imaginative, playful and full of energy; just the requirements to keep his Scorpio woman sexually satisfied. The Gemini guy has probably never encountered a woman as passionate as his Scorpio gal!

If the Gods of Mercury and Pluto (the ruling planets of Gemini and Scorpio respectively) make a special astrological agreement, this can be a passionate love match that lasts a lifetime! If they can't harmonise their differences, then they'll have no choice but to say 'hasta luego, baby!', and look back on the good ol' times with a wry smile.

GEMINI—SAGITTARIUS relationship

The *'I'm having the time of my life, are you too?'* relationship

STAR GEMINI–SAGITTARIUS COUPLE
Marilyn Monroe and Joe DiMaggio

Talk about the real romantic deal! When Cupid's love arrows hit this combination, you have all the trappings of a zodiac love affair to remember. In fact, when it comes to falling in love, this is the combination that makes that happen more than most. I even bet in the movie *An Affair to Remember*, that the characters were astrologically Gemini and Sagittarius: the Sagittarus being the role played by Cary Grant and the Gemini being the role played by Deborah Kerr. However, it could work out the other way round too. Certainly if they get into the right romantic mood, groove and opportunity to unfold their romantic charms upon each other, the Sagittarians are certainly going to have the time of their life.

No matter whether their union lasts a short time or a lifetime this will be a huge learning experience for them both. Karma or destiny plays a mammoth role when the Twin and the Archer fall into each other's arms. Mercury-ruled Gemini and Jupiter-governed Sagittarius are on opposite ends of the zodiac wheel where they gaze across at each other in mutual fascination. There's a magnetic attraction and on emotional, mental, spiritual and sexual levels, they simply just click.

Gemini woman—Sagittarius man

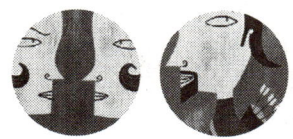

The *'I've heard a lot about you . . .
It's so nice to finally meet you'* relationship

'Hello, where have you been all my life?' is often what occurs when these two signs meet up. When the Gemini woman and Sagittarius man first get acquainted, there's usually no shortage of mutual admiration and sexual attraction. Sometimes there's a bit too much of both to comfortably handle.

These two adventurers often meet in extraordinary circumstances. A Gemini friend of mine on holiday met her Archer guy in a hut in the mountains of northern Spain. She'd hiked through rain, mud and fog to get there — the others she was hiking with turned back because of poor weather conditions — but she soldiered on, driven by fate. So you can imagine her surprise (and delight) upon finding her mountain-climbing Sag man at such high elevation! She moved to Spain to live with him (destiny plays a pivotal role in the Sag–Gemini match), and though their relationship which lasted for several wonderful, adventurous years) eventually fizzled, my friend looks back with fondness at the amazing adventures she experienced by his side. But did they go the total distance into marital bliss? No they didn't, as indeed many a Gemini gal and Sagittarian guy do not manage to do. Sometimes they are the affair to remember, rather than the full-on lifetime commitment, but who is to say that one is actually better than the other, certainly not I! There's a magic ingredient to 'an affair' that sometimes longer-running relationships cannot reproduce.

That's not to say that all Ms Gemini–Mr Sagittarius matches are destined to end up unhappily. Sometimes these two don't even notice each other at all — there's got to be more than just a casual encounter for this couple — and the timing also has to be right. However, if all the romantic pieces are in the right place, often when they first meet Twins and Archers get the feeling they're staring into the eyes of their soul mate. They resonate with each other. She loves his positive outlook, enthusiasm and visionary mind. He's an individual and a very smart guy. The Sag man walks his own path (he refuses to conform and is often extremely anti-establishment), and the Gemini woman loves nothing more than a man who has his own agenda. The typical Gemini gal is not the most starry-eyed of the zodiac sisters, so she'll even forgive her Archer guy for his lack of romance.

That doesn't mean that he won't surprise her with thoughtful presents (though you can forget flowers, chocolates and champagne). His gifts to her are practical, such as the latest ski boots, a sturdy backpack, or perhaps a gift voucher for language classes at the local evening college. She won't mind, because this guy has his heart in the right place and he truly adores her. What she might get sick of is hanging out with her Sag man *and* his buddies. He's a bit of a guy's guy. He likes his mates and seems occasionally, especially with Australian men, to prefer their company to that of his ladyloves. However, that doesn't mean she can't join him and his mates occasionally too. Whether it's down at the local pub or on a bushwalking expedition, she'll start to get the feeling that she's 'one of the boys'. But she can't always expect to be his one and only companion, he's a social creature who is going to have other attachments or interests, whether it's his mates, his children by another marriage, or some hobbies or pastimes that take up his time. There are also times when the Sag man wants to be alone and God help the woman who tries to sweet-talk him out of his solace. Like the statue of The Thinker, he'll sit, ponder life's philosophical questions, assimilate his deepest thoughts and plan his next adventure. He's a strange creature all right. But the Gemini girl is fascinated with her Sag guy and considers it a game trying to put the pieces of the puzzle together.

Meanwhile the Sagittarius guy is constantly surprised by his Gemini gal. He's impressed with her breeziness, independence and multiple interests and talents. She's a little girl, fascinating woman and genius all rolled into one. The trusting Archer loves a challenge, but if she's the kind of Gemini girl that weaves too many white lies with her verbal talents she'll push him away. He's a lover of honesty and can be seen on weekends aiming his Archer's arrows in preparation to shoot down hypocrisy and lies. Though while his Gemini babe is not a straight-faced liar, she does have a penchant for stretching the truth. In this love match each has qualities the other would like to cultivate. Ms Gemini admires her Sag guy's sincerity and his ability to shoot for a star and reach it. He'd like more of her poise and knack for keeping a cool head in the face of disaster. The most successful Sag–Gemini unions are those that admire (without envying) the other's positive qualities.

Both signs are wary of marriage. Even if the Archer guy and his Gemini gal have enjoyed a committed relationship for years, the subject of marriage is likely to remain untouched (much to the distress of both their families). But if Mr Sagittarius and Ms Gemini do, eventually, become husband and wife it's unlikely to be a conventional marriage. Adventure, study, work and interesting hobbies will be constant themes in their life, and they're likely to travel frequently (and often independently) because of these commitments. Fortunately for our Sag guy and Gemini gal lovers, absence will only make the heart grow fonder.

Gemini man—Sagittarius woman

 The *'You're my best friend as well as my true love'* relationship

Mr Gemini and Ms Sagittarius are astrologically opposed on the zodiac wheel and for this reason there's a powerful magnetic pull between the two. On a karmic level, they can teach each other marvellous things because each possesses what the other lacks. They find an instant empathy in each other's arms, for what they do share is an inquisitive mind and a need for freedom. The Gemini guy and Sag girl are trendsetters and go-getters, and together they'll achieve in a week what most couples would get done in a year!

Just think about it for a minute. Mr Gemini is air and Ms Sagittarius is fire. He can encourage his Archer maiden into action (air always fans fire into higher flames). While she might have a tendency to smother him (fire burns out the oxygen in the air), she is also very able to *warm* her airy Twin. The planetary ruler of Ms Sagittarius is Jupiter, the planet of abundance, and she just loves things in big quantities. Think loads of love, stacks of sex and lashings of laughter (plus, she's likely to have a very healthy appetite!) Mr Gemini, though, is more inclined to trying a tiny bit of everything. Ruled by whimsical Mercury, the planet of movement and communication, the Gemini guy wants to experience all that life has on offer. What they do share, though, is an unquenchable curiosity for life.

The Sagittarian woman has a mind of her own (just look at Jane Fonda, Sinead O'Connor and Bette Midler), and she's often very outspoken. She believes strongly in honesty, trust and sincerity and she doesn't mess around, especially where love, romance and relationships are concerned. In fact, it's very likely that she asked Mr Gemini out on their first date! When it comes to matters of the heart (and libido) the fire-ruled Sagittarius woman is very direct. She's a passionate, sexy woman — think of how Sagittarian Kim Bassinger steamed up the screen in *Nine And A Half Weeks*; she knows what she wants and how to get it. Mr Gemini and his Archer maiden soon discover that they are perfectly matched sexual partners. Even if their relationship begins to falter on other levels, it's usually the sex that keeps them together, at least for a while!

He also adores the fact that his Archeress is a guy's girl; she has no qualms about playing a game of pool with her Gemini guy or eating takeaway pizza and watching her favourite football team blitz his. She's up for anything, and this is truly a breath of fresh air for Mr Gemini. The Twin guy is seeking a lover, playmate and partner-in-crime all in one. Luckily, he finds it with adventurous Ms Sagittarius. She's a faithful lover, but that doesn't mean she won't entertain herself by just looking! A Sag girlfriend of mine is less than subtle when a good-looking guy walks past on the street. She'll turn around, peer over her sunglasses, stare lustily and wolf whistle until his cheeks turn lobster-red. But it's all in good fun. You see, the Sagittarian woman never takes herself (or others) too seriously. That's why she connects with her Gemini guy. He's unassuming and a spirited freethinker. Thankfully the male Twin is not a clingy man, so they'll give each other the freedom they mutually need.

One of the big problems in this relationship is the lack of stability and permanence. Both are experts at short-term *anything*. When it comes to planning a weekend away or an extravagant birthday party you can bet it will be the hottest event in town. Long-term projects, however, scare the living Jupiter and Mercury out of both of them. Watch Mr Gemini's eyes dart anxiously or the Sag girl's foot tap nervously at the mention of a five-year career plan, buying a house or raising children. Together they might fall into the temptation of only seeking life's quick thrills. But the Archer guys and Twins gals who *do* decide to 'build' a life together step by step will bond in amazing ways, and discover that it is possible to have their cake and eat it too!

GEMINI—CAPRICORN relationship

The *'All you need is to keep your sanity and everything will be fine'* relationship

STAR GEMINI–CAPRICORN COUPLE
Priscilla Presley and Elvis Presley

You might say that these two are from different planets, different solar systems, and different universes. But, 'hello', when these two snuggle up, put down some roots and decide to get cosy, you would never know they weren't perfect companions. Sometimes the fact that this couple are such poles apart in just about every way, works miracles in their favour. It's like the expression 'you can't teach an old dog new tricks'. Well, Gemini (the cosmic trickster) is quite capable of teaching Capricorn (often regarded as the most steadfast of the zodiac signs) lots of new tricks and vice versa.

Both of them look at life through separate vision of what they want. The Saturn-ruled Goat favours wisdom, stability and caution, while Mercury-influenced Gemini gets high on variety, change and movement. The Twin laughs in the face of Capricorn's 'stick-with-what-you-know' motto. The Capricorn queries the Twin's ideas about what's good, great or even possible. If it's new, hot-off-the-press or cutting edge, the Twin dives into the middle of it, eyes wide with child-like excitement. Meanwhile Caps prefer 'tried and tested' to anything new and experimental. The Twin likes to race light-footed into the future, while the Goat prefers the slow but sure path to the top of their chosen future mountain (*and* will stop to clean their boots at each rest stop). An impossible union? Not necessarily, but certainly one that will have its extreme tests, challenges and strange encounters of the romantic kind.

Gemini woman — Capricorn man

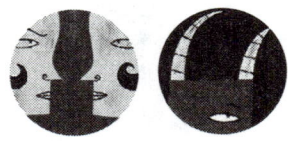

 The *'It's going to be very different than what we both expected'* relationship

'The World According to Capricorn' is seriously challenged from the moment Ms Gemini crosses his path. Stroking his chin seriously, he ponders the strange creature before him. She's like the wind, free and unpredictable, and it's impossible to guess in which direction she'll blow next. But there's something about her lightness and breeziness that tugs at his sleeve and ultimately at his heart. He adores watching her animated face light up, and her arms and hands waving furiously as she illustrates her point. The way she lives 'outside the box' entrances and confuses him to no end.

Gemini's curiosity is also ignited when she meets the Capricorn man. His serenity and dignified mountain goat bearing might even leave her at a loss for words (something that rarely occurs for Geminis!) Though chaos rules her life more often than not, what she really craves is a way to soothe her inner restlessness. She's impressed that his feet are so firmly planted on terra firma. His innate elegance, stable job and impressive assortment of degrees and diplomas will make her gush to her friends *'He's just sooooo together!'* But his conservative façade can be deceiving. She's thrilled to discover her Goat has a 'twinkle in his eye' and a wacky sense of humour that comes out at the most unexpected moments.

These two can really learn and benefit from each other. She admires his Zen-like discipline and will see her share portfolio and professional networks expand through her relationship with him. As the Goat flicks through her resumé, he'll shake his head in wonder, trying to find a pattern in her listing of jobs that include writer, waitress and road builder. Whether her Jill-of-all-trades career path has worked for her or not, you can bet that his connections and business savvy will catapult her working life to new heights.

Her adaptability, child-like wonder and sense of style are why he admires her, but the fact that she *adores* him is the reason he *loves* her. The Capricorn man wants the whole package: a wife, good job, money in the bank, a house and children (though not necessarily in that order). He likes to look good, and what can look better than a Gemini wife on his arm? He'll expand his horizons with her, and get swept up in her life of exotic travels, fascinating projects, offbeat friends and sense of aliveness. By her side, he gets to see that there's more to life than climbing the corporate rung and keeping up with the Joneses.

The commitment-phobic Twin *does see* that her Goat will be a loyal husband and doting father, but it takes a certain Ms Gemini to accept his proposal. She needs patience with a Capital 'P', while his best tool in this union (apart from his male one!) is a big dose of understanding. In the bedroom these two can be a great match. After their first sexual encounter, Ms Gemini is amazed. How can such a cool, calm and collected guy be so passionate? Earth-ruled Capricorn likes to take his time and make sure his partner is satisfied (after all, he wants to do a good job!) In fact, Goats can be kinky and even variety-is-the-spice-of-life Gemini might be caught off guard by his creativity in the boudoir! She plays 'prude' one night and 'prostitute' the next: a duality that keeps him turned on and begging for more.

The biggest challenge in the Gemini–Capricorn household is communication. Her need to constantly talk about her ever-changing feelings and thoughts can drive him crazy with frustration. His sulking and dark and silent moods, that can last for days, will have her turning to friends on the phone for solace. She'll try to charm and probe him, but a clever Gemini gal soon learns that Saturn guards its secrets very well. If these two understand that love means accepting someone exactly as they *are* and exactly as they're *not*, then the Gemini and Capricorn union can be a long and happy one.

Gemini man — Capricorn woman

The *'I think we both need to remain very patient with each other'* relationship

How can such different personalities find a happy, loving partnership and stay sane in the process? It isn't going to be easy for them, but it's certainly going to be a high-curve learning experience. The Gemini guy and the Capricorn gal are rather opposites when it comes to the way they look at life. This can provide them with a very broad arena to play out the scenes of their relationship and there's likely to be plenty of 'scenes' to play out.

Wise beyond her years, you get the feeling that the Capricorn woman has been around this planet before — many times. Intelligent and mature, she's a gal with a practical head on her shoulders. But she's likely to have all her worldly-wise experience put to the test when she teams up with Mr Gemini. By the way, what could she possibly see in an unpredictable, emotionally irresponsible Gemini who isn't even from the same planet? Then again, let's face it, what does the ethereal, avant-garde Twin find attractive in the Capricorn earth mother? After all, she'd rather browse antique shops than join Gemini in his search for the coolest bars and cafés around town.

The answer is easy — opposites attract. Sometimes they only attract for the initial lusty period of the relationship, but sometimes they click together like a key turning in a relationship lock and they stay bonded. Certainly many unions formed by a Gemini man and Capricorn woman sizzle and slowly burn out, but those who keep their love-fire alight can have long and happy relationships that last a lifetime. But whatever occurs between these two, the word 'compromise' is a key word they need to remember, especially for Ms Capricorn, as Mr Gemini is likely to keep her on her cosmic toes.

Usually if Ms Capricorn is truly interested in her Gemini man, she's in for the long haul and she's prepared to work at making the relationship succeed. Extremely loyal, the typical mountain Capricorn maiden is not interested in a passing love affair or a quick romantic interlude. She needs to make this clear right from the beginning, because Mr Gemini doesn't exactly have a reputation for longevity in the relationship arena. His fleet-footed zodiac ruler, Mercury, was the messenger of the Gods, so delivering quick love packages is more his style. But that's not to say that when he's in love, he can't commit. What he needs is the right woman to bring out the best in him.

Ms Capricorn's love is like a steady candle-lit flame, providing stability in Gemini's otherwise frenetic life. He adores her earth mother aura, which is a solid base from where he can safely explore the world and then return to her loving arms. As long as she allows him his freedom and self-expression (and that includes allowing him to flirt harmlessly), he'll thrive in this relationship. To stifle a Twin's yearnings is also a mistake. His wanderlust is infamous and interestingly enough, as she gets older, she'll be more open to exploring exotic shores, though he needs to realise that a luxury hotel is more her style than a mosquito-ridden camp site.

In their home life, she definitely wears the pants. Ms Capricorn is more likely to take control of the family purse strings and make decisions on their children's education. She's a born organiser and, as he might point out glibly when they argue, a control freak. The truth is, the Goat maiden is far better prepared to take care of their money matters. She believes in saving for a rainy day, whereas spontaneous Gemini's spending habits can be erratic and downright dangerous! Even though Ms Capricorn is one of the glamour girls of the zodiac, she'll scold him if he surprises her with expensive, spur-of-the-moment gifts.

One of the biggest challenges is their different outlooks on life. He's sunny, positive and excitable. Twins don't get bogged down in life's despairs and disappointments, and sometimes he makes the mistake of trying to cheer her up when all she wants to do is have him listen to her woes and offer her a loving hug. She can wallow in gloominess for days before she's ready to pull herself out. This can be draining for Gemini, who might flippantly tell her to *'Get Over It!'*, causing her to retort back, *'You're such a child!'* The difference is, the Gemini embraces problems, seeing them as a way to reinvent himself and, like Houdini, finds a new escape route. His Capricorn gal, however, will worry about her weight, her relationship, her money, her job, the in-laws, neighbours, the ozone layer etc, etc.

Gemini wears his heart on his sleeve, yet she keeps hers well and truly under wraps. But looks can be deceiving and while she can, at times, appear to be an Ice Maiden, the Capricorn woman (when in a loving, secure relationship) loves to let her hair down. Sex between these two is passionate, loving and affectionate, yet at times they will feel out of sync with each other in the bedroom. But when they hit the sexual jackpot, earth and heaven collide to produce a cosmic firework display!

GEMINI—AQUARIUS relationship

The *'I was made for loving you'* relationship

STAR GEMINI–AQUARIUS COUPLE
Kylie Minogue and Michael Hutchence

The combination of Gemini–Aquarius is definitely a strong contender as a powerful romantic relationship possibility, but not an everyday type of connection — it is going to be something out of the ordinary. Hold on to your hat, and get ready for an emotional, mental, physical and spiritual roller coaster ride! There are elements of theatre and the *bizarre* in this cosmic love partnership. Just think of a Star Trek movie starring Marilyn Monroe and directed by Woody Allen. It's just too strange for words.

Though don't be fazed if you are actually *experiencing* the Twin–Water Bearer love match. This can actually be one of the more successful cosmic couplings in the zodiac. For some peculiar reason this duo seems to work, and occasionally work really well. That's because Aquarius (ruled by unconventional Uranus) and Gemini (governed by fast-paced Mercury) are both air signs capable of harmonising on the same love-radio wave frequency. Let's hope that you both enjoy tuning into the same kind of cosmic music!

Gemini woman — Aquarius man

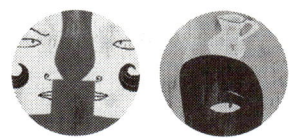

 The *'Is this as good as it gets, or what?'* relationship

Get the right Gemini gal together at the right time and phase of her life, with the appropriate Aquarian guy for her, and you'll have a couple who vibrate, gravitate and levitate on the same frequency of mental understanding. Quick-thinking, intelligent and with a knack for putting their stamp of individuality on everything they do, this cosmic couple can go through life together, hand in hand, in awe and wonder and find each other fascinating, extraordinary and intriguing. If they are lucky enough to have the added ingredient of finding each other sexually intoxicating, you could even think they 'had it made' in the relationship romance stakes. This of course will only apply if destiny has opened the doors of their hearts to each other in a major way. Then zany Mr Aquarius and quirky Ms Gemini, both air signs, can find a long-lasting harmony incorporating friendship, romance, love and passion.

However (eek!), if the wrong Ms Gemini and Mr Aquarius attempt to 'explore the romantic realms' together, they have the ability to drive each other totally nuts. When Ms Gemini and Mr Aquarius get out of each other's romantic orbit this relationship can turn out to be a relationship where early romantic bliss quickly transforms from passion to pain. What results is a great deal of relationship neurosis and ongoing panic attacks.

These two have much in common and a lot of major differences. Though both are seekers of variety and movement, Ms Gemini shouldn't expect her Aquarian guy to actually make changes within himself. Aquarius, you see, is a fixed sign, which means that the Aquarian guy can be stubborn, unmoving and opinionated. This might come as a shock to his Gemini gal who, when she first meets him, is dazzled by an unconventional and original guy who stands out in a crowd. He's different, and many Aquarian men *look* physically different, almost as if they're from another planet! So while he might be a humanitarian, hippy or freedom fighter looking for world change and evolution, he himself is a creature of habit!

My friend had a husband who was an Aquarian stickler to routine, who'd worked in the same job for sixteen years and only liked to talk if he had something to say. No matter how much she pleaded and begged him to look for something new, he simply became more and more intent on sticking it out in a job he really didn't like. She ended up throwing up her hands and letting him do things his way, but accepting defeat took a huge toll on her. She felt she failed him and he failed her. But if anyone can pull an Aquarian guy out of his routine and move him onto a new adventure it's going to be the Gemini gal. Ms Gemini's innate curiosity and her love of a challenge will open his eyes to another world. By her side, he'll see that anything is possible! In fact, when things flow well between them, they can add up to a super and highly creative team.

However, their merger into the love-affair business won't be a walk down easy street either. The truth is, life and love alongside the Aquarian man will never be easy-going or boring. He's a guy who loves to shock, and even the streetwise Gemini girl will have moments when he does actually surprise and shock her! All the better for keeping her taste for variety satisfied. Another thing she adores about him is his Aquarian love of truth. Though the Gemini gal typically loves her own exciting life, she often feels 'flaky' because of her inability to commit to one person, place, career etc. To her the Aquarian man can represent integrity, truth and responsibility, *and* she's likely to put him up on a pedestal.

She probably cries 'Eek!' in her heart at times, because he's so unreachable and comfortable living and existing in his own perfect and private mental world; his distance between himself, the world and sometimes even her, can drive her nuts. She can also become neurotically and even irrationally jealous. This jealousy arises because of his ease and harmony when he's around other members of the fairer sex.

Although he's not likely to wander or be unfaithful, she might feel threatened by the attention he manages to shower so happily upon the opposite sex, but generally she's foolish to worry. Sometimes her over-dramatic reactions to his involvement with others, pushes him into her competition's arms. She should let him have his female friends and not become overconcerned. After all, he doesn't like change and unless she's driving him nuts with her jealousy, he isn't likely to do much more than have a chat and share some fun times and innocent laughter with others.

Now conversely, when Ms Gemini flirts she's usually much more seriously intentioned about playing the field than he is, so *he* could have reason to wonder when she pays special attention to other men as to what she has on her romantic agenda. Even when Ms Gemini waves a romantic flag at some other man,

Mr Aquarius is so naturally cool and calm about emotional matters, he probably won't even notice her flirtatious side anyway. Instead, he'll be glad to see her having a nice time, which could possibly even aggravate her even more than him becoming jealous.

As mentioned earlier, this relationship team can make an intense couple. Both the Gemini gal and Aquarian guy are nervous, high-strung air signs, restless and quick-moving. In fact, just listen how Mr Aquarius complains that his Gemini gal sometimes 'gets on his nerves' and vice versa. Their body types are often typically lithe, long-limbed and slim, though much depends on other astro-influences in their horoscopes. Together they need to make a concerted effort to slow down and take care of their health. Too much coffee is a definite no-no for these two (and unfortunately they love nothing more than sitting elbow-to-elbow in a café discussing the world's problems!)

Taking a yoga or meditation class together is a fabulous way to slow themselves down and also share an activity in common. Of course, another way they can relax together is by making love! Luckily, Ms Gemini and Mr Aquarius are on the same level when it comes to sex. Their sex life is often thrilling and uncomplicated; though if they do get out of tune with each other it can be very half-hearted. This couple live more in their heads than in their bodies, which means that neither of them are the most highly sexed signs of the zodiac. However, usually their sex is inventive and unconventional and they'll always be trying something new.

In fact, the communication-specialist Gemini gal and her high-tech Aquarian guy have most likely tried phone sex, internet sex, text message sex and any other kind of sex requiring a phone line or computer! Their lovemaking will be non-conventional and varied, but they'll also enjoy romantic poetry-readings and sensual massages as a prelude to sex.

Gemini man—Aquarius woman

 The *'Let's get right out of control'* relationship

When this relationship works well, it can work romantic miracles. Naturally when it doesn't work well it is a total disaster! Fortunately, usually if time and space are in accord between them the Gemini man and the Aquarian woman often find that they make a perfect, well-suited zodiac match. However, it isn't usually an everyday, normal kinda match that these two forge when they align their lives together. The Gemini man and Aquarian woman often join forces to create the most unconventional love match in the zodiac neighbourhood. My Gemini friend and his Russian Aquarian lover operate a business importing decorative Native American totem poles into Australia. Their seven-year-old daughter is trilingual, and there's always plenty of extended family around (his son from a previous relationship and her visiting family from Moscow). They're not married, but they are starting to talk about a wedding ceremony involving Eskimo rituals and Celtic dancers. Go figure!

You see, the wired Gemini guy and his eccentric Aquarian gal are a couple who surf the same cosmic wavelengths. Though life is never simple between these signs, it is guaranteed to be fascinating (and even a tad exasperating). Ruled by the element air, they both live on a mental plane. They're ruled by their thoughts, not their emotions. And here's where it gets *really* interesting. Although they *think* about things a lot, don't expect them to be *rational* or *sensible*! The downside of so much mental energy is that it's easy for the Gemini guy and Aquarius gal to lose touch with their feelings (and the feelings of each other). To make this relationship last life's cosmic challenges, they need to regularly set aside time for romantic interludes. And they'd better mark them with red ink in their diaries in capital letters *and* circle them with a big heart! If not, absent-minded Ms Aquarius might just forget. Or head-ruled Mr Gemini might confuse it with another important engagement in his busy schedule. And they'll overlook once more the chance to make powerful romantic connections because of other distractions.

Not making time for each other can be the biggest problem, and it can even lead to the downfall of their relationship, especially if the time they miss out on is lovemaking time.

I'll let you in on a secret. If they *do* manage to schedule some sexy fun in their mutual agendas, they'll create enough electricity to light up Las Vegas. Sensual foreplay, especially a massage, is a Godsend to this airy couple. They need an earthy prelude to sex to pull them out of their heads and back into the world of emotions, sensuality and eroticism. Then, once they're in the mood, offbeat Aquarian gal and try-anything Mr Gemini have an amazing ability to let their imaginations run wild. You can bet this cosmic couple have a well-thumbed copy of the Karma Sutra on the bedside table!

Although the element air co-rules these signs (making them both lovers of free speech, knowledge, travel and social events), their natures are in many ways quite different. Ms Aquarius is a fixed sign, and this means when she makes up her mind about something, she's as *immovable* as the Rock of Gibraltar, a fact that's likely to confuse her Gemini guy. *'How can she be so out there and so stubborn at the same time?'* he asks himself. Her 'stick-with-it' attitude is often a blessing in disguise.

When it suits her, she'll wear the pants in this love match. Fortunately Mr Gemini won't mind too much. The Twin is a 'mutable' sign, which means he's extremely adaptable. This guy is a master at quickly turning things around. He can turn a 'tragedy' into a 'blessing' or her character 'flaw' into a charming 'nuance'. So, his dual-sided nature will allow him to sit back and enjoy the colour, sound and lighting in the magnificent show his Aquarian gal puts on in her daily life.

Despite her zany outlook on life, the female Water Bearer is a smart woman, and she knows she's onto a good thing with her Gemini guy. She's probably had plenty of affairs in her (mainly single) life, but when this girl finds her true soul mate she can be quite happy to settle into marriage and motherhood. The Twin male is very often the man she's been looking for all her life. He'll support her unconventional (and very often humanitarian) projects and interests; in return she'll give her sociable Gemini the freedom he so desperately needs. What else could they possibly need?

GEMINI — PISCES relationship

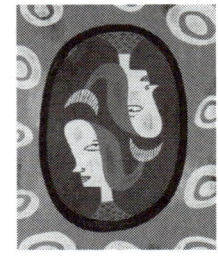

The *'Exactly who do you think you are?'* relationship

STAR GEMINI–PISCES COUPLE
Kim Clijsters and Lleyton Hewitt

Though it might not seem apparent at first, watery Neptune-ruled Pisces and airy Mercury-governed Gemini do have some things in common. Anybody with an inkling of astro-knowledge can tell you that Gemini, the Twin, is the infamous sign of duality. They're often in two places at once. They might own two cars, have serial romances or live in two cities or even two countries. Many work two jobs and yes, there are those Geminis who have two lovers!

Pisces is *also* a sign of duality. The astrological symbol of Pisces depicts two fish: one swims upstream while the other swims downstream. There is always an inner emotional or spiritual tug of war taking place. So, what does this tell us? In a nutshell, if you are part of a Gemini–Pisces love match, don't expect anything to be straightforward or clear-cut!

Gemini woman — Pisces man

 The *'Are we going anywhere or standing still?'* relationship

When this dreamy, romantic son of Neptune meets up with a flighty, elusive daughter of Mercury there's no telling what might happen. Hopefully though, Mr Pisces is not afraid of heights. Without his knowledge or consent, this amazing gal will lead him on one adventure after another, taking him to the top of the tallest pinnacle, right before she yells 'Geronimo!' and promptly leaps over the side. Whether he decides to follow or not is another thing altogether. His composed, more reserved nature is something of an enigma to most people, especially to the gung-ho Twin Ms. For the life of her, she can't understand — nor does she want to — what fun there could be in exercising *caution*. To her, the unknown possibilities are what excite her most about life. Without spontaneity, adventure and impulsiveness, Ms Gemini would be a dreary girl indeed.

Yet for all her love of excitement and 'fly-by-the-seat-of-her-pants' attitude, this carefree gal harbours a secret longing for some consistency and permanence in her life. Although she would never give up her lifetime pass to freedom or reckless abandon, Ms Gemini wants to know that when she does decide to fly the coop, her Pisces man will wait patiently for her to return (in her own good time, of course!) The unique duality of the Twins is the very essence of what makes this woman so amazingly inconsistent. Deep within her soul, Gemini gal is interestingly at odds with many of the traits that make her the remarkable individual she is. The equally dual nature of Pisces guy (represented by the image of two fish swimming in opposite directions) makes him more qualified than most to identify with his Twin gal's 'where should I go, who should I be, what do I want', quandary.

In her own sweet way, Gemini gal is full of love and admiration for her Pisces guy. It's just that — well, listening to corny love songs, gazing into each other's eyes (this makes her extremely nervous), and snuggling up after sex weren't quite what she had in mind when she uttered those three magic words. *I love you* was meant to be a kind of *invitation* — you know, to come sample the delights at the

 193

Gemini playground (while the 'Be A More Responsible Person Seminar' is further down the road). How was she supposed to know he'd fall head-over-heels in love with the most darned frustrating and exasperating woman in the known Universe? Her! Well, of course, that's only what other people say about her (and secretly — they just don't know it yet — even they adore her charming wit and winning smile). She's not an easy gal to understand but he does better than most!

Make no mistake however, Mr Pisces, though compassionate and sympathetic, is quite capable of cutting his ties swiftly and permanently should his own fragile soul be at risk of injury. He can endure only so much of the run-around from her. He can tolerate only so many broken dreams and disillusionments; so much criticism and hurt. Just as magically as he appeared in her life, Ms Gemini's one, true chance at happiness could easily disappear in a puff of smoke never to be seen, nor heard from again. (Mr Pisces is excellent at finding a new gal as a speedy replacement if he's had enough drama to last him for a while.)

Ms Gemini and Mr Pisces are two very complex and vastly diverse people. Gemini gal symbolises everything that is childlike and naive (in fact, Geminis are often called the Peter Pans of the zodiac), while Pisces is undoubtedly the Old Soul of the Universe. (This is one Fish who's swum around the cosmic block a few times!) Together, this unlikely couple can have the best of both worlds, though this isn't always apparent at first. To make this union last, Pisces man needs to leave his safe, watery sanctuary behind to fly high amongst the clouds with his Mercurial Gemini lover. He has to believe in her and have faith in the relationship enough to give her his trust. She, in return, must be prepared to swim with him to the great depths of his aquatic nirvana and not pester him too much about the small things that don't add up about him. Once each has tasted life with the other, there is little chance either is likely to turn back.

Gemini man — Pisces woman

 The *'You think that I love you . . . yes, in your dreams!'* relationship

The Pisces woman is a sensitive girl whose emotions ebb and flow like the tides. Like her astro-symbol, the Fish, there are times when she's in tune with life — swimming downstream easily and peacefully, just going with the flow with her Piscean ease and dreaminess. Then there are other times when life turns upside down and she's swimming upstream, against the universal flow. Water-ruled signs are extremely emotional and her moods can change several times in the space of an hour!

When the Pisces woman falls in love it's magical, but very seldom practical. Similarly, the Gemini man is impulsive when it comes to love and romance. Many relationships between the Pisces Mermaid and Gemini Twin begin when one of them (or both) is either married or going through a separation or divorce. Or even if both are physically and emotionally available, they're sometimes geographically challenged! Many a Mr Gemini–Ms Pisces relationship begins when they're living in different cities, states or countries! This theme of battling against the odds seems to be the karmic pattern in their union. But the truth is, the Twin guy and his Pisces gal each bring wonderful things to the relationship table.

There's something about the dreamy Piscean princess that Mr Gemini finds irresistible. He drowns in her eyes. She's vulnerable and mysterious and the Gemini man could spend hours just trying to figure her out. But he won't. *'But if she's not from this planet,'* he muses to himself, *'how is it that she understands me so well?'* And he's right. The Pisces woman is completely otherworldly, yet she intuitively recognises his needs, wants and desires. Such a sensitive soul is a handful for the Gemini guy. He's an air sign who's more in touch with his thoughts than his feelings. Highly emotional women send emergency service sirens wailing in his head and red lights flashing in front of his eyes. He doesn't have a handle on his own emotions, let alone somebody else's! Fortunately, by her side he can safely explore the depths of love, passion and emotions. Her empathy, especially for animals, small children and old people, touches his heart. The head-ruled Gemini man might even start talking about how 'Blending With the Great All' is what humankind should strive towards. This is when his friends at the pub look at him strangely and wonder what Ms Pisces is doing with his mind! Seriously, Ms Pisces will encourage her Gemini guy to explore his feminine, emotional side and this can only be a GOOD THING.

The Gemini man, on the other hand, can offer his Pisces gal focus and motivation. Ruled by communication planet Mercury, the Gemini man is a quick mover who knows how to talk his way into anything. The Pisces woman admires his poise, razor-sharp mind and ability to get what he wants in life. He loves variety and challenges, while she often feels overwhelmed at the thought of taking on the unknown. I have a Pisces girlfriend who calls her Gemini husband 'My Super Man'. Though I happen to think that *she* is Super Woman (she juggles two children, a husband, a beautiful home and a successful career). It's true that her Gemini guy has a wonderful way of helping her dreams become reality. The Twin man is a master at short cuts and quick escapes. He can also help pull her out of the Martyr–Victim Club in which many Pisces women have life-long memberships.

When it comes down to the nitty gritty, both the Gemini man and Pisces woman have a tendency to be easily impressed and their love match will quickly form into a mutual admiration society. Sex between the Twin guy and his Fish gal is sensual, passionate and imaginative. They both appreciate beautiful words, so exotic poetry or love letters are likely to feature in their prelude to lovemaking. These two just won't be into 'talking dirty'.

In the Gemini–Pisces household however, there's likely to be plenty of chaos. They may forget to pay bills or stock the fridge with food. The funny thing is, sometimes their house will be completely spotless, while other times it will look like a hurricane has blown through with piles of 'fall-where-they-may' clothes on the floor and unopened letters lying on the kitchen table. It will rarely be something in between.

But this can be a wonderful relationship, particular if they learn to love (and spend time in) each other's world. If the Pisces woman allows herself to be swept away on adventures atop Mercury's wings with her Gemini man; and if he willingly explores the emotional depths of dreamy Neptune with his Pisces Mermaid, then they'll discover the secret to true, unconditional love.

cancer cancer cancer cancer cancer
cancer cancer cancer cancer cancer
cancer cancer cancer cancer cancer
cancer cancer cancer cancer cancer
cancer cancer cancer cancer cancer
cancer cancer cancer cancer cancer
cancer cancer cancer cancer cancer
cancer cancer cancer cancer cancer
cancer cancer cancer cancer cancer

cancer cancer cancer cancer cancer
cancer cancer cancer cancer cancer
cancer cancer cancer cancer cancer
cancer cancer cancer cancer cancer
cancer cancer cancer cancer cancer
cancer cancer cancer cancer cancer
cancer cancer cancer cancer cancer
cancer cancer cancer cancer cancer
cancer cancer cancer cancer cancer

CANCER

[22 june – 23 july]

romantic pursuit: highly inconsistent

romantic vibration: tick-tocks

between 'I love you, I don't love you!'

secret love desire: to have a lover who is sexy,

gorgeous and loves them enough to deal with

their highs and lows

element: water

planetary ruler: the moon

symbol: the crab

quality: cardinal (= activity)

colours: silver, blue

gem: pearl, moonstone

best companions: pisces and scorpio

strongest virtues: inner soul power,

intuition, open heart

traits to improve: negative thinking,

cynical attitude, lack of focus on important

everyday matters

deepest desire: to be loved, and to love in return

Cancer celebrities

Anjelica Houston, Anthony Edwards, Athena Starwoman, Bert Newton,

Bill Cosby, Bryan Brown, Camilla Parker-Bowles, Carlos Santana,

Carly Simon, Cat Stevens, Chris Isaak, Chris O'Donnell, Clyde Packer,

Courtney Love, Cyndi Lauper, Dan Akroyd, David Hasselhoff, Deborah

Harry, Donald Sutherland, George Michael, George W. Bush, Gina

Lollobrigida, Giorgio Armani, Gough Whitlam, Harrison Ford,

Imelda Marcos, Janet Leigh, Jerry Hall, John Cusack, John Farnham,

Josh Harnett, Kevin Bacon, Linda Ronstadt, Liv Tyler, Mel Brooks, Meryl

Streep, Michael Flatley, Mike Tyson, Nancy Reagan, Nelson Mandela,

Nelson Rockefeller, O. J. Simpson, Pamela Anderson Lee, Princess

Diana, Richie Sambora, Ringo Starr, Robin Williams, Sir Edmund Hillary,

Sylvester Stallone, Terence Stamp, the Dalai Lama, the Sultan of Brunei,

Toby Maguire, Todd Marin, Tom Cruise, Tom Hanks, Yul Brynner

CANCER — CANCER relationship

The *'Get ready for a wild romantic ride'* relationship

STAR CANCER–CANCER COUPLE
Brigitte Nielsen and Sylvester Stallone

When a Cancer mates with another Cancer — eek! — anything can happen. This is no ordinary, everyday type zodiac relationship. Rather, it's a bizarre combination of erratic and unusual romantic moon-charged energy flows. For many, this coupling will result in a wild ride of emotions and highs and lows — some they will enjoy, other's they won't. Getting together with their same sign will involve lots of challenges, family issues and close encounters with strange fateful occurrences that alter both their destinies. However, it can also be an incredibly connected heart, mind and body zodiac alignment. If the right Cancers get together, it can sometimes work wonderfully because they share so many mutual goals and aims.

Initially, when Cancer meets up with Cancer they can forget about keeping both feet on the ground. These two are highly romantic, and if their hearts collide, the earth disappears and they instantly head for the moon and stars. Should two Cancers combine, their lives orbit in different directions from the rest of the world. This is a giddy experience and both individuals need to prepare to be taken through every rush of emotion under the sun, moon and stars. It will certainly help them both to enjoy this relationship much more if they love to play the role of a child or parent.

Cancer woman—Cancer man

The *'Hi Mum and Dad! I know I've only been married two days, but can I please come home and live with you both again?'* relationship

What can you say to explain what can and might happen when Cancer teams up with Cancer? One thing is certain, this relationship is not destined to be right for the faint-hearted. You need to be prepared to experience raw emotional energy when two people born under the most emotional sign of all, Cancer, fall in love. Two moon signs together is somewhat crazy relationship energy, but it has tremendous potential for being a fantastic love match if it can survive the craziness it often conjures up. This is an exciting connection, so exciting in fact, being enmeshed in a Cancer–Cancer relationship means that this couple could end up feeling like they are operating under full moon energy every day! That's why when two Cancers get together, they both tend to give each other a constant aerobic emotional workout. There'll be times when their Cancer partner will be their best mate, parent, child, soul mate or baby, while in other cranky times they'll be a maelstrom of irrational, headstrong, emotional energy stirring up their universe. Watch out too! If either partner hurts the other's feelings (which is *sooo* easy to do), they quickly build up walls between them that can be tougher than the Berlin Wall to pull down again.

Let's face it, moon children of both sexes are super-sensitive individuals, and it can take time (possibly even a lifetime spent together) for these two moon-driven people to totally let down their guards (especially emotionally). Certainly the time two Cancers spend together will definitely change their lives — or make or break them. Whether this is a short or long relationship, if it doesn't kill them, it will certainly make them stronger, as the saying goes!

Growing close to each other may take time, but it should prove well worth the time investment. Even after the first date, they shouldn't worry even if it is hard to totally win each other's trust. For if romantic magic casts its spell over them, it's very powerful magic indeed, because these people are ruled by their feelings. Cancer will love, honour and adore with a great depth of feeling, even if they don't hand over the keys to their heart on their first date. So don't be in a hurry for the true depths and breadth of this relationship to be established. Cancers are tough people to deal with when it comes to emotions and feelings. They require nurturing, gentleness and tenderness like a delicate flower, especially when it comes to matters of the heart.

Now Cancer gals will need to be very gentle with their Cancer guy, even if he is the macho man of his crowd. He doesn't give his heart enthusiastically because some Cancer men are never quite able to trust enough in their partner's ability 'not to hurt them' to ever be comfortable opening up completely. The one woman he has probably trusted in his life is his mother. So by finding out how he relates to her — if he loves his mum and thinks she's a great gal — then his partner will fare much better than they would with any Cancer guy who has a chip on his shoulder about his childhood and his mother. In fact, the 'I don't like my mother' Cancer male can be quite a meanie.

Before any Cancer guy tries to fathom the mystery of his Cancer gal, he should find out whatever he can, about how she rates her daddy. If she rates her dad top of the 'daddy' pops in any relationship with guys she will handle the exchanges far better than if she thinks her father was a disaster dad. If she unhappily considers her dad as no hero but more a zero, then she'll probably spend most of her time subliminally punishing all the men around her, especially for the wrongs she feels her daddy bestowed upon her. That, unfortunately, could turn her partner's life into a minefield of volatile emotions, so watch out. This gal is capable of being a formidable punisher, particularly on emotional levels. Let's hope she likes men; if she doesn't, hell hath no fury like a Cancer woman scorned.

While a Cancer gal often exudes with femininity (look at Cancer Pamela Anderson Lee as an example of exuding ultra-femininity), when assessing any Cancer man's strengths and weaknesses, don't be fooled by his appearance, attitudes or self-assured presence. He can be the mystery man of the zodiac. This Moon-ruled guy is a terrific actor (just look at fellow Cancers Tom Hanks and Tom Cruise). No matter if he's the managing director of a huge company, a truck driver, a professional wrestler or an iron-man footballer (and many top sportsmen are born under this sign) and everybody's best friend; that may not provide even a chink of a glimpse into who he truly is. Sure, any true Cancer guy has many of the same soft spots as the Cancer gal. He may even be capable of shedding a tear (and hiding it very effectively), loves having a foot or head rub, and has a tendency to indulge in comfort foods, but he's also a lot tougher when he needs to be.

Being male, he has likely developed more defensive mechanisms from an early age (to cover his vulnerability). For example, he may have built more of a crab shell around himself, providing him with a private world into which to withdraw. He can also yank up his emotional drawbridge if he wants people out of his life, with a skill that can be scary to observe.

Even if he is a toughie at times, whether he's a teenager, a young adult, or in his nineties, a Cancer man remains a big baby in many ways. And that one characteristic can be his most endearing quality or his most annoying one (depending on the time and the place). He's quite an organiser too, and he may love to organise his partner (something that they may not like or enjoy at all). He can be a bit bossy if he thinks something has room for improvement, particularly anything to do with his partner, home or family. He's touchy about all kinds of things too, particularly his weight, height and appearance. He isn't necessarily the most easy-going guy on the planet so it will be easy for his partner to upset him over nothing. And talking about upsetting him, here is a RELATIONSHIP MONEY ALERT: one of the things that can come between him and his partner is his money. In fact, money is sometimes his greatest 'love' of all.

A Cancer woman with a Cancer man are both constantly dealing with a whirlwind of emotions — his and hers. The fact that the Moon rules both of them ensures they will experience ongoing highs and lows. At least this combination of star signs indicates the exchange between these two is never destined to be dull or commonplace. There'll be times when they may wish their time together would settle into a safe, secure routine, but because the changing moods of the Cancer sign are so prevalent for both of them, changing energy flows and stormy emotions usually erupt sooner or later. So this will be a relationship adventure. There'll be an abundance of dramatics and sometimes even neurotic exchanges taking place between this couple. It will certainly be a bumpy, yet enjoyable ride, but how often do you have an opportunity to fly over the Moon holding hands with the one you love. Enjoy the ride!

CANCER—LEO relationship

The *'You say* tomarto, *I say* tomato' relationship

STAR CANCER–LEO COUPLE
Jerry Hall and Mick Jagger

This Cancer with a Leo romantic combination often creates a romance that starts off bigger then Ben Hur and sometimes grows from strength to strength. But, other times it ends up falling flatter than a pancake. Whichever way their relationship shapes up, before too long what's happening between them is established as either serious or nothing at all. As these two star signs don't mess about, their romance is either on or off — there's no maybes happening here. There appears to be no middle ground for romantic negotiation or flexibility between them either, so if they don't get along too well once they are married, they will soon get divorced. Staying in the relationship for the sake of keeping up appearances usually doesn't cut it for either of them.

Why are they so black and white and immovable about making this relationship an all-or-nothing affair? Well, Cancer is a water sign and Leo is a fire sign, so they both view life through different eyes. Both are also quite possessive and proud about their relationships, so if the other person can't live up to their high expectations, they soon get the message that they 'just aren't good enough'.

Extremes are always in force between them, and these extremes can be relationship adrenaline or relationship poison. Let's face it! The Cancer and Leo relationship is two extremes of astro-energy meeting each other. If they hit it off they'll be a wildly exciting couple with an explosive energy flowing between them; if they don't, they'll blast each other into fragments of broken-hearted pieces.

Cancer woman — Leo man

 The *'Tell me a fairy tale'* relationship

When the Cancer woman and the Leo man get together the Cancer gal sometimes resembles Little Red Riding Hood carrying her overflowing emotions in her love-basket. Naturally, if the Big Bad Wolf she runs into is Mr Leo Lion, he can certainly gobble this gal right up. Although their signs are slap bang next to each other on the zodiac wheel, they are both ruled by such profoundly different zodiac luminaries (she the Moon, he the Sun). So there are all kinds of indications that this couple is certain to be something of an odd couple (though perhaps this couple isn't really that odd after all). Sure she's Little Miss Crab and he's the Big Proud Lion — a funny combination and a funny picture to imagine in your head of the two of them walking around arm in arm, isn't it? Somehow their 'together' image doesn't seem to match visually, but of course, naturally that's not always true.

There are many queenly Crabs around, many of whom are very appropriately suited to the proud Lion's taste in the opposite sex. And there are more than a few Lions that probably don't exactly roar all the time either, some of them are more gentle, more cuddly and less threatening than that. Anyway, whether he's a lion or a cuddly pussy cat Ms Cancer can still wrap him around her feminine fingers if that's on her seduction agenda. She's got Moon Magic working on her side and it can trap even Mr Wiley Lion in its spell.

Without doubt, many a Cancer gal can be quite beauteous in her appearance, presence and feminine wiles. When she flutters her long eyelashes, many a Leo man forgets all about his role as the Fire God who wants to rule the world and have women aplenty. In fact, he can become a one-starwoman man, who feels the happiest he's ever been snuggling up with his loved one — and that's when he turns from the predatory Lion into a purring home-loving 'puddy' cat. Now the big question is: how long does this 'snuggle-up-and-be-nice-to-her' phase last for him? The answer is that only time will tell? Much depends on the way the Cancer woman plays the game of love, and how efficiently she keeps Mr Leo's wayward, masculine heart, dangling from her heartstrings.

If she's clingy, overly emotional and reveals any sign of weakness to him, he's going to pounce on what he considers to be shortcomings, turn tail and change in his attitude to her sooner or later. That's when he can transpose from the Mr happy-and-content pussy cat who loves being at home every night, into Mr out-all-night-and-missing-from-home-constantly Lion. The male Lion doesn't have much tolerance for too much overly emotional debate. While he may find it charming at first, he tires quickly of hearing the question repeated time and again: *'Do you love me? Do you love me? Do you love me?'* After all, he's the guy of the zodiac who was born with the biggest ego. He loves praise and wants his ego stroked, constantly. So fulfilling someone else's desires to be reassured — or told how beautiful they look — doesn't appeal to him for long.

He's also a natural heartbreaker, and if there's one thing Ms Cancer can't handle too well is anything that may play havoc with her delicate heart. Where he can fall in and out of love simply by catching the sniff of a new damsel's exotic perfume, then walk out the door from his old love and never look back; the same doesn't apply to little Ms Cancer. She's still probably angsting about the guy who never called her again in her teenage years, and pondering where she messed up and wondering how he could ever treat her that way. Now having said that, Mr Lion can move onto new love in an instant, but that's only when there's something wrong with his existing relationship. If all is hunky dory, he isn't going to stray, but keeping Mr Lion happy is no easy task, and Ms Cancer may not be up to it. She's a Moon Maiden through and through; she's inconsistent because she goes through the phases of the Moon in her outlook, mood and energy levels. She also lives in her fantasies and romantic fantasies are some of her favourites. So while Mr Leo can and will probably fulfil many of her fantasies, as much as he'll test her romantic metal, she'll test his too. His biggest test will be living up to her fantasies in reality.

Ms Cancer is one of the zodiac's most dedicated romantics, so she won't accept anything else but the real romantic package for too long. She may not exactly nag him if he isn't living up to her romantic expectations, but there'll be something (an undertone of resentment) in her tone of voice that grates through if Mr Leo doesn't fit his Prince Charming role to suit her desires. He often fails her, however, because he does grow weary of having to constantly conjure up a glass slipper every midnight; and she delights in letting him know when he has slipped up in producing, or fulfilling her romantic fantasy as well.

Now personalities aside, this is one romance that can go bust, or rise and shine in the bedroom. This combination of Ms Cancer and Mr Leo is likely to explode or erupt into arguments of passion in the bedroom. If he can light her sexual fire (and keep it alight), then she'll probably overlook even his greatest romantic insults, shortfalls or bad behaviour. However, their love life will mirror their changing moods too. Consequently you'll find them either unable to get enough of each other sexually, or avoiding each other like the plague and being quite celibate. As they are both demanding, self-absorbed individuals, they'll also need time to themselves. Therefore, they'll spend lots of their time making amends and making up after an explosive scene or argument has erupted between them. They are a volatile couple, destined to go through relationship cycles where they cool down or heat up.

Their biggest issue will be working out the best way to express their changing relationship barometer of emotions, needs or desires and stop themselves from being too reactive. If, after a tiff, they can kiss and cuddle their way back into loving each other again, then the bedroom will become the place where they unleash many of their pent-up emotions in passion. Often the Cancer–Leo relationship that lasts the distance is the one where the couple's passion ignites in the bedroom, overcomes all other considerations, and never fails to leave them all lovey-dovey again. But if they can't manage to keep things hot in the cot, then this relationship eventually fizzles out.

Cancer man — Leo woman

 The *'high love stakes'* relationship

If Mr Cancer plays his cosmic cards correctly and doesn't show any signs of real weakness, occasionally, but only occasionally (and if the Moon is in its correct phase), he can wrap the Leo lady up in a gift package and present it to himself.

Not many men can claim taming Ms Lioness as a romantic accomplishment. How can he do what many other men of the zodiac have tried so hard to accomplish? Simple, because he's different from them — very different — and other men of the zodiac don't have his ability to change the tides in their inner ocean of emotion in a second. But to rule over Ms Leo in the love stakes, he needs to keep his cool and not lose his head, even if under the pressure of a passionate relationship.

What's Mr Cancer's secret weapon? It's his ability to be so self absorbed by, and into, his own feelings and being so totally ignorant about what's happening in the Leo gal's life. Mr Cancer can be a man who feels everything when it pertains to what's important to him, but senses little when it comes to what other people expect. Another thing in Mr Cancer's favour in the balance-of-power energies between them, is that while his Leo woman likes to have all the pieces of her life humming along happily under her steady control, he's the one man of the zodiac who can turn the happy hum of her life into a more grating buzz-saw sound. The man of the Moon, Mr Cancer can be the individual that she will probably never totally manage to coerce, organise, manipulate or control, and that's possibly why she often feels out of her depth when she's fallen for him. Without effort, if he holds an upper hand, he keeps her on an emotional edge (whether or not she's sure if she's in his heart or out of it) and he does this naturally. Once he gets the hang of it he loves doing it too.

So where putting up emotional walls to other women of the zodiac might work against him, usually Mr Cancer finds that his natural moody, changeable tendency makes him tough to decode and extremely hard to fathom. And this often works for, not against him with the Leo lady (at least temporarily). He can be the man of her dreams and nightmares all rolled into one. The greatest power he has over her is his ability to pull the cosmic wool over her eyes time and again, and catch her out or leave her startled when he does the exact opposite to what she expected him to do. Now that doesn't mean he leads her on a merry chase (often she's the one leading him on the chase, or at least she thinks she is). However, he does seem to be able to keep her guessing on one level or another. He opens his heart and closes it to her, like a revolving door that spins around busily in a New York office block. She seldom knows whether she's totally in or out — and she is probably a little of both.

He is devoted, dependable and, at the same time, distracted — and if Ms Leo loves one thing from her man, it's his attention. Unfortunately, Mr Cancer is often so attentive towards or about his own moods, feelings or desires, he puts her (subliminally) second to his own needs. When Ms Leo feels (or imagines) that she isn't getting enough of any man's attention, that can encourage her to unsheathe her Lioness's claws and become quite a formidable opponent or romantic competitor. Her pride is one of the strongest driving forces in her life, and romantic rejection can weigh heavily on her ego — so much so that she can turn into a neurotic man-chaser. In fact, many men claim that the best way to win a Leo lady's heart is to ignore her and then she's certain to be theirs.

Now not all Leo gals are so easy to overwhelm with male Cancer energy, and some Leo gals certainly do run rings around their Cancer partners. But when relationship push comes to shove, it is often the Leo gal who's doing the work and the Cancer man who's cruising along (most of the time anyway).

CANCER—VIRGO relationship

The *'Don't get cute with anyone else but me'* relationship

STAR CANCER–VIRGO COUPLE
Bryan Brown and Rachel Ward

Here we sometimes have the match of the perfect couple. There's some kind of cuteness about them and they seem to really gravitate naturally towards each other. Even if the passion isn't the real strength of their romantic attachments (but it often is), then Ms Cancer and Mr Virgo are destined to have many wonderful conversations together.

They can argue, agree, and then disagree again in a matter of moments. They also laugh a lot, usually at different things, and yet, still nobody takes himself or herself more seriously than they do! They enjoy fussing over each other, shopping for books, shoes and food but most of all, they enjoy having something to worry about. If they don't have something to worry about between them, they'll invent a first-class worry to dwell on — just for kicks.

Cancer woman—Virgo man

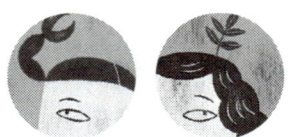

 The *'Can I offer you me?'* relationship

She's his cool drink of water; he's the strong tree under which to shelter when she needs to. Cancer is a water sign and Virgo is an earth sign, so this relationship merges the ocean of emotions with the more stable and solid ground-bound energy flows. Certainly the right Mr Virgo often provides a solid anchor for the Cancer gal, who needs a strong shoulder to lean on, a best friend and a loving partner all rolled up into one guy of the zodiac. But that's only if there's relationship magic in the air; if there isn't, these two can bore each other almost to death in the longer term.

Ruled by the Moon, there's not too much that is earth bound or ground bound about Ms Cancer. That's why Mr Virgo often suits her to a 'T' and why she appeals to his sense of values. Ms Cancer is first and foremost a feeler, and then if all else fails, she's a thinker; whereas Mr Virgo is a thinker first, and then if he still can't figure something out, as a last resort he's a feeler.

Now Ms Cancer is a mystery to Mr Virgo because she trusts her instincts and goes for it. Her instincts or intuition cuts a straight pathway through logical thinking. Mr Virgo admires her ability to cut to the chase. She thinks he's clever and likes the method to his madness. That's why if they gel together well, this couple can make a pretty great duo. So there's little wonder (when you know their differences) that this couple frequently find each other fascinating, devastatingly attractive and charmingly different. Many times this sense of wonder about their different energy flows or handling life's issues spills over to the more erotic sex zones too. In the love-making department, Ms Cancer and Mr Virgo can be highly passionate (and even inspired sexually) in very different ways from each other. If their physical chemistry is powerful they often become inventive sexual partners, which can provide a great relationship bonus to both of them, and something which helps to keep their relationship re-inventing itself on many different levels. However, if the sexual chemistry is low between them, the Ms Cancer–Mr Virgo relationship often develops into a good friendship instead of a lifetime romance.

Sex, unfortunately, won't be enough to save them from relationship disaster. Whether they are hot in the cot together or not, sizzling, sexual chemistry isn't enough to secure their relationship in the long term, but they'll sure have lots of fun in the sack while they are finding this fact out. When it gets down to the real core foundation of the Cancer gal with a Virgo guy relationship, they both need to have powerful mental links if this relationship is going to last. What happens between their ears can make their relationship fantastic or dismal; and their mind dances and psychic exchanges with each other are where they really have a true meeting of their minds. If this mind-match occurs this can be the most profound relationship exchange of all.

When a Cancer gal and a Virgo guy are in a relationship, sometimes the best parts of the exchange between them are likely to happen on the unspoken levels of operation. If science had created a machine that measured unspoken words it would run overtime when these two are thinking about what they think of each other, or what they would love to say to each other. When you're in their company, you may even feel as though you can hear a hint of a buzz in the air around them. Both Cancer and Virgo are highly tuned individuals. They pick up on all kinds of things subconsciously (they both operate somewhat like subliminal psychic radars), and this can make their relationship even a little scary, 'cos they know things about each other without knowing why exactly they 'know' them. They can read each other's thoughts and tune into things about each other and the world at large that other signs miss altogether.

Although this couple's relationship may appear straightforward, simple and easy-going on the exterior, underneath, it's likely to be more complex, multi-dimensional and quirky than what others guess. Because of their often psychic connection, the couple themselves often don't realise the depth of the process of exchange that takes place every time they walk together, talk together or think of each other. The Cancer gal and the Virgo guy are pretty close to cosmic-kindred spirits, especially if they can both laugh at themselves now and again. One of the biggest tests they will face is not to take themselves, life or each other too seriously.

Cancer man — Virgo woman

 The *'Please don't hurt me'* relationship

Tread warily and be gentle with each other because (uh-oh) Ms Virgo is one of the most fragile starwomen of the zodiac, and Mr Cancer is a big softy underneath his macho exterior. This relationship has two fragile hearts trying to survive the rigours of everyday relationship stress. And if these two don't take special, loving care of each other (something they often manage to do), the demands of work, family, finances etc can sometimes turn this relationship into a stressfest rather than romantic bliss.

So gently does it! This couple needs to be extremely sensitive, nurturing and caring towards each other if they want to keep this relationship buzzing along merrily and joyfully. Their motto needs to be: to have lots of fun together, otherwise their fragile relationship can shatter their delicate hearts into fragments of painful memories.

Both Ms Virgo and Mr Cancer are quite passive signs (neither has a natural tendency to race out and 'cut the rug' or party on). However, ensuring that they continue to have fun together (after they navigate their way through their initial romantic highs) can take special effort. That's because Mr Cancer and Ms Virgo tend to take themselves, their relationship and life in general, *too* seriously. Worry, stress and mental tension quickly takes those intoxicating buzzy love-tingles they were feeling when they were initially around each other, away from their passionate romance very quickly.

It's well worth Ms Virgo and Mr Cancer investing some time and effort into turning their problems into opportunities rather than arguments. If they work at it, this couple can be really good marriage material! After all, he's a Cancer (the astrological ideal father), and she's a Virgo (the astrological ideal home-maker). In astro-terms they have the components that add up to making them the perfect couple. Indeed, many Cancer men and Virgo women are as close to the perfect couple as you can get. Unfortunately, just because they have astro-positives holds no guarantees! Some Virgo woman–Cancer man couplings make it, and do have a 'happy-ever-after' romance, but unfortunately others hit the romantic wall very quickly. Why is it that this ideally matched relationship sometimes goes wrong? As Ms Virgo and Mr Cancer tend to go through the same kinds of lows, if they hit a low at the same time their relationship is thrust into a very, very low phase. When a Virgo gal and a Cancer guy feel negative about life, each other or anything else that's going on around them, Sad Sack has nothing to compare with how low these two can go should they get a dose of the blues together.

Even if you believe you know this couple very well, don't be too quick to judge what's happening between them. There are times when it isn't wise to be fooled by both these individuals' outwardly cool, calm and collected auras. The relationship between the Moon Man and the Earth Goddess takes many forms. It is passionate, romantic, endearing and surprisingly often a very feisty one. As they are combined feelers and thinkers, their relationship has hidden chinks, lots of dramas, and plenty of hidden and sometimes most apparent emotional baggage. However, having said all that, there are lots of very happily married Cancer men with Virgo wives. If they enjoy and applaud each other's eccentricities and complexities and don't drive themselves nuts trying to figure each other out, this relationship could turn out to be a match made in heaven.

This couple will have to learn to go with the flow and not be too nitpicky, otherwise they'll end up hitting a brick wall somewhere along the relationship lane of life, and both end up emotionally or psychologically scarred for a long time ahead. When instead, with a little forgiveness, compassion and respect for each other, they would have been flying off for a romantic time hanging out happily on cloud nine. 'Let's make love, not war' should be their motto, and when it is, relationship miracles happen.

CANCER—LIBRA relationship

The *'What a romantic fool I am'* relationship

STAR CANCER–LIBRA COUPLE
Richie Sambora and Heather Locklear

Hubble, bubble, toils and possibly plenty of romantic relationship trouble ahead. Somehow Cancer and Libra seem to have totally different morals, rules and regulations when it comes to romance. Sure they can fancy each other — and lust madly, truly and deeply over each other's every move — but they usually end up messing up somewhere along the road to romantic bliss and someone gets detoured off in another direction.

Certainly they are not going to have a smooth-running romance unless they both have heaps of patience and perseverance with each other. In fact, they often have highly volatile, temperamental-type relationships, not patient and persevering ones. If they are a public kind of couple, you'll probably read about their relationship highs and lows in the tabloids; sometimes they are discreet enough for you to not hear about them. However, if they aim for the longer term, many times this relationship ends up in trouble, especially romantically. This couple tends to lack relationship cohesion. Their diverse outlooks often lead them into love, hate, passion, disinterest, broken hearts, law courts, second times around or even emotional bankruptcy.

Linking up Cancers with Librans is like stirring up an astrological hornet's nest. Though sometimes a good hornet's nest can be a sexual experience for some; and occasionally a bit of a stir up can be just what these two passive signs need, to get them cranking. That's why just as often as they can upset each other, they can also inspire each other to be better than they ever would be without each other, or if they were romantically involved with anyone else.

Cancer woman—Libra man

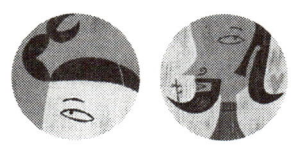

The *'Where were you last night when you should have been home with me?'* relationship

No wonder when Mr Libra meets her he often falls in love with this Moon maiden gal of the zodiac. After all, the Cancer woman is a shaft of moonlight, captured in living flesh. She's the Moon goddess of the zodiac; she's ethereal, imaginative and very unpredictable. She's also the most emotionally charged up and needy gal of the zodiac. The Libra man is cute and very appealing to her maternal instincts too, but before she leaps into his most sexy arms she wants to do a quick astrological check on his cosmic genetics. Maybe they don't match up with hers. After all he's the zodiac man who is often emotionally immature, while she's someone who craves emotional closeness. She also wants a man with a plan, while he's constantly caught up in an inner dilemma about which step to take next.

On many levels of existence, Mr Libra (as gorgeous and appealing as he is) goes through many stops and starts. He loves an easy-going life and he hates to be under pressure, as he's under enough pressure from himself as it is. Consequently when it comes to love, romance, relationships and emotions, he can run for cover if the pressure of his feelings overwhelms him.

So as the Cancer gal loves to plunge heart first into the emotional heady stuff that relationships produce, Mr Libra will go through fire amd brimstone to carefully detour around emotional matters. And who could blame him? He's wise enough to know he doesn't handle complications too well, and there are certain challenges that emotional commitments make on him that he isn't comfortable fulfilling. Now having said all that, *well*, what does this mean? It means, *'Hello, is anyone home in this relationship?'* The answer to that question is: yes. If somebody's home, it is Ms Cancer, and maybe she's sitting up waiting for Mr Libra who should have been home hours ago.

Certainly there's a few hassles ahead for this couple. It isn't hard to find out why either, if you look to the practice of astrology for answers. Ms Cancer needs commitment, support and endurance. And what does Mr Libra usually lack the most in terms of his natural attributes or tendencies — commitment, a supportive personality and endurance. Although these two may fair well in the short-term romantic stakes, when it comes to the long-term pressure of maintaining a relationship, too often Mr Libra flies the coop or somehow breaks the rules that Ms Cancer has set him. He doesn't take her relationship expectations or demands well. Usually — though he may not react when she sets them out to him — he will let her know very quickly that he isn't going to play the relationship game by her rules, even if he does pass this message back to her in a very roundabout, evasive fashion.

Though this couple's perfect meeting place can be found with some hard work and true love, it tends to exist in 'the middle of nowhere'. It has to be found in their deepest heart areas where time, space and reality don't count. To reach this place of ultimate trust and commitment demands that they both step over the edge of their relationship fears and enter into unknown territory. So the big test is, can they both take the pressures that this relationship will eventually create? The answer, probably not in the long term; 'cos Ms Cancer or Mr Libra will both go to great lengths to avoid taking emotional or lifestyle chances. Rest assured if you meet a content Cancer gal and Libra guy who are together, it is probably some other part of their horoscopes that's allowing them to be that way. Good luck!

Cancer man — Libra woman

 The *'You certainly are very confusing to be around'* relationship

Though he may have many factors operating in his favour, when it comes to romance and relationships in general, Mr Cancer is often not an easy guy to please. He is usually fixed in his tastes, desires and demands regarding life in general at an early age and he can be tough to change. His expectations, especially regarding relationships, women, romance and commitment, are especially high, often rather unrealistic and unreasonable. Therefore it's no wonder, that very few gals ever quite manage to measure up to his mother.

Often it is his mother who covets the key to his heart. She's his number one gal, but fate usually ensures that his mother meets her 'control Waterloo' eventually. If perhaps, like a sweet summer breeze of femininity, the right Ms Libra happens to be the one that fate tantalisingly sends to cross Mr Cancer's path (and steal the key to his heart away from his mother), this zodiac gal will not pass by unnoticed. She's an expert (subliminally of course) at leaving a waft of seductive perfume lingering behind her. This Venus-ruled gal of the zodiac without even realising her own subliminal powers, knows how to cast a romantic spell around her; and should she decide to cast one in Mr Cancer's direction he's going to be a romantic pushover. If and when this magic exchange of romance occurs, Mr Cancer can be love struck in such a positive way that it transforms his life. Under her direction, he'll get a new haircut, smarten up his wardrobe, change his image, alter his outlook and also adopt a new religion if that's what Ms Libra wants. He'll even do the 'unthinkable' for a Cancer man — forget his mother! Although this lapse could prove more temporary than permanent!

What does Mr Cancer have to offer Ms Libra? Plenty, though possibly what he offers isn't so apparent on everyday levels, but she'll probably be savvy enough to recognise his values. He's highly sentimental and he'll warm her heart with his affectionate displays of attention (even if he only displays this affection in private). He's moody and sometimes cranky if he doesn't get enough sleep or if he's having a bad time. However, he also has a huge conscience, and if he knows that he's been tough or difficult with her he'll move the Earth, Moon and stars to make up for it after he's fallen from grace. He's an excellent provider (and Ms Libra has expensive tastes), and he's a wonderful, dedicated husband and father.

They both love decorating, houses, gardens, making things pretty or playing host and hostess. Many a Cancer man and Libra woman's home is a show place. It will have all the trappings of elegance, comfort and serenity that make it more than a show place — it will suit their needs and fulfil their desires perfectly. They probably won't wait too long either to hear the patter of little feet. They both love the idea and concept of 'family', although there may be times in the future when they question if they raced into having a family a little too quickly. Possibly they should have allowed their own relationship more time to unfold, like the wonderful flower it has the potential to be.

So what can go wrong with this magical match? Plenty. Ms Libra may be too fussy for him, too flirtatious around other men, or too much bother. Or, she may spend his money too comfortably in which case he could quickly build up resentments towards her. Mr Cancer truly loves his money, and though he can be generous he hates to see his hard-work savings being squandered. Or, he may be too complacent, passive and disinterested in her desires, plans or projects to keep her interest. And she may flirt, dilly-dally with others out of boredom or sometimes even out of spite; or he may do the same to stir her up.

While there are great opportunities for romantic Venus, the love planet, to make a magical match with Mr Cancer and Ms Libra, only time will tell if the magic that's cast between them holds strong, or is broken by the grinding harsh tests of time.

CANCER — SCORPIO relationship

The *'You're perfect ... but I want to put you through some more tests'* relationship

STAR CANCER–SCORPIO COUPLE
Camilla Parker-Bowles and Prince Charles

This is probably one of the more 'royal' zodiac romantic relationships. Love often blossoms and survives when these two find their hearts colliding in the love realms. On all kinds of levels, this romantic relationship is truly written in the stars. If the astrologer gypsy gazes into her crystal ball and sees a Cancer and Scorpio figuring there, she instantly knows that she's looking at a love match. But if you know even a little about the stars, you don't need to be a crystal-ball gazer to see that Cancer and Scorpio are wired astrologically on most levels.

Even if these signs don't figure in a romantic relationship, some of the best friendships, business associations or work associations occur between these two signs. But when romance is their magical link, then a Cancer and a Scorpio have exactly what it takes to build their own 'Stairway to Heaven'.

Cancer woman — Scorpio man

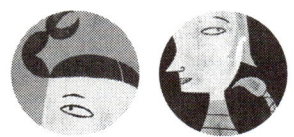

The *'You better be nice to me, or else!'* relationship

Ms Cancer is a water-sign Princess; Mr Scorpio is a water-sign Prince. So naturally when these two meet and fall in love, this truly is an accurate translation of a 'match made in heaven', because *it is indeed* a match made in heaven. The bonding rites of the true Cancer gal with her Scorpio guy counterpart is similar to an astrological royal wedding taking place. It's quite a zodiac occasion! Having said that, it is quite ironic that Princess Diana was a Cancer and Prince Charles is a Scorpio, and their royal wedding didn't exactly turn out to be a 'happy-ever-after event'. So not all Cancer gals with Scorpio guys find their true love blossoms to fullness; sometimes the love flower withers on the vine before it gets a chance to reveal its true beauty. However, it is also interesting to note that Camilla Parker-Bowles (Prince Charles' supposed soul mate) is also a Cancer, so there's plenty of astro-royal magic still in force, even though the partners have changed.

When it comes to Ms Cancer and Mr Scorpio finding each other, on many occasions this couple meet in a unique, memorable and fateful way. Right through their time together they are also likely to have many strange fateful stories to tell about their experiences together. They are likely to meet by the sea, by a swimming pool or on a luxury liner; or even at a bar or party close to the kitchen or bar. But it's mostly that the effect they immediately have on each other will be powerful, and by meeting their lives will be radically transformed.

As so many strong forces are in flow between these two, they may feel so overwhelmed at first meeting that they suddenly find themselves tongue-tied or becoming clumsy, or acting out of character in some form or fashion. They may not make contact at first meeting, just glimpse each other from afar. Nevertheless, even a glance in each other's direction will make such a powerful impact that they will never forget their first meeting experience. They will also be very sentimental about their romantic journey. They'll collect memorabilia, and years after an event took place that was especially dear to them, they'll be able to recollect it in perfect detail as if it had occurred just yesterday.

This cosmic pair will undoubtedly have their arguments, possibly some powerful screaming matches where they both sulk for days after the event. They'll have their upsets and often hurt each other's feelings because they are born under the sign of water; and the changeable ocean forces run their emotions, ensuring they'll have their high tide of emotional times and their smooth-flowing emotional times as well. Jealousy and possessiveness may plague them, or there may be power struggles to deal with, but if the magical forces that bind them are strong, nothing will rock their relationship boat long enough to upset it sufficiently to tear them apart.

Being water signs both individuals are emotionally highly strung, although this vulnerability in their emotional status will be much more apparent from the behaviour of Ms Cancer than it will be with her Scorpio mate. After all, Mr Scorpio is a master of the art of secrecy and he has spent a lifetime hiding his feelings from public view. Though if anyone has the power to bring out his tender side, it will be the Cancer gal. She seems to know exactly what to say, what move to make, and what information to share, to keep him perpetually fascinated by her. In many ways she is a gentler, female counterpart of himself, and when he spends time with her he has the unique opportunity of enjoying his own company much more than usual, because he's so comfortable and well-suited to her.

Cancer man—Scorpio woman

 The *'Don't mess this thing up'* relationship

Ms Scorpio is probably wearing sunglasses when she meets her Cancer man, shielding her sensitive eyes from the sun's glare or using them to deflect the dingy glow from the nightclub scene. Night and day she often likes to keep her eyes hidden from public view (after all, they are the windows of her brilliant and secretive soul), and there are many Scorpio gals who will go to great lengths to keep their feelings secret from others.

She has an incredible knack of seeming to appear out of nowhere and Mr Cancer is likely to be immediately fascinated and surprised by her. He probably feels intense feelings erupting within him, but his initial feelings may concern him rather than make him feel thrilled. This is because the feelings that Ms Scorpio evokes in him are likely to be amazingly different from anything he's experienced before. If the chemistry is intense between these two, the world may even seem to stop turning for an instant at their first meeting. And possibly, there will be instant sexual electricity in the air too, where a brush of an arm against each other sets unseen sexual sparks shooting off everywhere.

Why does Mr Cancer often feel the full effect of Ms Scorpio's seductive and feminine aura when some other men are oblivious to it? He experiences her 'vibe' because he's one of the few men of the zodiac who attunes to her without any effort. He's got this ability because he has similar astro-genetics to those she has (they are both water signs), and this connection wires them up to the same cosmic spark plugs. If the spark plug chemistry ignites between them, this is likely to turn out to be a highly passionate, tempestuous, feisty, and sometimes uncontrollable and obsessive relationship. Or, it may be one that burns super bright then quickly fades. Or it could turn into a power struggle that puts them both through hell. Or it may even be a 'happy-ever-after' matching. One thing is certain, if there's any powerful reactions between them, before their relationship is over both of them are going to have been through a great deal — for better and worse results.

So like Abracadabra! There's powerful magic happening when the Cancer man's journey through life leads him into a Scorpio woman's loving arms. He's likely to lose his heart and soul in a moment and feel lost and out of his depth (and sometimes totally under her control) from the first seductive flick of her gorgeous eyelashes. Once he enters into her magical sphere of influence, wham! His world shifts orbit; and while this relationship is certain to be a life-changing experience for both parties, it will be especially life transforming for the Cancer man.

If the chemistry is strong (and it often is between this duo), from the 'get-go' this is going to be an intense relationship ride and he'll need to learn to hold on tight to his sanity, 'cos there'll be times he may imagine he's 'losing' it — over her. If she wins his heart — and he's one of the most emotional guys of the zodiac, so his heart overrules all logic and common sense — before long, Ms Scorpio is likely to be organising his life, reprogramming his schedule, and opening up his mind, imagination and plans to a whole new way of living, loving, thinking, dressing, working and socialising. She doesn't stop when it comes to transforming her man; in fact she thrives on it. She's the gal who will take him shopping for clothes (and he probably needs to go shopping too), will redecorate his apartment and tell him nicely that it is time he got that cosmetic dentistry job done.

After all, this water maiden Scorpio is not just *one* of the most powerful gals of the zodiac — *she is the most powerful gal in the zodiac*. Although she usually wields her enormous powers of persuasion in a hidden fashion, it is wise not to underestimate her on any level. She may be very cute, very innocent and very vulnerable, but she's also fiercely strong and undefeatable if she wants something or has her sights set on accomplishing a mission. If mating up with a Cancer man becomes her mission to accomplish, if he isn't ready to mate with her, he had better leave town in a hurry, leaving no forwarding address — and even then she may track him down.

CANCER—SAGITTARIUS relationship

The *'Sit down, you're rocking the (relationship) boat'* relationship

STAR CANCER–SAGITTARIUS COUPLE
Tom Hanks and Rita Wilson

It's not easy for the Cancer and the Sagittarian to see eye to eye about most things, except for the magical matter being discussed in this book — love. Surprisingly these two very different individuals can actually find each other extremely attractive and experience a very powerful, true love connection. However, it could be tougher on both of them to survive the different viewpoint sthey have about life than they probably guess or expect. When the sizzling intoxication of new love is running through their passionate veins they often overlook just how wide the gap is between them in their everyday outlooks. Adjusting to each other's views, desires and lifestyles may prove tough especially on the Cancer.

When Cancer teams up with Sagittarius in a romantic relationship, they'll need a gigantic sense of humour and heaps of forgiveness and patience for the relationship to go the distance. After all, Cancer is the most sensitive sign of the zodiac, and Sagittarius the most insensitive. So between the two of them they are likely to have moments in their relationship of total disenchantment and experience some amazing mental and emotional ping-pong matches. Now here's the biggest issue. The Cancer's personality is composed of a strange mix of independence and dependence; they change their minds about how they feel as often as some people change their shoes. They also usually need loads of reassurance and Sagittarians hate to be kept dangling; to be fenced in; and they don't like to be badgered by someone who requires lots of attention — all things that they need to face, being with a Cancer. However, as opposites do attract and because life is all about evolving, learning and expanding, these two signs are often intensely attracted and long-lastingly attached to each other. With a little TLC and lots of kissing and making up, they often end up spending a wonderful (sometimes even hilarious) lifetime together, but not always!

Cancer woman — Sagittarius man

 The *'This could easily turn into a love-hate affair'* relationship

Mr Sagittarius is a bit of a 'Jack-the-lad', light-hearted, spring-footed type of guy. Ms Cancer is subliminally a nurturing, serious-minded zodiac gal, so often this guy's boyishness and fun-filled nature appeals enormously to her nurturing, more serious nature. The same (once) endearing quality about him, can also one day become the very thing that 'turns her off'.

Naturally to his credit, Mr Sag has a lot more going for him than his 'boyishness' because he can be ultra sexy as well, and his sex appeal helps Ms Cancer look twice in his direction. He's a man of fire too (Sagittarius is a fire sign), so he has a natural enthusiasm for life, an extremely positive attitude and he considers himself to be a winner. If he does get 'down' in mood about something, whatever's happening generally doesn't manage to keep him down for long.

Ms Cancer on the other hand tends to view life with some fear, angst and general trepidation. She worries about the state of the world, the ever-increasing threat of terrorists, the unpredictable financial downturns, and the possibility that it might rain on Sunday. When she shares her many assorted fears with Mr Sag, he just laughs, turns the next page of the newspaper and says, *'Don't worry honey bunny, it'll all turn out fine. Always has, always will!'* Amazingly he is usually right, too.

It's Mr Sag's free-spirited approach to life that works all kinds of magic. Somehow his confidence about the future helps her feel better about the world in general. So, while these two are coming from two different psychological zones, even against all logic, somehow they seem to blend. If they find each other at the right time and place in their lives, and if the romantic chemistry ignites, they may stick! Many a Cancer gal and a Sag guy enjoy the companionship of old age together — that is, after having a whirlwind romance, a family life and a work-busy career time as well (sometimes they even work together). But, not all of them!

Many of these Cancer gal and Sag guy romances do *not* end up happy ever after! If things go badly or poorly, and they fail to live up to each other's romantic expectations, then this can be a heavenly romance that suddenly falls straight to hell and explodes like an atom bomb into disintegrated, sour and bitter, unhappy memories. Certainly this is one relationship that often ends up with bad vibes, calling in the lawyers and suing each other for each and every thing. If these two go their separate ways, their parting usually doesn't conclude with a friendly 'goodbye' over a glass of nice wine.

Though if this unusual zodiac duo passes their initial cosmic tests, possibly the fact that they are coming from two such different 'places' is what works in their favour. And if they are so different in personality traits, even under mundane conditions, this difference ensures that they share lots of unique adventures together. Most times, she'll provide a wonderful home for him, be a fantastic support to him on all kinds of levels and keep him constantly evolving by what he goes through dealing with her many ups and downs. She can turn out to be his best teacher of patience (something he usually lacks). In turn, he'll teach her oodles of fascinating trends, outlooks and philosophies; provide her with a powerful love base and take her on all kinds of emotional, spiritual, sexual and travelling adventures.

Foreign places are likely to somehow come into their lives because Mr Sagittarius is the voyager, the gypsy traveller of the zodiac, and as much as Ms Cancer is reported astrologically to be a 'there's no place like home' home maker, she's quite an explorer of the globe too. Mr Sag may be content living in a tent on the shores of Hawaii going surfing every day. Ms Cancer though may complain that she would prefer something more civilised and comfortable, but she can probably even shack up in the tent if their love and passion is still pumping at full blast. And Mr Sag in a cavalier moment may even write a funny sign for the tent stating, 'Our Love Shack'!

The fact is, Ms Cancer is a lot more adaptable than she realises, and Mr Sagittarius (who is one of the most adaptable signs of the zodiac) awakens this hidden adaptability characteristic within her. Most importantly for Ms Cancer, Mr Sag encourages her to laugh (and laugher is often in short supply in her world before he makes his entrance). He also makes her feel young because of his youthful approach to life.

What does she do for him? Well if he really clicks with her, he'll totally adore her. He'll love her weird mood swings (he may even find them entertaining), he'll be touched by her tenderness, vulnerability and her inability to hide her true feelings. He will however, hate any possessive, jealous side to her character or insecurities she throws around like swords that cut him to the quick. So if she wants to keep him, she may need to learn to trust him, especially if he journeys without her for work or other reasons (something he is likely to do). But her trust in him is likely to be rewarded and he'll bounce home full of tales of his adventures (always relating the story with him in the starring role of 'hero' of course). He never leaves her out of the story, he'll tell her how he thought of her at the appropriate moment of his adventure, and tells her of his plans to take her somewhere wonderful in the not too distant future. Then he'll waltz her off to the bedroom and make up for any leave-of-absence he has had, with some gentle but passionate lovemaking, and they'll be all very lovey-dovey again in no time at all. When this occurs, they can be assured that many happy travels are ahead!

Cancer man—Sagittarius woman

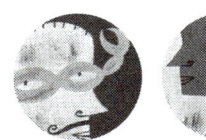

 The *'You truly are quite amazing at times!'* relationship

The Moon may not be full, the stars may not be twinkling, and there may not be a flash of cosmic lightening filling the air when Mr Cancer meets his Ms Sagittarius. Nevertheless there's likely to be a fantastic feeling of joy, hope and possibly some sense 'this could be an affair to remember' in the air. If the right Mr Cancer links up with his special Ms Sagittarius, they can both feel something like the cosmic cat that got the cream. There's almost a purr in the air between them. Jupiter, the ruling planet of Ms Sagittarius, has a special connection towards the sign of Cancer — it likes them a lot — and this acknowledgement from above is an invisible thread that links these two together. This is because they have the blessing of the most magnanimous planet of all, Jupiter, and you can't do too much better than that if you want some support from the celestial realms.

Naturally not all Cancer men are going to connect with their right Ms Sagittarius, and sometimes this can turn out to be a battle of the sexes instead of a love match. But if they do both find the right person in each other magic happens. Often this couple has previously been primed by fate to be 'ready' for each other (and yes, fate frequently plays a role in what occurs between them). Possibly before she meets up with Mr Cancer, Ms Sag is quite jaded with romance. She may have been burned in previous relationships and left feeling as if she cannot depend on any man any more. She might be *sooo* disillusioned with men that she has started to think of most men as 'hopeless', 'desperates' or 'losers'. Or she may refuse to even give any form of acknowledgement to past liaisons by making any reference to them at all (that is, she'll erase those encounters she has had with others from her memory bank). Mr Cancer may also have been left emotionally bankrupt by past flirtatious flings and feel as if he 'has had enough of romance to last him a lifetime'. But if the cosmic chemistry ignites between these two — like a blast of renewed relationship fresh air — the past is forgotten and a new beginning is forged. They can truly light up and excite each other's lives.

Now while you may not 'get it' from looking at this couple from the outside, they actually have lots of things in common. To see them together one might wonder what on earth are those two doing together? Possibly the best times these two 'share' together take place when they are on their own, removed from the rest of the world and 'doing their own things' together. They can actually have lots of fun and laughs together. Though Mr Cancer may seem a little dull, serious or predictable to some other gals of the zodiac, Ms Sagittarius finds him appealing, cuddly, funny and vulnerable. She may also sense an innocence or gullibility about him that others can't see at all. She'll love his ability to be true and reliable and she'll laugh as he attempts to learn to Rollerblade, as she whirls past him in crazy circles on her expert Rollerblading feet. Her heart will go out to him as he kindly but rather uncomfortably attempts to help her out with the oldies when she does her community duty for 'Meals On Wheels' at the local retirement village. He's often got a heart of gold and he'll be her special Knight in Shining Armour, her helper, adviser, daddy and (yippee) also her big-boy super lover; and she'll be amazed that there are actually 'men like him on this planet'. Rightly, she'll count her blessings that she is the lucky one who found him.

In her, Mr Cancer will see a beautiful brave, bold, honest, talented, happy and most lovable gal. She's someone who has kindness written all over her, who goes out of her way to think those around her have a great time, and will go right out of her way to think of those in need. He'll love the freckles on her nose, the shine in her hair and the sparkle in her eyes. He'll adore her as the mother of his children, especially when she gets right into the kid's stuff and plays all their games with them. He'll have a real emotional 'Kodak' moment when he returns from his office to find her on the floor covered in finger paint with the children, laughing at the pictures she and the kids have produced.

So this daughter of Jupiter (Sagittarian's ruling planet), and this man of the Moon (Cancer's ruling planet), can do marvellous things together if the chemistry is right and they are prepared to open up their hearts and love each other from an unchallenging, trusting, unconditional level.

What might, could, should, maybe go wrong? Oodles, especially if trust is broken or feelings are hurt. Resentment between this duo can run riot, especially if Mr Cancer feels he's being taken for any kind of emotional, psychological or financial 'ride'. Ms Sagittarius can sometimes overstep the mark and Mr Cancer can sometimes be a cad, and they can end up totally despising each other. If they do, hell will freeze over before either of them give an inch to the other. But if these two tread warily, realise the value of what they have, and set jointly inspired goals to create a relationship of integrity between them, they have a special opportunity to transform a unique and special romantic relationship into a lifetime party.

CANCER—CAPRICORN relationship

The *'Should auld acquaintance be forgot'* relationship

STAR CANCER–CAPRICORN COUPLE
Pamela Anderson and Kid Rock

This relationship can often be one of the more solid, committed and enduring relationships of the zodiac. There's real relationship value in this romance. They can make wonderful romance, music, love and even money together if their stars are in alignment. Usually this couple makes a success of a romantic relationship if the time and place is right for both of them; this occurs as there's a powerful karmic astro-connection between them. Cancer and Capricorn are positioned on opposite sides of the zodiac wheel from each other. Consequently this relationship is made up of two opposite zodiac signs. What does this mean? Well, imagine that there's some special psychic connections in force between these two; some special kind of psychic wiring that makes them have stronger links to each other on unconscious levels than most people have with each other. One of them probably expresses the personality traits the other one represses. Together, they actually make quite a nice complete zodiac package.

Destiny probably plays a huge role in determining the outcome of their romance too. If they are meant to meet and fall in love, fate will move mountains or uproot their lives around them to ensure that they do. And if the relationship is not meant to last, no matter how much they love each other, circumstances beyond their control will dictate their relationship's ending. But whether the romantic relationship survives the test of time or fate decides its eventual downfall, if they have a true, heartfelt connection then this relationship is likely to have a powerful effect on each of their lives one way or another.

Cancer woman — Capricorn man

 The *'Love is beautiful, the second time around'* relationship

Remember the line that's so often used in movies or takes place at a bar where singles hang out; where one person strolls casually up to another and asks, *'Say, haven't I met you somewhere else before?'* As much as this approach is a well-used pick-up line, in the case of Ms Cancer meeting Mr Capricorn it mightn't be such a line at all. There are some strange attachments, vibes and even karmic forces associated with these two signs, and often their soul connections are powerful ones. Many astrologers believe that when this combination of Cancer woman and Capricorn man link romantically, it is sometimes a connection based on their past union in previous lives. That's why, sometimes, when a Cancer woman meets up with the right Capricorn man — the right one for her — she often has a quick flash of déjà vu, a feeling of excitement, trepidation, fear or relief all occurring at the same time; or a sudden surprising sense that she has 'completed' a mission or quest in some way.

If the right Ms Cancer hooks up with the right Mr Capricorn, it may indeed take place on a blind date, at a single's bar, through a website dating service, through family or friend's introducing them or through work. But if the pieces of their heart fit well together, this can be one of those rare relationship meetings that truly is written in the stars. How do these two suit each other? The ever-changing Moon rules Ms Cancer, and she needs a steadying force, a Rock of Gibraltar kind of man to keep her on an even keel. The steadiest, sturdiest and most patient and persevering planet of all, Saturn, rules Mr Capricorn and that helps him keep both his feet firmly planted on terra firma. As he's prepared to take his time with whatever he's doing and doesn't enjoy getting worked up over nothing, this makes him Mr Cool, Calm and Collected most of the time. This works wonders for Ms Cancer who loses her cool the moment her emotions become stirred. So while she may fluctuate in her feelings, moods and emotions with the regularity of the tick-tock of a clock's pendulum, he can be exactly the opposite. Sometimes one of the things that will bug her most about him ironically, is that he doesn't change enough! Perhaps this ability of his to be steadfast and unchanging is actually her blessing in disguise, although she may not view it that way!

One of the greatest bonuses Mr Capricorn can provide Ms Cancer often becomes known once their relationship has progressed into the bedroom. While she may have problems in the love-making department due to her intense feeling nature, he again can be Mr Patient and Persevering. As he's prepared to take his time and focus totally on the love-making task at hand, she often ends up a very sexually happy gal, sometimes as a direct result of his excellent work ethic that fortunately for her often spills over into the bedroom as well.

So while she may occasionally complain about some of his foibles, she'll love him for his wonderful way of dealing with her highs and lows, his ability to be patient and help her overcome life's challenges, burdens and upsets. Conversely, he'll adore her charming vulnerability, her openness and emotional frailty. Most of all he'll love the way she makes him feel that he's 'the real man' of the house. And there'll be times when she does even more than that — making him feel that he's the most 'loved' man in the world.

Cancer man — Capricorn woman

 The *'Someone to watch over me'* relationship

This Moon Man can be rather naive when it comes to social interaction with the opposite sex. That's why he may prefer to continue throughout life with the gal he dated first in his teenage years, rather than test his chances in the big, wide relationship world with someone who could turn out to be a challenge. When it comes to emotional areas, he likes to feel secure about what he's doing and doesn't fancy uncertainty or the unknown as options. As he's more of a romance philosopher, if he is approaching life after twenty-five alone, he may expect his special true love to magically manifest before him in a puff of smoke or somehow to propel herself into his life and land — kerplop — in his waiting arms. Amazingly, she often does!

Unless the magic happens, however, many Cancer men actually lead rather lonely lives; in fact some of them are confirmed bachelors. How does he get that way? Sometimes his mother has something to do with that state of affairs. As much as his mum loves him to be a bachelor, she's also torn between that and finding him a mate and seeing him have his own little 'uns. His well-intentioned mother may line him up with eligible gals she selects from here or there, but unless his mother is right on target in her choices, her mission to help him to meet a mate may scare him off meeting eligible gals altogether.

Often his matchmaking requirements add up to a tall order. While he might not know too much about what he wants in his future partner, he does, however, expect that they will need to be perfect! He's not a man who surrenders his heart to any starmaiden without putting her through a few cosmic hoops. It isn't that he means to be difficult, it's just that he probably has got a few hang-ups where the opposite sex is concerned, and he also takes himself extremely seriously.

Now should the right Capricorn starmaiden enter his life, then Mr Cancer's quest for the 'perfect partner' may have reached its final destination. She may even be his perfect match because Ms Capricorn has a most remarkable feminine stargal personality. She's wise beyond her years, strongly independent, self-secure (well, at least in many areas, but not in all of them), and generally extremely capable. She also exudes a calm exterior (even if it veils a rather hassled interior). She is reliable, steadfast and capable. Being ruled by the planet Saturn (the most steadfast of planetary energies), she's usually a stargal you can count on. Most of the above is just what the Cancer man is looking for, though he may not have realised it at the time.

What's more, she's usually not shy! She's quite capable of taking control of the dating situation and sweeping him off his feet before he even realises it. If the magic works, the moment she comes into his world and they fall in love, his life seems to re-arrange before his very eyes. Suddenly he's at the opera, he's travelling to Italy for holidays and he's buying a new apartment. If she's interested in the business world and its options (as these are often areas that this zodiac gal has expert knowledge), he may even find himself with a new stock portfolio and career as well. In return, she finds his eccentricities to be charming. She'll laugh at the way he wears odd socks. She'll adore the way he cries at sad movies (even though he tries to hide it), and best of all, she'll even admire the way he takes care of his parents.

Now where she may have a tough time with him is that he's super sensitive. She may not be able to throw out his favourite chair immediately, even if the leather is hanging off in threads. Although some of his clothes date back to the sixties, he'll still love to wear them (even if she hates them), so she may have to operate within certain, stringent boundaries. But when they are in the bedroom making love, she'll be well rewarded for having been especially patient and persevering. He'll be very adventurous, kinky and surprisingly adept in the sex department, and she'll love him for that.

How will he feel about her? She'll dazzle him with her feminine wiles, talents and general brilliance. He probably won't have that much time to ponder his feelings about her too much — he's too busy. He won't have time to slump into blue moods because he's probably got heaps of projects to finish around the home, friends or family coming to visit, plus there's plants to buy, and plants for the garden, and kitty litter to purchase for the cat. He may even now be coaching the local boys' footy team or doing more surfing than usual. So if this match works, it's a bonus for both parties. When put under the pressure of relentless test-of-time and this combination doesn't work, you can bet it wasn't due to both partners not giving this relationship a good old-fashioned 'go'.

CANCER—AQUARIUS relationship

The *'I can't figure out whether I'm crazy about you, or you're just driving me crazy?'* relationship

STAR CANCER–AQUARIUS COUPLE
Ronald Reagan and Nancy Reagan

When these two most 'eccentric' signs of the zodiac discover the fascination they offer each other and settle down to explore romance together, some of the most unusual, unique and creative partnerships on the planet are formed. Although at first assessment this pair may seem strangely ill-suited, they do have something quite special in common — their 'off-the-wall' unique form of individuality.

It is the Moon that rules the sign of Cancer (the Moon is the most changeable astro-energy field of all), and the planet Uranus that rules the sign of Aquarius (and Uranus is the zodiac's most unpredictable planetary force). So combine the forces of Cancer's changeability with the unpredictable energy flow surrounding Aquarians and you end up with something special, unusual and sometimes a relationship that could easily be termed 'out of this world'.

Cancer woman — Aquarius man

 The *'anything can happen'* relationship

The Aquarian man does everything he can to establish a quiet, peaceful life for himself. He actually loves routine and the safety of a regular, everyday existence, even if he does sometimes decide to go out and have a wild adventure or to live dangerously every now and again. Generally he lives in a nice neighbourhood, has a secure job, drives a reliable car, and he handles his finances with extreme care. His desire is for his world to be ordered, structured and predictable. But, if he falls in love with a Cancer gal he's about to throw all his well-laid plans into a jumbled heap of uncertainty and often (because of the influence she holds over him), the predictable quality of his structured life flies straight out the cosmic window.

So what does the Aquarian man often end up creating if he matches up with a Moon Maiden? A very unpredictable life indeed! Teaming up with the most changeable, moody, creative and erratic female of the zodiac, the Cancer Moon gal is, for this eccentric man of the zodiac, a little like trying to drive a car without a steering wheel. This relationship could end up going just about anywhere, but it's certain to involve hitting a few emotional skids or heartbreaking road blocks along the way. Even if Ms Cancer brings some drama, challenge and chaos into his existence, in many ways she's great for him because she livens up (in no uncertain terms) his otherwise extremely, overly-structured existence. She brings some new dimensions into his existence — often fantasy dimensions of experience that he would never have without her — and that's often of great value to him, in more ways than one.

Now to be fair to Ms Cancer, from her perspective when dealing with Mr Aquarian, he isn't always Mr Easy-To-Get-To-Know or Mr Easy-Going himself. Frequently she finds the time she spends with her Aquarian man almost as challenging as he does with her. But she also finds him stimulating, exciting and extremely sexy, and if he is one of the more creative Aquarian males around (and there are many of these), he's likely to introduce her to some trendy scenes as well. However, on emotional levels, being around him, for her, is like attempting to navigate her way through a field of potential emotional time bombs or doing the tango with heartache itself. He doesn't relate (or sometimes doesn't want to relate) to her emotional side at all. In fact he can totally ignore it, especially when she needs him to notice it the most. He wants to be affectionate, but not twenty-four hours a day. He also doesn't want to have to shower her with reassurance, affection or compliments, something she expects as part of her zodiac sign's natural birthright.

Mr Aquarius is almost impossible to predict, read or tune into, so the Cancer gal will never know what he's likely to come up with next. Though while this uncertainty in their exchanges in many ways thrills her, it also leads to plenty of strange tensions lurking under cover within the relationship. She's never really quite certain what to expect of him and he feels the same with her. But he's possibly more a mystery to her than she is to him. You may ask her, 'What's he like?' and although she may give you a glib, clever answer, chances are she hasn't really got a clue about what actually makes this man tick, and he possibly feels exactly the same about her. Sometimes, this kind of unknown quality is just what this couple needs to keep them dangling on each other's relationship string.

So why does this couple often find each other fascinating? Probably their attraction to each other can be explained as simply as that crazy temptation one feels when seeing a sign that reads: Wet Paint, Don't Touch! There's almost an invisible pull, or that subliminal desire and chemistry that makes a person want to reach out and 'test' that the paint is truly wet. So although he sees warning flashes of high potential for emotional upheaval ahead when he meets the Cancer gal, the Aquarian guy usually chooses to ignore it. Instead, he focuses on her cuteness, feminine allure, and her ability to make him feel outrageously sexy at the most unusual times and in the most unusual way. Perhaps not too long into their relationship — when she throws a minor tizzy fit — he reconsiders his feelings towards her. But as he is a fixed sign, if he's made up his mind that she's the one and a honey-bunny, then she usually has to throw a super-duper tizzy fit to really make him say, 'That's enough', and go away, leaving her wounded in her heartache. He doesn't like to hurt her, and that can be a strong force that binds them together too.

What pulls her away from him? If he really is too distracted all the time, if he's constantly disinterested in her whims or wishes or attention-seeking actions, eventually (especially if they are lacking some excitement in the sack) she may look elsewhere for what she needs. In the meantime, if their love stars are in alignment, then these two can play some of the strangest and most intriguing relationship games of the zodiac; and be very content to be together, even if they don't truly understand why they are!

Cancer man — Aquarius woman

 The *'mystery package'* relationship

When the Moon-ruled man of the zodiac teams up with the Uranus-ruled Aquarian woman, he is usually heading into a very unusual relationship experience, and so is she. These two zodiac children definitely didn't emerge from the same cosmic genetic pool and it won't be hard to see that they don't have much in common, except something very important — each other! That's why it is quite amazing how they can turn out to be each other's mutual admiration society when they usually don't truly have a clue exactly who or what they are dealing with. Sometimes romances are strange experiences and this is likely to be one of them.

One reason they often seem out of each other's romantic zones is because their outlooks are generally poles apart. She's likely to be modern-thinking, and he's possibly a trifle old-fashioned. She'll debunk his greatest theories on the Universe or politics, and he'll laugh at her idea of what she considers to be terrific photography, music or art. He may only read novels, while she'll only read magazines and do crosswords. He'll like home-cooking, she'll prefer dining out. They may go to the movies together, but they probably won't agree on what movie to see, what the movie's plot was about, or what was going on between the actors. They may even enjoy playing some sports together, probably tennis or golf, but many of their interests will differ.

This cosmic pair also handle conversations extremely differently. He tends to play the role of listener, she tends to play the role of communicator. Sometimes he won't be able to get a word in edgewise because she does (occasionally) ramble on, but he doesn't worry about her effervescent conversation, as he usually enjoys her ramblings. Ms Aquarius is a great researcher. She usually knows the latest trends, what's happening in the world at large, and what the weather is going to be like tomorrow — all information that he probably needs to know about, so she keeps Mr Cancer informed and up-to-date. However, there are occasions when she spills the beans disclosing personal information or secrets to others that he would expect her to keep under wraps. Occasionally her lack of tact or outspokeness can lead to conflict between them.

Certainly Mr Cancer and Ms Aquarius are a strange mix of astro-energies, and the biggest surprise is that they probably get a buzz from it and enjoy having it that way. In many ways he'll envy her ability to view life from multi dimensional perspectives, when he knows he lacks the visionary power to be so creative in outlook. She'll love the way he always seems to take life seriously, goes out of his way to be supportive and generally is 'there for her when she needs some TLC'. Also she adores the way he snuggles up to her in bed at night, whispers sweet nothings in her ear, and surprises her when she gets home from work late — he will have prepared a great meal, put on some music, arranged some flowers and have a bottle of her favourite wine on the table. He's quite a romantic and that means a great deal to her, although at times she may tend to take it for granted and not appreciate just how significant his affectionate, caring nature is in their relationship.

His secret to her rather preoccupied heart is that he knows how to 'woo' her and that means a lot to this gal, because she often has been taken for granted by other guys in her life. If they move past the infatuation stage into a more permanent relationship, often this duo not only turn out to be fantastic lovers (they both usually surprise each other with their ability to be inventive, exciting and adventurous in the sack), partners and team mates, but also best friends. Why they 'click' is because they can learn so much from each other, and can see the world in a new and different way simply by spending time together.

When their children come along, they often seem to reverse roles. He may suddenly become a Mr Mom and she may spend a lot more time at the office than she used to, but this also works well for them. They seem to have an ability to go with the flow when outside circumstances demand it, and unless they try hard to change each other (something they will never manage to do long term), this rather 'offbeat' relationship often has all the ingredients to help make it last.

CANCER—PISCES relationship

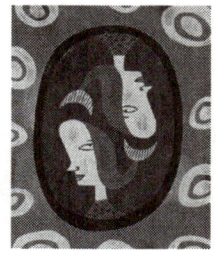

The *'Let's build ourselves a boat and sail away'* relationship

STAR CANCER–PISCES COUPLE
Courtney Love and Kurt Cobain

Tread warily. There are two sensitive, romantic hearts beating in each of these delicate individuals. When the Crab meets the Fish they certainly swim around in the same 'emotional ocean'. So no wonder if they do fall in love, it is love that is radiating with flashing technicolour passion lights. This is one of the great zodiac relationship combinations that can turn out to be the greatest romantic experience they ever have in their lives. However, it doesn't necessarily have long-lasting staying power. Just in case it doesn't, this couple would be wise to make the best of the intoxicating, juicy aspects of this romance while it lasts. Too often this love connection quickly turns into a love experience that could be compared to either dreamingly swimming along with the dolphins, or alternatively swimming desperately trying to survive emotionally with the sharks!

Zodiac-wise, these two are peas out of the same cosmic romance pod. As both Cancer and Pisces are water signs, they are psychic, sensitive and insecure. If they connect romantically with true love power, their connection can be powerful. It can both energise and uplift them. Unfortunately, due to their sensitive natures (and ability to feel scared of giving too much of themselves to another and leaving themselves vulnerable), neither of them is really strong enough emotionally to deal with any romantic upsets or adversity. They are not fighters like some of the other signs, and seem content to crumble if love goes wrong, rather than make some resolutions. Consequently at the first sign of problems or if their relationship hits a major bump in the relationship road, then their love for each other can quickly fizzle out. The shock of the emptiness they feel as a result can leave them emotionally scarred, psychologically despondent, and feeling like an emotional bulldozer ran over them, for years to come.

Cancer woman — Pisces man

 The *'You're nobody until somebody loves you'* relationship

Okay, the Cancer woman and the Pisces man are star-linked in a romantic way. In fact, astrologically they're kindred spirits. Yes, they are astro-mates and they have similar feelings, moods and desires. Yet though they can indeed be perfect zodiac mates — and many couples of this combination have amazing long-term relationships, there's still plenty of cases where Ms Cancer and Mr Pisces just can't take the relationship heat and consequently they just won't last the distance. These two may even be meant for each other, yet still make a great mess of it. Why? Because they are so effective and efficient at hurting each other.

Sometimes two people who have so much in common in a love relationship actually end up with more problems than those who don't really know each other at all. That's what happens with this couple. There's so much zodiac magic flowing between them that they expect unrealistic things out of their union. It's an overload of sensory, physical and emotional input, and that often creates a relationship burnout. There's a lot happening in this relationship — lots of mixed feelings, different agendas and a broad range of sometimes impossible dreams or ideals that each holds for the other. A Cancer woman with a Pisces man creates a couple who are comprised of mixed-up, jigsaw-puzzle type personality traits.

Some pieces fit together nicely, yet other aspects of their individual characters, no matter how much you try to force them to, don't fit at all.

Ms Cancer is also very possessive (often neurotically possessive), and Mr Pisces often loves to party, flirt, raise the roof and live for the moment. If he's one of those more slippery Fish, Ms Cancer suffers greatly from constant bouts of jealousy and is often insecure. But whether he's the flirtatious type of Pisces, or the more committed-relationship kind, most Pisces guys are free spirits. They love to suit themselves, go with their emotional flow, and if they feel like doing something risky they'll often say 'to hell with the consequences', and they'll do it. This can leave Ms Cancer fuming, and it may take some time after she feels he's somehow dropped the relationship ball for them to re-connect again.

As much as they can have a truly loving connection, inadvertently Ms Crab and Mr Fish often end up in a battle of wits. Both of them are easily hurt, too, which means those arguments, disagreements or any breach of trust (no matter how small), leave some scars hovering over the 'big picture' of their relationship. So, unless each of these individuals learns to enjoy the sometimes, imperfect side to their love match, and overlook the occasional shortcomings, they gradually end up building a brick wall between them. Now their stubbornness can prove to be their undoing, though they may experience some problems at times, that certainly doesn't mean they should give up too easily on each other. Sometimes both Ms Cancer and Mr Pisces just don't try enough to make things work.

Avoiding pain and seeking pleasure, they tend to run from angst-ridden emotions, rather than to deal with them and resolve problems. Though they have so much in common, can learn so much from each other, have an abundance of feelings, tenderness and concepts to share, there's no guarantee the Crab and Fish will automatically love each other 'forever after'. One thing they can expect during their time together, is that they are likely to experience the total gamut of relationship highs and lows — from the best relationship, the worst relationship and everything in between! Certainly they can bank on hot kisses, passionate caresses, dancing under the moon and the stars aplenty.

Cancer man—Pisces woman

The *'I think I could get into this romantic stuff . . . big time!'* relationship

If ever two lovers could summon up sufficient magic between them to fly over the rainbow and enter the world of Oz, it's a Cancer man and his surreal Pisces love-gal. This zodiac water sign liaison is forged from the same mould as a romantic novel. The Cancer man is naturally entwined with the feminine part of his nature because the Moon, the most mothering force of the zodiac, rules him. The ocean's mighty ruler Neptune rules the Pisces gal. This means that she's also affected subliminally by the elements that change the tides and rule our ocean, and that's the Moon above. So the Moon provides a powerful zodiac link between them and it's a romantic one as well.

This couple is naturally romantic. They innately attract romantic circumstances, experiences and opportunities because that is part of their soul's evolution. The stories of their romances from teenage years through to old age, fill the Hollywood movie screens. He's her astrological knight on his shining white horse racing to her rescue, and she's the pretty princess sometimes trapped and defenseless in her ivory tower. So in astro-terms, the Cancer man and the Pisces woman represent the fairy tale couple of old, brought into modern time. Like the romantic couple in the movie *Pretty Woman* portrayed by Richard Gere and Julia Roberts — who in the movie displayed the characteristics of the Cancer man and the Pisces woman — behind the glitter of fairy tale, there's frequently a kinky, sexual, seedy side to this Moon guy and Mermaid gal relationship, just to make life interesting.

Now just because they are perfect zodiac partners, is no guarantee that their relationship will make it through life's maze of tests, challenges and responsibilities. Some of their biggest 'relationship' drawbacks occur because they are both so imaginative — they imagine problems that don't exist in their relationship. They both tend to analyse their relationship, mental connection or emotional feelings as well. Insecurity can run right off the Richter Scale for both Cancer and Pisces, so two insecure people together can create double insecurity.

Despite their foibles, this couple will have wonderful times together. They will share incredible love-making sessions, have many interests in common, and probably be the best of friends. However, all it takes is a tiny little chink in their relationship exchange, and like the Walls of Jericho, their relationship connection comes falling down! Having sensitive egos, when either of their feelings get hurt, there's likely to be hell to pay. Both he and she become rather daunting figures when they experience real or imagined emotional pain. Sometimes they can spend the rest of their lives suffering angst, dwelling on the pain (real or imagined) they experienced, and may even go to great lengths, paying back the one who they feel 'did them wrong'.

Forgiving and forgetting (and getting on with living life) doesn't often flow easily for either of these two. Kissing and making up also doesn't seem to work for them; it may work temporarily but usually over time they remember old hurts, and fling them around like mud at their partner. Getting over upsets of the past doesn't come naturally to them unless they make a super effort. The problem is that both Mr Cancer and Ms Pisces are professionals when it comes to holding grudges. They sometimes make promises to each other that they fail to keep and usually, they don't let the one who failed to keep their promise forget it. Jealousies and insecurities can drive them nuts too, and often they imagine more negatives about their partners than is fair or really warranted. Sometimes they can tend to live their lives under the heading 'do as I say, not as I do'.

So, although this couple has the opportunity to sail through life together on their own form of wonderful love boat, avoiding stormy emotional seas won't always be easy, but they'll certainly have a heap of intense emotional exchange and fun along the way.

leo leo leo leo leo leo leo leo leo leo
leo leo leo leo leo leo leo leo leo leo
    leo leo leo leo leo leo leo leo leo leo
leo leo leo leo leo leo leo leo leo leo
leo leo leo leo leo leo leo leo leo leo
    leo leo leo leo leo leo leo leo leo leo
leo leo leo leo leo leo leo leo leo leo
leo leo leo leo leo leo leo leo leo leo
    leo leo leo leo leo leo leo leo leo leo

leo leo leo leo leo leo leo leo leo leo
leo leo leo leo leo leo leo leo leo leo
    leo leo leo leo leo leo leo leo leo leo
    leo leo leo leo leo leo leo leo leo leo
leo leo leo leo leo leo leo leo leo leo
    leo leo leo leo leo leo leo leo leo leo
    leo leo leo leo leo leo leo leo leo leo
leo leo leo leo leo leo leo leo leo leo
    leo leo leo leo leo leo leo leo leo leo

LEO

[24 july – 23 august]

romantic pursuit: similar to an athlete going for

Olympic gold

romantic vibration: has a tendency

to run hot and cold

secret love desire: to seduce anyone they want!

element: fire

planetary ruler: the sun

symbol: the lion

quality: fixed (= stability)

colour: gold

gems: amber, chrysolite, neroli

best companions: aries and sagittarius

strongest virtues: bravery, loyalty and

big-picture attitude to life, love and

everything else

traits to improve: bossiness, vanity, arrogance

deepest desire: to live all your dreams

and more

Leo celebrities

Anna Paquin, Antonio Banderas, Arnold Schwarzenegger, Ben Affleck,

Ben Chaplin, Bill Clinton, Billy Bob Thornton, Charlize Theron, Christian

Slater, Daryl Somers, David Duchovny, Dean Cain, Dustin Hoffman,

Edward Norton, Eric Bana, George Hamilton, Geri Halliwell, Gillian

Anderson, Halle Berry, Hulk Hogan, J. K. Rowling, Jacqueline Kennedy

Onassis, James Cameron, Jennifer Lopez, John Howard, John Laws,

Julian McMahon, Kate Beckingsale, Kevin Spacey, Lisa Kudrow,

Madeleine Stowe, Madonna, Magic Johnson, Martin Sheen, Matt Le

Blanc, Matthew Perry, Melanie Griffith, Melissa George, Michael Klim,

Michael Richards, Mick Jagger, Neil Armstrong, Patrick Swayze, Pete

Sampras, Peter Weir, Robert De Niro, Robert Redford, Roman Polanski,

Sandra Bullock, Sean Penn, Simon Baker, Stanley Kubrick, Stephen

Dorff, Susie O'Neill, Vanessa Amorosi, Wesley Snipes, Whitney Houston

LEO—LEO relationship

The *'When Tarzan meets Jane'* relationship

STAR LEO–LEO COUPLE
Jennifer Lopez and Ben Affleck

Grrr! Get ready to rumble in the relationship jungle. With this Leo–Leo zodiac combination there's going to be plenty of growling, prowling and scowling, plus bold and erotic sexcapades too! When two Leo the Lions match up it's destined to develop into some kind of love battle. Similar to scenarios that occur in the jungle when real lions stalk mates and selectively choose their breeding partner, in human terms, two Leos are destined to test each other's strength, power and commitment before they totally surrender their hearts to each other.

So what happens when a Leo woman and a Leo man successfully pass each other's mating test and decide to get together to play the cosmic love game? Trying to work out their relationship dynamic is fairly easy (compared to other more complex, internalised signs). Imagine the dynamic that occurs when two rock stars, celebrities or actors come together (not that the Leos have to be these things, just consider this possibility). It can be the basis of a very competitive union. Throw into the mix loads of passion, two egos bumping into each other; blend up their union with dynamism, arrogance, high romance, drama, jealousy and an abundance of affection and adoration, and you have everything that a Leo with another Leo relationship is likely to offer. *Purr-fect* stuff for a romantic soap opera.

Of course, sometimes this feisty union will blossom, like husband and wife team Antonio Banderas and Melanie Griffith. Other times it will rush along like a romantic wildfire and then burn out, like competitive ex-lovers Madonna and Sean Penn. One thing's for sure, there's no room for weakness, disloyalty or boredom when the Sun God and Goddess join forces in the romance stakes if you don't want to be seriously mauled and clawed. Certainly if these two really get serious with each other they can be heading for quite dangerous, murky, but also highly intense and exciting relationship realms.

Leo woman — Leo man

 The *'C'mon . . . you must have heard about me before'* relationship

If ever a couple thrived on creating and sharing what they perceive to be 'the entire romantic deal' then it's two Leos together playing their roles as King and Queen of romance. Romantic dinners, passionate weekends away, or exchanging gifts of chocolates, flowers and expensive jewellery are the kind of things they savour. There is always a reason for them to celebrate and you can expect to find a chilled bottle of champagne (usually French!) in their fridge — and Mr and Ms Leo *don't* really need any excuse to open it. Just being 'them' is enough! Self-confessed eternal romantics, Leos are ruled by their hearts not their heads, and romance is the cornerstone of their entire life's existence. When love pervades the air and they are snug in the security of it, this regal couple rules the love realms supreme. Their positive Leonine characteristics are accentuated and their negative tendencies are diminished when they are in love and loved in return. (Just look at how your newly-in-love Leo employer changes overnight from an egotistical dictator to a warm and generous boss!) Love can truly lift them up where they belong — in the celestial realms up amongst the stars.

Yep, love and romance rule their world and the Leo couple bask in the glory of their warm and cosy love nest. This can be a romance made in heaven or, if and when things fall apart, watch out! Ouch, this can truly become a love match destined for hell. Much depends on the individual egos of the Leo lovebirds. One of the biggest challenges they will have is dealing (diplomatically) with their mutual need for top billing. You see Leos need big doses of attention and adoration. It's likely that one Leo will roar loudly in outrage if his or her lover claims too much of the limelight; or one of them will sulk and withdraw their attention and affections (which is the beginning of the romantic end for this ego-driven, proud couple).

Both of them need to be equal and share the limelight. Of course they'll try all kinds of different role-playing but ideally (unless you truly love being a home-maker), the Leo woman should never play Stay-At-Home-Housewife to the Leo man's Big-Daddy-Provider role. It usually just won't work. In the Leo–Leo love match both woman and man need to exercise *outside* of the relationship their common need for self-affirmation, expression and leadership. This way, there's less likelihood of an ego-fest happening once they close the office door and come home to each other and feel a need to vie for attention or to outshine each other. They'll be more able to relax in each other's arms, listen to each other and support each other emotionally. Top-billing actors Melanie Griffiths and Antonio Banderas seemed for a while to have mastered the trick of supporting each other emotionally while managing their mutually hot careers. They 'take it in turns' to make movies, accompanying the other to their respective movie sets with children in tow. Allowing the other 'to shine' in his or her own right and to star in their own form of life movie is the secret to ongoing long-term happiness for the King and Queen of the jungle.

Magnetically attracted to each other, the Leo couple is more often than not one of those couples simply dubbed 'beautiful'. When they walk into a room their combined magnetism is striking. They're endowed with attractive smiles, luxurious manes of hair and warm skin tones (and they adore gold jewellery). There's loads of sexual chemistry between the fiery Sun-ruled Leo lovers and their expressive body language shows that these two are deeply in love and passionately in lust. They'll drape arms around each other's shoulders and waists, hug frequently, and kiss and canoodle in public. In fact, Leos are born exhibitionists, often fond of exciting sexual trysts in public where there's a chance they'll be caught. Both have a natural tendency to turn into the Green-Eyed Monster. Small doses of jealousy, however, are often a good thing in the Leonine love match. It can make the other feel loved and desired (as opposed to mistrusted), which can be a sexy turn-on for Leo. The truth is, Mr and Ms Leo are both loyal and unlikely to stray (unless there is a major problem in the relationship).

The Leo household is full of excitement and quite often drama. There is always something going on in their home — expect tears, tantrums and laughter, but more than anything, plenty of fun. They both adore children and can be doting, affectionate parents to their offspring. Although their home is beautifully decorated, housework is *definitely* not their forte. Leo couples shouldn't think twice about hiring a cleaner as it will save them stress and give them the freedom to enjoy their favourite pastime — loving each other!

LEO — VIRGO relationship

The *'If you don't want me to be purr-fect, keep patting me on the head'* relationship

STAR LEO–VIRGO COUPLE
Madonna and Guy Ritchie

Step into the 'world-wrestling' romantic ring. This combination of earth element (Virgo) and fire element (Leo) is likely to turn into something of an emotional struggle at times. While Leo is definitely the stronger of the signs when it comes to dealing with the outside world, don't count Virgo out! After all, Virgo is head-ruled and Leo is heart-ruled. So Virgo can outsmart Leo every now again, (not that they'd ever let Leo know they've done just that!) However, even if the Virgo is street-smart and romantically savvy enough to temper and control the powerful Lion or Lioness, there are still lots of issues that this couple will need to deal with diplomatically if they want their love to survive. It can take a long time before these two finally trust each other and settle down comfortably together to share their domestic bliss. So if you're reading this because you're in a Leo–Virgo relationship and things are not going too well, don't give up! Those love sparks you share together require lots of nurturing to continue to shine.

There's a lot of patience needed to nurture this relationship along. Especially in the early stages of love, lust and romance, fussy Virgo and bossy Leo need tolerance and understanding in order to establish trust and any long-term possibility for this love quest to continue. Damage can be done if Virgo is too coldly critical, hurting Leo's excessive pride; or if Leo upsets sensible Virgo's nervous system with typical Leonine drama and extravagance.

In the best of cases, this couple become devoted companions and faithful lovers who love to organise and support each other's lives (and both are lost without their Filofaxes!) Leo's unshakeable optimism makes Virgo feel cosily secure, and Virgo provides a mental, physical and spiritual equal that Leo has been waiting for. Mutual respect and curbing habits that drive the other crazy is the key to their fairy-tale romance. If the love stars are shining in their favour, then their first meeting was destiny. Though they might not know it, if their stars are karmically united in the love zones, then they've been waiting for each other for a long, long time.

Leo woman — Virgo man

 The *'Are you sure you're ready for me?'* relationship

One of the most famous Ms Leo–Mr Virgo couples on the planet would be Madonna and her film-director husband, Guy Ritchie (or 'Mr Madonna' as he has been called; and you can bet he just cringes when he's called that!) But any Virgo guy (Guy Ritchie included) who is partnering a Leo gal will have his buttons pushed one way or another; and sometimes that's just the challenge Mr Virgo needs to lift his game anyway. He probably realises very quickly into this relationship that Ms Leo is not an ordinary, everyday female — she's a feisty gal with the spirit of a proud, regal Lioness. Consequently she is going to give any man of the zodiac a wild run for his money. Now if he decides she's worth the work, he knows what's ahead of him and he chooses to tame Ms Leo, then Mr Virgo needs to prepare himself to put on his best romantic Lion-taming magic, sexual, financial and charismatic act. Even once he assembles the whole romantic package to present to her, she's still no easy gal to tame, influence or win.

Although she's a powerful stargal in her own right, for all her fiery impulsiveness, independence and seeming appearance of being 'on top of her world', the Leo woman is still anxiously looking for the right man to bring stability, balance and calmness into her life. Though she's highly independent, savvy and most well organised, she doesn't want to be alone. She knows that she needs to find herself a man with a plan. That's where Mr Virgo suits her requirements extremely well. He is great at putting the different pieces of his and her everyday life together into an effective, efficient joint package. She appreciates this natural skill of his because she wants to have it all, and more, in life. She enjoys being able to raise a family, have a gorgeous, sexy man who loves her, and continue to have a career. If he's the right guy for her, then Mr Virgo is one Astrological Star Lord who can usually help her accomplish this task. As a bonus, he may even be prepared to help out around the home more than most men of the zodiac. While this may scund a minor asset, remember Ms Royal-cosmic-blooded Leo is often not too fond of housework and other mundane tasks! But her Virgo guy — a perennial lover of law and order— is often most supportive in those little mundane areas (those that can make or break a relationship). His ability to be the perfectionist, the organiser and the assembler helps her live out her dreams in more ways than one.

Now he's going to have to put up with some of her sometimes overwhelming characteristics, and occasionally he may find she goes a bit too far for his true enjoyment. She can tend to be quite a show-off or attention-seeker, and there will be occasions when her attitude, vanity and arrogance will annoy him. But, unless he's having a lot of stress elsewhere making him overly cranky, even her over-the-top behaviour usually makes him smile knowingly. You see, Mr Virgo is a very smart man and he knows she's just a little pussy cat under her big brave Lioness front. He'll put up with her attention-seeking tactics because he knows that even if she can be a pistol at times (who likes to shoot him down in flames or poke fun of those she shouldn't), she's also warm, generous, good fun, creative, wise and very sexy. Plus, she brings a special zippiness and expansiveness to his life that was not there before she entered his heart's door. She has a way of making every day somehow much more special than they were before, and he adores her enthusiasm and spontaneity. 'Come on honey,' she'll say, dragging him outside for a walk on a sunny day when he's quite content to spend the entire day sorting out bills and filing paperwork. And he 'comes on', and they go and do things together that he would never have considered before, and that's good for him too.

She changes his routines and habits, which is sometimes just what is needed to help him move onto the next level of his life. It is important to point out now that Mr Virgo is a man of habits who likes to surround himself with tranquillity, and this is why many Virgo men remain bachelors (or marry late in life); they like to live in a peaceful, clean, ordered environment. So in meeting Ms Leo he's met his opposite, she is not a quiet, reflective person. And it will take a special Leo lady to pull him out of his 'I love peace and quiet'; 'I want everything and everyone to be totally perfect'; and 'cleanliness is next to Godliness' Virgo world!

She'll work hard to make him adapt to her ways, because she adores him for his cute concepts, great capabilities and precision in handling everyday affairs. However, much of his fastidiousness may annoy her at times, but his cool sweetness and slight boyish vulnerability is refreshing to Ms Leo. She's probably been sorely romantically jaded by some of the smart-set type guys she's surrounded herself with in the past, so he'll seem like a romantic breath of fresh air to her. She is also thrilled because he can be funny (even quite hilarious) when he wants to be. And don't discount the fact that he's often a good businessman too and she enjoys that money-making aspect in his character tremendously.

Now, if she could change anything about him, she'd like him to be more awe-struck by her and to pay her more attention. The Leo woman needs to be worshipped, loved and admired — and *this* is where they differ. Her Virgo guy is discreet, analytical and laidback. He may not kiss and cuddle her in public or say 'I love you' ten times a day or on cue when she hints she needs to hear it. He's a practical kind of guy and is more likely to show he loves her in practical ways. He'll hang picture frames in her apartment, wash her car, cook her dinner or buy her a year's subscription to her favourite magazine; he may even massage her back when she needs it, but he probably won't pay her huge compliments or hang onto her every word.

Early on in their relationship she might mistake his lack of demonstrative affection and cool detachment as lack of love. But if he doesn't sprout forth with words of ongoing praise, don't be too quick to judge him as feeling less or lacking in love for Lady Leo! There is more to the Virgo man than meets the eye. He's quite emotional but he just *doesn't* show it or reveal it to you or anyone else up front. He just isn't a person who can wear his heart on his sleeve. But to keep her contentedly purring, Mr Virgo possibly needs to learn to loosen up his emotions a tad more and risk showing a little bit of emotional vulnerability. His lady needs the equivalent of a rewarding pat on her Lioness head at least twice a day. And if he puts out some special attention in her direction he'll be rewarded. Being more emotionally expressive towards her will be worth it.

Now there will be times when she'll be sulky, but most of the time she'll easily fuss over him, especially if he's being attentive to her. She adores her Virgo guy because he's everything she isn't. He's quiet, controlled and there's something secretive she can sense that's locked up inside him which makes him very intriguing. His sexuality is more the secretive, brooding type (just think of super cool Virgos Richard Gere, Keanu Reeves, Sean Connery and Jeremy Irons), and that is highly attractive to her. He oozes with something special and sexual, but he isn't flashy about it at all.

As they have such a different approach to everyday life, their different ways of dealing with money (particularly the way they both spend and save it) is an issue that is (sometimes) likely to create headaches and angst between the Leo woman and Virgo man. He may have it, but not spend it too easily. She may not have it, but she'll spend it anyway! The Leo woman can be a high maintenance and an extremely extravagant gal; and he can be a guy who worries about money and frets over its foolish handling or spendthrift use more than most. In fact, the Virgo man worries about a lot of things, but most frequently his biggest worries can surround his financial security, and sometimes he can even be a penny-pincher. Wheatever it is that he worries about, worry can turn him into a very cranky person, too. In many cases, if he gets on a downward spiral in this regard, he can turn worry into an art form and fret about his health (always a huge worry for him), job, finances *and* relationship. If Ms Leo is too feisty, pushy and challenging, her dramatic and emotional outbursts can literally make him feel sick and upset his entire physical energy levels. Naturally this isn't going to help their relationship and she'll need to make certain she isn't pushing his sensitive buttons too often or too hard.

Apart from the diplomacy of being gentle with each other, also living life at the same pace may prove difficult because they both have different ideas about most things (including the use of time). Though he's often rattled by her impetuous plans, the Virgo male is versatile enough to go along with them *as long* as they are logical. He can be a little on the eccentric side, but he likes and can often see the value of her creative ideas. He is not a clingy man and he'll encourage her to explore and expand outside of the relationship, and continue in her career and other pursuits. Most Leo gals are ambitious career women and he's also incredibly hardworking (because of his perfectionist streak he needs to do everything 'just right'). Together they can run a very successful business, however, they should establish *who* is in charge of *what* before they begin; otherwise sparks will definitely fly. If they work together they could bring their work worries home with them and that could prove detrimental (big time) to their happiness at home.

If there's a major complaint Ms Leo has about her Virgo guy it might be that he doesn't challenge her enough; he's a bit too passive for her. He's dependable, punctual, modest and low-key and he's not interested in dramatic confrontations or relationship theatrics; and maybe she's missing out on just how much of a bonus that side of his character can be to her. Even if he's passive or overly patient, he's certainly not boring! Ruled by Mercury, the planet of communication and the mind, he's a very, very smart guy and many Virgo men can be quite eccentric. He'll go out on a limb for her and change a little to jazz himself up so that he fits more with her flamboyant style or expectations. He adores her, however she can sometimes spoil things unnecessarily.

Some immature Leo women are likely to create drama in their relationship (yes, she's a Drama Queen from way back!) She may cause a fracas simply to 'spice things up'. She might flirt with other men in front of him, just to see if it will spark a reaction, or employ some other kind of attention-attracting scheme. If she uses this type of romantic ploy, she could be creating her own romantic Nemesis. Ms Leo is sometimes a bit too frisky for her own good. She may make merry in silly, self-cantered ways that rebound back on her. That doesn't mean that Ms Leo isn't faithful or that her occasional wild-child behaviour means that she doesn't love him; it's just that she easily adopts the role of a sensationalist. When in love, she can be the most loyal woman in the zodiac. The Leo woman can be the wise Sphinx one moment and then a playful cub the next, innocently playing games where she maybe oughtn't, especially if she wants to keep her Virgo man loving her eternally.

Leo man — Virgo woman

 The *'When I'm with you I somehow feel anxious'* relationship

Cupid's love arrows smite the Leo man's heart with a bull's-eye when it aligns him with a Virgo beauty. Although he bounds around the social world looking like he'll never settle down with one gal, that's just a part of his 'Leo man on the prowl' act. He's not really as happy being 'single' as he makes out he is. Underneath his 'out-having-a-good-time' veneer, he is looking to settle down with the right woman with beauty *and* brains, and hopefully a trust account that's big enough to impress him, too. But once a delicate, sensitive and alluring Virgo gal steals the key to his tender heart, whether she's rich, poor, a stunning knockout or plain Jane, the Leo man will adore her and surrender his heart without a whimper. She's likely to be thrilled that she has succeeded where many other stargals have failed, but she now faces a whole set of other problems. Now that she has his heart, living up to his high, romantic expectations could turn out to be a full-time job and place enormous demands on her.

After all, the Leo guy is no small-time romantic man who just wants a little TLC from his ladylove. He needs constant attention, endless compliments and sincere, devoted admiration. This is where there may be future (if not immediate) problems hitting this relationship's agenda. You see Ms Virgo is a very giving, caring, generous person. She loves to make a fuss of other people but she's also got her *own* agenda. Sometimes she's prepared to be his constant companion and hang spellbound onto his every word, but often she's not the kind of gal to sit by his feet in his Lion's lair and worship him all day long! No, the exquisite and lovely Virgo woman often has places to go, people to meet and things to do. She's frequently got a business, a hobby, or a project that she's working on that means a great deal to her. He may want her to change her plans, job or even location, dramatically, to be with him, and that can be tough for her to do (even if she really wants to).

MR LEO: *(Sweeping her into his arms and dipping her backwards in a dramatic Mills and Boon-type cover shot)* Darling, I'm going to take you away this weekend and shower you with love and kisses and . . . hmmm . . . you smell really good . . . then we can spend some time together just the two of us . . .

MS VIRGO: Honey, that sounds fantastic, but — I actually have commitments this weekend. You know, I've got yoga on Saturday and I promised mum on Sunday I'd go work in her garden and clear out all that mess of weeds that's been driving her nuts . . . She's not been feeling the best anyway, remember?

MR LEO: *(Sounding a little crestfallen)* But darling, can't you get your brother to go pull some weeds and check out how your mother feels? After all, he's not working at the moment and the exercise would do him good. Anyway, you do too much for other people — you don't *have* to be the Mother Teresa of your family. And I *need* to be with you . . .

MS VIRGO: Honey. It's my mother we're talking about. Surely you understand that she needs me? You aren't the only one who needs attention — honestly — maybe you should go and visit *your* family. That feud with your sister has gone on long enough, and you know what? It's your pride stopping you from picking up the phone and calling her.

MR LEO: *(Turning red for having being reprimanded)* And it's your nagging that's stopping me from asking you to marry me! *(Stands up and slams door behind him)*

Now when these two have a falling out things are usually patched up very quickly. But sometimes the damage is done. If he's been too demanding on her, she thinks he's being too selfish. If she's not been prepared to sacrifice something to be with him, he thinks she's being too selfish and perhaps she doesn't really love him. And while Ms Virgo is most likely able to forgive and forget, and kiss and make up, the noble Leo has enormous pride and can't stand being made a fool of or criticised or left in the lurch. No matter how much he expects it of her, try as she might to be his perfect partner, Ms Virgo can't always keep him happy. After all, she's a woman of honour, and family duty and responsibilities mean a great deal to her. She's dutiful to her family, friends, boss, work colleagues and neighbours . . . and her pets. Oh, and her neighbours' pets, too. She simply can't help it. 'To serve others' is her personal motto (though her Leo guy wishes it sometimes read: 'To serve the Leo King only'). This particular gal of the zodiac is a romantic enigma because she'll be nicer to him when he's down than when he's up, and he's going to have to have plenty of patience and love to fathom her out.

But with some work, this couple do have a great chance of making a success of this extremely complex relationship. They will definitely need to be gentle with each other and be prepared to compromise on many occasions. There are plenty of potential pitfalls awaiting them, even if they do tread warily. She has a tendency to be super critical, while he has a tendency to be a tad bossy. Both of them possibly have unrealistically high standards to live up to (particularly when it comes to choosing a love partner), and that can put them both through some extremely tough love tests. However, sometimes their mutually high expectations mean that they are both forced to lift their romantic game, and they actually end up working harder at being better partners to each other than they have ever been before.

One thing is certain, it is going to take a lot of effort to make this relationship work. But Ms Virgo will put in her best effort because with Mr Leo she'll finally feel she's found someone worthy of her love, trust and admiration. She adores him for his dependability, love and generosity. When she's feeling low he'll be over in a flash to cheer her up and envelop her in his protective arms; and he'll make her feel loved — that's a hugely important feeling for her to experience. He'll try hard to make their romance a success, 'cos he'll sense that she's a gal in a million and someone well worthy of his love and affection.

Although these two may have the highest intentions, she may discover keeping Mr Leo happy over the long haul is not an easy task. He'll expect her to be a whole sphere of fantastic women created in one human physical form. Fortunately, being a very clever gal, she's adept enough to accomplish this close-to-impossible feat. Plus, he may prove to be quite temperamental, moody, self-centred and highly strung. Though his sulking moments may frustrate her at times, the Virgo gal knows that it's worth putting up with his occasional cranky bouts of frustration. Luckily he doesn't stay shadowed in the blues for long.

Of course, he is sexy, *very* sexy. That sexy side to his character fits Ms Virgo's list of high priorities too. Earthy Ms Virgo knows a thing or two about pleasing her man, but she has probably never had so much unbridled passion (and fun) in bed before meeting Mr Lusty Leo. Fire signs are naturally combustible in bed and he'll certainly steam up the sheets. His wild brand of jungle passion is arduous yet tender, natural and gentle. She has a special innocent aura that naturally turns on his sexual radar full force. It drives him wild that in public she is demure, innocent and always composed; and that behind closed bedroom doors she can turn into an incredibly erotic and earthy lover. Down-to-earth Ms Virgo responds well to his honest lovemaking and feels uninhibited enough to explore new and creative sexual realms. The only thing that is likely to turn him off in a matter of moments is if she brings up some problems or criticise him *just* as he's starting to get 'in the mood'!

If they can get over the obvious hurdles in front of them, this couple will prosper and gain from their relationship union. Certainly most Leo men are generally more faithful, happier and more relaxed after they are married. Also Ms Virgo becomes more in line with her feminine, earth goddess element when she is situated in a secure, loving relationship. So marriage for these two can definitely provide them both with a solid loving basis. The Lion King loves returning to his castle after a hard day's work to find his Virgo Queen (and baby cubs) waiting eagerly for his appearance. Though she may have been hard at work herself, the Virgo woman is smart enough to make him feel that he's her courageous provider and protector, and that his efforts are appreciated. Even if she has to underplay her own contribution and overplay his, what's a small detail like that matter when she knows she has him to snuggle up to and feel cosy, safe and secure for the rest of her life? Purr-fect.

LEO—LIBRA relationship

The *'I want to be wanted, you want to be wanted. So why don't we just want each other?'* relationship

STAR LEO–LIBRA COUPLE
Ben Affleck and Gwyneth Paltrow

Romance is the astro-realm where those born under the signs of Leo and Libra often meet successfully and discover that as a couple they can shine brightly. These two are ideal romantic companions because they usually have heaps in common, especially when it comes to love, romance and the fun and games of bedroom antics. Now these are their wonderful compatible areas in the romantic dimensions. However, in other areas, they may have to stumble through their relationship exchanges, rather than enjoy a smooth run through it. They aren't always going to find the going between them is happy-ever-after and easy-peasy, because when you mix fire (Leo) and air (Libra) what do you get? Well, in the worst case you get a dangerous fire that runs rampant and eventually has to be put out (usually by the entire fire department). Their love can run super hot and then turn freezing cold in a short span of time. But if the sharing, caring and diplomatic energies of both are applied carefully, the passionate prompting they both fall prey to doesn't need to burn out of control.

Wisely utilised, fire and air can create a warm, sensual and balmy breeze that caresses the skin in an unforgettable way. As both these signs have a primary desire to love and be loved in return, I prefer to picture the balmy breeze when I think of fire-ruled Leo and air-ruled Libra uniting in the game of astro-love. There's extremely good planetary energy flowing between Leo and Libra and the potential for companionship, love and passion is high. But, as in any astro-match, it all depends on the individuals involved as to whether they create longer-term relationship heaven or hell!

Leo woman — Libra man

The *'Think of a romantic song that we'll forever remember as our song'* relationship

People will notice this couple when they walk into a restaurant. The Queen of the Jungle is ruled by the Sun, and true to form she radiates an enormous warmth and irresistible sexual power. She's dramatic and vibrates with a vital energy that screams, 'Look At Me!' She's flamboyant and striking, and just check out the guy on her arm! Her Libra guy is well-groomed, carefully-shaven, completely colour-coordinated and most likely *very* handsome, very sexy and most desirable (exactly how she likes it). He's usually born with sexual appeal and charisma because the planet of beauty, Venus, is his ruling planet and it smiles brightly when the Libra man is born. He captures some of this smile in his energy field and it is spellbinding (not only to the opposite sex but frequently to his same sex as well). Even if he's not textbook-type devastatingly handsome, he's still got that extra 'something special'. Many a Libran man is so charming and debonair that people will always remember him. He usually has 'it' whatever the invisible 'it' is; and as he's *born* with it he doesn't flaunt it, abuse it or spoil it; he just wears this sense of 'attraction' around him like a Venus-designed aura.

His planetary ruler, Venus, also governs love relationships and the Libran man adores women (sometimes lots of them as he can be quite a Casanova). But he does want to end up with his true heart's companion, his soul mate, so he has his inner romantic compass pointed at admiring, romancing and marrying his own starwoman. While he enjoys the social scene, and the dating and mating games, he is a guy happiest when in love and married. Now he often takes time to settle down — even when he's married — 'cos sometimes he just can't let go of his urge to explore the female realms even more than most men. A male Libra friend of mine has been married four times (wife number four is an exotic Leo beauty from India), but he has never become disillusioned with the institution of marriage, he just likes to be adventurous in his experiences. He is completely and utterly in love with being in love. Fortunately, his beautiful wife is a passionate Leo with a heart of gold. They're a perfect match, but will it last? Only time will tell.

Mr Libra is not exactly the most predictable man of the zodiac when it comes to knowing how he'll react romantically or in the marriage stakes. That's why the Leo woman feels a trifle out of her depth. She knows she's dealing with a somewhat unknown male quantity. She also realises that while she can control him to a certain extent, there's a side to him that can be super elusive and therefore tough to pin down. The Leo woman needs to feel special and adored, and her Libra guy is able to make her feel like she's the most unique woman in the world (something she truly laps up).

When they meet there's probably a hot surge in the air, an instant physical attraction. Romance and lovemaking is an important part of their relationship, perhaps more so than other sign combinations. The Leo woman is more inclined to desire raw, lusty sex (typical of fire signs), while her Libra guy favours beautiful and refined preludes to lovemaking. He'll take her out for a romantic dinner or weekend away and sprinkle rose petals on their bed before a night of lovemaking. He loves the preamble to sex. Ms Leo adores his romantic touches but she is often more impulsive in her attitude to pleasures of the flesh. She'll occasionally grab him from behind (just think of the feisty Lioness of the Jungle!), rip his clothes off and make passionate love, right there and then. Both of these exhibitionists adore making love in a room with mirrors on the ceiling and walls. As nothing quite turns them on as much as themselves, and seeing the two of them together in acts of intimacy can be more erotic to them than just about anything else under the sun, moon and stars.

Outside the bedroom the Leo gal and Libra guy have a way of balancing out each other's very different personalities. The air-ruled Libra guy is very communicative, and he'll draw her out in those times when she feels insecure, is going through one of her more sulky moods and doesn't want to talk. But one thing they probably will never quite come to grips with between them is his ability to charm the birds out of the trees. She only wants his charms to be utilised on her, so one thing that Ms Leo is going to have to get used to is her guy's innate flirtatiousness. His charm oozes from his every pore, he just can't help it — that's who he is, Mr Charm of the zodiac. So, even if he has no intention of straying from his Leo lady, he'll still chat and smile coyly with the pretty waitress serving them or the attractive neighbour next door. It might help some Leo women to know (especially those inclined to jealousy) that he uses the same charm in his business life too. There is simply something about him that has people falling over themselves to say 'yes'. He isn't looking to run off with someone (although he might), but he just can't stop himself from being a turn-on.

When single, the Libra man is likely to fall in and out of lust many times. But, when he TRULY, MADLY AND DEEPLY meets the woman of his dreams and falls in love, he usually wants to get married; so does Ms Leo when she meets her true heart's desire. Now if they decide to turn their romance into a permanent relationship both Mr Libra and Ms Leo usually have expensive tastes. So they'd better go out of their way to secure good incomes (ie good investments and well-paid jobs) that will set them up for a good life together. They'll need plenty of 'dollars' to support their spending habits, especially as both of them love good food and wine, luxury hotels and expensive clothes.

If they marry and have children, it's likely that Ms Leo will decide on where they buy their house and how they raise their children, simply because she has a tendency to dominate. The Libra man is more flexible and will usually let her get her own way. After all, he's undecided on most issues and could find either the pros or cons in anything. He hates to argue, so generally he'll let her have free reign over home, hearth and general affairs. That's because maintaining harmony, balance and peace are sacred goals to the Libra man and so-called 'ugly' emotion (anger or fear especially) makes him feel extremely nervous. If she gets out of line, becomes unreasonably jealous or possessive, he'll argue with her for a while, but when push comes to shove, he'll back off. However, if she is too pushy, controlling or unreasonable, he may not say too much but one day he'll walk out the door without looking back. Similarly, if he is disloyal to her, unfaithful, unreliable, or a spendthrift, she'll also pull back and eventually leave or throw him out the door.

So these two need to treat each other with kid gloves most of the time, as there are definitely areas where they need to tread cautiously if they want to keep their true love alive. But if true love prevails, and they both remain heart-connected, the Leo gal and the Libra guy can turn out to be one of the most successful cosmic couples on the planet.

Leo man—Libra woman

 The *'I would love to dance with you tonight . . . horizontally'* relationship

When they join forces, the Leo man and Libra woman can create absolute magic. From marriage to life-long friendship and business deals, they simply vibrate on the same levels. They'll float through life with cheer, optimism and love. After all, Ms Libra and Mr Leo are from the same astrological neighbourhood. She's from Venus, the planet of love and beauty, and he's from the life-giving exuberant Sun; and these planets are galactically harmonious. In fact, you might say that the Libra woman and her Leo man are like the zodiac's boy-and-girl-next-door.

My close Libra friend and her Leo husband have a wonderful life together. They started a business buying expensive art overseas and selling it in Australia. Both have an eye for beautiful and exotic objects d'art, and they have carved out a niche for themselves in a very competitive market. Their dinner parties are incredible, as Leo and Libra are the zodiac's host and hostess par excellence! They are a very glamorous couple and the fabulous thing is that they are so much in love.

Yes, Leos and Libras really have the possibility of creating a dream life together of the happy-ever-after kind. They each bring to the relationship what the other lacks and the result is pure physical, mental, spiritual, emotional and sexual chemistry. In fact, it was probably the sexual chemistry that first brought them together. Ms Libra is the kind of gal who loves to be swept off her feet by a charming man (as a little girl her favourite bedtime stories involved chivalrous knights fighting dragons to save the beautiful princess). Of course, the Leo man is one of the most charming and magnetic men in the zodiac. It's likely he wooed her with extravagant gifts and wonderful dinners; she in turn would have charmed the pants off (literally!) her Leo suitor with grace, elegant conversation and feminine wiles, leading him finally to her romantic bedroom, complete with four-poster bed and white, lacy bed linen. Both are heavily into pleasure and their love-making sessions are blissfully long and sensual. Neither likes to be rushed when it comes to sex.

Outside the bedroom, Ms Libra has a tendency to be . . . well . . . a little lazy. Ruled by pleasure-loving planet Venus, the Libra woman prefers enjoying herself than the monotony of hard work. This is the kind of gal who really needs to follow the saying, 'do what you love and love what you do'. The perfect job for her involves being with people (she's naturally very sociable), and surrounding herself with beauty (many work in art-related professions). There are many career-orientated Libra girls who work hard, but there are also others who prefer to stay in a beautiful house, raise beautiful children and have their beautiful husband be the breadwinner. Thankfully, the Leo guy is a perfect candidate. You see, his astrological symbol is the Lion and he's a natural provider. He's quite happy for his Libran Queen of the Jungle to remain in the lair while he goes to hunt.

The Leo man has a tendency to be extremely temperamental. He's often moody and dominating, and his bossy manner can sometimes be too much for his soft, gentle-mannered Libra gal. If there's one thing she can't stand it's unfairness, aggression and fighting. Well, just think about it. The astrological symbol of Libra is the Scales, and she is constantly trying to find a balance in life. She's just and impartial (in fact many Libras make great lawyers or human rights fighters). In the Leo–Libra household, she's often the peace-keeper (especially if her children are sparring). Luckily the Libra gal knows exactly how to handle her Leo man's ego and turn his Lion's roar into a pussy cat's purr. She's a master of flattery, and it gets her *everywhere*, especially where her Leo lover is concerned.

LEO — SCORPIO relationship

The *'Are you really sure this is going to work?'* relationship

STAR LEO–SCORPIO COUPLE
Bill Clinton and Hillary Rodham Clinton

Anything and everything can and possibly will happen with this zodiac exchange of passionate energy. If you are in the near vicinity of this duo meeting and matching up, then get ready to run! Get ready to hide! Because when there's a Scorpio–Leo love match starting to burst into fiery love flames, it is explosive and drama-packed, and has the same effect as a romantic wildfire. Unfortunately, for some strange karmic reason, when these two fall in love usually somebody ends up getting burned (often a current partner who is about to be replaced in an instant). But this union often has the effect or impact of turning everybody's life inside out and upside down around them. This is one of those relationships often labelled Love–Hate. It definitely isn't for the faint-hearted and both members of these two signs should enter into it at their own risk, fully aware that they are heading into uncharted, uncontrollable, romantic realms.

Let's look at this duo astrologically. Here you are combining the Lion with the Scorpion. That's enough of an image to give you cosmic insight that both individuals are forceful, deadly and not someone to play around with. In human terms, intense Pluto-ruled Scorpio and fiery Sun-dominated Leo are both, by nature, hot signs to handle by any means. But put them together and the words POWER, DOMINANCE and PASSION light up in front of your eyes. Both Leo and Scorpio have an intense desire to be in control, at any price. When things are going well for these two, you can have the most dynamic couple in the world. They can expect high passion, intensity and a strong love connection. But when things go bad between them, well, to put it mildly what occurs can be severely bad. If infidelities or other mishaps occur between them, then the relationship storm clouds that can brew over these two can be scary.

Leo woman — Scorpio man

The *'Aahh . . . oooh . . . scratch a little higher'* relationship

If only astrology were taught at school, we'd be much more ready for the astrological love game — at least Ms Leo and Mr Scorpio could prepare themselves for the power plays in their own love match. Passion, control and intense emotions rule when the Leo woman and Scorpio man dance into each other's arms and gaze up into each other's powerful eyes with expressions of love, lust and romantic promises. This union unleashes the love furies in all its most intense and powerful forms.

Feelings run super deep when warm, gregarious and expressive Ms Leo meets the intensely private and secretive Mr Scorpio. His deep, steady gaze immediately begins probing the very workings of her soul. Does it feel good to her, this sense of being invaded? Only if she really is attracted to him. If he isn't the right guy for her, she'll sense his intensity, turn tail and run. Though it's not like a Leo woman to feel intimidated, even if she madly fancies him, she probably still had a sense that his advances were a little too close for comfort. Ms Leo is, after all, the regal Queen of the Jungle. Well, *how dare* Mr Scorpio cut to the chase *sooo* quickly and break romantic play, the game of romance protocol, when he should be bowing graciously to Her Majesty (along with her many other faithful followers).

He'll vibrate with hidden passion and she'll act haughty for a while, but devastatingly sexy Mr Scorpio will soon work his sexual 'come to my bed immediately' voodoo magic on her, seducing her into his boudoir. Once she's between his sheets, then she'll have a chance to consider, if he's as good as he promised he was going to be when he projected his love vibes in her direction. If he shapes up to her expectations, she is going to be his devoted slave. If he flunks the sex test, she's gone from his abode and his arms, probably before he returns from his post-sex trip to the bathroom.

But if the sex magic does its job (and it usually does), it unleashes all kinds of unusual possessive passions between these two intense individuals. And, no matter how much he loves his magnetic Leo gal, Mr Scorpio is unlikely to *ever* act like her subject, unless in extreme private where nobody can see him. It won't be an easy exchange of energy because two large egos clash together loudly in this classic Love–Hate relationship. Ultimately though, the passion, loyalty and a mutual respect for each other's magnificence can create a powerful and long-lasting union between the Scorpion and Lioness (even though it's a romance destined to go through dramatic ups and downs along the way). The karma between this couple suggests that they have valuable life lessons to teach each other, so whether or not they experience a short-lived love affair or a long-lasting romance, they are going to impact on each other's lives dramatically.

What they will *feel* along the way is the full gamut of emotions from complete adoration to uncontrollable lust; burning jealousy and absolute hate! Her Scorpio guy's creativity and deep, strong emotions fascinate the Leo woman. But a deep insecurity lies beneath her extroverted and courageous exterior. If he criticises her, she's likely to feel it very, very deeply. And he'll soon learn that the Leonine displeasure can be icy cold.

Like his astrological symbol, the Scorpion, the Scorpio man has a sting that is downright deadly. I once had an interesting conversation with a Scorpio friend about this very point. Interrupting me ever so smoothly, he said that I was mistaken, and that death by a Scorpion sting was actually very rare. '*Yes — alright,*' I told him, '*. . . sometimes the venom doesn't kill, but it will cause severe pain and suffering, difficulty in breathing, muscle-twitching and convulsions.*' Well that's not too bad, it could be worse, was his response. That said, if you are a Leo woman involved with a Scorpio man, observe two golden rules here: a) Get on the bad side of Mr Scorpio and the price you pay will involve suffering and pain, and b) Never think you can tell him the truth about himself, others or the world at large. As far as he's concerned he's always 'right'.

Mr Scorpio is a water sign, the most powerful of all elements. When up against the flames of fire sign Ms Leo, he has the ability to douse her flames and put out her light. But typically, the Scorpio man needs her flame to light up his life. What fun is his existence without her boundless energy, sunny smile, generosity and warm embrace? His big lesson in their union is to allow her room to shine. The magnetic Leo woman will *always* have people (especially men) in orbit around her. It's a fact of life, and the Scorpio man needs to keep tabs on his own jealousy and possessiveness. You see, a Leo woman in love is extremely loyal. These two lovers need to spend lots of time together but leave some things separate (like their bank accounts!) Following these few simple guidelines, Ms Leo and Mr Scorpio can live passionately and powerfully with each other forever.

Leo man—Scorpio woman

♡ The '*"Sorry" isn't the best way to start off a romance'* relationship

Are we going to be great mates, start a business together, or fall head-over-heels in love and go and get hot in the cot? Often the Leo man and Scorpio woman are confused about exactly where this relationship or the feelings they have for each other should lead. They certainly have loads of options because together (on almost any level of operation they choose), they are a relationship force to be reckoned with. If love is their chosen way of joining forces, drawn together by each other's strength, confidence and magnetism, there are plenty of intense emotions and power games ahead. To understand this passionate relationship, just consider the dynamic between Leo ex-US president, Bill Clinton and his wife, Scorpio senator Hillary Rodham Clinton. In life and in love, the Scorpio gal and her Leo lover don't hold back; they are often in the relationship for the long haul — even if it tests their true grit — and they'll smile and carry on regardless. Usually being a public kind of couple, they play out their relationship on centre court. It's no wonder there are so many famous politicians, actors and other performers who make up the Ms Scorpio–Mr Leo combination.

The chemistry is intensely strong between them. Often, if their love stars are tuned into each other, when the Leo man and Scorpio woman first meet there's so much sexual chemistry that the sidewalk they're standing on 'literally' starts to sizzle. The first thing he notices are her eyes. This woman has the most penetrating eyes in the zodiac — they speak volumes. With one intense gaze Ms Scorpio will show whether she's ready to indulge her sexual fantasies with him or whether she's playing hard-to-get. If she's angry she'll give him the 'dagger eyes'. Even though her eyes give away everything, she'll *never* verbalise her desires or fears. You see, the Scorpio woman is very secretive; and why would she give up her mystery by wearing her heart on her sleeve? It would be akin to shooting herself in the foot! So she decides to keep her intense emotions hidden underneath a controlled façade.

Depending on the planetary placements in her personal horoscope, the Scorpio woman can be highly romantic or, alternatively, extremely detached from romance. *What* really excites her is the anticipation of a night of hot sex with her Leo lover. The Scorpio woman is a sultry sexpot who typically knows exactly what to do to drive her man wild with desire. The Leo man is also a Casanova — he's confident, dramatic and he radiates an irresistible sexual power that draws women into orbit around him. His ruler, the Sun, gives him an abundance of enthusiasm and an ability to enjoy life (and especially sex!) Together, Ms Scorpio and Mr Leo can access a sexual nirvana that makes their past sexual encounters pale in comparison. Although the Scorpio woman has no inhibitions when it comes to sex, don't think for a minute that this girl is all body and no brains.

The sexy Scorpio gal is intelligent and intuitive, and she knows how to wrap a man around her little finger. But her love of control can be very self-destructive. A Scorpio gal pal of mine tried to manipulate her Leo husband into becoming someone else! She liked the 'raw material' but wanted him to be more cultured and intellectual. It didn't work and trying to get him to change his job (he'd been in the same business for ten years) and become an opera buff (when he much preferred football!) gave him the constant message of *'I'm not good enough for her'*. Needless to say this Leo man and Scorpio woman ended up in the divorce courts.

The Leo man is quick to fall in love *and* he's very loyal, but if his pride is hurt and he feels rejected he can turn into a roaring beast (and believe me, that ain't a pretty sight!) When it comes to the crunch, the Leo man is simply a big pussy cat (parading as a lion) who wants to be loved. It won't take long for the love-struck Leo to realise Ms Scorpio's game. He'll be running her errands and suddenly stop and think, *'What the hell am I doing?'* when he realises he's stopped playing King of the Jungle and turned into a playful and bland Cheetah! Hence the power play between these two dominating signs begins once more.

If Ms Scorpio and Mr Leo haven't progressed very far along the astro-evolutionary ladder, it's unlikely that good sex alone will keep them together. These fixed signs have too many power struggles going on to be able to maintain a truly loving, peaceful and balanced relationship. And if either Ms Scorpio or Mr Leo lose respect for each other, it's over, for good. Successful Scorpio woman–Leo man partnerships have learned to give and take, to forgive and forget and to put their egos aside long enough to let the love in. If they do work through their astro-challenges, this couple will enjoy a loving, lusty relationship forever.

LEO — SAGITTARIUS relationship

The *'Why am I so lucky in love . . . sometimes?'* relationship

STAR LEO–SAGITTARIUS COUPLE
Melanie Griffith and Don Johnson

There's gonna be emotional and sexual fireworks and a whole lotta dancing (most of it horizontal), romancing and partying going on when this gregarious, 'let's have a party' Leo–Sagittarius couple unite. Naturally to keep up with their desire to live a full, romantic life, they'll need loads of money, time and energy to keep up with each other's high expectations; and sometimes any lack of supply in these areas tends to slow things down. Yet generally if the love magic is potent between them, everything about the love match between Leo and Sagittarius happens in a larger-than-life, let's-boogie-on-to-the-romantic-realms way.

It's likely these two pleasure-seekers even met in extraordinary circumstances; had a dramatic courtship; starred in their big wedding; came up with a most flamboyant kind of honeymoon and now live in a big house and are on their way to having beautiful children. Words such as 'ordinary' and 'moderation' rarely exist in the combined Leo–Sagittarius vocabulary. You see, when Sagittarius (ruled by Jupiter, the planet of abundance) and Leo (governed by the life-giving Sun) unite, there is combined power, passion and plentifulness. And they are often both born lucky, which helps a great deal too. One thing's for sure, Leo and Sagittarius weren't designed in the zodiac realms to play for small stakes in life *or* love, so this isn't going to be a meek, cautious, waltz-me-around-the-kitchen-sink type of relationship — it's going to be a romantic hula-hula dance kind of affair.

Leo woman—Sagittarius man

 The *'C'mon, stop trying to stop the inevitable'* relationship

The love match between Ms Leo and Mr Sagittarius is often that once-in-a-lifetime love connection that comes once *only*. Whether it lasts five days or fifty years, theirs is an intensely powerful, profound connection. The Archer and his Lioness are both fire signs and by birth they are fiery, active and enthusiastic. They love life and, in each other, have found a soul mate with whom to share life's adventures. Unfortunately, tactless Mr Sagittarius has a way of arousing the fury of his Lioness. He knows exactly how to push her emotional buttons and make her growl, and he's foolish enough not to learn his lesson and keep quiet when he should (for peace's sake, too!) The following scenario may sound familiar to the Ms Leo–Mr Sagittarius couple:

MS LEO:	Hi sweetie, ready to go? Do you like my new shoes?
MR SAGITTARIUS:	Yeah, I love them. Ya know, you did really good buying those shoes because they really make your feet look better.
MS LEO:	What do you mean — look better?
MR SAGITTARIUS:	Oh . . . smaller I guess. The strappy gold ones the other night made your feet look really big. They kinda looked really strange.
MS LEO:	*(Silence. Lioness purring has stopped, now replaced by a deep throaty growl)*
MR SAGITTARIUS:	*(Silence. Starts to get nervous, shrugs his shoulders and attempts to smile broadly. Then tries to make amends)* Darling, you have beautiful feet, would you like me to massage them for you.
MS LEO:	*(Snarling)* You keep your nasty little hands to yourself — big ears!

Well, sometimes these two can be so ridiculously childish it is quite hilarious. Hilarious, maybe, to everyone else, but probably not too funny and hilarious to them.

Unfortunately, candid Mr Sag is too honest for his own good (especially where love and romance are concerned). He has a tendency to be too frank, too outspoken, and too direct at the wrong time. If he hurts her pride or treads too heavily on her Lioness' paws, Ms Leo is likely to retreat — wounded — to her Lioness' lair (she often seeks out close girlfriends at this time and has a good long sulk). You see, the Leo woman needs and desires a man who loves, cherishes and looks up to her. She doesn't want to be thought of as anything *less* than totally gorgeous 24/7 — even if this is an impossible image to uphold. For all her confidence, the Leo gal (while always appearing regal, proud and in control) often feels deep down that she's not good, pretty, desirable, attractive, smart or rich enough. She *cares* what people think about her.

Mr Sag, however, respects his Leo lover; he adores her for who she is, but he'll never worship adoringly at her altar. Grovelling is just not his style. Luckily, no matter how much he frustrates her or fails to boost her ego at times Ms Leo will fall deeply in love with her philosophical Archer. He's a wise sage, naughty little boy and sensual lover wrapped up in one package and not many gals of the zodiac can resist his mischievous, fresh, sex appeal (certainly not her). Plus, he's independent and doesn't care what people think about him and that's quite attractive and appealing to her, because she cares *sooo* much what the world thinks of her. His Leo woman somehow hopes (maybe through osmosis) that like him, she'll have a carefree relaxed attitude to the outside world, and she'll become immune to other people's opinions about her.

The Leo woman, meanwhile, brings plenty of love, affection and wonderful sex into Mr Sag's life! Both are fire signs with big sexual appetites. She's a lot of fun and a lot of dramas all wrapped into one; and he loves adventure more than most. Their bedtime antics are fiery, passionate and plentiful. This woman exudes carnal desire and she's a mistress of seduction. Luckily, her Sag guy has a strong (but sometimes erratic) sex drive and is able to fulfil her needs. Neither tolerate boredom when it comes to sex — and he, especially, needs plenty of mental stimulation to keep his sexual longing alive. Both of them love those mirrors on the ceiling that reflect back their karma sutra positions so erotically.

While her Sag man enjoys her need to dominate in the bedroom, many times he gets frustrated when she tries to control him outside the *boudoir*. He won't be ruled by her whims, wishes or insecurities and it certainly won't work for her to try and rein him in. Trust is a big issue here because he needs plenty of space. He's the not the kind of guy who enjoys twenty-four-hours-a-day togetherness. If she gives him some rope, he is unlikely to stray (especially if he is completely smitten by his Leo gal).

Freedom-loving Sagittarius is one of the male signs most likely to win the zodiac's Confirmed Bachelor award. When in love, however, he's loyal and affectionate. Fortunately the Leo woman is one of the most promising candidates to bring an end to his bachelorhood status. She's intensely alive and intensely individual; and the Sag man will find a ready playmate to join him in a tennis match, a walk in the mountains, a game of chess (or whatever other activity he has added to his repertoire!)

Leo man—Sagittarius woman

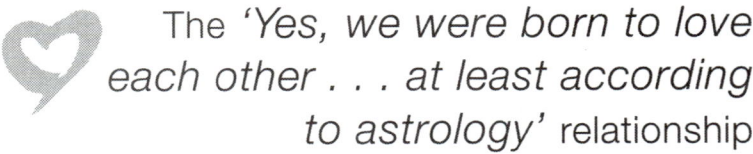

The *'Yes, we were born to love each other . . . at least according to astrology'* relationship

When the Archeress and Lion King get together in the love game it's going to be an all-or-nothing affair. And whether their connection ends up being a hot one-night stand, an intense affair, a long-term romance, a great friendship or a lifetime marriage, it will be a relationship that changes their very being. Emotionally, mentally, spiritually and sexually, there are amazing possibilities between the Leo man and Sagittarian woman to make their dreams come true — *if*, of course, they are both looking for the same thing. For example, if a Sagittarian woman, ready to settle down, meets a Leo man still in the throes of bachelorhood, then there will definitely be tears before bedtime.

In many cases, however, it might be the Sagittarius woman who is shy of long-term commitment. This is one of the most independent gals in the zodiac. Courageous, strong and idealistic, she doesn't want a relationship to feel like a ball and chain around her ankle. There is so much in life that the fire-ruled Sag woman wants to experience. She's feisty, self-expressive and optimistic, and these are the things that the Leo man loves in a woman.

The Sagittarian woman, however, is a rebel at heart. My friend's ninety-four-year-old Sagittarian grandmother fought tooth and nail to remain in her own home when the subject of a nursing home was brought up in a family discussion. And so she stayed in her own home! You see, even in old age the Sagittarian is like a teenager; tell her *not* to do something and she's likely to go right out and do it! Mr Leo is likely to call this rebellious streak of hers 'irresponsible'. If he self-righteously tries to lecture her (as the dominating Lion is want to do), Ms Sag will fire one of her Archer's arrows of truth straight into the Leo's ego with one swift movement of her bow. There's nothing worse than seeing a Leo man's warm heart instantly frozen when his pride has been hurt or his ego deflated. She needs to remember that her Leo man has the biggest ego of his zodiac brothers.

Despite their fiery discussions, there is plenty of *positive* energy between the Sagittarian gal and the Leo guy. They find an instant empathy and understanding in each other's arms. Mr Leo admires her integrity, unshakeable optimism, free spirit and her cheerful outlook on life. She is attracted to his noble bearing, creativity, high energy and warmth. She loves to take on new adventures in life and he can be a willing companion to help her design, plan and lead the expedition!

Sometimes the competitive energy between one another is a magical prelude to lovemaking. These fire signs simply sizzle between the sheets. The Sag gal is magnetically attracted to her Leo guy's charm and chemistry. He's romantic and expressive and he'll sweep her off her feet with dinners-for-two and champagne toasts. But basically they know how to laugh and have fun together, and this might be the most powerful aphrodisiac of all!

If Mr Leo and Ms Sagittarius marry and set up house together, it's likely to be a home full of extravagant furniture (his), sporting equipment (hers), books, art and plenty of social invitations stuck to the fridge! If they have children, he'll make a doting and affectionate dad, and she will instil a sense of independence in them. Both parents will plan fun activities for the whole family to do together.

The wonderful thing in this cosmic partnership is the ability they have to lift each other's spirits. When the Lion feels glum, his Sagittarian lady will cheer him up and help him find his lost roar. And when the Archer girl's arrows have all misfired, her gentle Leo man will help guide her back on track, and harmony will prevail in the cosmic jungle once more.

LEO — CAPRICORN relationship

The *'We've been dating for ten years. Isn't it about time for us to get serious?'* relationship

STAR LEO–CAPRICORN COUPLE
Jaqueline Kennedy Onassis and Aristotle Onassis

Hello — is anybody home? Probably not too often at the Leo–Capricorn home. The big relationship question is: are they out together or going their own separate ways? That's probably the best way of gauging whether this romantic relationship is rocking on, or already on the rocks. It isn't easy for the Leo and

Capricorn to always get along (unless they have such super times in the cot that they can't wait to get back into it together again). Or, perhaps they are building a family world together (their own dynasty) or a big company or they share some huge mutual goal, then this couple can be a relationship and romantic force to behold. But usually it takes more than one of Cupid's smaller love darts to make this love match pass the everyday tests; he needs to shoot them both up with a love-guided super missile.

After all, in astro-theory, the Leo–Capricorn love match just *shouldn't* work (which is often exactly the reason why it does — this relationship operates out of the ordinary range or accepted realms of relationships). Sun-ruled Leo is proud, expressive and very often extremely bossy. Lions are born to bask in the attention of their loyal subjects and their speciality is telling *everyone* how they feel and what they think. Discreet Capricorns, on the other hand, have a tendency to hide their emotions, look like they are calm when they really are having a tizzy fit; and they also love to be in control, but in a less upfront fashion.

Now it's this control situation (deciding who is going to hold the control in their relationship) that can become their tough love issue. The Capricorn's planetary ruler, Saturn, holds a gripping influence on them, endowing them with wisdom and self-discipline (and a variety of hang-ups that keep their therapists in work for years!) Whereas Sun-ruled Leos just spill the beans if they've got issues that are burning them up and they express themselves outwardly rather than hold everything back. But opposites have a tendency to attract, and as these two come from such different zodiac realms, the very differences are often what works for them, not against them.

Leo woman — Capricorn man

 The *'Remember, diamonds are a girl's best friend'* relationship

'The Armani suit?' he asks her.

'No, I think the more outrageous Versace is actually better on you — it has more flair.'

'Mmm, but I actually prefer the classic cut of the Armani,' he says, choosing, in the end, the understated Armani suit.

If there's one couple destined to favour designer clothes (or designer *anything*!) it's the Ms Leo–Mr Capricorn match. And this couple is also possibly destined to find themselves featured in the social pages of the newspapers or magazines. They have different styles, different ideals and different expectations, but nevertheless they do have one big thing in common — they want to make it to the top of whatever ladder they think is the right one for them; and they'll go about their tasks diligently to make their mark and lead the way. Sometimes this couple are true fashion trendsetters too. While he's into quiet elegance; luxurious flamboyance is more her style. This couple is destined to live the high life together (even if in a very humble home-maker setting; somehow they'll jazz things up so it has a special beauty, appeal or comfort to it).

Right from the start of their relationship they seem to gravitate towards each other, as if magnetically connected. The very regal Ms Leo catches the eye of her Mountain Goat guy because she has some kind of power that exudes out of her. You see, this is a man with a special quality — he has something different to offer her (she's not quite sure what, but she can sense it). Possibly it's sex appeal, but she isn't sure if that's all it is; there's more to him than she can fathom. At her first appraisal she feels the Capricorn man loves fine clothes, exquisite furnishings in his house and eating out in the best restaurants. Even if he's a Capricorn of modest means, he's likely to save in order to buy 'quality' over 'quantity'.

To him, the Leo woman is a living, breathing 'quality' item that is wrapped up in a very exciting physical package. He falls in love with her Leonine ability to light up a room and her sophisticated (but not stuffy) style. She's an individualist and he admires the way she wields magnetism over her followers. Both are natural leaders, yet Mr Capricorn's approach is definitely more conservative (his astrological ruler, serious Saturn, won't allow him to be anything else). He's a Mountain Goat determined to reach his chosen pinnacle, step by step on a well-trodden path. His Leo gal is more of a risk taker. She will do something he never does, and that's take short cuts or go off on side trips as she winds her way to the top. Courageous and strong, she'll try a new path that promises a quick journey with cappuccino stops along the way. If they join forces, however, both will enrich the other's journey and enjoy plenty of laughs on the way to the top. The Capricorn man is often surprisingly funny and offbeat, while the Leo woman also has a healthy sense of humour. So often you'll see them laughing together in a corner, sharing a joke or an aside that nobody else would understand or get the funny side to, except for them.

If she's his super stargal, then Mr Capricorn man might put her up on an unrealistic type of pedestal at times, and seem to only focus on her good side without seeing some of her lesser qualities. But that's just where the Leo gal, ruled by the dominating Sun, loves to be. Sitting atop her pedestal and emitting a warm, proud glow like the Queen of the Jungle, she'll bask in the warmth of his love and respect. Mr Capricorn is made for marriage and if they *do* tie the knot expect a lavish, Hollywood-style wedding. The typical Capricorn guy wants to do everything by the book, insisting that life occurs in the 'right order'. He aims for a nice engagement first and then a big family-style marriage followed by babies.

Even if Ms Leo decides her biological clock is ready before the nuptials occur, she's unlikely to talk him into premarital fatherhood. The Cap man's need to follow protocol can drive her insane, causing her to roar loudly *'Who cares what people think, forget about your stuffy values, just step outside the box for once!'* Yet if the truth be known, she wouldn't want him any other way. He has good manners, he's reliable, steadfast and a trifle old-fashioned at times, and he's surprisingly patient with her. He's a real man and she's a real woman; and that's just what this couple needs — an equal; but not someone who is so alike them otherwise their union becomes humdrum.

There are also times when Mr Capricorn won't be so compassionate or understanding and will pick flaws in his Leo sweetheart. *Why does she need so much attention? Doesn't she know that I love her? Why do I need to keep proving myself to her?* He's not the kind of guy who'll be pushed around and he's certainly not going to obey her every wish, command and order. In fact he's probably never loved someone with such depth *or* argued with such passion but that doesn't mean she should try to walk all over him! You see, both Mr Capricorn and Ms Leo are very stubborn when it comes to affairs of the heart. There are many Lion–Goat couples that find it impossible to keep their strong personalities in balance, and these ones won't continue their friendship after the romance fades. Sometimes this relationship burns out because there's too much of a challenge of power plays in force between them.

To make it work the Lion gal needs to let her Capricorn guy shine in his own particular way (he's not a flamboyant performer so he can shine without outshining her). He, in turn, needs to indulge her need for attention, affection and adoration and her desire to explore her spiritual, emotional and physical self. Capricorn men can sometimes come across as being cool and distant on the outside but most are surprisingly passionate when they're with the woman they love.

Now where this couple may find they have a great advantage as a couple is in their physical lovemaking. They can both be great partners for each other, and their lovemaking can be passionate and always exciting. They have the same philosophy on sex. Both are romantics at heart, and they'll plan a candle-lit dinner as a prelude to a night of lovemaking between, naturally, designer sheets.

Leo man — Capricorn woman

 The *'Please don't get cranky with me, I'm doing my best'* relationship

When Mr Leo is attracted to a Capricorn woman he might feel a little confused, even uncomfortable, and this sensation will come as a great surprise to him. Most women do not have the power to make him feel out of his comfort zone at all. But Ms Capricorn is different. She has the power to sometimes run rings around him and that makes him giddy. Ms Capricorn is classy, funny and she's a subtle seductress. In fact, a Capricorn girlfriend of mine has flirting down to a fine art. She knows how to catch a man's eye, smile shyly with *that* twinkle in her eye, hold his gaze and then walk away, looking slowly over her shoulder one last time. If her feminine wiles catch the attention of a confident, regal Lion of the Jungle, then sparks are definitely going to fly!

Although the Capricorn woman is typically softly-spoken and feminine, she *ain't* some flighty little pushover who'll be content languishing in the Lion's pride. The Leo man instinctively feels that life could change (and dramatically) alongside the Cap woman. She's certainly going to be a mystery to him. What he'll soon learn is that the Mountain Goat maid doesn't wear her heart on her sleeve, she's smart enough to always maintain some sort of independence. OK, she might get a little sensitive, feminine and gloomy sometimes, but she's not the kind of woman to break down and cry in public. The Capricorn gal is ruled by Saturn, the planet of restraint, and since childhood she's been taught to 'behave and be strong' (and that includes hiding her emotions). She can run hot and cold; and so can he so that can sometimes complicate things. Both of them are likely to get frustrated in those moments when their partner switches off and retreats to their own form of inward emotional hidey-hole or criticises them coldly. If he's doing it to her he'll pay a big price, 'cos she'll build up an emotional brick wall between them which will require a lot of good behaviour on his behalf to tear down. If she's doing it to him, she'll soon learn that rejection doesn't become the proud Lion; it can cause him to react in all sorts of ways that might damage the fine balance of their relationship or he may find another gal to cheer him up.

Here is where the difference lies in their personalities. The Leo man is expressive, enthusiastic and positive, while she's more inclined to caution and pessimism. But with time, the Leo man's generosity and warmth is likely to envelop Ms Capricorn, prompting her to share hidden secrets, long-held desires and more than anything — her fears. His sunny disposition can coax her out of the depths of despair and she'll return to his loving arms once more.

There's plenty that Ms Capricorn contributes to her Leo lover in this cosmic love match. She's one of the most supportive females in the zodiac and will encourage him in his grandiose plans and goals. You see, the Capricorn gal is ambitious and likely to have a career as successful (if not more so) than her Leonine partner. Mr Leo needs to realise that he's not going to change her — not her clothes, her career, her friends and definitely not her family. If he's the kind of Leo man looking to mould a woman to fit his lifestyle, then this union is not going to work. Neither will it make the distance if he's the type who flirts incessantly and surrounds himself with beautiful women (even if he is one hundred per cent faithful). His Capricorn lover is a determined, no-nonsense kind of gal and she won't put up with his game-playing for long.

Accepting each other for who they are is the secret to the Mr Leo–Ms Capricorn love match. Fortunately, where sex is concerned the Mountain Goat maid is an earthy woman who's magnetically attracted to her Leo guy's overt sex appeal. The sex can be powerful, but trust is a big issue here. Ms Capricorn needs to feel it in order to abandon herself physically and emotionally. She'll let her hair down and explore new realms of sexual possibility alongside her passionate Leo man. If they sort through their differences and make it to the altar, odds are they'll have a wonderful life together.

When in love, these two are fiercely loyal, making a wonderful base for a happy family life together. To the Leo man, his home is his castle and the two of them are likely to fill it with antiques, objects of art and lots of children. She is very attached to her family and her mother, father, siblings, cousins, aunties and uncles will drop by often. In fact, with a healthy dose of mutual respect, Mr Leo and Ms Capricorn have the ability to surprise friends, family (and themselves!) and live happily ever after.

LEO — AQUARIUS relationship

The *'Has anybody else ever told you you're romantically weird?'* relationship

STAR LEO–AQUARIUS COUPLE
Loni Anderson and Burt Reynolds

Opposites attract and that's exactly what occurs in the Leo–Aquarius relationship. On the astrological chart, these two signs are exactly opposite each other. On physical, mental, emotional and spiritual levels, there is definitely a strong attraction that takes place between them and it's a mystery how it happens. This 'pull-push' zodiac dynamic certainly provides an abundance of sexual chemistry; and Leo and Aquarius find each other sexually irresistible even when they are experiencing tensions or problems in other areas of their relationship.

Many of these tensions occur because Leo and Aquarius belong to the zodiac's fixed sign group, which means they are both very immovable. So, what happens when two of the most stubborn signs of the zodiac get together in the name of love and lust? Well, as you can imagine there is plenty of head-butting and foot-stamping (à *la* their fixed sign buddy, Taurus). While a mutual love of having things 'their own way' can lead to problems, so can the unfortunate habit of trying to 'change' the other. If Leo and Aquarius are emotionally mature, this relationship can be a sizzler, but if they don't know how to give-and-take it is sure to end up a fizzler!

Leo woman—Aquarius man

 The *'I'll handle this romance my way . . . do you have any objections?'* relationship

We all know couples that bring out *the best* in each other. I'm sorry to tell you but when Mr Aquarius and Ms Leo pair up in the zodiac love game, the majority of couples born under these two star signs tend to . . . well . . . bring out *the worst* in each other. Now, before I get a barrage of letters from happily married Leo gals and Aquarian guys disputing this claim, just read on a little!

Let's face it: Leo and Aquarius (along with Taurus and Scorpio) are the zodiac's 'fixed' signs, which mean they can be pretty downright stubborn! Both have strong opinions and find it difficult giving in or giving up their point of view. Ms Leo and Mr Aquarius also have problems admitting they are wrong, even if they blatantly have been. So what happens when two 'It's-my-way-or-the-highway!' signs join up for love, lust and romance? As both can be bossy, large dollops of give-and-take are needed for this relationship to make it to long-term status. Whether this relationship sizzles or fizzles lies fairly and squarely in the hands of these two powerful individuals.

On the zodiac wheel they are situated 'opposite' each other, which means that there's plenty of physical attraction and mutual fascination between them. Sexually, the Leo gal and Aquarian guy is a powerful, passionate match. They both love surprises and variety in their sex life and they are both generous in giving the other plenty of pleasure. In fact, Mr Aquarius (ruled by the 'out there' planet of Uranus) is one of the kinkiest men in the zodiac. He's imaginative and certainly left-of-centre where sex is concerned. If Mr Aquarius keeps the excitement levels in their sex life at peak level, then his Leo gal will have no reason to wander.

The Leo woman needs plenty of challenges in her life and that includes love, lust and romance. She loves fantasy and theatre and she's often fond of extravagant lingerie, erotic photography or videos and role-playing. They often make a very striking couple. He's usually tall and slim and though not traditionally 'handsome' there's normally something very striking about his facial features. The Leo woman exudes sensuality and often has a Lioness mane of hair, a voluptuous body and a hearty, sexy laugh.

The funny thing about this relationship is that Ms Leo has what Mr Aquarius lacks, and vice versa. She has a warm personality, whereas the Aquarian male can sometimes come across as being detached and distant. She's responsible and has a true sense of dignity; Mr Aquarius on the other hand is often not very reliable and tends to forget promises or commitments he's made. What he does have is humility to admit that he may have been wrong; whereas saying 'I'm sorry' is a hard task for a Leo! Criticism tends to fall off him like water off a duck's back. He's quick to admit his faults and can be very self-effacing (he's very often the butt of his own jokes!) This is where the Leo woman can learn from him. The Royal Lion Queen won't put up with criticism or any behaviour from anyone not giving her the credit, admiration and appreciation that she deserves!

It is common that this couple have known each other for some time before beginning their romance. They may have worked together or, alternatively, been in the same social circle. My Leo girlfriend was a friend with her now-husband, an Aquarian, for five years before they started dating. Both had been in and out of relationships and *boom!* They suddenly found themselves single at the same time. An interest in foreign film brought them together and they went to see a romantic French comedy on their first date. They married a year later, and together started a company importing independent foreign films. In fact, Leo's courage and daring mixed with the Aquarian's eccentricity and unique ideas, makes them formidable entrepreneurs. Both are born organisers who love a challenge, and it's this 'make things happen' attitude that makes them excellent businessmen and women.

Not a lot offends or bothers the Aquarian man. And thankfully so. The spirited Leo lady is an expert at 'pushing the buttons' of her lovers (in more than one way!) She can be incredibly bossy, but deep down she wants a man who will stand up to her, adore her and love her — all in one package. In fact, a man needs to be very sure of himself if he takes on a Leo gal. Fiery, passionate and very sexy, she's the kind of woman who naturally attracts men. Few can resist the sensual charms of the Leo woman. Her Aquarian guy, thankfully, is not the jealous type. He likes his independence and will grant her freedom, too. He's not the kind of guy to worry if male admirers suddenly surround her. No true Leo woman ever gives up on flirting — so he'd better get used to it!

Both are friendly, intelligent and outgoing and they can talk for hours on end! When they *do* argue other people will duck for cover. Both Leo and Aquarius are extremely stubborn and neither will budge an inch when they believe they are right and justified in their view. Ms Leo (like fellow fire signs Aries and Sagittarius) can be pretty volatile during the heat of a fight. She'll exaggerate and dramatise and she'll put on an award-winning soap opera performance that may leave her Aquarian guy spellbound. Thankfully, he's not the kind to get ruffled for long. He's more likely to burst out laughing halfway through her dramatic argument and present her with a mock Golden Globe Award for her performance. She may feign humiliation at first (don't forget that Ms Leo is the regal 'Queen' of the Jungle) and sulk for an hour or so, but she'll soon be her loving, extroverted self once more. They'll kiss and make up and then kiss again — and remember why they fell in love in the first place.

Leo man—Aquarius woman

 The *'You're a very confusing but very sexy person to be around'* relationship

Mr Leo has never met anyone like Ms Aquarius before. She's one of a kind and when the Aquarian woman enters his sphere the Leo man can become very confused, even speechless! You see, the Aquarian gal doesn't care about being another member of the Regal Lion King's pride. Independent and often quite eccentric, Ms Aquarius enjoys being 'herself'. She doesn't *need* to be in a love relationship to be happy or fulfilled. At first, the Leo guy is sure to feel a little taken aback by her eccentricities; though his initial reaction will be to take it all in his stride. You see, he's not the kind of guy to show that his composure has been completely rattled by a woman!

The King of the Jungle is noble, with a deep sense of pride and showing *too* much surprise at her spontaneous antics is beneath his dignity! She will poke fun at his pompousness at times but deep down she truly admires him. She adores her Leo guy because he's fun, warm, magnanimous and very sexy. She is sometimes in awe at how he can 'make' things happen. Practical and organised, he commands respect from people wherever he goes.

Even though she does respect him, there are times the Aquarian gal acts like a naughty little school girl. She'll try and destroy his smooth composure and upset his dignity. Though he loves to joke and have fun, Mr Leo doesn't appreciate a woman who makes *him* look like a fool. God forbid his Aquarian gal play too many practical jokes or make him look anything other than regal! Leo can be quick to anger, just like fellow fire signs Aries and Sagittarius. If he feels threatened he can rise to the position of King of the Jungle, establishing his authority and enforcing his very own 'Law of the Jungle' on his Aquarian gal. If she 'gets burned' by his reprisals it's unlikely she'll want a repeat performance! He can be a formidable opponent. She, too, is very fixed in her views, so if they differ in opinion their best bet is to 'agree to disagree' rather than attempt to change each other's mind (a next-to-impossible task).

Their quarrels, however, usually create an 'energy' that turns quickly from frustration to desire! There is a powerful and magnetic sexual attraction between Aquarius and Leo. The Leo man tends to associate powerful emotions with sex, and so arguments between them often end in a passionate session of 'Kiss and Make Up'. Their feuds turn them from fighters into lovers within a very short space of time, and the calm that follows the storm renews their sense of desire and love for each other. The Leo man (ruled by the warm Sun) will always wish that his Aquarian lady were capable of more tenderness. He is an extremely 'touchy feely' person who is physically very affectionate. Being ruled by the chilly planet of Uranus, she can sometimes be unintentionally cool and detached.

Despite the fact there are times when he thinks she could use a few sessions with a therapist, Mr Leo actually loves being with such an adorably *unconventional* woman! Though eccentric, the Aquarian woman is usually intelligent, and quite often bordering on genius.

Thankfully, with a bit of give and take the Leo man and Aquarian woman can be compatible. Mr Leo is usually tender, gentle and supportive of his Water Bearer lady. No matter if she's a high school dropout, stay-at-home mum, or high-flying executive, he will forever be encouraging her to reach her potential. If Mr Organised and Ms Genius decide to start a business or enterprise together it can be an outstanding success. He is certainly the more practical of the two and, if they live together, he'll be the one to pay the bills on time, remember dental appointments or that her mother is coming over for dinner on Friday night.

He'll teach her to focus her energy on fulfilling her dreams and she'll teach him that being different certainly has its advantages. She teaches him that there really isn't anything that can be called 'normal'. She breaks the rules constantly. The Aquarian woman is likely to have very interesting hobbies, such as brewing her own beer or she may be an expert in hot-air ballooning. She may have grown up in a non-traditional family unit, being raised by parents from different cultures or surrounded by stepbrothers and stepsisters. The Leo man needs to adjust to the fact that he won't always have the undivided attention of Ms Aquarius. She's a busy lady with a wide range of friends and interests. He'll show his infamous pout if he doesn't receive the attention he needs. A smart Aquarian gal will learn early in their relationship that to ignore Mr Leo is to lose him! Similarly, a wise Leo should understand that attempting to stifle his Aquarian gal's spontaneity is a big mistake.

One thing that Ms Aquarius will never quite understand about her Leo guy is his vanity. Mr Leo is probably the most vain man she has ever dated! Not that that's a bad thing, it's simply that the typical Water Bearer gal is a 'no frills' kind of girl. She doesn't make a big fuss over her appearance. If she does hold a corporate position, she's inclined to wear a dash of lip-gloss and mascara, with her hair pulled back sleekly in a ponytail rather than full-face make-up and blow-dried coiffure. She is very natural and simply prefers spending money on things like travel, books, outdoor equipment, music and her hobbies, rather than designer clothes, expensive make-up and gym memberships.

Her Big Cat guy, however, is likely to occupy more space in the bathroom cabinet than she does with his assortment of hair and skin-care products! He's typically immaculately groomed and beautifully dressed. Even if he's slumming around the house on a Sunday morning reading the papers he'll give the term 'smart casual' a new meaning.

If they want to stay together, the formula for eternal happiness is to accept each other for who they *are*, instead of who they *aren't*. That may sound simple enough, but the Aquarian woman and Leo man are two very stubborn people with a leaning towards self-righteousness. Their life lessons together are to learn tolerance, patience and understanding. Both live life in an 'aggressive' manner, so learning to be a little 'passive' at times is not such a bad thing.

LEO — PISCES relationship

The *'Don't you dare go out without me'* relationship

STAR LEO–PISCES COUPLE
Lucille Ball and Desi Arnaz

What can I say? The Leo–Pisces match has the potential to reach a high pitch of relationship bliss or fall into chaos and become living partnership hell. The way it is going to turn out however, is certain to be extreme and how it turns out (for better or worse) greatly depends on the individual Leo and Pisces. In the worst-case scenario it can turn into a battle between Bossy Leo and Wimpy Pisces, where the Leo superiority complex heightens Pisces' feelings of inferiority. In the best of cases Leo can learn lessons of humility, spirituality and tenderness from emotional sensitive Pisces. In return, Leo will boost Pisces' confidence and show him or her that reality, responsibility and discipline are not such nasty words!

There is certainly an element of student–teacher roles in their love relationship and the roles will change, depending on what is occurring in their lives. To avoid their relationship turning into a dramatic soap opera starring Weeping Fish and Sulking Lion, tolerance, patience and understanding are necessary. Thankfully, there's no shortage of romance. When amorous Leo and starry-eyed Pisces unite in a love match, you can rest assured there will be an endless amount of flowers, candle-lit dinners and whispered 'I love you's'!

Leo woman — Pisces man

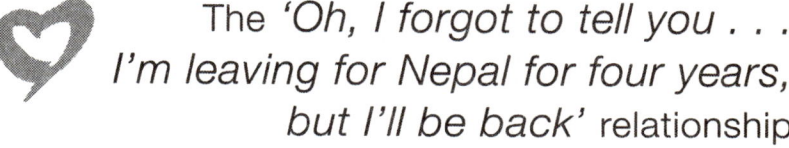

The *'Oh, I forgot to tell you . . . I'm leaving for Nepal for four years, but I'll be back'* relationship

She's a feisty gal of the zodiac, the Leo Lioness. One guess as to who 'wears the pants' in this relationship! Yep, it's the Lion Queen. In the astro-love game between Ms Leo and Mr Pisces, a role reversal takes place; that's because Leo is a 'masculine' sign and Pisces a 'feminine' sign. The life-giving force of the Sun (Leo's ruling planet) manifests itself in Leo women with the traditional 'male' characteristics of leadership, self-confidence and dominance. Though bossy at times the Leo woman is one of the most charming, lively, affectionate and fun-loving women of the zodiac.

Now it might be starting to sound as though the Pisces man has gotten the short end of the cosmic-straw. Well, nothing could be further from the truth. The Pisces man *doesn't really mind* being dominated, just as long as it's done with kindness! In fact, he'd much rather let her 'run the show' if it means that he can concentrate on daydreaming and his creative inner world. Mr Pisces has the ability to tap into dreams, intuition and other worlds. He has enormous vision, creativity and talent and many Piscean men are either involved in the arts (dance, music, art, writing) or in positions where they can help and counsel people. His psychic attunement means that he has great empathy for people and he has friends from all walks of life. He chats with the homeless guy on the corner, he'll listen to telemarketers until they finish their spiel, and he's a good mate with the company CEO. In fact, his Leo lady is likely to become infuriated and demand more of his time and attention. Mr Pisces will soon learn that his regal Lion Queen needs, desires and demands attention from her loyal subjects!

Even though she will sometimes annoy him with her bossiness and 'I know best' attitude, the Pisces man adores his Leo gal because she's kind and warm-hearted. He will also discover that Ms Leo has a tremendous sense of pride. He will listen in amazement as she tells him how she lived on a diet of cheese sandwiches during her university days. Of course she *couldn't* ask her parents for money, she'll tell him with a horrified look on her face!

Born under the mystical planet of Neptune, the Pisces man is quite a mystery himself. People might think they know him, but he's constantly doing things that surprise the people around him, including his Leo gal! It's not that he is out to shock, it's simply that Mr Pisces is not consistent and predictable. *Which* is why the Leo woman is so attracted to him. She's a practical gal with a sensible head on her shoulders (though romance is one area of life where she is completely and utterly impulsive), and sometimes she just doesn't 'get' him.

One thing that's guaranteed, the Leo woman–Pisces man match will be a romantic and dramatic story to rival Romeo and Juliet. Romance makes Leo's world go around. Born to be loved, she's never without a queue of potential suitors waiting to sweep her off her feet. She can also be quite a Drama Queen (just ask her girlfriends), but she's an impossible romantic with a true belief in the happy-ever-after, fairy-tale romance.

Thankfully, dreamy Mr Pisces matches her romantic vision. When a new romance enters his life, the Pisces man has a special spring in his step and twinkle in his eye. He'll put his Leo gal up onto a romantic pedestal and no matter what she does (within reason!) he'll love and adore her. In love and romance, he tends to don a pair of rose-coloured glasses. But the Pisces guy is also one of the most appreciative men of the zodiac. His Leo gal's sunny disposition truly lights up his life and he'll be the number one fan in her admiration club. There will be times, however, when he has big outbursts of emotions. Just as the ocean can suddenly become stormy, Mr Pisces is capable of pulling surprise emotional punches that will leave her speechless and even sorry for her thoughtless words or actions.

The more typical scenario, however, is that Ms Leo's fiery nature offsets Mr Pisces laidback attitude. Leo is a fixed sign and Pisces is mutable, which in astrological terms means that he is more likely to give in when there's an argument. The Leo woman can be quite stubborn and unmoving in her viewpoint. She does, nevertheless, have her feet firmly planted in reality, whereas her Pisces guy is a bit of a dreamer. She is capable of giving him a kick in the seat of his pants when he most needs it (especially where his career, business or financial affairs are concerned). He, on the other hand, will introduce her to new and exciting 'inner' worlds. One thing's for sure, he'll bring an abundance of tenderness and sensitivity into his Leo gal's life. What she loves about him is his ability to *listen* to her without trying to solve her problems. He's probably the most empathetic listeners in the zodiac and Ms Leo (talkative by nature) will adore being able to pour her heart out to him!

Mr Pisces and Ms Leo need to work together at creating harmony and balance in their partnership if they are to survive the 'honeymoon' period. If Leo learns to curb her brashness and treat sensitive Mr Pisces with gentleness, and he showers his Lion Queen with the admiration and appreciation she desires, then this truly could be a match made in heaven.

Leo man—Pisces woman

 The *'If you want my body let me know! If you want anything else from me, we could have a problem'* relationship

There is a puzzling and *very* strong attraction that draws Mr Leo and Ms Pisces together in the game of love and romance. In fact, you could say that the Law of Opposites applies to this zodiac matching. He's outwardly expressive, while she lives in her secret, fantasy-driven, inner world. The Leo guy is super confident, whereas Ms Pisces is prone to insecurities. He's a fire sign and she's a water sign. They are right out of each other's element. And that feeling of being 'out of your element' and exploring new dimensions (especially with romance) can be a most intoxicating mutual attraction!

In fact, the different elements of their respective zodiac signs are quite revealing. Fire (Leo) can dehydrate even a small amount of water with too much heat, while a large amount of Water (Pisces) can extinguish fire and put out its flames. Water signs intuitively fear or respect Fire signs *and* vice versa. Both sense on subconscious levels that the other could be extremely hazardous. Though Leo might get the inkling that he's in 'deep water', with Ms Pisces he is actually quite fond of dangerous liaisons! He's a daring guy and when it comes to matters of love, lust and libido, he adores a challenge. Ms Pisces, on the other hand, senses from the beginning (and she is quite psychic) that she might get 'burned' if she gets involved with fiery Mr Leo. It doesn't matter that dreamy Ms Pisces has thrown away common sense in the name of love before, so why should she stop now?

Born under watery Neptune, the mysterious and sensual Pisces Mermaid can initially seem to be a 'cold fish' to the hot-blooded Leo guy. His perception couldn't be further from the truth. Ms Pisces is a caring, compassionate and emotional gal, but she'll keep her feelings hidden beneath the surface until she knows and trusts him. The Pisces woman is sensitive and her emotions run *very, very* deep. She's romantic and dreamy and her deepest desire is to meet her true soul mate. Although her mission is pure, Ms Pisces is very impressionable. She's adept at picking the wrong guy. So, when she meets Mr Leo it's understandable she keeps him at arms' length — at *least* to begin with!

You see, the Pisces woman is very much like her zodiac symbol — two fish swimming in opposite directions. There is always a two-way conversation going on in her head. 'Don't fool yourself, he's just a wolf in sheep's clothing!' A minute later she'll be convinced he's her Knight in Shining Armour. Most things in her life occur for her in this kind of 'pull-push' way. Part of her wants a serious relationship and yet she is scared to death of commitment and, more than anything else, getting hurt. Her sensitive Mermaid flesh has been hurt before by carelessly cast love hooks.

Mr Leo, on the other hand, is fiery, passionate and impulsive where matters of the heart are concerned. He's charming and (until he finds the right gal) he can be a real 'Ladies' Man'. Ms Pisces is instantly attracted to the Leo man but he is normally not her usual 'type'. In fact, when they first meet Ms Pisces is likely to think he's a little too arrogant and showy. But little by little, Mr Leo's magnetism works on her — in both subtle and overt ways! He'll sweep her off her feet with extravagant romantic gestures, buying her flowers, chocolates or champagne followed by a romantic dinner for two. Dancing (one of his greatest pastimes) is sure to follow. Thankfully, the sign of Pisces rules the 'feet' and most Pisces women are agile and graceful dancers. Move over Fred and Ginger! When these two hit the dance floor they're likely to receive plenty of admiring glances.

Even though the Pisces woman will have loads of fun with her Leo date, it's the 'little things' he does that will win over her heart. Like when he brings her chicken soup when she's sick in bed, or buys her a seashell charm bracelet from the local craft market. He's demonstrative and will shower her in hugs and kisses. He's constantly touching her; whether his hand rests on her knee as they travel on the train, his arm around her shoulder as they walk down the street or he'll play with her long flowing hair as they watch television. She adores his fun-loving outlook on life (it balances her melancholy spells), his optimism and his warmth.

But her Leo guy is going to have to work to gain her love, trust and hand in marriage (if that's what he wants). It can either take Ms Pisces a long time to decide whether marriage is for her or, she'll impulsively jump into marriage more than once, like romantic and idealistic Pisces actress Liz Taylor. Intuitive, adaptable and creative, the Pisces woman is a mystery to Mr Leo. He's highly organised and knows what he wants in life, and it can drive him crazy when she changes her mind constantly, forgets things or tries to dodge responsibility. He can get bossy and arrogant, when in fact; all she needs is for someone to listen to her. Every day is different for Ms Pisces and much depends on her mood. If she's at a low ebb, she'll be self-indulgent and stay in bed all day, and not even Mr Leo's motivational talks will rouse her out of her depression. When she's happy, healthy and on top of things, she's a magical person to be around and her creativity and intuition are truly inspiring.

There will be times when communication between the two seems impossible. If Mr Leo and Ms Pisces make the crossover from passionate love affair to life-long commitment much will depend on the tolerance they develop for the other's weaknesses. The astrological vibrational pattern between them is often one of destiny or karma. They certainly can learn from each other. Both are very charismatic and tend to lead other people on, almost without realising it. Jealousy is a very common emotion in the Mr Leo–Ms Pisces union and can be felt deeply by both. What else do they expect considering her enchanting wiles and his debonair charms?

When they are dwelling on the shadow side of their signs, their relationship will be like an incessant soap opera with punctuated highs and lows that will leave them giddier than a roller coaster ride. If it reaches this stage, it's better to end it and remain friends. However, if they both manifest the 'bright' sides of their zodiac signs (rather than the shadow side), the Leo man and Pisces woman will create magic together and prove that their differences complement each other, instead of causing clashes between them.

virgo virgo virgo virgo virgo virgo virgo
virgo virgo virgo virgo virgo virgo virgo
virgo virgo virgo virgo virgo virgo virgo
virgo virgo virgo virgo virgo virgo virgo
virgo virgo virgo virgo virgo virgo virgo
virgo virgo virgo virgo virgo virgo virgo
virgo virgo virgo virgo virgo virgo virgo
virgo virgo virgo virgo virgo virgo virgo
virgo virgo virgo virgo virgo virgo virgo

virgo virgo virgo virgo virgo virgo virgo
virgo virgo virgo virgo virgo virgo virgo
virgo virgo virgo virgo virgo virgo virgo
virgo virgo virgo virgo virgo virgo virgo
virgo virgo virgo virgo virgo virgo virgo
virgo virgo virgo virgo virgo virgo virgo
virgo virgo virgo virgo virgo virgo virgo
virgo virgo virgo virgo virgo virgo virgo
virgo virgo virgo virgo virgo virgo virgo

VIRGO

[24 august – 23 september]

romantic pursuit: tentative

romantic vibration: sensitive (easily hurt)

secret love desire: to have a more exciting and

erotic sex life with their lover

element: earth

planetary ruler: mercury

symbol: the virgin

quality: mutable (= flexibility)

colours: earth colours, ochre, orange, yellow

gem: agate, hyacinth

best companions: capricorn and taurus

strongest virtues: creativity, tolerance,

determination

traits to improve: self-esteem,

worrying about everything, looking for

gold at the wrong end of the rainbow

deepest desire: to be perfect

Virgo celebrities

Agatha Christie, Baz Luhrmann, Ben Lee, Bill Murray, Buddy Holly,

Cameron Diaz, Charlie Sheen, Claudia Schiffer, David Arquette, David

Copperfield, Elliott Gould, Elvis Costello, Freddie Mercury, Gene

Simmons, Gloria Estefan, Harry Connick Jnr, Hugh Grant, Ingrid

Bergman, Jacqueline Bisset, Jada Pinkett Smith, James Packer, Jason

Alexander, Jason Priestley, Jeremy Irons, Jimmy Connors, Keanu

Reeves, Lachlan Murdoch, Lauren Bacall, Lily Tomlin, Macaulay Culkin,

Mark Harmon, Michael Jackson, Michael Keaton, Mickey Rourke,

Mother Teresa, Noah Taylor, Oliver Stone, Peter Phelps, Peter Sellers,

Prince Harry, Rachel Hunter, Rachel Ward, Raquel Welch, Richard

Attenborough, Richard Gere, Ricki Lake, Robin Leach, Ryan Phillippe,

Salma Hayek, Sam Neill, Sean Connery, Shania Twain, Sophia Loren,

Stephen King, Steve Waugh, Tommy Lee Jones, Van Morrison

VIRGO — VIRGO relationship

The *'Someone likes me, and I think it's you'* relationship

STAR VIRGO–VIRGO COUPLE
Claudia Schiffer and David Copperfield

When lovers of the same sun sign meet and start a relationship, especially when it's two Virgos, their compatibility factor is so in tune that the feeling they have when being together is often akin to slipping into a favourite pair of well-worn shoes. This couple often just fit well together. Their relationship can be cosy, comfortable and they feel good around each other. If their energies flow along together merrily, then Mr and Ms Virgo will spend many happy hours talking, analysing, discussing and perfecting their theories on everything under the sun, moon and stars.

When they stop talking, they'll go about their day-to-day chores like the busy bees they naturally are; putting order, structure, systems and sense into everything they do. Once that's done and they're feeling tired, they'll get into their neatly made bed, read a few passages from their novels and when they turn off their matching bedside lamps, they'll explore each other's earthy, tender, sensual charms.

Together, they'll take themselves (and each other) way too seriously, and then they'll pause to laugh at their quirky idiosyncrasies and go out to celebrate with vegetarian pizza and a glass of freshly squeezed orange juice or something more intoxicating. They'll help their friends and family, plan for the future and live long and healthy lives. It doesn't get much better than this.

Virgo woman — Virgo man

 The *'I've done the calculations and I think you and I could make a terrific team'* relationship

It's hard to imagine a more organised household than Mr and Ms Virgo's abode. Bills are paid on time, dental check-ups scheduled regularly, the dirty laundry basket is rarely overflowing and there's no lint on the sofa, despite the fact they own a white, long-haired shih tsu. Though not all Virgos are neat-freaks, the majority do like order in their lives. But that's when they've got over the dating and initial getting-to-know-you-better stage, so let's backtrack just a little.

When Mr and Ms Virgo meet, usually there's an immediate sense of recognition in the clear and sparkling eyes of the other. It's as if they're meeting a kindred spirit and they know it and often comment upon it to each other. They share a purity of spirit and a quick mind. Perhaps more importantly, they are looking for the same thing in a partner. Sometimes this closeness in their identities can help or hinder them. What decides this issue depends on how much they like each other in physical terms. If they don't find each other physically attractive, or if they don't have a sexual chemistry, then their mutual interests may be overlooked and they don't even notice each other.

In love and romance, earth-ruled Virgos seek stability and the typical Virgo is not into one-night stands or fleeting affairs. The Virgo gal (for all the rumours about her virginal airs) is a beautiful, natural and earthy woman who loves to be adored and desired. She's looking for an 'honest' kind of love. In fact, she will often make the first move on her Virgo guy, as he is prone to forget the fact that his Virgo gal is a live, flesh-and-blood woman! She's gentle, earthy and sensual and his slow-to-act style can leave her discouraged. Thankfully, determined Ms Virgo knows clever ways to let her man know that she desires him; but it takes Mr Virgo a while to give his heart and body away. He's a gentleman and his mother probably taught him to respect women and put them up on a pedestal.

Both are discriminating when it comes to choosing their partner, though Mr Virgo (in particular) can be a 'latent lover'. He may need a little encouragement to actually race her off to bed. Sometimes he thinks too much about the implications of a sexual relationship with her, such as what will happen if they're not a good sexual match; or whether she'll want to move in with him once they start making love.

The Virgo man needs to forget about the future sometimes and just give in to the moment! When he does surrender to the sexual chemistry between them, it's likely to be a blissful event! They know exactly what turns the other on and both are tender and gentle but passionate lovers. Pure-hearted Virgos believe that sex is a wholesome and earthy expression of love. They often feel uncomfortable talking about (let alone experimenting with) pornography, prostitution, sex toys and anything else they deem to be 'dirty'. Now, that doesn't mean that Virgos are frigid or asexual, as some astrology books will have you believe. It's simply that they don't like to cheapen sex. (Although I do need to make a note here that there are some Virgos who are very much into kinky or unusual sex, but for the purpose of this book I'll be looking at the ones more interested in developing a meaningful, loving relationship.)

Our Virgo couple can be highly sexed and they're usually methodical, careful lovers though this can present a double-edged sword. Mr Virgo, in particular, can be too intent on 'getting it right', leaving his lovemaking lacking in spontaneity. On the other hand, his slow and careful approach means that his Virgo gal gets plenty of special attention! He wants her to be satisfied and with time and trust, their sexual relationship gains more depth. Both Mr and Ms Virgo possess a detached, critical eye and they need to be careful that they don't start to over-analyse their lovemaking (especially during the sexual act and start conversing about what is going right or wrong at the time!)

This couple often fall for each other's minds even before the physical chemistry becomes apparent. Ruled by Mercury — the planet of the mind and communication — Virgo is an intelligent sign and their minds are quick and analytical. The wonderful thing is that Mr and Ms Virgo will never run out of fascinating conversation. The bright Virgo man and woman make a wonderful team as romantic and business partners and they can be very successful if they put their business heads together.

Both are courteous, logical and intelligent and they have an earthy sense of humour. There's generally no drama in this union and the chances are for a long and happy life together (and Virgos do tend to live to a ripe old age). They are typically health-conscious and clean-living and very few smoke, drink to excess or eat junk food. They love being with somebody who shares the same healthy living philosophy, and they'll share mock-horror stories about their ex-partners' frequent trips to McDonalds or Burger King.

The problem is, when two Virgos get together in the name of love, lust and romance, their negative and positive traits are magnified. On the positive side, they are dutiful and possess a need for selfless service. Many Virgos give money to charities or volunteer their time to help people or are involved in some type of work that serves or helps others. They are staunch humanitarians, but as much as they love people they also feel very protective of animals. Many Virgo couples may even forgo having children and shower their affections instead on a special four-legged friend. They adore animals because they are loyal and pure of heart (unlike many humans they know!) The Virgo couple are dutiful and they want to do the right thing by people. They'll send thank you notes to their friends and they'll nurse their own family members when they are sick.

On the downside, they need to be careful that they don't become too rigid in their outlook on life. They can be tough critics on themselves and their nitpicking and nagging can reach new heights if they live together. You see, problems arise if they choose the same day to wake up on the wrong side of the bed. They are prone to falling into depressions and there is nothing worse than a moody Virgo. They become critical and turn little worries, mistakes or setbacks into huge problems in a 'much-ado-about-nothing' kind of way. When things go wrong, they are quick to point the finger (either at themselves or their partner) and then they suffer the guilt associated with it!

It's times like these they should get away and take a break together and stop taking life so seriously. Fresh mountain breezes and country air do wonders for Virgo; and as they both like to take care of themselves, spending time at a spa or meditation retreat will do them a world of good. Going to funny movies and spending time with young children (who are so beautifully non-judgmental) also provide great therapy for the Virgo couple. These humble souls need to concentrate on loosening up and accepting themselves — and each other — with all the character virtues and flaws. Once they learn that perfection is an unrealistic state of being (and that there is a little bit of the saint and sinner in all of us), there's no reason why they won't happily spend the rest of their lives together. Well, as long as she washes the dishes on Monday and he mows the lawn on Saturday.

VIRGO—LIBRA relationship

The *'I thought you said that it was a sunny day, not that you're running away'* relationship

STAR VIRGO–LIBRA COUPLE
Jada Pinkett Smith and Will Smith

Earthy Virgo and ethereal Libra come from two different zodiac planets; and watching them in the decision-making process can actually tell you a lot about their dynamics as a couple. No-nonsense, practical Virgos carefully (but quickly) analyse in detail all the pros and cons of the matter at hand and efficiently make their choice without looking back. Libras, on the other hand, can spend agonisingly long periods balancing two thoughts at the same time in their symbolic Scales, until one comes out the winner. Then they'll agonise some more. But neither is wrong or right — they are simply different.

The attraction between Virgo and Libra initially tends to be very physical or very cerebral. But once they get to know each other, these next-door-neighbour zodiac signs discover that they have a strong heart connection. In love they both seek affection, respect, harmony, balance and acceptance and this is why the Virgo–Libra combination can be a winner. Virgo and Libra are serene and neither like raised voices or confrontation. But in any relationship, it's not always wine and roses. Virgos need to keep a check on their tendency to criticise (a sure-fire way to burst Libra's balloon); and busy, popular Libra needs to make time to show how much they appreciate helpful Virgo.

Virgo woman — Libra man

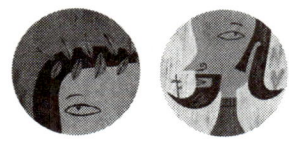

The *'If you don't treat me right, you won't get to heaven'* relationship

Young Hollywood actors Will Smith and his wife, Jada Pinkett Smith may give you an idea of the workable dynamic that exists between Mr Libra and Ms Virgo. They are compatible in many ways, but they have enough differences between them to keep an element of surprise and interest in their relationship.

You see, when the Libra man meets Ms Virgo, he's struck by her appealing feminine nature, mild-mannered personality, sweet smile and witty sense of humour. There's something refreshing about her and she has an aura of purity and goodness. Despite popular belief, the Virgo woman doesn't spend all her time doing selfless service and she's not a puritanical virgin (though of course these Virgo straight-laced type of women do exist). She's independent, intelligent and she has a mind of her own. Virgo women are accomplished workers and businesswomen and many have extremely successful careers. If there's a job to be done and you want it done well, Ms Virgo is the woman to ask! She's a realist and she knows (and typically more so than the men she dates) that relationships require give-and-take if they are going to work. She's a hard worker and she doesn't mind giving time, energy and whatever else to make her relationship work.

But the Virgo woman is discriminating and she won't give her heart away to any old zodiac Tom, Dick or Harry. She's attracted to the Venus-ruled Mr Libra because he's tender, a gentleman and a master at romance. He's chivalrous and affectionate; he surprises her with sweet gifts, and he would have to be one of the most charming men of the zodiac. And he's usually *very* attractive. The Libra man has a subtle way of commanding attention when he walks into a room. He may not be the most handsome or outrageously dressed, but he has own kinda style and his charming understated smile and his magnetic aura are his best assets. He may be happy as a bachelor boy, but nevertheless a happy life makes more sense to Mr Libra when he is in a loving partnership and he counts marriage as a life goal.

Ruled by Venus — the planet of relationships, love and romance — he comes alive when he's in love and he also adores being seen in the company of a lovely woman like Ms Virgo. He innately seeks the right partner to complete his life. He loves candle-lit dinners for two, whisking his true love away for a romantic weekend or buying her sexy lingerie. He is a devoted lover (as he is a highly sensual guy) and the earthy and tactile Virgo woman adores his tender touch. (He'll be an expert at massaging her neck, shoulders and back, and will help release her pent-up tensions and put her in the right mood for love!) Meanwhile, his erogenous zone is in his mind and his Virgo gal will soon learn that sexy bedtime talk and ideas (and maybe erotic books and movies of the more tasteful artistic type) are what turn him on.

So, you'd think that everything would be hunky dory in a relationship between romantic Mr Libra and devoted Ms Virgo. Well, yes and no. Virgo and Libra are two very different personalities and at times their differences will cause tension. The Virgo woman is ultra-sensitive, and she has a tendency to take their relationship very seriously (almost too seriously). He, on the other hand, sometimes forgets that he's in a relationship! Now that doesn't mean that he doesn't love her, or that he is out chasing after other women. It's simply that the Libra man is ruled by the element of air and, like the wind, he needs to be free and constantly active and moving. She values security over freedom and this is where they differ.

Although he might be deeply in love with his Virgo gal, there are times when he appears detached and that can be unbearable for an earth sign gal like Ms Virgo. While his Virgo gal has a razor-sharp mind and is extremely intelligent, she is more sensitive than he realises. She doesn't wear her heart on her sleeve, so people often don't realise that she's not as emotionally cool as she first appears. She's hurt by every promise he fails to keep and every time he arrives late to pick her up. If he is serious about a long-term relationship with Ms Virgo he needs to show that he appreciates her. Thankfully, Libra men possess silken diplomacy and he will make it up to her in no time.

The Virgo woman can fall into pity-party type gloomy periods and these depressions are often caused by feeling she hasn't lived up to her own high standards or that she's not pretty, good or special enough; or she may become hurt and feel that others have let her down. This is often when she starts to fault-find, nitpick and criticise him and nothing he does will be enough. He can feel hurt, but normally his easy-going sense of humour and 'tomorrow is another day' attitude help to cheer her up and allows her to laugh at her own behaviour. She thinks he's sweetly naive, though she does think it's amazing that he creates such wonderful things in his life simply because he believes that anything is possible. He loves her because she's gentle, intelligent, wise and a wonderful listener, who'll patiently listen as he goes back and forth, up and down in his quest to examine an issue from all sides in an attempt to make up his mind.

They need to create as much tranquillity and calm in their relationship as possible, as worrying makes them both suffer physically. If Ms Virgo has too many problems on her mind, she tends to get indigestion or insomnia. Her Libra guy, on the other hand, simply runs out of energy and he can spend days recovering from mental and physical exhaustion. Tiredness also makes him cranky and although it doesn't happen often, he can get surprisingly irritable if he's not getting enough rest or not eating properly. Though they can find each other frustrating at times, they can also find long-lasting happiness. Compromise is the key. Ms Virgo should strive not to take their relationship so seriously and he, in turn, should remember to appreciate her. Little things count to his Virgo gal and bringing her breakfast in bed, buying her a book by her favourite author, or giving her a cute puppy from the RSPCA are the kind of small gestures that will win her heart forever. Of course, a marriage proposal on a mountain under the stars will also do the trick.

Virgo man — Libra woman

 The *'Show me a man I can walk all over and I'll show you my man!'* relationship

Peaceful Mr Virgo doesn't go looking for love. Neither does he try and attract disruptions or surprises in his life. And just when life is moving along smoothly and quietly the vibrant, charming, lovely, irresistible and beautiful Libra gal floats into his life on a billowy cloud and torpedoes his heart into fractured, love-blown pieces that only she can put together again. This is one romantic situation where Mr Virgo can get lost in love, when Ms Libra steals his heart. Ruled by Venus —

the planet of love, relationships, beauty and femininity — this gal of the zodiac is cheerful, smart, an eternal optimist and her smile makes his head spin, and all his usual Virgo common sense flies out of his ears. Famous Libra gals like actresses Gwyneth Paltrow, Catherine Zeta-Jones and Brigitte Bardot personify the Libran belle's many feminine charms.

Even if it's Ms Libra's sex appeal and general feminine charms that initially attracts him, he soon learns that she is not just a pretty face. Ms Libra is born under a cardinal zodiac sign, which means that she's an alpha female by nature, an innate leader who likes (or must have) her own way. Though the Libra gal is not as aggressive or up-front in getting her way as, for example, Ms Aries (also a cardinal sign), her sweet voice, beautiful smile, sparkling eyes and diplomatic words are secret weapons to get what she wants! She's sweet but firm and she can wield her 'iron fist in a velvet glove'. She is a much more strong and powerful force to be reckoned with than her personal appearance or outer energies may suggest.

Because of their differences, there will definitely be some power struggles to go through between them before this relationship finds its true level ground. Now, easy-going, courteous and dependable Mr Virgo is one of the most helpful guys in the zodiac and he'll do all he can to help her have her way — at least initially (and he'll often go along with her plans, desires or needs instead of following his own). But as time goes by, he might discover that he is constantly helping her do all the things she wants to do. Eventually he can become so caught up in her life that he'll wake up one morning and wonder how did this all happen?

Her Virgo guy will put up with being Mr Nice Guy who does everything 'she says' for a while, but not even her sweet-talking ways will blind him indefinitely and he'll soon let her know that she's being unfair. If there's one thing Ms Libra can't stand, that's unfairness; even though she's probably an expert at it at times. Her astrological symbol is the Scales and she will admit that perhaps she was leaning on him a bit too excessively. This is when Ms Libra will swing like a pendulum the other way, and do all she can to please her Virgo guy. She'll take on more responsibilities and even iron his shirts to show how sorry she is for having been such a spoilt little girl! Courteous Mr Virgo will accept her apology, but in the same breath he'll mention that she forgot to iron the collar or that he found a wrinkle in the lower left sleeve. Mmmmm. The Virgo man strives for perfection and he has a tendency to nitpick and even cordial Ms Libra (the zodiac's people pleaser) will have a hard time living up to his high standards. So these two are going to have some sorting out to do of their various peculiarities or expectations where relationships are concerned.

Yet usually this sorting out is manageable. After all, she knows that if he weren't so discriminating, he wouldn't be with her. And Mr Virgo doesn't give his heart away lightly. Some Virgo men remain bachelors all their life (or marry very late) because of their quest for perfection and their discriminating eye. But if anyone can come close to living up to his high standards, it's charming Ms Libra. She's an optimist and possesses an ability to light up a room when she walks in. She brings a breath of fresh air into his ordered and scheduled life; she teaches him that some plans are made to be broken, and that it's good to experience change every once in a while. If he's the kind of Virgo who prefers a neat house and punctual meals she will need to compromise and make the effort to be on time and keep everything in tip-top shape around him. He, on the other hand, can bring a much-needed sense of stability into her life. He's practical, honest and responsible and unlike some other lovers before him she'll greatly appreciate the fact that he won't let her down.

Though her ability to see both sides of the coin and her inability to make up her mind can annoy him at times; he will listen patiently as she plays a game of intellectual ping-pong with herself. He'll try and analyse her, but may simply give up trying to understand her logic. Virgo is an earth sign and Libra is an air sign and these elements have little in common. One of his most admirable qualities is his honesty and he's direct. She, on the other hand, likes to prettily paint a picture with a thousand words and even then he might not know whether she said yes or no to his question. Ms Libra is a complex woman. She makes a perfect judge, lawyer or marital counsellor because she has the ability to see both sides of complicated issues.

Their social life could be a cause for tension. The Virgo guy is not into making superficial chitchat at parties, openings or other social events. He finds them boring and he'd much rather go out for dinner with two or three close friends. He can be a loner and he doesn't care if he doesn't win a popularity contest. Ms Libra, on the other hand, is a social butterfly. She loves meeting people, exchanging opinions and gossiping. There will be times when Mr Virgo opts for a night at home to watch his favourite documentary with a good glass of aged whisky, while she paints the town red with her friends. Time apart is actually very good for them.

At times he can turn off his emotions and retreat into sulky silence without talking to her for days. This is the worst punishment he can present to talkative Ms Libra. When things are out of balance (with her lover, friends, job, family etc) it affects her nervous system and she may also have a cranky moment once in a while. Thankfully, Mr Virgo is a practical guy and he knows that marriage and love has its ups-and-downs. There are times when he will bore her to tears and she'll annoy him with her contrariness. He might criticise her tendency to procrastinate and her eternal search for pleasure, but when it comes down to the nitty-gritty he adores her. His Libra gal fills those lonely moments with her beautiful smile and charming ways and he gives her the stability and warm comforting arms she's been waiting for.

VIRGO — SCORPIO relationship

The *'Don't be mean, say something nice to me'* relationship

STAR VIRGO–SCORPIO COUPLE
Shania Twain and Mutt Lange

Hands up if you are a Virgo–Scorpio couple, sitting side by side and about to read my book? Now, hands up if one (or both) of you have on your serious face today? Enough said. There's something about the Virgo and Scorpio love match that creates a serious tone and heavy atmosphere. That's not to say that they don't have fun together. But, a Virgo–Scorpio match simply has the ability to win the Astrological Award for Relationship Doom and Gloom year after year.

You have to go out of your way to keep the magic flowing or you both become the most worried couple of the zodiac rather than the most loving ones. Watch comedy movies, go to the circus, and hang out with bright and breezy Gemini and Sag friends! Bring lightness, laughter and good times into your romance and you can throw away that top Worry Sign Award forever!

Virgo woman — Scorpio man

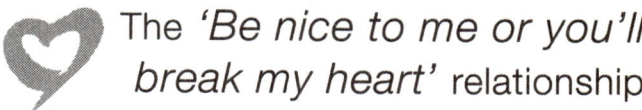

The *'Be nice to me or you'll break my heart'* relationship

When the demure Virgo gal meets sexy Mr Scorpio she's likely to blush under his penetrative gaze. He's mysterious, magnetic and a master of seduction. Mr Scorpio, ruled by the intense planet of Pluto, has a way of making a woman feel as though he knows her every secret. Thankfully, Ms Virgo is not the kind of gal to keep secrets. But neither is she a completely open book. The earth-ruled Virgo gal can appear demure, tranquil and in control on the outside, but underneath she can be surprisingly tense and worried. The Scorpio man is similarly a quiet and secretive soul. He is ruled by the element of water, and his controlled exterior hides emotions that can transform from a peaceful ocean into a tumultuous storm in a matter of moments.

Neither Scorpio nor Virgo likes to wear their hearts on their sleeves and there's always more going on than their façades will reveal. Mr Scorpio is a fascinating mix of passion and intellect that Ms Virgo finds irresistible. He has the powerful ability to bewitch her and she (normally a most sensible gal) will find herself falling head-over-heels in love and lust. Though he's the zodiac's sex symbol (and sex is very important to him), it doesn't mean that he's unfaithful or disloyal, as many astrology books would have you believe. When he's in love, he's one of the most loyal men around, and in many cases he can become obsessed with the object of his affection. He adores Ms Virgo because she's honest (he can't stand dishonesty), grounded, intelligent and very loving. He is a suspicious man by nature, but he knows he can trust his heart in the hands of the earthy, upfront Virgo gal. But that won't stop him from feeling jealous or possessive when other men pay her attention. Ms Virgo has an aura of purity and goodness about her that men adore. Plus, her natural beauty and no-fuss style is classical, earthy and sensual.

Yes, being in a relationship with Mr Scorpio is exciting (and volatile at times) and there are many Virgo women who just aren't prepared for the intensity of a lifetime relationship with this man. Sex between them is dynamite and his passionate intensity blends well with her earthy and tender approach to making love. Outside the bedroom, trusting Ms Virgo is a dutiful and devoted partner but she has to learn to stand her ground with Mr Scorpio. He's a powerful personality and he can be controlling. As she's a woman who's willing to do almost anything to make her relationship work, it's easy for her to succumb to his needs and wants and forget about her own. The Scorpio man is born under a fixed sign, which means that he likes to have things 'his way'. The Virgo woman, on the other hand, is born under a mutable sign, giving her the ability to adapt and go with the flow.

However, Ms Virgo is a perfectionist who sets high standards for herself and her loved ones. She can be a know-it-all and try to correct, nitpick and criticise her Scorpio guy. But Mr Scorpio is determined and unyielding and once he has made up his mind about something he's rarely swayed (and he certainly won't humour his Virgo girlfriend, lover or wife who tries to tell him what to do!) If self-confident Scorpio sniffs that she is trying to control him, he will put her in her place with a Scorpio 'sting' that cuts like a knife. He has the ability to wound with a few words and he knows how to push her emotional buttons. His Virgo gal is more sensitive than he realises and her plaintive cry of 'I was only trying to help' usually makes him regret his words afterwards. Mr Scorpio adores his Virgo gal, and although she can be tough on him she is always more critical of herself. Ms Virgo is fully aware of her own imperfections and he knows that she wouldn't ask something of him that she wouldn't ask of herself.

If they do decide to give one hundred per cent to the relationship (and most Virgos and Scorpios are 'all-or-nothing' kind of people when it comes to love), this can be a loving relationship with great potential for long-term happiness. They share the values of determination, loyalty, honesty and self-discipline, and both are ambitious. Ms Virgo and Mr Scorpio are survivors who have overcome immense obstacles in their lives, and this common bond creates intimacy. So when she tells him how she worked behind a bar six nights a week to pay her way through university and take care of her bed-ridden mother, he loves her even more. And when he describes how he clawed his way back up from bankruptcy, after his marriage and business collapsed in the same year, she knows she's found a kindred spirit. He thrives in a crisis and she, too, has a keen ability to find an escape route when her back is up against the wall.

As both are inclined to negativity at times, their relationship often has a heaviness, intensity and serious tone that can pull them both down. Scorpio and Virgo guard their feelings inside, and so regular exercise or playing sport will help them release built-up tensions. Work, duty and obligations tend to come first for this couple, so it's important they inject a sense of fun and frivolity in their relationship every once and a while. Going ice-skating, visiting the zoo, renting comedy movies or anything that makes them laugh will work wonders and help them share the good as well as the tough times!

With a little give and take, this couple can be very compatible. Mysterious Mr Scorpio is a puzzle to Ms Virgo, but as she is curious and analytical by nature, she will never get bored trying to work him out. Maybe due to his self-confidence and 'everything-is-under-control' personality she worries less when he is around. He feels relaxed and 'at home' when he's with her and the practical Virgo woman has a way of helping him make his dreams, goals and desires come true. When they truly pledge their love to each other, this relationship can become solid, firm and secure and last a lifetime!

Virgo man—Scorpio woman

 The *'Where's the aspirin, I think you give me a headache'* relationship

In many Virgo man–Scorpio woman matches you get the feeling that this couple are completely out of sync. The following scenario is a true story as told to me by a male Virgo friend. The Virgo man and his Scorpio woman plan to meet at the bar on the fifteenth floor at seven o'clock. He's reserved the best table with a stunning view of the city below. He arrives punctually, steps out of the elevator, looks around for her and checks his watch (he couldn't be more punctual). Meanwhile, Ms Scorpio saunters into the lobby on ground floor. The doors slide open; she walks in; presses fifteen; reapplies her lipstick and starts to ascend. Mr Virgo looks impatiently at his watch again and worries that maybe she forgot the name and floor number of the bar. He steps in the other elevator, goes down to the lobby and looks around for her, flowers in hand. Glancing at his watch again, he checks his mobile phone for messages (there are none) and decides to go up again. The elevator door slides open and he sees Ms Scorpio, perched at the bar in her little black dress, sipping a vodka and tonic and chatting with the handsome barman. *'Hi,'* she says coolly to Mr Virgo, *'Greg here told me the window table's already taken — some guy is proposing to his girlfriend tonight.'* Needless to say my Virgo friend listened to his instincts and didn't propose to her that night — or any other night.

If ever a woman knew how to take the wind from under the wings of Mr Virgo, it's the Scorpio woman. It's impossible to surprise this gal and she lacks a sense of spontaneity. Not that Mr Virgo is the most impulsive of signs, but he's an old-fashioned romantic who'll use tried-and-true methods to sweep his lady off her feet. Which is why his Scorpio gal presents such a challenge. In this cosmic love game between cat and mouse, it's usually the Virgo man who plays mouse. She's a woman who makes the rules (but she also loves to break them!); and he's a law-abiding citizen who wants to know where he stands. Mr Virgo wants a simple life; a good career, healthy body, a woman who loves him and a nice place to live. Nothing too complicated just everything nice and perfect (ha ha).

The funny thing is, Ms Scorpio is one of the most complex women in the zodiac! She needs plenty of emotional, physical and mental challenges to keep her satisfied, while her Virgo guy is a perfectionist who likes to file, sort and catalogue his life into neat compartments. But he's unlikely to come close to classifying the deep and passionate Scorpio woman into his mental filing cabinet!

The Scorpio woman is often attracted to the Virgo man because he poses no kind of threat to her powerful character. He's tolerant, intelligent (but not too opinionated), witty and polite. Ruled by communicative Mercury, the planet of the mind, he's analytical and perceptive. She adores these qualities. Pluto, the powerful planet of regeneration and depth, influences her. The Virgo man appreciates her compassion, inner strength and emotional loyalty. The sex between them is often extremely sensual and earthy; and while they're not the kind of couple to show off their love and lust in public, behind closed doors the passion comes alive. The Scorpio woman, however, is often more highly sexed than her Virgo guy. With a little patience, she'll soon ignite his libido and imagination!

Many times their common respect and love will lead Mr Virgo and Ms Scorpio to the altar, but in the domestic realm they have many challenges. God forbid the Virgo man who starts to lecture, nag or criticise his Scorpio woman. Before he has the chance to say *'Honey, why can't you be a bit neater around the house?'*

she'll have transformed from a loving woman into a scathing creature who throws an 'if-looks-could-kill' glare in his general direction. This poison dart is enough to send the sensitive Virgo man into a sulking silence for days!

Though there are many differences in their astrological make up, the Virgo man and Scorpio woman share some similarities that act as the cement from which they can build a life together. Both are consistent, intelligent and great at organising their lives; and they both know how to keep a part of themselves under lock and key. When Mr Virgo and Ms Scorpio recognise this self-protective characteristic in the other, they can begin to build up trust and start to share deep feelings.

VIRGO — SAGITTARIUS relationship

The 'I've got a romantic problem, and I think it's you' relationship

STAR VIRGO–SAGITTARIUS COUPLE
Sophia Loren and Carlo Ponti

There's something about Virgo's purity, goodness and earthy nature that captures the imagination of fiery Sagittarius. Similarly, it's the Sagittarius' lust for life that makes practical and sensible Virgo an admiring fan. Their different ways of living and loving are often very extreme but there is enough appreciation and respect between earth-ruled Virgo and fire-ruled Sagittarius to create a harmonious and long-term relationship.

That doesn't mean that their differences won't cause tensions. After all, Virgo's negativity knocks fiercely against the Archer's positive outlook on life. And sometimes the Sagittarius belief that 'anything is possible' is just too naive for realistic and practical Virgo. But if they try hard, this couple can prove that opposites not only attract, but that they can find long-term happiness too. Both are honest, bright and intelligent and they have a mental connection in addition to their physical and emotional attraction. In fact, when Virgo and Sagittarius have major differences it's their good communication that ensures they make up instead of break up.

Virgo woman — Sagittarius man

 The *'Are there any relationship books we can read that might help us?'* relationship

Ms Virgo and Mr Sagittarius are often the first to admit that they're an 'odd couple', but they'll probably also quickly admit that they wouldn't want it any other way. They enjoy and appreciate their differences and that's why this earth sign–fire sign combination often results in a solid relationship. Certainly many Ms Virgo–Mr Sagittarius couples have a great track record. You only have to look at the long and enduring relationship between Virgo actress Sophia Loren and her late Sagittarian director/producer husband, Carlo Ponti as an example. Singer Lee Ann Rimes and her husband Dean Sheremet are another example of the attraction that exists between Ms Virgo and Mr Sagittarius (but whether they'll last the distance only time will tell as they are both so young).

It is their different approaches to life that make Virgo and Sagittarius *sooo* fascinating to each other and they often end up enacting teacher–student roles, with the role of teacher changing according to what is happening in their lives. Naturally the role of romantic, sexual and home-making teacher is the one exchange they both usually enjoy the most! This zodiac combination often forges some great connections between them, operating on all kinds of diverse levels.

When Mr Sagittarius meets Ms Virgo, he's often lost for words, an unusual occurrence for the silver-tongued Archer. He's usually not so easily stunned by femininity as he can be when he encounters this zodiac gal. You see, the Virgo gal is not just a pretty face. In physical appearance it may not matter whether she is plain, pretty or absolutely stunning, but it's normally more than her looks that leaves him spellbound. She's unique, and she's like a rare jewel to him if the magic of love shines brightly between them.

Ruled by Mercury, the planet of communication and the mind, the Virgo gal has a quick-thinking and analytical mind and her first conversation with him is intelligent, down-to-earth and punctuated with her clever wit. There's no pretense about the Virgo gal and he adores the natural way she talks, looks and acts. So, once Mr Sagittarius remembers how to string a few words together himself, the Virgo gal is soon in awe of him (though she won't show it immediately). He's unlike any man she's met. He's confident, intelligent, candid and funny, and he's incredibly optimistic. His eyes sparkle when he talks and the Virgo woman can't help but get swept up in his enthusiasm (and neither will his other admirers). His popularity might have something to do with his planetary ruler, Jupiter, who in Greek mythology was the King of all the Gods, the party thrower and the gift giver. He can certainly be the life of the party!

The demure Virgo gal typically won't go chasing men, but she'll give him a few subtle but well-designed hints that she is attracted to him. When Mr Sagittarius gets the hint and finally asks her out, she shouldn't expect a romantic wooing worthy of Romeo and Juliet! No, the typical Sag guy won't sweep her off her feet with romantic details such as flowers, chocolates, champagne, poetry and candle-lit dinners. He is more likely to take her to the circus, Rollerblading in the park or to a night of live comedy. Sex between this couple is passionate but extremely tender. She feels completely safe to be herself with him and explore new realms of sexual possibility. He adores her gentleness and lingering, profound way of loving. At times his impulsive need for sex can be at odds with her 'take it slow' approach, but if trust and love are there they will learn to get in sync with each other on emotional and physical levels. Both Virgo and Sagittarius are mutable signs, which means they are good communicators and adaptable. Good communication gives a solid basis to their relationship.

He adores her patience and persistence, and at first he finds her need for law and order, systems and financial security endearing. Though he admires her work ethics, self-discipline and organised approach to life, he doesn't necessarily want to be that way himself. Ms Virgo needs to be careful that she doesn't start to nag and criticise him. 'Everything in moderation' is Ms Virgo's catch-cry; while his tends to be 'eat, drink and be merry'! Mr Sagittarius has a tendency to overdo things, and this often includes drinking, eating, partying or gambling or spending too much money on 'toys'. She, on the other hand is sensible and thrifty; sometimes he'll call it being 'stingy'. His need for 'expansion' is completely at odds with her need for 'restriction' and many of their arguments will be surrounding this theme:

MS VIRGO: *(Beginning sweetly and gently)* Honey, that idea of yours to buy a new flat-screen television seems extravagant to me. Do you think we really need a second television? The old one works just fine.

MR SAGITTARIUS: Yeah. But this one is bigger and better and the thirty-six-inch flat screen is so much clearer and it's really incredible for watching sport. And you know the boys are coming around next week to watch the big game.

MS VIRGO: It's a huge waste of money — and how typical that you'd do anything to please and impress your buddies, but when was the last time you helped me with any housework. I'm constantly picking up after you — you're so irresponsible.

MR SAGITTARIUS: *(Impulsively, shooting his harsh arrow of truth)* That's not true. It's just that you're obsessively neat and have nothing better to do, that's why you fuss around the house so much. The excitement in your life revolves around dusting shelves, paying bills and being on time. Why don't you just get a life!

MS VIRGO: *(Fights back tears and answers quietly)* Well, if that's the way you feel, I think I'll just leave now . . .

So, it's 'not always easy loving you baby' for any Mr Sagittarius and Ms Virgo. Life can be hell, not heaven, if she regularly indulges her penchant for criticising and he clumsily shoves his foot in his mouth in response. In order to keep the harmony both needs to keep a check on these natural habits. Tact and diplomacy can make or break this relationship, as they are both somewhat challenged in being sensitive and receptive to each other's needs. But there are positive vibes between Ms Virgo and Mr Sagittarius and so it's worthwhile diluting the behaviour that tends to push the other's buttons. His love and appreciation of life is contagious and she'll get swept up with him on the ride. With him, she'll climb mountains, travel to foreign shores and float in a hot-air balloon. He truly lives life to the fullest, and this encourages Ms Virgo to follow her own dreams, regardless of the outcome. The Virgo woman is often lacking in self-confidence and she can be her own worst critic. Her Sag guy teaches her to appreciate herself and to give herself a pat on the back when she succeeds. He is optimistic and if he fails, he is wise enough to learn from the experience.

She, on the other hand, is a solid rock of stability for gadabout Mr Sag. In her arms he finally feels as though he belongs somewhere. She teaches her boisterous Sagittarius some courtesy and patience (he has a tendency to be tactless and this can hurt sensitive egos). Many times she'll act as a gentle buffer when he says or does the wrong thing in public. Practical Ms Virgo also encourages him to think before aimlessly firing his Archer's arrows in the wrong directions. Practical Ms Virgo understands that all dreams need a little bit of structure in order to become reality, and she forces him to slow down and think before he acts. Even though there are sometimes tensions between them, a combination of devotion, trust and loyalty help them keep the Virgin and Archer on the path to happiness.

Virgo man — Sagittarius woman

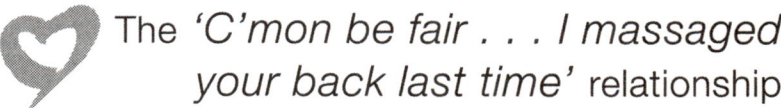 The *'C'mon be fair . . . I massaged your back last time'* relationship

This gentle man of the zodiac is not renowned for risk taking, but he's likely to bend all his most steadfast rules of romance when he meets and falls in love with a feisty, exciting gal born under the zodiac sign of Sagittarius. Usually Mr Virgo doesn't plunge into a serious relationship quickly, nor is he the kind of guy to leap into marriage; but there are always exceptions, and this zodiac combination could prove to be the exception for him. You see, earth-ruled Virgo is very discriminating when it comes to relationships and he wants to be really — but really — sure before he gives away his heart (and bachelor pad). So when Ms Sagittarius walks (or bounds) into his life he is often quite taken aback. She can be quite dramatic and she likes to use her arms and body when she's telling a story. She's playful but wise; fun loving but well read and knowledgeable. Her outrageous antics, enthusiasm and spontaneity excite him and he admires her honesty and philosophical way of looking at life. She takes him to romantic places he has never been before, and it is generally a very uplifting experience for him.

When Mr Virgo is sure he wants to give up his treasured bachelor's existence, he will give one hundred per cent to the relationship. The Virgo man is extremely devoted and he'll help his Sag gal in all sorts of practical ways. Funnily enough, there are times when intelligent and capable Mr Virgo feels downright inadequate by her side. She's bright, cheerful and self-confident and she's been Ms Popularity throughout her entire life. Her inner spark and fiery ideals can make him feel lacking in passion but then again, once he thinks it over he wouldn't want to be like her. Her honesty is sometimes confusing to him, especially if he's used to coy women who rarely say what's on their minds. He can be critical of her bluntness and the effect it has on people. Mr Virgo is courteous and gentle, and although he appreciates her honesty he will often wince when she bluntly speaks her mind, shooting her Centaur's arrows impulsively in all directions, wounding people with her careless words and actions. He teaches her to soften the tips of her arrows and to think before she talks.

When it comes to love and romance, Ms Sagittarius is looking for a firm, tender, intelligent and honest guy. Although he may sometimes be a little sedate or unadventurous for her real liking, in most matters of life Mr Virgo fits the bill. She especially loves the fact that he's self-sufficient and independent and that he has his own life to live. Personal freedom and trust are all important to the Sagittarius gal and she simply can't stand being in a relationship with a jealous or possessive man. Earthy and tender Mr Virgo is often just what the love doctor ordered for Ms Sagittarius. She's a trusting soul who's fallen down many times and has had her heart broken, and although she's super confident on the outside she is sensitive to rejection.

The loving and loyal Virgo guy gives her stability and warm arms to come home to after her many adventures. And she doesn't mind if he occasionally firmly holds the reins on her Centaur behaviour that so often gets her into trouble. You see, the Sagittarian gal is a prolific adventurer who loves challenges and taking risks. She's normally well travelled and a born nature-lover. She may love camping, hiking, horseback riding, white-water rafting, climbing mountains or skiing. Her Virgo guy also loves the great outdoors. If they plan a camping trip together you can bet that she'll choose the destination and he will meticulously organise the details, creating the most perfect expedition known to mankind! Together they can make a wonderful team.

Whether Ms Sagittarius is a company executive, teacher or stay-at-home mother, you can bet that she loves what she does. Archer girls tend to choose an occupation that they love and being happy is more important than the money she makes. This fact can shock Mr Virgo. Some Virgo men choose a well-paid but unsatisfying job instead of doing something they adore that pays peanuts. Like all earth-ruled men, he is attached to material and financial security because it makes him feel safe. In any case, Ms Sagittarius is a creative trailblazer and her optimistic attitude energises him. She teaches him the values of generosity of spirit, open-mindedness and tolerance, and that there's nothing constant in life except change. The Sagittarian gal embraces change whole-heartedly and there's nothing she likes more than taking on a challenge or risk. This explains her love of gambling (which can include the lottery, poker machines, betting on the horses etc), and he is always amazed at how lucky she is! Ms Sagittarius also teaches him the futility of trying to be 'perfect' all the time and trying to please everyone. With the Sag gal by his side, Mr Virgo starts to loosen up.

There are times, however, when her free spirit and trailblazing nature can shock his Virgo sensibilities. Her quest for freedom and frankness can hurt his feelings deeply and he's likely to cringe every time she shoots her blunt 'arrows' in his direction. Her practical jokes can also go too far and when he's hurt, Mr Virgo's self-protection mechanisms shift into action and he can retreat into moody silence for days on end. Thanks to her Virgo guy, Ms Sagittarius learns the valuable lesson of thinking before she talks and acts, instead of hurting the people she loves most. He needs love, respect, tenderness and appreciation in a relationship and if he doesn't get it, Mr Virgo is likely to pack his bags and leave. He will do almost anything to make his relationship or marriage work, but once an earth sign decides to leave, they rarely return.

The Sagittarius woman might complain at times about his stinginess with money or his nagging when she leaves her clothes lying on the bedroom floor, but she knows she's lucky to have found such a kind, loyal and caring guy. He, too, is willing to put up with her verbal faux pas, clumsiness and tendency to act before she thinks because he knows she brings sunshine into his life. If they marry, their house will be full of children and animals. Both have a soft spot for animals, and they'll have at least one pet, lots of books and a telling bedroom where his side is beautifully ordered and her side is busy and chaotic.

Ms Sagittarius and Mr Virgo both have intelligent and inquiring minds and they open up each other's eyes to different ways of viewing the world. Once he learns to temper his criticism and she to dilute her frankness, they'll discover that opposites can live happily ever after in harmony and peace.

VIRGO — CAPRICORN relationship

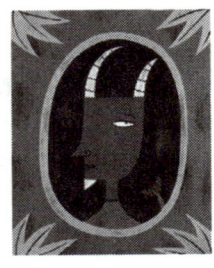

The *'I promise to love you until you do something that upsets me'* relationship

STAR VIRGO–CAPRICORN COUPLE
Cameron Diaz and Jared Leto

Get serious! Are you guys truly expecting to cruise off into the romantic sunset hand in hand with never a worry, care or disagreement taking place between you? If so, you are in for a rude romantic awakening. You may possibly have the perfect romance, but if you are born a Virgo or a Capricorn you know you usually have to do whatever you are tackling the hard way. You can do it easily in this partnership, but you won't. You both seem to have this belief that if you're going to do something, do it properly (but properly can mean turning pleasure into pain, or fun into a chore); and that goes for relationships, too. As far as this earthy couple are concerned the stars of romantic happiness are stacked in their favour.

Even if they could fly to cloud nine effortlessly they will resist the urge. With all their respective four feet planted firmly on the ground the Virgo–Capricorn match have just about everything in the zodiac happening in their favour, except the ability to let love be the wind beneath their wings. Both often worry too much about little things that may or may not go wrong, and expect too much of each other and themselves to simply cruise along. These lovers believe there is a right way and a wrong way to go about their business, even when it is the 'love business'. These are two ultra serious folks we're talking about here, who believe that falling in love is no reason to lose one's head and become silly, sentimental and soppy (for goodness' sake). They want even their love fever to come structured, tied up in red tape and organised to the nnnth-degree dosage. So will they fall in love? (yes); will they have a great deal in common? (yes); but will they manage to live happily ever after? What on earth are you thinking?

Virgo woman — Capricorn man

 The *'It's never easy, no matter what they say . . . loving you is tough'* relationship

Ms Virgo knows a great deal about most things. She reads a lot, watches documentaries and spends hours researching her latest 'thing'. What she doesn't know is a whole lot about *herself*. Not that she's completely in the dark, mind you. A Virgo gal understands why she has to drink two glasses of water each morning before she eats breakfast (otherwise it will ruin her entire day), and why she never sleeps on the left side of the bed. The bit that's unclear involves love, romance and how to act around the handsome Capricorn guy she met the other night. She'll fret, angst, stress, lose sleep and suffer an upset tummy (which may take her straight to the twenty-four-hour medical clinic), wondering whether she can handle another person complicating her already frantic life.

And that's all before the first date.

It's a big deal for Ms Virgo to take the plunge, putting her trust and faith in another human being (let alone a guy). She's used to being self-sufficient; capable of doing anything on her own (and mostly preferring it that way too). Or so she thinks. What this daughter of Mercury also failed to realise while she was reading up on the Laws of Human Nature, was that everyone, even super-efficient Virgo gals, need someone to complete them. Now if you're a Virgo woman reading this, you'll shake your head obstinately and dismiss the whole concept as hogwash. Ask any Virgo (man or woman) and they're as whole and complete as they need to be. Why complicate matters further with unnecessary attachments?

Well, it's nice to feel confident, but somehow, when the Virgo woman crosses paths with a Capricorn man, something just clicks between the two of them. Call it destiny if you will, but these two souls have a connection that stretches all the way back to the dawn of time. And both of them will feel it too. It may be confusing or even unsettling at first, but once these two earth folks make the connection, more often than not, it's for life.

You see, in many instances, Ms Virgo feels obliged to get married. It may be that the idea of marriage itself doesn't particularly appeal to her, it's just that Virgos tend to be people-pleasers, and they would much rather conform to the norm, than make a spectacle of themselves. (What would people say?) So, rather than anguish over living a life of sin in unwedded bliss, many a Virgin beauty will compromise her true desire to remain unattached, and walk purposefully down the aisle at the earliest possible moment.

Her Goat man is similarly endowed with a strong sense of what is right and proper in the eyes of other people, especially his family. There's just no point in dancing around the subject of marriage when it's wholly and totally expected of you. In that sense at least, these two share a common directive. He will very happily make her his wife (what else could she be?); and she will feel lucky to have a husband who thinks, acts and feels the same way she does.

Once the initial shock of uncomfortable silences, dating, and ultimately matrimony wears off, this is a relationship to rival Lancelot and Guinevere's. They take life and every aspect of it seriously and that includes the vows to love, honour and obey. (Okay, the obey reference might be a little bit of a stretch, but two out of three ain't bad!)

Even if at some point in their relationship, the road down relationship bliss becomes rocky, causing disharmony or worse, separation, you can bet it won't be permanent. For all their cleverness, industriousness and practical meeting of minds, these two share a profound respect and love for each other that will inevitably, always save the day.

Virgo man—Capricorn woman

 The *'What's love got to do with leaving the top off the toothpaste?'* relationship

You might be forgiven for thinking the typical Mr Virgo is more machine than human; and more prone to cool detachment than active involvement when it comes to matters of the heart. By the same token, you may consider Ms Capricorn a rather standoffish type gal, whose main concern is whether her love affair interferes with a productive day at the office. In some respects you might even be right.

Everybody has priorities, right? Right. And no one has a list as long, or as precisely detailed as a Virgo man and his Cappie mate. There are projects to finish, places to go, people to see, investments to take care of, properties to purchase, promotions to secure and health scares to investigate. Life is full of responsibility when these two team up, and unfortunately, some of those responsibilities don't leave much time for anything else.

The Mercury-ruled Virgo man though, is something of a zodiac trickster. He's *sooo* cool on the outside yet often tumult-filled on the inside. He is abundant with emotions that only flutter beneath his surface, like a butterfly trying to enter into a room via a closed glass window. Occasionally an emotion may break through to the surface and suddenly appear as a small tear in his eye — a tear that is quickly brushed aside. However, his poker-faced, composed exterior belies a deeply loyal and devoted lover, capable of unwavering commitment in the face of adversity and one who can internalise great depths of emotion. His earthy determination (some call it stubbornness), tireless commitment to the truth and lightning-quick intellect make him a worthy opponent to any who stand in his (or his lover's) way. He'd never admit to it, of course, but he loves his Capricorn sweetheart truly, madly and deeply, even if she does blur his vision of orderliness from time to time and unsettle his rational outlook.

But don't be fooled. The Goat maiden is no slouch when it comes to all things orderly and has a great deal in common with Mr Virgo. She too has her emotional boundaries and often keeps her truest of deep feelings hidden from him. She's also quite a material girl in many ways. Some women were born to shop, while others find their niche having babies. Ms Capricorn has enough feminine savvy to master being both a stargal who is able to go out on the town, and a fantastic mother as well. While many Cap gals are a force to be reckoned with at any department store sale, in any boardroom and in any kind of social company; they can also make wonderful (if not conservative) mothers.

However, their sense of achievement comes from being in control. Whatever they are doing they need to be the one calling the shots. Yes sir! These gals can be bossy, self-centred and even a little tactless at times, but that doesn't mean they're not capable of great kindness, generosity and love. Even the most sensible, practical Goat gal needs a little tender lovin' in her life and oddly enough, Virgo boy might be just the man for the job. (So long as his CV is in order and he can start at six each morning.) Once the 'getting-to-know-you' or rather 'getting-to-check-you-out' romantic formalities are out of the way, earth man and earth woman can get on with the job of being in love.

What a great job it will be! Rarely do two people complement each other the way Virgo man and Capricorn woman do. They share a similar outlook on love (it's nice, but don't get too carried away in case something goes wrong); money (save, invest, then save again); and careers (the more responsibility, the better). Both share a common need to be useful and dependable; and both understand the hurt the other feels when these qualities go unnoticed and worse, unappreciated. Even Saturnian Ms Capricorn, who has at times been unfairly labelled the Ice Queen of the zodiac, suffers deeply beneath her outwardly unemotional façade when she is truly unhappy. It takes one to know one, and that's of great comfort to Mr Virgo and his Capricorn love when no one else seems capable of grasping the circumstances before them. Virgo man and his mountain beauty are alike in other ways too. But sometimes you can have too much of a good (bad?) thing. Possessing a strong resolve is a real plus, but downright inflexibility is another matter all together. When they decide to, this couple can remain locked in a stalemate for days, even months, without the slightest hint of compromise. He wants what he wants, and she wants what she wants. That's it. No ifs, buts or maybes. It's my way or the highway, sunshine. Take it or leave it.

Thankfully, somewhere through the dusty haze of this earthy stand-off, a truce (or rather, an agreement to disagree) generally emerges. Emotions are once again put away for another day, and it's back to work for our no-nonsense couple.

VIRGO—AQUARIUS relationship

The *'Since we met I'm having panic attacks'* relationship

STAR VIRGO–AQUARIUS COUPLE
Michael Jackson and Lisa Marie Presley

Well aren't you guys in for a surprising, unpredictable, romantic experience? If you're embarking upon a Virgo–Aquarius love affair, then get ready for an emotional and mental roller coaster ride and the ultimate romantic challenge. It takes patience, compromise, tolerance and respect for these two extremely different signs to find a workable 'harmony' together. After all, rebellious Aquarius is obsessed with doing their 'own thing' and sensible Virgo loves perfection.

In this relationship the Aquarian Water Bearer creates disorder out of order and the Virgin sets about putting the order back into the disorder. Confused? That makes you, the happy couple *and* me. Together they are a riddle that simply can't be solved. But somewhere, in the midst of their differences, they find enough similarities to be able to relate to each other. Both are intelligent, analytical, creative and curious. They will spend hours trying to work out what makes the other tick (and they might never find out). But that's what keep things interesting. Some Virgo–Aquarius romances never make it further than an exciting but short-lived love affair, while others find their eternal soul mate. As both are as relationship-shy as the other, at least they start on common ground! One thing is for sure: no matter how long this couple stay together, earth-ruled Virgo and air-governed Aquarius will march to the beat of their own cosmic drum.

Virgo woman—Aquarius man

 The *'Forget your previous plans, you're with me'* relationship

Yes, there is definitely proof that 'Men are from Mars and Women are from Venus', and this odd couple can reveal just that. However, with this couple you can take this astro-summary one giant leap further. Not only are Ms Virgo and Mr Aquarius zooming into planet earth from different planets, but on top of that, Ms Virgo is an earth goddess and the Aquarian man is an air god. Naturally opposites or different energies often find each other fascinating and sometimes this is exactly what occurs with this dynamic zodiac relationship duo. But it can turn out to be a very quirky and most unpredictable kind of stressfest sooner or later.

Even when the love-lights burn brightly between them at the beginning, it soon turns into a relationship that either sinks or swims or somehow does a back-flip back and forth between sinking and swimming. Why is it tough for this zodiac couple to keep the love fires burning brightly? Because they have so many differences in their personalities to work through before they can find real, ongoing compatibility. However, those differences can be a bonus or a cross that they have to bear in this relationship, depending on their attitudes and, of course, how powerful the chemistry of sexual and romantic attraction is between them.

If and when these two get together their combination is certain to make an unusual and interesting mix of female and male outlooks, energies and desires. Exactly what do they have in common? Well, very little actually, but that lack of common interests still doesn't really need to be a problem. Indeed it could expand their horizons and open them both up to all kinds of new adventures. After all, in relationships what one person lacks and the other person offers creates the buzz. Opposites or the differences between people are frequently *sooo* beguiling. The fact that they are so removed on many levels could be exactly the magical magnetism that attracts them to each other. It's a small wonder that if the 'sexual' chemistry ignites, this couple could find each other fascinating, intriguing and extremely sexy.

Now from the Aquarian guy's point of view, Ms Virgo is like the best friend he's ever had (and she is often his best friend, too). For him, she may have real 'girl-next-door' appeal and ironically, as a twist of fate, she may even have grown up in his neighbourhood or lived next door to him.

She's good at making him laugh too! And he needs a good laugh. He's a guy who tends to take life seriously, and she sometimes will clown around with him, or say something witty to break the ice and he loves and adores her for it. Most times, when he's in her presence, he may feel a peace or comfortable feeling generating within him — a feeling he doesn't experience anywhere else. She completes him in many ways, and many an Aquarian man has fallen for a Virgo woman because she seems able to understand him, read his innermost thoughts and nurture him in a way that makes him feel loved, appreciated and special. Of course, on top of how good she makes him feel, she's usually organised, intelligent, a great home-maker and a good cook as well. Sure they have different focuses, dreams, desires and expectations, but what she needs he can deliver and vice versa. They somehow manage to fill in each other's gaps; they sort out their affairs and they get the best from each other.

When she looks to nature or earthly pursuits for her pleasure, solace and grounding, he looks to the skies. While she's taking care of earthly pursuits, he's allowed the time to sort through his thoughts, gaze at the clouds, drift through his musings without feeling disconnected to her. She's sensitive enough to give him time to think, to have some mental space, to work through his innermost thoughts and feelings.

And what he does for her is that he makes her feel appreciated. She's a dedicated person who makes the most of whatever she is handed in life and he admires her for her commitment and support. This couple combination is often a long-lasting, strongly committed relationship. Sometimes they miss the highs and lows that other couples go through because they tend to assume a level approach to life. But they'd rather have a comfortable, safe existence than get involved in risky business or go for a walk on the wild side together. You'll usually find them doing whatever it is that they enjoy doing, yet not necessarily doing it together. They have their quality times together and their quality times apart, and this arrangement generally suits them both, just fine!

Virgo man—Aquarius woman

 The *'Are you stark raving mad?'* relationship

The relationship between Mr Virgo and Ms Aquarius has a strong, unconventional tone to it. Unexpected, uncommon and unpredictable turns of events will guarantee that the two of them will be anything but bored with each other; and sometimes they'll shock each other when they do everything they probably shouldn't. This relationship often works because sensible Mr Virgo balances out the eccentricities of his Aquarian gal. And if Mr Virgo is flexible enough to enjoy some wild ups and downs, then he's found the right partner. Though Ms Aquarius is an eccentric woman, she is slightly old-fashioned when it comes to love and romance, and that's why there's great chance of success with the Virgo man. As there is so much chaos in her own life, she is attracted to him because, typically, he's a practical, sensible and reliable guy.

Ms Aquarius runs hot and cold like no other woman in the zodiac. She can be flirty and seductive one minute and then uninterested and detached the next. She can be sweet and charming but at the same time standoffish and distant. Even the Aquarian gals who look conventional are always shocking or surprising people in some way. She's highly unpredictable and not even she knows what's going to happen next. She loves hanging out with her friends but one-on-one romantic relationships are not always comfortable for her. The Aquarian gal lives so much in her mind that getting in touch with her heart is not always an easy task. Being in love can shake her world and send her into a spin. Independent Ms Aquarius likes to be free and in control of her own life, which is why many single Aquarian gals have no qualms about having no-strings-attached affairs once in a while. Earth-ruled Mr Virgo is also tentative when it comes to starting a new romance. Some Virgo men remain bachelors well into their forties or fifties and having the occasional fling because 1) he's very choosy; 2) he's basically a loner; and 3) he's afraid of failure, and if it's not going to be perfect he doesn't even want to try. Both can be marriage-shy so if anyone is going to understand Ms Aquarius' concerns about getting serious it's Mr Virgo.

They often start out as 'just friends' and a common interest is sometimes what brings them together. They may meet at a course, seminar or class or through their involvement with a hobby or sport. But as both Mr Virgo and Ms Aquarius are reticent to jump into a serious relationship, they take their time getting to know one another. Both guard their independence fiercely and sometimes they need a little push to get together (often a mutual friend or family member acts as 'matchmaker'). Once they do take the plunge and start a romance, their relationship is anything but dull. In fact, once Ms Aquarius falls in love with her Virgo guy, she might propose marriage a week later. The Virgo man should expect the unexpected with his unpredictable Aquarian gal! When they do consummate their relationship, the sex is unexpectedly sensual and steamy, and they bring out a raw and passionate side in each other. Mr Virgo is a very tender and earthy lover, but he needs to learn to surprise her every now and again with something completely unexpected. Ms Aquarius needs variety in all areas of her life and that includes sex! With her imagination and his earthy gentleness they can be an explosive couple. Nevertheless, she needs to understand that her Virgo guy needs time to get in the mood for sex and things like romantic dinners, sexy pillow talk and sensual back massages will work wonders.

Ms Aquarius is looking for a guy who's sexy, intelligent, good-natured, kind and someone who'll be a good lover, husband and father. The Virgo man fits the bill, as he's a multi-talented guy who is not fazed by having a 'busy life' In fact, Mr Virgo is an expert in time management. I once watched in amazement as a male Virgo friend of mine managed to prepare a two-course dinner, speak to his mother-in-law on the phone and rock his baby to sleep, all within a half-hour period! The Virgo guy is a magician in more ways than one. Ms Aquarius, on the other hand, is better concentrating on one thing at a time. She often has a far-away, detached look in her eyes that initially fascinates (and later frustrates) her Virgo guy. His life is in his Filofax or hand-held computer, and he is able to retrieve within seconds any bit of information concerning where he has to be, with whom and at what time. Yes, the Virgo man is methodical, systematic and he's extremely punctual. He's the kind of guy who remembers not only his Aquarian gal's birthday, the day they met and the day they married; he also knows her favourite flower, perfume, chocolates, shoe size and bra cup size. It can annoy him immensely when she forgets to pay bills on time, gets her niece's and nephew's birthdays mixed up, leaves wet towels on the bed or absent-mindedly puts the milk in the cupboard and the rice in the fridge.

But attempting to change his gal's habits is like trying to turn back the hands of time. Though she doesn't do these things on purpose. You see, Aquarius is ruled by Uranus, the planet of ingenius thinking, the higher mind, technology and scientific breakthrough. She's extremely intelligent, but she can be like an absent-minded professor at times. While she may not remember names, faces, birthdays and other simple data, her mind works in more complex ways when she comes up with brilliant observations, original ideas and accurate hunches and predictions. She sees the 'big picture' in life rather than focuses on the small details. Funny thing is, though rebellious Ms Aquarius would love to change the world and everyone else in it, she isn't too keen on changing herself. She is a fixed sign and that means she's very stubborn when she wants to be. Ironically, as much as she despises authority, convention and routine, she can fall into her very own 'rut' with the greatest of ease. Ms Aquarius isn't good at admitting she's wrong or apologising for her mistakes and when they argue it's usually Mr Virgo who says 'I'm sorry' first.

Although her unconventional approach to life can get on his nerves, he adores her because she is big-hearted and good-natured. This gal never takes herself or life too seriously and she has a way of making everything she touches completely unique. Ms Aquarius teaches her Virgo guy to be more spontaneous and that you can't please all of the people all of the time. Though his tendency to nag and criticise annoys her at times, thanks to Mr Virgo she's more careful not to hurt people by being outrageous simply for the shock value. When they strike the right balance between Virgo realism and Aquarian idealism, this couple go together like apple pie and cream.

VIRGO — PISCES relationship

The *'Love walked in and then walked straight out again'* relationship

STAR VIRGO–PISCES COUPLE
Richard Gere and Cindy Crawford

Sitting opposite each other on the zodiac wheel, Virgo and Pisces smile and wave flirtatiously at each other and yet there are other times they snarl, glare and frown. That's because Pisces and Virgo each have qualities that the other lacks, fears, envies or would like to have! While opposites certainly attract, there are also times that the tension between them is too close for comfort.

Pisces is a sign of duality and their astrological symbol depicts two fish swimming in opposing directions. This explains why those born under Pisces often feel torn and confused in life. On the other hand, their duality makes them extremely adaptable and able to accept change in their lives. They know deep down that everything around them happens for a reason. No such confusion for Virgo. Ruled by Mercury, the planet of communication and the mind, Virgos know where they've been, where they are, where they're going to and at what time they are going to arrive. A change in routine for Virgo has been known to create all sorts of physical ailments (including lack of sleep, indigestion and constipation).

Their combined energy gives this relationship somewhat of a green light–red light dynamic. Plus, the negative traits they share are a handful of fears, phobias, worries and neuroses. Of course, when these two lovers share a relationship their double-trouble anxieties are going to be multiplied. But whether they decide to find a good therapist together or find other healthy ways to relax, they'll feel better because they are in it together!

Virgo woman — Pisces man

 The *'Things between us are looking good today, aren't they?'* relationship

Just as his astrological symbol depicts one fish swimming upstream and the other moving downstream, life is never a simple process for Mr Pisces. In fact, it can be downright confusing. And as the ocean tides rise and fall, so do the moods of the Pisces man change constantly. So you can imagine how comforting it is when Mr Merman meets Ms Virgo, the epitome of femininity, tenderness and sensuality. Her soothing mannerisms, soft voice and gentle touch are a healing tonic for Mr Pisces, and he's mesmerised by the way her eyes sparkle when she laughs. Yep. He's a romantic all right, and once he's decided that she's 'The One' he will set about seducing her in his subtle and mysterious way that constantly leaves her guessing.

Now, if you are a practical Virgo woman falling for the charms of elusive Mr Pisces I can certainly understand your concerns. You've probably got that sense of uneasiness about him, even if you feel he's the love of your life. Don't fret and think you are neurotic. It's quite normal for you to want to know whether he's a fishy swimming upstream or a fishy swimming downstream. The questions Ms Virgo most likely wants to know are:

> Will he have a good job?
> Can he pay the bills?
> Will he be a good husband?
> Is he punctual?

> Is he neat around the house?

> And eek! Can he remain faithful?

Unfortunately Ms Virgo, when you get involved with a Pisces man it's impossible to answer any of these questions. Yes? No? Maybe? Yes on Monday, but No on Thursday? Mr Pisces is one of the most complicated men of the zodiac and he's constantly changing. He is also one of the most charming, compassionate, gentle, kind, scattered, melancholy and emotional men under the cosmos; and not even clever, patient, curious and analytical Ms Virgo can comprehend his many moods. This, quite frankly, is his charm. Funny thing is, whereas Mr Pisces can't tell you exactly what he looks for in a woman (he just knows it when he sees it), Ms Virgo has her very own 'perfect man' list. She often lists compassion, kindness, tenderness and sensitivity among the qualities she'd like her perfect lover/boyfriend/husband to have (and Mr Pisces has them all). But then she goes and spoils everything by putting down methodical, perfectionist, logical and disciplined. If she's serious about her 'better the devil you know' attitude, then she should forget Mr Pisces and look for a Virgo man who will mirror herself. However, if she's prepared to throw caution to the wind and follow her heart, not her head, then Mr Pisces is her man.

Though it might sound like I'm making a 'hard sell', the truth is, both the Virgo woman and Pisces man are very aware of the sexual attraction that exists between them. It's normally a very powerful and high adrenaline-rushing physical magnetism that brings them together, but Ms Virgo and Mr Pisces soon find they have more in common than just sex. Both are mutable signs, which means they are good communicators who have the ability to express themselves and listen to each other. Both are understanding, gentle and kind; and their caring attitudes toward people (and animals!) they love gives them a common bond. That's not to say there won't be ups-and-downs on the relationship roller coaster ride for this couple. There may be times they hold hands and squeal for joy. Other times, they might even try and wrestle each other out of the roller coaster carriage! Whatever occurs, this is a relationship that will impact upon them both greatly.

Ms Virgo adores her Pisces guy because he's truly interested in what she does and how she spends her day. He's the kind of guy who sympathises when she comes home from a long day at the office and he'll offer her a warm cup of tea and a foot rub. Though it's true that the Pisces man can be downright lazy at certain times in his life, he tends to be more invigorated and active when he's in love. He loves taking care of her in sweet and romantic ways. Ms Virgo is also besotted and she may even joke to her friends that her Pisces guy cast a magical spell to entrap her! She senses that he can read her mind and heart before she says a single word. And he probably can at times. The Pisces man is very attuned to the invisible and intangible world and he can be very psychic. He is also attracted to the occult, meditation, yoga, personal growth, astrology, tarot cards and other esoteric subjects.

At times earth-bound Ms Virgo finds it difficult to relate to his spiritual nature and his lack of practicality. She can be quite horrified when he casually remarks that his cheque for the rent bounced or that he forgot to pay a parking ticket. Organised Ms Virgo will be equally aghast when she finds out that his health insurance expired five months ago or that he's been meaning to go to the dentist about a tooth that's been aching for six weeks. When it comes to money, insurance and health, Ms Virgo is super efficient. Particularly where her health is concerned, she is very careful. In fact, some Virgo women are hypochondriacs who visit the doctor at the slightest ache or pain. This often occurs because she suffers more from psychosomatic conditions than most people. When the Virgo gal is drained, stressed or worried about something, her health tends to suffer immediately. She is particularly susceptible to insomnia, indigestion and constipation; and her medicine cabinet contains practically every kind of vitamin and pharmaceutical drug known to mankind!

Ms Virgo can be very critical about her lover's carelessness, lateness and messy apartment amongst other things but she'll soon learn that her Pisces lover responds badly to criticism. He is super sensitive and emotional and her cold criticism can cut him like a knife. The Pisces man is like a sponge and when there are bad feelings around him, he soaks them up completely. If his periods of insecurity and woe occur at the same time as her episodes of fear and neurosis, their household will be a gloomy place indeed. Not to worry (seriously!) Before too long gentle and compassionate Mr Pisces and Ms Virgo will remember that the sun is shining outside and that there's no greater thing than being in love.

Virgo man—Pisces woman

 The *'I think you have my heart, what do I have to do to get it back?'* relationship

These two often look like the perfect couple, and indeed they sometimes are. But frequently there's a lot of broken hearts occurring between this couple as well. They certainly come from two different zodiac realms, which sometimes can be too far a distance to really merge together. Though if they do successfully merge, it's like building a stairway to romantic paradise.

Ruled by Neptune — in Greek mythology the God of the hidden depths of the sea — the Pisces gal is the mysterious Mermaid of the zodiac. She's beautiful, seductive, timid and mysterious, and she has the ability to hypnotise men with her dreamy eyes and flirty femininity. When Mr Virgo meets Ms Pisces he's interested and very confused. The Pisces woman is childlike but wise, intelligent but dreamy, funny but melancholy, sweet but temperamental, innocent but sexy, emotional but calm. Although she can come across as being a 'helpless female', there is always method behind her madness. Whether its romance, sex or marriage she has on her mind, she can be quite audacious when it comes to getting her man. (Think of actress Elizabeth Taylor and you can picture the seductive Pisces woman instantly.)

Meanwhile, Mr Virgo's analytical mind is working overtime as he tries to categorise her, but he'll soon learn that Ms Pisces will never fit into a pigeonhole. She is many women rolled into one. Apart from her obvious feminine charms the Virgo man falls for Ms Pisces because she's compassionate and a wonderful listener. He's dated women who have talked non-stop and he's patiently listened, so it's a treat to meet such a lovely woman who is sympathetic and interested in what he has to say. He trusts his secrets with her and that means a great deal to Mr Virgo.

Ms Pisces is attracted to the Virgo guy's inner strength, stability, tenderness and goodness. She's looking for a real man; the kind who'll offer his strong shoulder for her to lean on. He has his feet firmly planted on terra firma and as she often has her head in the clouds, Ms Pisces senses that this is a good thing. The physical attraction between them is magnetic and their sex life is sensual, deep and intense. Trust is a big issue for the Virgo man and because he feels safe with his Pisces gal he allows himself to relax and completely abandon himself to the moment. She, too, feels safe and peaceful in his arms. Though there is plenty of physical attraction to keep them entertained, this couple often fail to keep the fire burning because of the immense differences in their personalities. The famous but short-lived Hollywood marriage between actor Richard Gere and model Cindy Crawford illustrates the strong Virgo man–Pisces woman connection that begins sizzling yet ends fizzling. Their differences in personality, lifestyle, life goals (she wanted children, he didn't) and values (his commitment to Buddhism and her disinterest in it) should have been an indication. However, romantic Pisces and devoted Virgo believe that love will conquer all. And sometimes it will. Not all Virgo–Pisces marriages are destined for the divorce courts.

One very big difference between Ms Pisces and Mr Virgo is their attitude to money. Ask Mr Virgo how much money he has in his bank account and he'll probably give you a figure right down to the very cent. Ask Ms Pisces the same question and you won't get a straight answer. In fact, she might duck and weave past the question and start talking about how bank fees have gone up again and how she would really prefer to keep her cash stashed under the bed. The fact is, she probably doesn't know. Depending on the other influences in her astrological chart, Ms Pisces can be financially astute, but typically she is a little on the careless side when it comes to money. Money and financial security don't drive her life. She's more concerned with feeling emotionally secure and allowing her creativity and intuition to guide her through life. The Pisces gal has an enormous talent for daydreaming and wishing. She's intuitive, very often psychic and she has the amazing ability to make her dreams come true. Whether she does it by traditional prayer, visualisation or white witchcraft, she has a special touch to create whatever it is she wants in life. As Ms Pisces isn't content to believe only in the physical world, she is open to many experiences that her Virgo guy simply misses out on.

Here's an example. An out-of-work Pisces girlfriend of mine, a journalist, woke up one day and decided that she wanted to travel through Bolivia and Peru for a couple of months. Her bank balance was running on empty and so she began to visualise that someone would offer her a job that would help pay for the trip. Her sensible Virgo boyfriend laughed at her unusual approach and gave her the name of his bank manager to organise a loan to pay for the trip. A week later the editor of an airline magazine (who had received her CV three months prior) phoned to see if she was free to fly to Lima the following week. The in-house journalist had fallen sick and they needed a replacement to write a feature article on Peru's Machu Pichu. Her Virgo guy simply shook his head in disbelief.

It simply doesn't make sense to the earth-bound Virgo man when Ms Pisces conjures things out of thin air. He can be highly critical of her unconventional approach to life but even so, there are times when he feels a little envious of his magical woman. After all, Mr Virgo doesn't leave a lot of room in his life for dreaming or relaxing. His mind is like an efficient card indexing system where all information is filed, sorted and stored in its proper place. Most Virgo men keep everything in their lives under control and orderly. He balances his cheque book every month, pays his bills on time, he won't miss a dentist appointment and he always remembers to put out the recycling bin on the correct day. In a nutshell, he's highly efficient.

Ms Pisces just wasn't made to fit into systems or routines, and many Piscean women work from home or have their own businesses simply because they don't like to work between the constraining hours of nine and five! She moves to her own rhythm. Ms Pisces is talented, creative, imaginative and empathetic. She can excel in jobs where she uses her creativity or in the counselling professions where she is a wonderful listener and communicator. Even though the Pisces gal loves to relax and 'go with the flow', part of her senses that she could benefit from more self-discipline and less procrastination. She's fascinated with how efficiently her Virgo guy manages his own life and his efficiency will rub off on her in a very good way. But he will also benefit from taking a leaf out of Ms Pisces' Book of Life and learn that dreaming is good for the soul. When they are out of sync with each other, Ms Pisces and Mr Virgo are the living, breathing example of that old saying 'relationships weren't meant to be easy'. On the other hand, when they are in tune with each other, this thoughtful and compassionate couple show that two very different souls can share the most wonderful romantic, cosmic journey of all.

libra libra libra libra libra libra libra
libra libra libra libra libra libra libra
libra libra libra libra libra libra libra
libra libra libra libra libra libra libra
libra libra libra libra libra libra libra
libra libra libra libra libra libra libra
libra libra libra libra libra libra libra
libra libra libra libra libra libra libra
libra libra libra libra libra libra libra

libra libra libra libra libra libra libra
libra libra libra libra libra libra libra
libra libra libra libra libra libra libra
libra libra libra libra libra libra libra
libra libra libra libra libra libra libra
libra libra libra libra libra libra libra
libra libra libra libra libra libra libra
libra libra libra libra libra libra libra
libra libra libra libra libra libra libra

LIBRA

[24 september – 23 october]

romantic pursuit: confident but also wary of commitment

romantic vibration: seductive and sensual

secret love desire: to be spoilt and indulged by their

lover particularly sexually

element: air

planetary ruler: venus

symbol: the scales

quality: cardinal (= activity)

colours: blue and turquoise

gem: diamonds and opals

best companions: gemini and aquarius

strongest virtues: eye for design, social

charm and diplomacy

traits to improve: feeling helpless, lacking

direction and handing your power over

to others

deepest desire: a life filled with romance

Libra celebrities

Alicia Silverstone, Angie Dickinson, Barbara Walters, Bob Geldof,

Brigitte Bardot, Britt Ekland, Bruce Springsteen, Catherine Zeta-Jones,

Colin Friels, Dannii Minogue, Deepak Chopra, Donna Karan, Elisabeth

Shue, Fran Drescher, Guy Pearce, Gwyneth Paltrow, Heather Locklear,

Hugh Jackman, Ian Thorpe, Jean-Claude Van Damme, Joan Cusack,

John Lennon, Julie Andrews, Julio Iglesias, Kate Winslet, Kelly Preston,

Linda McCartney, Luciano Pavarotti, Luke Perry, Mahatma Gandhi,

Margaret Thatcher, Mario Puzo, Martina Hingis, Martina Navratilova,

Matt Damon, Matt Day, Meatloaf, Michael Douglas, Mickey Rooney, Mira

Sorvino, Naomi Watts, Neve Campbell, Olivia Newton-John, Paul Hogan,

Paul Simon, Penny Marshall, Ralph Lauren, Randy Quaid, Roger Moore,

Sarah Ferguson, Serena Williams, Shaun Cassidy, Sigourney Weaver,

Sting, Susan Sarandon, Tim Robbins, Viggo Martensen, Will Smith

LIBRA — LIBRA relationship

The *'You're the closest thing to perfect that I've ever met'* relationship

STAR LIBRA–LIBRA COUPLE
Michael Douglas and Catherine Zeta-Jones

Admire a Libran couple from afar and you might get the feeling you're watching a fairy tale about the handsome prince meeting the beauteous princess romance unfold into reality. He's a success; she's beautiful; they have lovely children, a nice home — it all looks so hunky dory and wonderful. Charming Ms Libra and her chivalrous companion morph into the host and hostess of the moment when they combine their beguiling forces. Only Venus, their ruling planet of love, harmony, art and beauty could have bestowed on them such crowd-pleasing virtues.

The wonderful thing is, this couple look fabulous together and what's amazing is that in most cases (yes truly, madly and deeply) they ARE fabulous together. Fortunately, their interests are more than just skin deep, as they can keep each other amused for hours on end with their chatty rapport and intellectual compatibility. So in many cases this is indeed a relationship that is made in the stars.

Will it last forever? Yikes, only time will tell, as unfortunately just because something's good, doesn't mean it has staying power, especially when two very undecided Librans are in command of the state of the affair.

Libra woman—Libra man

 The *'This romance we're sharing is a kind of crazy thing'* relationship

There is a special kind of magic that occurs when two Libras are together as a romantic couple; they simply resonate with each other. In fact, it's difficult to see two more charismatic individuals together — charm literally oozes out of their every pore.

You only have to look at the on-screen chemistry and real-life magic between same-day birthday Librans, Catherine Zeta-Jones and husband Michael Douglas. Love, passion, romance, magnetism and elegant chic define this union, making them one of Hollywood's most popular golden couples. Tracing their whirlwind courtship (it's said that Douglas pursued Zeta-Jones with hugely romantic gestures), it's easy to see the Libra touch at work.

Those born under the sign of Libra are true lovers of romance. They are in love with being in love and both the Libra guy and gal are blessed with intimate knowledge of the art of flirtation. Notice the lingering glances, seductive smiles, gently batting eyelashes and other well-honed flirtation techniques. Even ordinary looking Librans (and most are *very* attractive) know how to use their natural assets to their advantage in the game of romance and courtship. What you will also see is a physical attraction that sizzles with electricity!

But Libras are united *not only* in their social charm, diplomacy and sexual attraction. On a mental plane, Ms Libra and Mr Libra also find a solid connection. Ruled by the logical and intellectual element of air, this couple will talk, discuss and deliberate, and can spend hours (preferably at a cosy dinner table for two) talking well into the night. They are well versed in current affairs and world events and are true fighters of truth and justice. In fact, many Libra couples meet through their interests in human rights, law, politics, the environment etc. Their conversations are lively affairs but they know how to see and understand the other side of a debate. A good conversation will mentally energise this couple.

One of the biggest challenges in this relationship is their inability to make decisions. If one Libra *alone* has problems making up his or her mind, imagine what happens with the *double* equation! Carefully weighing all the options on the Libra Scales, they have the ability to *put off* making important decisions — forever. Libras find it difficult to make up their minds because they are obsessed by a moral compulsion to do the right thing. They genuinely try to do what's fair and just, yet other zodiac signs will often accuse Librans of being fence sitters. Thankfully, two Librans in love understand each other's contrary nature.

Although the Libra couple might not take a solid stance on any given subject, they do possess a strong will. Ms Libra, in particular, has a mind of her own and *she* is the one likely to wear the pants in the double-whammy Libra relationship! When it comes to love and romance, Libras are more inclined to be *in* a relationship than single. Ruled by the relationship goddess, Venus, Libras thrive when in love and will cite getting married as the most important event of their lives. They are devoted to each other and know how to compromise.

If Mr and Ms Libra marry (and of course many *do*) the dual Libra household will have a peaceful, beautiful and gracious ambience. Those born under the sign of the Scales have a knack for creating balance in their surroundings. Their home is an oasis full of beautiful objects chosen for their shape, form, design and colour. The Libra couple like their home to be ordered and harmonious and they generally prefer to live in a quiet, peaceful part of town rather than the bustling heart of the action. They need plenty of rest and if they *don't* get it they become overtired and cranky. Hopefully the Libra couple can synchronise their mood swings so that only one Libra is out of sorts at any given time!

The Libra couple strive for balance in their outer world because their *inner* world is often a tug of war between what they consider to be right and wrong or good and bad. This couple feel a sense of duty to live up to the other's expectations and at times they struggle between what they *want* to do and what they *think* they should be doing. Though complicated emotions can rule this relationship, their household is full of love, warmth, creativity and good times. The Libra couple are wonderful parents and likely to raise a big family. Then, as in the best of fairy tale romances, they'll live happily ever after.

LIBRA — SCORPIO relationship

The *'We're just good friends'* relationship

STAR LIBRA–SCORPIO COUPLE
Matt Damon and Winona Ryder

Libra and Scorpio are two star signs located next door to each other on the zodiac wheel. That's about all they really have in common (unless of course the love bug bites them), because their outlooks, desires and the way they structure their lives are not very connected at all. Libra likes to take life as easily as possible, while Scorpio seems intent upon taking the pressures or tests that life offers to their limit.

So, that's where these two can suddenly find each other a very valuable companion. Libra can take away some of Scorpio's pressures and Scorpio can bring a new buzz of adventure, challenge and excitement into the realm of the Libran. Plus, there's an element of teacher–student vibration in the Libra–Scorpio love match. Libra gets the feeling that wise Scorpio has been around the cosmic block before; while Scorpio really understands his or her chosen Libra is vulnerable and needs protecting much more than they possibly realise themselves.

Though whatever occurs in the Scorpio–Libra relationship, there's plenty of sexual admiration and true passion for the other. They probably don't think too much alike, as Libras live on a mental 'air' plane while it's the 'water' element that rules emotional Scorpio, but they can kiss really well. With such different *modus operandi* driving these two next-door-neighbour signs, it's no wonder there's mutual attraction and fascination between them which often makes this couple's love relationship quite a sizzling one.

Libra woman—Scorpio man

 The *'What's this love we share? It's a mystery'* relationship

Mr Scorpio is a lover of mysteries and if there's one woman of the zodiac who comes delicately surrounded by an aura of seven feminine veils — which she only removes one by one, slowly and tantalisingly for certain males she wants to captivate — it's Ms Libra. On this dimension alone the right Ms Libra can turn Mr Scorpio into romantic jelly. She does so well with her feminine wiles because the Libra woman innately knows how to intrigue him. She doesn't even use this skill consciously because it comes as part of her zodiac birthright. What works so well for her with Mr Scorpio is that he's probably one of the zodiac guys who will feel her subconscious wiles (or tap into them) more than most, as he's an extremely psychic kind of guy.

Ruled by the feminine planet of Venus, she's attractive and womanly, yet armed with high intelligence, a quick wit and a very strong will. She's cute, cuddly and adorable, but she's no little girl lost either. The concept of the 'iron fist in a velvet glove' sums up many Libran women. Just think of Libra Hollywood icon and animal rights crusader, Brigitte Bardot; or Britain's ex-Prime Minister and 'ball breaker', Margaret Thatcher, who can wrap a man around her little finger with one feminine arm tied behind her back.

When Ms Libra meets her Scorpio man, she gets a delicious shiver down her backbone, her eyes are magnetically drawn towards him and psychologically she has the feeling she has met someone who could teach her a lot (hopefully between the sheets). It is said in astrological circles that the Scorpio man is the most highly sexed of the zodiac, a claim he both deserves but sometimes cannot live up to. Whether he's the real sexual deal or not, being a very sensual stargal Ms Libra is very tuned into his potential of high sex appeal. Now not all Scorpios of either sex are certain to be hot in the cot all the time (but many are). That kinda constant sex drive depends on each individual Scorpio, but it *is* true that the Scorpio man is an extremely sensual, magnetic and seductive lover. He's also sometimes deeply emotional, focused, and has an innate ability to tap into his intuitive powers. So much so that he's able to read his partner's needs, thoughts and desires. No wonder Ms Libra sometimes feels as though he can read her every thought because often he instinctively can! He can be an intimidating man, but luckily the Libran woman is not easily intimidated so he truly can have a gal on his hands who challenges him, again something he likes.

Small wonder that the Scorpio man adores being around his charming, attractive and lovely Libran gal. She's sexual, challenging, flexible, cooperative, supportive and fun to be around. The Libran woman has a way with people *and* a far-reaching network of friends, business and social connections. She has a way of getting what she wants (almost subconsciously) with her beguiling wiles and gentle, but firm, tone of voice. But Mr Scorpio is no pushover for Ms Libra's eyelash-batting ultra-feminine strategy *if* he feels she is manipulating him. He doesn't like to be manipulated. And he also possesses a detective's nose and will soon realise if she's sweetly cajoling him into doing something 'her' way. That can make him withdraw and come up with a counter-attack, and that's when this relationship can sometimes enter into a quagmire of confusion. Who is really in control? Both of them try to overcome or over-impress the other, and eventually if they don't give an inch, everybody eventually loses!

Ms Libra does like to be pampered and though she is normally the picture of amicability, she does have her dark days if she's frustrated, stressed, tired or burnt out. Thankfully, Mr Scorpio won't be fazed when his Libra gal has manic mood swings, transforming from docile princess to grumpy, mean-spirited ogre in a matter of moments. He's one of the most perceptive males of the zodiac *and* one of the few who truly understands her. He'll appreciate that she's suffering one of her 'bad mood' days. The Scorpio man will soon learn to recognise Ms Libra's moods and her need to relax and re-energise in order to face the world again. He can sense *when* to back off and leave her alone; *when* to indulge and pamper her; and *when* to cheer her up with a spontaneous song-and-dance routine! That's one of his special talents which is extremely valuable to all and sundry.

He doesn't mess around, pretend or play games. She'll soon learn that in a Scorpio world, things are black or white but rarely a middle shade of grey. He has decided likes and dislikes and Ms Libra will cringe when he explains how he *hates* something or someone with a passion because she knows he means it. His intensity and black or white stance is often at odds with her sense of fair play and justice, and her natural tendency for fence sitting. If any issue is likely to rock their relationship this is where it lies. Adaptable Ms Libra sees all sides of an issue while her Scorpio counterpart is fixed in his view.

While Scorpio must learn to be fair around Ms Libra, she needs to be sensitive to his feelings. Scorpio is a water-ruled sign and his powerful exterior hides an intensely sensitive man. The wonderful thing about this relationship is that her optimism and 'tomorrow-is-another-day' attitude balances his intense and somewhat suspicious outlook. In fact, Ms Libra will soon learn that he is suspicious of *everyone's* motives. She, on the other hand, trusts people until they prove her wrong. In the middle of both of their judgments is probably where the truth exists.

Though she may wear the pants in the day-to-day running of the house, their social life and how they raise their children, you can bet that Mr Scorpio will take it upon himself to make what he considers to be the 'important decisions'. When it comes to give-and-take, the balance often tips in his favour. In many Ms Libra–Mr Scorpio matches, she'll support him while he finishes his studies or simply work in a 'behind-the-scenes' way to further his endeavours. Whatever makes *him* happy makes *her* happy and she'll 'stand by her man' until the end. That doesn't mean that she's a flighty pushover or 'just a pretty face'. Mr Scorpio had better learn (and fast) that his Libra lady is a miserable companion unless she has mental stimulation and feels responsible for her own life. If he doesn't make her happy (or try to) eventually she'll find someone who does, so Mr Scorpio can't rest on his romantic laurels either.

In the worst case scenario, Ms Libra hands over her personal power to dominating Mr Scorpio and allows him to walk all over her. In the best of cases they are mutually supportive of each other, sharing authority and decision-making and encouraging each other to reach their personal goals. This is definitely an unusual coupling, but one that does have plenty of successful aspects helping it to become a happy, sexy and exciting union.

Libra man—Scorpio woman

 The *'Love certainly moves in mysterious ways'* relationship

This is an amazing combination of zodiac signs because they have an ability to put each other through just about every kind of pinnacle of both pain and pleasure. And that little combination of sensual input can be something that is almost impossible to find elsewhere. That's why often when Mr Libra and Ms Scorpio are out on their first date, it's a meeting of the master of flirtation and the mistress of seduction. Mr Libra is one of the most charming, beguiling men of the zodiac. Brilliant, handsome, gentle and attentive, he is a romantic guy who takes pleasure in sweeping a woman off her feet. You see, the Libra man is born under a *masculine* sign but he is also ruled by the *feminine* touch of ruling planet Venus. This makes him a true gentleman, soft, sensitive and charming. He treats his Scorpio lady impeccably and this is what she adores.

Ms Scorpio, on the other hand, is the mistress of sex, power and seduction. The explosive power of her planetary ruler Pluto, makes her one of the most intense women of the zodiac. She doesn't do things by half measure and her desires are revealed in her 'come-to-bed-and-don't-try-to-mess-with-me' eyes. She's no shrinking violet. In fact, ex-lovers will look back fondly on their relationship with her and recall, with a wistful smile, how she wanted to 'possess' them. And they are right! She wants to feel the full gamut of emotions from passion to everlasting love with her chosen man. She's extremely loyal and needs to know that he, too, is faithful.

In this case, if Mr Libra treats her anything less than the most important woman in the world she'll start feeling uneasy and she may drop him like an anchor. Libran men have reputations for being heartbreakers, so he had better watch out if he's playing games with this gal's heart! If his intentions are anything less than honourable, she will feel it, know it and pay him back big time. Revenge is sweet for her. The Scorpio woman is a water sign, which means her emotions run deep. Very rarely is she satisfied with casual flings. More than likely, however, Mr Libra will

 351

succumb to her thrilling magic spell. He'll become hypnotised and mesmerised by anything and everything that his Scorpio gal conjures up (especially in the bedroom). He may even explain to his friends that this 'is the real thing!' But 'What is the real thing?' they may ask. To that he is likely to have no reply.

One thing is for sure, his friends will be treated to quite a sight if they encounter an argument between Ms Scorpio and Mr Libra. It's quite amazing to view the Libra man, giving his side of the story in his fair, logical and balanced way and all the time keeping his zodiac Scales in good balance. His Scorpio gal will give her evidence and listen to his. But when she's had enough of the conversation she'll give him that 'if-looks-could-kill' glare or leave him cold with a drop-dead comment that screams, 'I'm right'. One of the biggest tensions in their relationship is that neither find it easy to give in or give up their own point of view.

Thankfully, this is the kind of couple who kiss and make up in the nicest of ways. And before you ask, the answer is a definitive 'yes' — the physical magnetism between these two is intense. Mr Libra is romantic and sentimental and will no doubt sweep his Scorpio maid off her feet with his amorous gestures. It's unlikely he's met a sexual match to rival the Scorpio gal. Sex between them is passionate and dynamic and Ms Scorpio is sure to teach her man a thing or two about lovemaking. To her credit, she is incredibly patient with her Libra guy. He can be indecisive and cranky at times, but she knows deep down that his bad points fade away when compared to his winning cache of good points. Where else in the zodiac would she find such an attractive, intelligent, tender and romantic man?

Ruled by Venus, the planet of relationships, the Libran man is made for marriage. With the right partner, he is in bliss. Yes, these two can make a good couple, but whether their relationship will be long-lasting depends a lot on their ability to 'choose their battles'. A little bit of give-and-take will work wonders. The question is, might Ms Scorpio be too intense for Mr Libra? She can be possessive and jealous and needs to know constantly that he loves her, adores her, and that she's the only one. If he is up for the challenge, this can be a match made in heaven.

LIBRA—SAGITTARIUS relationship

The *'You're a riddle. I can't figure you out but I like it anyway'* relationship

STAR LIBRA–SAGITTARIUS COUPLE
Soon-Yi Previn and Woody Allen

When the zodiac signs of Libra and Sagittarius unite it's like the romantic dice are being rolled in romantic heaven. When these two get together it can either turn out to be a snake's-eye roll, or a high roller. There're so many variables, consistencies and inconsistencies operating between them, and what results could transport this relationship into heaven or hell. Consequently when Libra and Sagittarius unite in the game of love and romance, it's hard to predict what's going to happen. Destiny plays a huge part in whether this relationship finishes in the 'magical but short-lived' relationship dossier *or* whether it develops into the 'really wonderful total romance thing'. One thing's for sure, there'll never be a quiet or dull moment.

Both Libra and Sagittarius love to talk, debate and perform mental gymnastics. They also love to express their feelings in a passionate manner. However, to keep their interest piqued, they both need intellectual challenges and physical passion in equal doses. Thankfully, Libra and Sagittarius know how to keep each other on their toes. One thing they will enjoy is keeping each other guessing, as neither partner in this relationship is ever really likely to be able to gauge *exactly* where they truly stand with the other.

Libra woman — Sagittarius man

 The *'I forgot all my previous appointments while you were kissing me'* relationship

I once lived next door to a middle-aged married couple who constantly argued. Their conversations were baffling games of verbal ping-pong and I silently predicted (and somewhat secretly wagered with myself) divorce within the year. Yet, it all made sense when they told me she was a Libra and he a Sagittarius. *And,* that they were perfectly happy and simply thrived on a good rowdy debate (before they went to bed to make love at night). You see, Libra and Sagittarius LOVE to discuss and debate. Air signs like Libra flourish on mental stimulation, while fire signs such as Sagittarius simply need 'action'. Put these two together and you'll certainly not have too much peace and quiet, unless they decide to go into the sulks and then that's another cosmic story.

Usually, these two have loads of fun together and there's an intellectual rapport between these two outgoing and optimistic lovers; so no wonder Sag and Libra consider their 'arguments' good-humoured debates! With her balanced judgment and his love of philosophy some of their conversations will be very interesting indeed. In her fair and just way, she'll take both sides of the issue and will usually settle somewhere in the middle. Mr Sagittarius, however, is more stubborn and unmoving in his view (in astrology he's referred to as a 'fixed' sign), and he'll back up his theories with citations from great philosophers, historians, politicians and social reformers.

Ms Libra is more often than not the leader in this relationship. That's perfectly okay by her Sagittarian guy, as he much prefers to busy himself with one of thousands of projects he is working on than worry about making trivial decisions like where to eat, what clothes to buy or where to take a vacation. Well, I take that last bit back. When it comes to travel, Mr Sagittarius is the expert and he'll open his Libra lady's eyes to new countries, cultures, languages and ways of thinking.

He's funny, smart and well travelled, and she is mesmerised by his worldly knowledge. Mr Sagittarius is not the kind of guy who gets flustered easily and he has a calming effect on his Libran gal. This works wonders on her, especially when she gets impatient or restless when things don't quite go to plan. Meanwhile, he loves that she's *more* than just a pretty face. With the smart and sassy Libra gal by his side, the Sagittarian guy is a very happy man. Mr Sagittarius is a 'big kid' at heart and he loves to have fun. He adores the fact that she's intellectual *and* streetwise; feminine *and* strong. She's also the kind of girl who looks equally as comfortable in a ball gown as hiking clothes.

When the Queen of Diplomacy and the King of Tactlessness unite in the game of love it's a case of Ms Libra cleaning up the mess behind him, both literally and figuratively! Sag is sloppy around the house, and though the Libra gal is a great hostess she doesn't enjoy housework! He's the kind of guy who leaves his wet towel on the bed and his clothes lying where they may fall! She'll tidy up after him, only because she likes the house to 'look nice'.

She's also deft at covering up his *faux pas* at social events. She'll smile sweetly and apologise for his tactless comments, and with a wave of her politically correct wand Ms Libra will make everyone feel comfortable again. But lo and behold he let loose his tactless comments towards his Libra gal! His blunt comments can wound her sense of fairness and balance.

One issue that might cause some foot-stomping arguments is the issue of marriage. The Libra woman is wont to marry early. She believes in togetherness in every sense of the word and when she's in love, she'll naturally stop outside wedding dress shops and hear bells ringing each time she passes a church. Mr Sagittarius, on the other hand, is a die-hard bachelor, particularly in his youth. Though the words 'until death do us part' frighten the living daylights out of him, he *does* have the ability to love deeply *and* be faithful.

Put simply, Mr Sagittarius was born with a true case of wanderlust. There are so many oceans to cross, people to meet and things to learn. Where does marriage fit this picture? This will be his rationale to Ms Libra. The funny thing is, if this couple *do* tie the knot they're likely to have a wonderfully exciting marriage full of adventures at home and afar. Convincing the Sagittarius man of this will take Ms Libra time and patience. But knowing the Libra woman, I have no doubt that her charm, intelligence and diplomacy will help her get exactly what she wants in the nicest possible way.

Libra man—Sagittarius woman

 The *'You know how to make me tingle all over'* relationship

Mr Libra can be quite a playboy, that is, until he meets his perfect zodiac match who takes her earthly form as a Sag fast-thinking, fast-moving and fast-action gal. He's not used to *sooo* much excitement and life radiating out of one person, and this kinda overwhelms him. Ruled by Venus — the planet of love, beauty and art — the Libra man is a lover of aesthetics and all things beautiful. He appreciates beautiful women and has most likely dated some of the most attractive girls in town. However, born under a 'mental' air sign Mr Libra soon discovers when he has played the dating game for a while, that he needs more than just a pretty face. He craves someone with whom he can talk well into the night. Intellectual rapport is what he seeks as well as passion. He also needs someone to light up his life and inspire him, and Ms Sag is quite capable of doing just that — and more!

So, this is where Ms Sagittarius sashays into the picture, a little frisky, breathless and energised, possibly shaking herself a little like a puppy dog just emerging from the water. This gal has an ability to present herself as all cute, cuddly and radiating with a sensual energy flow that surrounds her like a natural man-magnet. She might not be a 'classic' beauty in everyday terms, but there is something extremely attractive, eye-catching and enormously appealing about her. Although she has a cute façade, she's no little girl lost either. She's strong, self-sufficient and determined. She's also outgoing, independent, funny, intelligent and has strong opinions of her own (just think of Sag superstars Jane Fonda, Kim Bassinger and Maggie Tabberer). And if she's the right stargal for Mr Libra, she can make him forget his previous playboy ways in a magic minute.

Now Mr Libra can be a little shy, mollycoddled and indulgent, and he needs someone to get him moving, fuelled up and excited. Fortunately there's a powerful chemistry between the air-governed Libra man and the fire-ruled Sagittarius woman, so she can turn his sexual tides in her favour very quickly. Since these two elements mix well in sexual compatibility, the Archer girl can arouse waves of previously unfelt ardour in him; and she can do it in the most effortless way with a mere glance or innocent touch on his arm. As he's a man ruled by the love planet Venus, he can pack a powerful sexual punch towards her too. He's not going to be flamboyant in his approach; he'll come onto her in an understated fashion, something that she finds most alluring. He'll flirt with her in a subtle manner and without appearing to be paying her too many compliments.

Without even trying to make a huge impression, the attractive Libra man will sweep her off her feet with his unique form of masculine attentions and if she's ready to surrender to his charms, the Sag gal will fall willingly under his special form of masculine love spell. Because of their natures, it usually doesn't take long for this couple to consummate their relationship, but independent Ms Sagittarius is unlikely to rush into the relationship — at least not *emotionally*. She's the kind of gal who can quite easily separate love from sex (something that her Libra guy finds more difficult to do). As with all fire signs, she is a very 'physical' person and an active lover.

The Libra man is a devoted lover and once he is involved in a sexual relationship he falls head-over-heels in love. Watch how, after one or two dates, Mr Libra introduces her as his 'girlfriend'. In front of his friends she'll be quick to correct him, stating that although they sleep together they are still *just friends*. Ms Sagittarius will be blissfully unaware that she just demolished his ego with a few words. One thing's for sure, if Mr Libra loves the well-meaning Archer girl he had better get used to her 'two-left-feet' approach to love and life.

Though the Sagittarian woman guards her independence, she is not a loner who wants to steer a course away from other people. In fact, she loves people and she can be quite dramatic at times when she's telling a joke or funny story. The Libran man is a wonderful companion for her. He's good fun, caring, open-minded *and* he'll keep her entertained with his wonderful anecdotes. When she is emotionally mature and ready for a life-altering relationship, this is when a relationship with the Libran man has more chance of eternal happiness. She's then quite able to 'turn into mush' when he calls her on the phone professing his love and adoration. Yes, there comes a time when the 'closet romantic' Ms Sagittarius will give in, *possibly* marry, but *definitely* raise a family. They both love children and their house will be big, beautiful and full of fun. They are incurable optimists and their grandiose schemes are more often plans of true genius than pipe dreams. If they ever start a business together it's likely to be a great success.

Both are interesting and social people and as a couple they'll be invited to the hottest events around town. They adore meeting people and forming strong friendships, though Ms Sagittarius is sometimes likely to cancel a dinner party at the last minute and talk her Libra guy into a weekend away in the mountains for some fresh air and long mountain walks. He had better get used to his Sag gal's high energy and active hobbies. If she's a typical Archer girl she'll love hiking, climbing, skiing, snowboarding, paragliding or any other sport that takes place in the great outdoors. Mr Libra prefers the arts, music and bar scene of the city, but when he's sitting shoulder-to-shoulder with his Sag girl cooking marshmallows over an open fire and staring up at the stars, he knows this is where he'd rather be.

LIBRA—CAPRICORN relationship

The *'This romance will either go very right or very wrong, very soon!'* relationship

STAR LIBRA–CAPRICORN COUPLE
Paul Hogan and Linda Kozlowski

This can be a very hot and heavy relationship, but even those relationships of these two signs, which run super hot at the beginning often turn into a stressfest later. If you're already involved in a Libra– Capricorn relationship, then you'll understand when I say that this coupling of astrological opposites brings great lessons in human patience (and unfortunately sometimes long suffering as well!) If you are contemplating embarking upon a Libra–Capricorn relationship and you're just reading this 'out of curiosity', then heed my words: if you sense that there may already be huge obstacles appearing before you, it's not too late to stop it!

You should know if this is a 'go-er' or not, because if it's going to pass the cosmic relationship tests it is certain to face, the Libra and Capricorn union is a challenging but ultimately satisfying relationship. However, you should get ready for the romantic tumultuous ride of your life, as you two are both born under 'cardinal' signs of the zodiac. Cardinal signs are those whcih may appear to be easy-going, but they actually have fixed agendas, rules, morals and expectations. Unless your agendas match you may love each other a lot but find you just can't seem to merge your dreams, goals and plans together. This is one of the more confusing relationships of the zodiac because what you both say to each other or express outwardly, could sometimes not be truly what either of you really feel or mean. This is definitely one combo that truly can either sink or swim.

Libra woman — Capricorn man

 The *'fate is in control, so does it all really matter anyway in the end?'* relationship

Ms Libra and Mr Capricorn often find each other to be devastatingly attractive. He thinks she's the cutest gal in the entire world; she thinks he is the most sexy, charming and exciting guy. *Sooo*, they date, fall in love, marry, mate and start a family (a boy for him, a girl for her). This union is often a most successful, loving and long-lasting one. Frequently though, with this couple, after the initial passionate honeymoon period is over they (alarmingly) discover that their ideas of future happiness and where it is to be found are poles apart.

MS LIBRA: Hey Honey! Wouldn't it be wonderful to quit our jobs, take the kids out of school for a year and rent a farmhouse in Tuscany? We could all learn Italian and I could take Art History lessons! It would be fantastic for us, terrific for the kids and we would have an amazing holiday adventure.

MR CAPRICORN:	Honey, sometimes you are so naive. Who do you think would take care of the business? What would we do with the house? Anyway, Tuscany is full of tourists these days — it's not as romantic as you think. It would be super expensive and you can bet that our careers would suffer in our absence.
MS LIBRA:	No you're wrong. It would be a beautiful experience and the kids would learn so much. Your brother Steven is a strong manager, he could easily handle and enjoy running the business for a year.
MR CAPRICORN:	Listen. Steven's no where near ready to take over the reins. It's a pie-in-the-sky idea. You're chasing rainbows. Forget about it — it is most unrealistic.
MS LIBRA:	Don't be so stuffy. Why don't you lighten up and enjoy life for once! You have very little imagination really.

Mmmm. Get the picture. Conservative Capricorn and optimistic, 'let-it-all-hang-loose' Libra are (once their initial mating game is over) often at definite odds. One longs for a dream world; the other wants to keep their pairs of feet planted firmly on safe terra firma; and you can't get either of them to really give an inch in their ideals, dreams or desires. Both are 'cardinal' signs. That positioning in the astrological world means they are born leaders with an iron will and often the attitude of 'it's either as I want it, or not at all'. Underneath their social exterior they have only one way of thinking, and that's their way. The main tension likely to arise in this relationship is that both are competitive and born organisers accustomed to 'running the show'. Two leaders together often end up butting heads, so Libra and Capricorn can often find that they spend most of their relationship disagreeing.

In the best of worlds, Ms Libra and Mr Capricorn learn how to share the balance of power. In the worst case scenario one dominates the relationship, while the other slowly becomes a reluctant (often resentful) follower. Of course, often this battle of egos only ends in tears. They need to discover for themselves that it's better to sometimes give in, rather than insisting on their own way all the time. But learning to compromise constantly doesn't come easily to either of them, unless one is much more evolved and compassionate than the other. So unless they learn to give-and-take, this relationship can have them constantly facing one crisis following another.

Once (and if) they master the game of give and take (and it *can* take years) however, then things look ripe and rosy for Ms Libra and Mr Capricorn. This can turn into a real win-win relationship exchange. Both are hard workers and high achievers with a strong belief in only the best for them. They can become great support systems in each other's life. When things look glum, Ms Libra holds true to her belief that 'tomorrow is another day' and that 'things will work themselves out'. Even if she doesn't *quite* believe it, she'll do her best to convince herself, *and others*, that things really aren't that bad. That's a bonus for Mr Capricorn because she can help lift him out of his natural doldrums very quickly and look at life again with a positive outlook.

He needs a good lift up every now and again because he's more inclined to pessimism and his stern and disciplined outlook on life can sometimes even crush her optimistic spirit. He can be very disapproving at times, especially if she procrastinates (his pet hate), spends too much money, or impulsively suggests they move to Tuscany for a year! He can't understand her irrational logic and occasionally thinks of her as 'foolish, fickle or far-fetched'.

If he wants to keep love alive, Mr Capricorn needs to limit his sternness with his Libra gal, otherwise her Scales will quickly plummet out of balance. She might appear tough and independent but underneath she just wants people to love and accept her for who she is. Be warned! An out-of-balance Libra gal is not a pretty sight! She's grumpy, cranky and avoids people at all costs. Typically, she'll retreat to the soothing calmness of her bed and escapes with a few fashion or gossip magazines. Most Libra gals decorate their bedrooms or 'hidey holes' with plush pillows, comforting doonas, the odd teddy bear and soothing colour schemes. And, of course, her hands-free phone to call girlfriends.

The sure-fire way for her Capricorn guy to pull her out of her glumness (and hidey-hole!) is to thoroughly spoil and dote on her. Take her shopping, out for lunch and then a walk in the park and she'll be just about back to new. Oh, he shouldn't forget to whisper sweet nothings in her ear and of course a big kiss, cuddle and some passionate lovemaking does a world of good too. The Libra woman adores to be romanced.

When Ms Libra and Mr Capricorn learn to work as a team instead of two competing power brokers, they can achieve *anything* together. Both possess amazing will power. In social and business networks they are much more powerful as a team than operating on their own. They are determined to get what they want and can make any dream (starting a business, buying a house, raising a family etc) come true.

Interestingly, in the Libra woman–Capricorn man romance, he is sometimes much older than she. That can make their relationship both easier and harder on different levels. Both believe strongly in the institutions of marriage and family, yet he prefers to be settled in his career and financially stable before saying '*I do*'. When they marry, this couple tend to fall into traditional male–female roles with the Capricorn man as the breadwinner and the Libra woman as the stay-at-home child carer. If they work together to carefully measure the magic ingredients, her optimism, combined with his realism, will ensure they keep the relationship scales well balanced and they can live out their relationship in 'happy-ever-after' fairy tale style.

Libra man — Capricorn woman

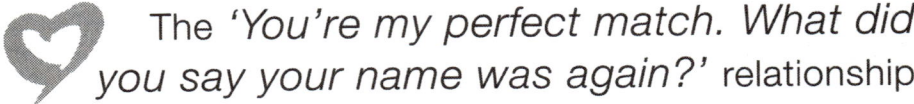

The *'You're my perfect match. What did you say your name was again?'* relationship

It's amazing how many people I've met born under this cosmic combination who are in a successful (or what appears at least outwardly to be successful) relationship. Certainly the zodiac chemistry is high and the sexual sparks often fly when Mr Libra and Ms Capricorn first meet. She is overcome by his charm, intelligence and attentiveness. He is struck by her classic beauty, style and down-to-earth manner. The law of opposites attracting definitely plays a part in their connection. Plus, they are both social, great at business and enjoy similar pursuits.

Just think of the romance that started to blossom during the filming of Crocodile Dundee between co-stars Libra Paul Hogan and Capricorn Linda Kozlowski. People said the relationship between the unlikely pair would never last. They went through all kinds of trouble because Paul was already married etc; but they believed that love conquered all and it seems that at least currently for Linda and Paul, many years later they've proved their critics wrong.

Ruled by Venus, the Libran man is friendly, charming and entertaining in a light, easy-to-digest way. Ms Capricorn — under the influence of serious Saturn — is more cautious, deep thinking and practical. He's intrigued by her worldly wisdom, combined with fun-loving ways and dedication to living life to its fullest. Though she's enchanted by his boyish optimism, she won't allow herself to melt *immediately* into Mr Libra's charismatic arms. No, that would be far too easy. She is wise enough to give him a good run for his romantic money. And he often keeps her at an arm's distance for a while, so occasionally this can turn into a real cat 'n' mouse romantic chase (but who is the cat and who is the mouse?)

The Capricorn woman won't waste her time in a relationship that starts as a sizzler but ends as a fizzler, unless Mr Libra's offering her a unique kind of emotional or financial security. In fact, Ms Capricorn can come across as the ultimate Ice Princess until she is very, very sure of her Libra guy's true intentions. Ruled by Saturn, the planet of restriction and caution, the Capricorn woman is naturally reserved when it comes to love and romance. She prefers to have her man prove himself before she hands over the keys to her heart, or allows herself to be connected with him socially.

This is where Mr Lover-Boy Libra gets confused. If he doesn't have enough patience (and many Libran men don't), he'll be inclined to give up his courting methods and go looking for romance elsewhere. The Libran man is very romantic in both words and actions. And he's not used to being shut out. *'Why is she so cold and unresponsive,'* he'll ask himself. *'What do I have to do to make her mine?'* Put simply, love, trust, patience and tenderness are the key to her heart, mind and body.

Even if they *do* begin a relationship, his light and airy lovemaking style is often at odds with her need for slow and sensual affection. She's an earth sign who needs solid shows of physical affection in order to get 'in the mood'. Possibly the right gift, promise of a future holiday somewhere wonderful or even a new decorator house can be what it takes, but often just a compliment is sufficient. As the relationship develops on all levels, she can teach him a lot about the deep earthiness of sexual intimacy. He will teach her to become more verbally expressive about her needs and desires.

When they get their sexual and emotional differences balanced, the Libran man is the perfect companion for the Capricorn woman. He's fair, tolerant and willing to listen to her point of view. He's also extremely supportive of her ambitions. This is very important, as his Capricorn gal is likely to be a successful career women. She's naturally attracted to positions with high responsibility and there are probably more female executives and business owners born under the sign of Capricorn than any other sign.

She is powerful, wise and she likes to be in charge of her own life. Her Libra guy loves this about her and does not feel threatened by her success or drive. One thing that earth-ruled Ms Capricorn needs to learn about air-governed Mr Libra is his need for freedom and movement. If she tries to restrict or contain him in any way, she is likely to lose him.

Just like air needs to circulate in order to remain fresh, the Libran man is at his best in a relationship where he can breezily be himself. He values the trust placed in him and when he's in love, he's unlikely to stray. She also needs to avoid talking to him in a disapproving tone of voice when she's angry. It has a way of reminding him of how his mother used to talk to him and this can be a big turn-off!

Both the Capricorn woman and Libran man are drawn to marriage and family. She, particularly, is close to her parents and social activities are likely to involve their families and close mutual friends. This relationship can reach a state of bliss when both learn to hold back doing those things that really get under the skin of the other. If you are in a Libra–Capricorn match, you'll know *exactly* what I mean. It's easy to resort to name-calling and bringing up incidents from the past. Mr Libra and Ms Capricorn need to stay above petty arguing if they are going to stay together. Treating each other with respect will ensure that the 'opposites attract' light burns brightly for the rest of their lives together.

LIBRA — AQUARIUS relationship

The *'Just when you think you've figured me out, that's when I change partners'* relationship

It is usually pretty easy for these two to fall in love. In fact, they naturally gravitate towards each other. They share mutual goals, ideals and expectations and often find each other devastatingly attractive. But they can also live in separate universes in their minds. They think a lot, often similar in thoughts or musings, but they don't necessarily tune into the same broadcast wave band. Even if they sometimes fail to properly communicate or express themselves to each other, that won't stop them initially falling for each other.

When these two air signs get together in the game of love, marriage or romance, there is a speediness, zippiness and high-energy feel to the relationship. Air-ruled signs are often highly intelligent types who run on nervous energy. If you are a Libra or an Aquarius and crave a 'no-challenge' relationship, then make your exit now. Together, these two signs conjure up surprises, impulsiveness and erratic behaviour. If you know how to give and take, then plunge right in. But be warned. When unpredictable Aquarius and 'I-can't-make-up-my-mind' Libra get to together, it *ain't* going to be easy. But where sparks fly, there is sure to be plenty of fun, passion and good times, plus a little bit of cranky-franky times too.

Libra woman—Aquarius man

 The 'Don't get too cute or comfortable with me' relationship

Mr Aquarius is no ordinary man. He seems all charm, appeal and diplomacy — and he is. He's also a very one-eyed, one-minded, stubborn guy. While he may smile and nod at what others are saying, it doesn't necessarily mean that he agrees with their ideas. He has very clear opinions about what he thinks, feels and believes in. As he's quite a private person, he frequently is happiest keeping his opinions to himself. However, that doesn't mean he won't change his mind if destiny somehow taps him on the shoulder and gives him a chance to see things differently! To him, the world is not a black-and-white place. But when he truly believes in something he's like the Rock of Gibraltar, completely immovable! One thing is certain, he's complex, sometimes distant and not a regular guy who is easy to figure out.

Now Ms Libra has all the charms, skills and feminine wiles to wrap this determined, unique man around her little finger. Though even if he falls for her hook, line and sinker, she still may not be able to order him around or get him to live life her way (at least once they pass the honeymoon stage). He's a man who innately marches to the beat of his own private drum. He can't help but do this, as it's part of his whole internal wiring. So she often needs to fall into romantic step with him if she wants to remain his true companion. That sometimes isn't easy for her because Ms Libra is used to getting her own way (after all, that's what she's managed to do ever since she was born). Consequently there can be a few ego battles ahead for this duo.

They sometimes have trouble sorting out their priorities or future plans (or even their social agenda). When they disagree on an issue she'll accuse him of being obstinate; while he'll turn right around and call her bossy. Now she may never have had anyone else call her this before, but Mr Aquarius is extremely discerning and he possibly can see through her 'cover' more than most. His accusation that she is bossy is often true of Ms Libra. She is a 'cardinal' sign which means she's a born leader accustomed to running the show. Now, Ms Libra needs to know that Mr Aquarius is born under a 'fixed' sign of the zodiac, and that's an indication he isn't likely to budge. He's stubborn and she's bossy, so their romantic dalliance could turn into a stressfest if they aren't prepared to compromise. So before Ms Libra starts getting involved with Mr Aquarius, she had better realise that her chosen guy is used to winning arguments! But look out Aquarius! When it comes to debating and discussing, Ms Libra is an expert. So that skill does give her a slight advantage over him in the long run.

The balance of personal power is a delicate balance in the Libra–Aquarius match. One thing's for sure. If they don't take it all too seriously, the 'debates' between Mr Stubborn and Ms Bossy can be stimulating and mentally challenging, rather than destructive to their relationship. Aquarius and Libra are both born under the mental 'air' element and they need plenty of mental activity in their lives.

Mr Aquarius is immediately drawn to the Libran woman, whose intelligence and genius match his own. She's a fun and intelligent companion and he, like many men, is likely to fall under her charming spell. She'll admit to being a tad self-involved and apologise sweetly with the flash of her dimpled Libra smile. There is nothing more beguiling than the Libran woman when she smiles. She's a sweet girl, down-to-earth woman and sexy siren wrapped up in one beguiling package; and she has the ability to make him feel 'himself' and 'at home'.

The Aquarian guy is a fighter for humanitarian causes and will always stick up for the underdog. He's tolerant of different lifestyles and, with Ms Libra's ability to plan great social events, their party list will include animal activists, homosexual couples, indigenous activists, left-wing politicians and other social rights reformers. In fact, this element of his personality is what appeals to Ms Libra's ideals of justice and fair play. Though the Aquarian man finds it hard to admit to having character flaws, the Libran woman can live with his. If she loves him and is committed to making the relationship work, she should carefully pick her battles with her Aquarian guy. That doesn't mean she should let him walk all over her. But for the sake of tranquillity (and without peace Ms Libra is NOT a happy girl), she should only argue for what is *really* important to her. A smart Libran woman will let him have his own way where petty issues are concerned.

One issue that she *should* stand up for is the right to get married. Ms Libra, you see, is pre-destined to marriage. Ruled by relationship and love planet, Venus, she sees marriage as the natural progression of a loving, lasting relationship. Her Aquarian guy, on the other hand, might be quite happy with their status quo as lovers or 'friends'. An eccentric Aquarian friend of mine referred to his beautiful Libran lover as his 'friend', even after having dated her for six years. Ever the optimist, his patient Libran lady pointed out in a balanced, just and fair debate that marriage would benefit his life enormously. She got what she wanted and they married the following spring!

When the Aquarian man settles down with Ms Libra he *does* enjoy life more. Many people don't understand his different way of looking at things, but with his Libran wife he can be 'himself'. She understands his brilliance and tolerates his eccentricity. And when he *does* become momentarily illogical she'll learn to remain peaceful by retreating to the comfort of a bubble bath; night out with the girls or afternoon of shopping!

The wonderful thing about this couple is that they share common interests. Be it music, art, literature, theatre, travel or their own children — they enjoy each other's company. In the big scheme of things, Mr Aquarius and Ms Libra realise that working together as a team will help them make their own personal dreams come true.

Libra man—Aquarius woman

 The *'I can't get enough of you baby'* relationship

When Mr Libra and Ms Aquarius first meet, there is a mental connection between the two of them that immediately forges a bond of friendship and a strong attraction. Born under the element of 'air', both Libra and Aquarius live on a mental plane. Like most air signs (Gemini is the third air sign), they share a highly-strung nature and quick wit. Observing them talk is akin to watching an exciting game of tennis with her driving forehand matching his rapid backhand, and with the occasional power serve leaving the other mesmerised.

Ms Aquarius is very comfortable with her own 'high circuit' *modus operandi*. Ruled by the unpredictable planet of Uranus, she thrives in frenzied and chaotic environments and situations. However, she'll soon discover that her Libran man's *own* restless nature leaves him prone to mental, physical and emotional burn-out. Mr Libra's astrological symbol is the Scales and he's constantly weighing things up, unable to make a decision. For example, in the space of thirty seconds he'll ponder whether they should get married now, later, in the future, never and then go back to base one again. His difficulty in making decisions drives Ms Aquarius insane, though *her* penchant for changing her mind *after* she's *made* a decision completely rattles Mr Libra.

Though he is usually an easy-going guy, he can turn downright nasty if she disrupts the delicate balance of his astrological Scales with the abruptness of her Uranian behaviour. When angry or upset, the Aquarian woman can be extremely emotional and this can actually make him physically ill. The Libran man craves peace and harmony in his life and when his own mental juggling act wears him out, he has a tendency to collapse. He operates at a one hundred per cent energy output until he crumples spread-eagled on the couch to watch re-runs of *The Bold and the Beautiful*, with a far-away look in his eyes.

Yes, there's something about being in a relationship with Ms Aquarius that might just push Mr Libra's astrological Scales completely out of balance. When they meet, she completely rocks his world. She's unpredictable, unique and fascinating. Her genius and eccentricity bewitch him, and she's infuriatingly stubborn! Although Ms Aquarius is never going to lead a normal 'white picket fence' life, a wise Water Bearer should do her utmost to create a sense of peace and tranquillity in their love relationship. The interesting thing is (as the Aquarian woman is quick to point out) her Libra guy does a lot to create his *own* disharmony.

In the astrological world, those born under the sign of Libra are notorious for spending their energy trying to be 'everything to everybody'. Such is his need to create peace and harmony. In this respect, the Libran guy could do well learning a thing or two from his down-to-earth Aquarian gal. She *doesn't* allow people to take advantage of her and she won't be pushed into doing something that goes against her grain of thought.

His sweetness, intelligence and diplomacy are what make Ms Aquarius fall in love with her Libran guy. With his sunny smile, warmth and caring nature, he touches her heart. Love makes his world go around, and he'll indulge her with his romantic gestures. He always tries to be fair and impartial, and the women in his life (his mother, sisters, aunties, grandmothers, female friends and colleagues etc) completely adore and spoil him.

Although Mr Libra and Ms Aquarius sometimes move to a different groove in life, they really are quite compatible. Just look at the 'meeting of minds' between Libran John Lennon and Aquarian Yoko Ono. The famous Beatles member fell in love with her genius and eccentricity; and Ono joined Lennon in his personal campaign for world peace and harmony. Together they united love, respect and friendship in a marriage that fascinated the world.

Both Mr Libra and Ms Aquarius have loads of interests, friends, hobbies and projects to fill up their busy lives. Friendship is an important element in their relationship and will ensure that they stay together long after the 'honeymoon' period is over. You'll see them growing old together, sitting on the front porch, smiling and shaking their heads at how the years passed by so quickly.

LIBRA—PISCES relationship

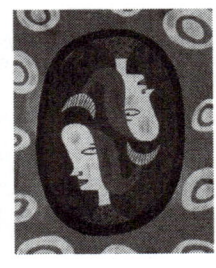

The *'When I'm with you
I lose the plot'* relationship

STAR LIBRA-PISCES COUPLE
Prince Andrew and Sarah Ferguson

Ask Libra–Pisces couples how they met and the answer is uncannily similar. They'll often say that they met 'by fate'. Strange meetings or situations tend to bring them into each other's arms. Though they don't seem to consciously 'choose' each other (fate seems to nudge them together), it's undoubtedly the law of opposites that keeps them together.

Ruled by water, Pisces is emotional, sensitive and imaginative. Libra, an air sign, lives on a mental plane and is constantly weighing up the pros and cons of any issue. Pisces simply *goes with the flow.* Thankfully, in this match of magical alchemy both share a love of beauty, romance and harmony. But frequently sharing the same ideals doesn't necessarily mean they're heading towards a relationship with a happy ending. Many couples born under these signs seem to only make it through the night, not the longer term.

Libra woman—Pisces man

 The *'You could quickly become my worst bad habit'* relationship

Ms Libra is the kind of beautiful woman who naturally attracts men into her life. She has the endearing, sweet femininity that made her the apple of her daddy's eye or the spoilt little sister amongst her brothers, as well as her teacher's pet. Later, as an adult, men have an innate desire to protect, admire and love her. So, you'd think the Libran woman would have a good understanding of what makes men tick, wouldn't you? Well, in Mr Pisces' case, she has NO idea; and no matter how many years she may spend with him, she's not likely to find out (because possibly deep down inside his secret self Mr Pisces doesn't really have any idea who he is either).

The Pisces man is a complex mixture of little boy, sensual lover and caring companion rolled into one mysterious package. There's something about him that is elusive and otherworldly and the Libran girl is, quite frankly, puzzled. She's a sensible girl (well, apart from the odd impulsive shoe-shopping spree), and for once in her life, she doesn't know what's going to happen next. He constantly keeps her guessing, confused and a little uncertain about him and it can, at first, make her uneasy. Not that Ms Libra wants to *tame* him or analyse his heart and soul. It's simply that she likes to have control and to use this control to set the relationship pace. She's a cardinal sign, which means she likes to be the leader in all areas of her life, *especially* relationships. And Mr Pisces is definitely one romantic sailor who will give her a run for her romantic money (especially if he turns out to be the type who likes to have a gal in every port, which of course, is another story).

If they hit it off after the initial first couple of meetings, Mr Pisces discovers he adores his Libra lady's creativity and romantic nature. She's dynamic, intelligent and she has a way of making people from all walks of life feel comfortable. He loves this about her because Mr Pisces is *everybody's* buddy and his friends include the local preacher, greengrocer and homeless guy who lives on the corner. Together they make a very popular duo, and usually everybody likes them (except perhaps their ex-partners, ex-boyfriends or ex-girlfriends who probably would prefer to see hell freeze over before these two new lovers found happiness in each other's arms).

Even though it all looks hunky dory at the beginning of its romantic phase, this relationship could quickly transcend into a soap opera drama entitled 'Much Ado About Nothing'. When the daughter of Venus and son of Neptune team up they are dangerously susceptible to drama, distractions and temptations. He has lofty, romantic (and other) dreams, but without self-discipline he can easily forget about the practical steps needed to make them come true. For example, he can forget arrangements he's made with her, run terribly late and generally be tough going to put up with in a romantic exchange of energy. Ms Libra, too, can be frustrating to deal with. She has a tendency to procrastinate and say one thing, then go out and do the opposite. Ruled by sensual Venus — the planet of love, relationships and beauty — she also holds high expectations of what a man should offer her (usually a lot of security), and she has a taste for the finer things in life. She also has lazy spells where all she wants to do is have fun and socialise or, alternatively, stay in bed all day. Mr Pisces may love to laze around too, so between the two of them sometimes they don't really manage their lives as well as they need to, to live their desired existence.

Aside from their momentary lapses of 'direction' and their mutual love of drama, confusion and mayhem, Mr Pisces and Ms Libra make a good team. And sometimes they even make a dynamic business team too. If they find their niche they can become magicians at making a business a success (and even making money). In the Pisces man, Ms Libra finds one of the most supportive men in the universe. He'll tolerate her inconsistencies more than most (sometimes because he has so many himself, so he could hardly complain about hers). She can talk around and around in circles, and he doesn't seem to notice. Thankfully, Mr Pisces is a very good listener and he doesn't even put her down when she messes up.

MS LIBRA: *(The door opens and Ms Libra enters like a tornado)* Honey! Guess what? I think I'm going to be offered a job with that new public relations agency — you know, the one Carol has started with. Well, you know how she's been putting in a good word for me. I have an appointment with the MD on Friday. I really think they want me!

MR PISCES: *(Giving her a bear hug and kiss on the cheek)* That's wonderful darling!

MS LIBRA: *(Her face momentarily darkens)* But if I do get the job what am I

	going to do? I can't just *leave* the college now. It wouldn't be fair on them and I'm committed to a year's contract . . . but . . . the PR agency would be a dream job. And the people there are great!
MR PISCES:	*(Nodding his head with empathy)*
MS LIBRA:	But I guess I shouldn't worry. I mean — I'll decide when and *if* I'm offered the job. I haven't been offered anything yet! Right?
MR PISCES:	Exactly.
MS LIBRA:	Thanks sweetie — I love you! *(She says, rushing to hug him and lighting up the room with her Venusian smile)*

Being around both of these people can be extremely confusing, except sometimes for each other. Unless they really get on top of their game and one of them turns into the ruler of the relationship. If both of them are running the show it can be a little like the blind leading the blind. And, if either of them get into depression or negative thinking it can often create big troubles for their partner. Though the Pisces man is very supportive, the downside is that he picks up negativity from others. It is often his misfortune that people naturally feel comfortable telling him their woes, and if he spends too much time with someone who's depressed, he'll actually start to absorb their feelings. Ms Libra, too, easily gets out-of-balance, especially if people around her are arguing. More than anything, she craves peace! So between the two of them, if they get into a pity-party it can quickly turn into a major stressfest.

As chaotic conditions and energy-draining people can wear them down, Mr Pisces and Ms Libra should concentrate on seeking 'balance' together. If they live together, their home needs to be *more* than just a cosy, peaceful, harmonious love nest. It needs to be their magical retreat. It's a place that recharges their batteries and stimulates their senses. They like soft lighting, soothing music, sweet-smelling incense and flowers and gentle colour schemes. Their bedroom is a true homage to romanticism, complete with flowing fabrics and plush pillows. Not that these two need to work much at creating a 'mood'. They're born romantics and sensual lovers, and their lovemaking is creative, sexy and tender. Ms Libra might be 'bossy' in other areas of their lives, but when it comes to lovemaking Mr Pisces shows that he's not passive at all — he can really stir up a sexual storm. And some sexual thunder and lightning is exactly what Ms Libra needs to get her feeling inspired. Sounds just what this girl ruled by Venus needs!

Libra man—Pisces woman

 The *'I think you and I should head immediately for the hills and stay there'* relationship

Romantic Mr Libra meets his match when he encounters beguiling Ms Pisces. Her dreamy eyes have the same effect on him as his dazzling Libra smile has on her! She's a captivating creature from the mystical planet of Neptune. Like the mythological Mermaid, she's enchanting, graceful and very appealing. In fact, whether she knows it or not, Ms Pisces uses her magical, mystical energy to her advantage. Born under one of the most psychic signs of the zodiac, the Pisces woman is able to tune into different levels of perception and *send* romantic messages to her Libra guy without even speaking.

This is why Mr Libra picks up on her vibration. He adores feminine, romantic girls and he's very attracted to Ms Pisces (though he might not be able to pinpoint *exactly* what it is that draws him to her). Their first date is likely to include a romantic candle-lit dinner for two with flowers and soft music. The way they talk about each other with starry eyes will make less romantic friends either sigh with envy or roll their eyes back with a 'this is *too* soppy' gesture!

The Libran man is gentle, charming and tender, and has many characteristics traditionally labelled 'feminine'. He might be a good cook, have an eye for interior decoration or wear beautifully designed clothes. He surprises her with gifts of lingerie, flowers, chocolates or her favourite perfume and she'll feel completely swept off her feet. But then again, it's not the first time that Ms Pisces has felt this way. She's had plenty of crushes before *and* she's fallen in love countless times. The Pisces woman believes in the happy-ever-after fairy tale and she has an enormous amount of love to give.

Mr Libra, however, can be a bit of a Casanova. She needs to take things slowly if she doesn't want her heart broken into a thousand tiny pieces! It's simply that Ms Pisces can 'create' a romance out of thin air and begin to imagine that a flirtation equals life-long love. That's not to say that Mr Libra's intentions aren't honourable. When he's with the right woman, the Libra man can be the most loyal and attentive of lovers. In fact, the Libran who lives alone is downright miserable. In the very depths of his soul, he has a burning desire to marry. She, too, *loves* to be in love, but the Pisces woman is not necessarily a strong advocate of marriage. She tends to either view it as something that restricts her freedom (something akin to a fish hook) or, she'll dive in headfirst such as married-more-than-once Pisces actresses Elizabeth Taylor and Drew Barrymore.

The Pisces woman loves the soft side to the Libran man that's mixed with a very powerful masculinity (just think of sexy Librans Julio Iglesias, Roger Moore and Jean-Claude Van Damme). He adores her compassion and great sense of humour. She doesn't take herself *too seriously* and in her most hysterical anecdotes she is constantly sending herself up.

Neither one of them really understand what makes the other tick, but even so, they find a soothing connection in each other's arms and an innate understanding. Like her Libran man, she becomes sick when her emotions are out-of-balance. The sensitive Pisces woman is like a sponge and negative vibrations and harsh words can affect her health and wellbeing. As both Ms Pisces and Mr Libra avoid confrontation, they need to be careful; instead of dealing with problems they'll have a tendency to push them under the carpet. If they are not committed to making their relationship work, one (or both) is likely to drift away emotionally when conflict arises.

When they do make an effort to 'stick it out together' through thick and thin (and various highs, lows and changes of heart and mind), Mr Libra and Ms Pisces can (with some dedicated work and staying power) create a beautiful love nest full of harmony and peace. They are sexually compatible and he will give her the tenderness she needs in their lovemaking. In bed she's imaginative and has the knack of anticipating *exactly* what is needed in order to turn him on. Passionate yet gentle, they find in each other a dream lover. When they start to understand and respect the differences between natives from Venus (he) and people from Neptune (she), then their star-crossed relationship is destined for even better things to come.

scorpio scorpio scorpio scorpio scorpio
scorpio scorpio scorpio scorpio scorpio
scorpio scorpio scorpio scorpio scorpio
scorpio scorpio scorpio scorpio scorpio
scorpio scorpio scorpio scorpio scorpio
scorpio scorpio scorpio scorpio scorpio
scorpio scorpio scorpio scorpio scorpio
scorpio scorpio scorpio scorpio scorpio
scorpio scorpio scorpio scorpio scorpio

scorpio scorpio scorpio scorpio scorpio
scorpio scorpio scorpio scorpio scorpio
scorpio scorpio scorpio scorpio scorpio
scorpio scorpio scorpio scorpio scorpio
scorpio scorpio scorpio scorpio scorpio
scorpio scorpio scorpio scorpio scorpio
scorpio scorpio scorpio scorpio scorpio
scorpio scorpio scorpio scorpio scorpio
scorpio scorpio scorpio scorpio scorpio

SCORPIO

[24 october – 22 november]

romantic pursuit: focused, highly organised and effective

romantic vibration: intensely sexual

secret love desire: to have great on-going exciting

sex with the one they love

element: water

planetary ruler: pluto

symbol: the scorpion

quality: fixed (= stability)

colours: deep reds and soft creams

gem: topaz and malachite

best companions: pisces and cancer

strongest virtues: tenacity, loyalty,

and self-honesty

traits to improve: intolerance, fear of change,

rushing to judgments of others

deepest desire: to live your truths, yet still do

whatever else you want (and not be caught for it)

Scorpio celebrities

Alex Lloyd, Art Garfunkel, Bill Gates, Billy Graham, Bo Derek, Bryan Adams, Calista Flockhart, Calvin Klein, Carl Sagan, Cary Elwes, Charles Bronson, Danny De Vito, David Schwimmer, Demi Moore, Dolph Lundgren, Ethan Hawke, Goldie Hawn, Helen Reddy, Henry Winkler, Hillary Rodham Clinton, Ike Turner, Indira Gandhi, Jaclyn Smith, Jane Pauley, Joan Sutherland, Joaquin Phoenix, Jodie Foster, John Cleese, John Singleton, Johnny Carson, Julia Roberts, Kelly Osbourne, Lauren Holly, Leonardo DiCaprio, Linda Evans, Lisa Bonet, Lyle Lovett, Maria Shriver, Marie Antoinette, Mark Philippoussis, Marla Maples Trump, Martin Scorcese, Meg Ryan, Nadia Comaneci, Pablo Picasso, Pelé, Prince Charles, Richard Dreyfuss, Roseanne Barr, Ru Paul, Sally Field, Sam Shepherd, Sean 'Puff Daddy' Combs, Ted Turner, Tina Arena, Tonya Harding, Vivien Leigh, Whoopi Goldberg, Winona Ryder, Yanni

SCORPIO—SCORPIO relationship

The *'Let's test the power of love'* relationship

STAR SCORPIO–SCORPIO COUPLE
Julia Roberts and Lyle Lovett

Eeek! What are the astro-odds for these two dynamic, powerful people snuggling up and attaining happy-ever-after status? Actually not very high. But as this couple is born under Scorpio — the most bloody-minded, stubborn and willful sign of the zodiac — if they want their love to last, come hell or high water they'll make sure it does!

Now a Scorpio–Scorpio romance isn't likely to be a fun-and-games type of romantic fling. These are the most serious, disciplined and determined folks of the zodiac. They don't know the meaning of 'no', and if they have set their inner compass on a particular course, they won't change it. When two Scorpios fall in love, it is an intensely emotional, physical and spiritual experience. Fortunately against all kinds of odds, this couple often seems to work things out between them. After some initial relationship dramas and other trials and errors, sometimes they eventually become (surprise, surprise) perfect partners. But this accomplishment is no easy feat. Along the pathway to romantic bliss, they have to temper their desire to control everything that's happening between them, and sometimes be prepared to compromise — big time.

But these unions between same-sign Scorpios (to my experience) have a great track record. In my many years as an astrologer, I have been associated with several Scorpios who married other Scorpios and their partnerships were (from appearance) huge successes. Now of course, one has to also consider that Scorpios can be extremely secretive individuals, so outer appearances can be deceptive. Though the cases I observed seemed very devoted, committed and loving to each other. However, Scorpios together will be involved in an 'all-or-nothing' affair, where anything can or could happen — and what occurs between them will add up to either 'love' or 'war'. This dual Scorpio combination is a highly volatile, controlling, strong-willed and stubborn dynamic in astrology. It exists in a zodiac relationship ball park all on its own and will get to bat more than a few emotional curve balls before it reaches a safe relationship home base.

Scorpio woman—Scorpio man

 The *'You've got me under your love-spell'* relationship

When the Scorpio gal and the Scorpio guy become a romantic couple, watch out! This union merges the most powerful zodiac guy with the most powerful zodiac gal so there's weird magic happening astrologically! This union may indeed be 'their destiny'. And if things don't work out, they can give a totally new meaning to the expression 'hell hath no fury as a Scorpio man or Scorpio woman scorned'.

This zodiac relationship operates on a mega-high level or sinks to an all-time low. Should these two really connect in mind, soul, heart and body, I bet your bottom dollar that their stars are in some kind of complementary alignment. In the zodiac hierarchy of relationships, there's truly nothing to compare to two Scorpios together. Now the zillion-dollar relationship question is — will the Scorpio with another Scorpio combination create positive or negative relationship magic? If this couple is blessed with positive magic, then they'll have a wonderful union. But eek! if their connection is not so positive (and meant to teach them lessons about loving), uh-oh, there could be heavy-duty relationship dramas, showdowns and ugly ultimatums ahead!

Sometimes when Ms Scorpio meets a Mr Scorpio and they fall in love, mountains of emotions begin to move within them. This may feel like a volcano, or if they are really comfortable together, a sense of calm or smooth-sailing sensation may prevail. Their initial exchange may even conjure up a sense of dislike for each other. But whatever occurs, they are likely to be affected on a deep-seated level. If the attraction chemistry ignites quickly and is powerful enough, usually both know something is happening in their hearts, minds and bodies that is out of the ordinary. However, there's also probably a scary feeling as well — a sense of walking into a potential relationship mine field and this can make them anxious around each other. If they feel the love power generated between them, depending upon how secure they feel within themselves, they'll either be excited or afraid of their feelings.

Any Scorpio desires to be in total control, and love conjures up human emotions that leave them vulnerable; and the Scorpio doesn't like that vulnerability angle at all! Also, the Scorpio experience with Scorpio won't be an easy-going relationship combination. It's not for the faint-hearted and nobody knows where this romance is likely to end up. No wonder this Scorpio merger is a super 'intense' exchange of abundantly powerful energy, and it can send one or both of them running in the opposite direction. There will be battles of will. Scorpio is one of the more fixed and stubborn signs of the zodiac, so getting these two to meet on middle ground and see eye to eye or compromise could create some massive problems. But if their love is true (and they are likely to be tested on a 'true unconditional love' level), they'll pass their tests with flying colours.

There may be some past-life connections happening here, too. This relationship may be a union that has strong 'karmic ties' and fate is likely to play an enormous role in the way this relationship unfolds. If this couple successfully passes the dating and mating courtship tests and they marry, they usually are committed to each other for life. However, should anything or anyone come between them, their separation from each other can be devastatingly destructive emotionally and cause dramas to unfold for a long time to come. Sometimes breaking up can be a debilitating, heartbreaking experience for both of them, which can leave them with a bitter residue of pain, anger, distrust and remorse for years and years.

The big, possessive thing with Scorpios is that they can't let go of anything or anyone easily, so they're not likely to let go of each other without a major showdown occurring. The possibility of politely shaking hands and wishing each other well in the future if they decide to go separate ways isn't likely to be a reality. Their separation is likely to be more like a version of *War of the Roses* or *The English Patient*; there's passion aplenty to be dealt with and organised or eventually some kind of real disaster is created.

So, due to the unique forces that flow around all Scorpios, it would be unwise to expect this to be a non-stop flight to cloud nine. They'll need to decode together what works in their relationship and what doesn't. Through each other they'll explore a range of pluses and minuses when it comes to relationship credits and debits. And there's likely to be extreme highs and lows between them as this is the kind of relationship that's designed to push them towards expanding their love boundaries for both better or worse.

Disloyalty, infidelity or criticism can be their undoing. And it would be foolish for either of these partners to imagine they can pull the wool over each other's eyes. Scorpios can sense or feel things that other people don't observe. This is a highly sensitive, psychic sign and consequently it is important for them both to be totally open and upfront with each other. Any attempts at deceit or subterfuge are likely to be short-lived. The sixth sense of the Scorpio can be uncanny (however, they do need to beware of allowing their tendency to have suspicious minds to create problems in their relationships). Pride is also a key factor for both of these individuals, as their egos are ultra delicate.

Scorpio is also a sign connected strongly with sexuality. The part of the body governed by the sign of Scorpio is the genitalia, so there's a powerful sex connection driving all Scorpios of both sexes. Put these two people together and if passion is their link, their sexual connection is likely to be a major role-player in bringing them together. Even if this relationship is launched under extremely passionate conditions — due to the highly sexual nature of their shared sign — this Scorpio–Scorpio relationship has the capacity to merge passion with friendship, camaraderie and affection, and has the astrological makings of a very special, life-transforming romance.

SCORPIO—SAGITTARIUS relationship

The *'It takes two to tango'* relationship

STAR SCORPIO–SAGITTARIUS COUPLE
Julia Roberts and Benjamin Bratt

The movie *When Harry Met Sally* is what I consider, astrologically, an example of a typical Scorpio meets Sagittarius movie. For those of you who haven't seen it, the couple in the movie story-line has a merry-relationship dance before they eventually get together. Before they reach this point, they both explore other relationships; they're best friends, they despise each other, they weep and laugh on each other's shoulders, and it takes ages before they realise their true feelings for each other.

Deep feelings, merged with strong friendship and hidden passion: that combustive combination of friendship, sex and deep feelings is very Scorpio–Sagittarius! So while the feelings they share often times fool them into thinking 'this is more a great friendship than a full-blooded passionate love affair', Scorpio and Sagittarius can be suited for a powerful love and romantic relationship.

Scorpio woman — Sagittarius man

 The *'If you break my heart be warned, you'll pay for it'* relationship

Often when Ms Scorpio meets up with Mr Sagittarius and romance is in their stars, they are likely to gaze into each other's eyes and — horrors — they become love-spooked! They'll ask themselves, *Have I got a fever? Should I go to the doctor to see if I'm coming down with the flu? Have I eaten something bad?* And generally, they try to rationalise what on earth is happening to them.

Initially, their feelings for each other may be interpreted as more of a bout of tummy troubles, fright or just general bad vibes. It may take time before they recognise that it's actually a heavy dose of romantic bliss. So if the chemistry is combustive, they'll confuse everyone by acting quite the opposite of what they are feeling. Why do they rebound? In astrology their characters don't fit comfortably together. There are issues of control (and strong will) in force, and when their two ruling planets: hers (Pluto) and his (Jupiter) collide in the love realms, it can become a romantic stressfest. Emotions burgeon all over the place (and scary ones too). What they feel can be a bit too close for comfort, and neither likes to deal with feelings they can't control. They realise these feelings place them under the power of someone else — and that can hurt!

Of course not all Scorpio gals and Sag guys become overwhelmed or get spooked by the strong feelings that erupt between them. Some meet, gaze into each other's eyes and see wonderful things reflected back at them. But this 'Hello, I'm in love and I like what I'm feeling' scenario is rarer than the first 'eek, head for the hills' example. Underneath their confident veneer both Scorpio and Sagittarius are childishly afraid of losing their hearts to someone else. Subliminally they know that if the magic darts from Cupid's love arrows pierce and claim them as love slaves, they are going to have to change. They may need to give up something, sacrifice freedom or power, and unfortunately neither Ms Scorpio nor Mr Sagittarius is very good at giving up anything, unless they feel they are going to get something very valuable, unique and special in return.

Teaming up with each other means they will probably give up a great deal, in fact, a large chunk of their identity. After all Ms Scorpio is the more steadfast, dedicated, reliable gal of the zodiac, and Mr Sag is one of the most erratic, free-spirited and changeable guys of the zodiac. To meet each other in the middle they are going to have to bend over backwards and really love, love, love each other. It takes work — plenty of work — to make things fit between them, but if they manage it, they can do each other 'a whole lotta loving good!'

How will they be good for each other? Well in the bedroom that's one place they'll probably fit together like a sexual treat. Ms Scorpio will also provide Mr Sagittarius with a sense of real security, loyalty, devotion and a sense of belonging that was previously missing in his life. He'll provide Ms Scorpio with abundant options, fun, games, enthusiasm, laughter, travel, passionate lovemaking and new values, ingredients in her life that she's been looking for. So often these two — while very different — if they give it a hundred per cent, joyfully discover they suit each other down to the ground.

Having covered what is good between them, let's check where the problems in this relationship are likely to arise. Mr Sagittarius is a freedom lover. He hates to be scrutinised, distrusted, placed under emotional pressure, or put in a position where he feels he doesn't have room to move. Sometimes Ms Scorpio is a bit too 'watchful' over her Sag partner's behaviour, spending habits, friends and other associations and general opinions and responses. To keep this relationship in flow, Ms Scorpio may need to lighten up in the way she deals with Mr Sag. She can be extremely intense, demanding and confrontational, and he may not appreciate this aspect of their relationship. If she wedges him into too many tight corners, Mr Sag will feel restricted and break free from her sooner or later.

This couple will operate under two different routines or time clocks too. While Mr Sagittarius may travel, have lots of friends or be an outgoing individual, Ms Scorpio may prefer to keep a quieter lifestyle. If she attempts to impose this 'stay-home-more' restriction upon him it may have a suffocating effect on their relationship. Consequently it can be vital for Ms Scorpio to remain trusting as much as possible, because if she worries too much about what her Sagittarian man is up to or becomes jealous and suspicious, inadvertently she may propel him straight into someone else's arms.

To keep in harmony, these two need to become 'relationship diplomats'. They should tread warily and watch their p's and q's when they're together, and be quick to kiss and make-up after any upset. To keep this relationship operating on higher loving ground, will demand that they both come up with some patience, perseverance and hard work, but the rewards will be well worth the effort.

Scorpio man — Sagittarius woman

 The *'I don't want anybody else but you . . .
at least I think I don't'* relationship

Here we have two extremes of personalities meeting up on romantic terms and surprisingly, it is the extreme differences that can keep them interested (especially if their passions are ignited by each other as is often the case with this zodiac combination). In this Scorpio guy and Sagittarius gal situation, you'll have one person expressing certain characteristics and the other repressing these same aspects. Put these two together in a great relationship and they will make a terrific all-round team. Put them together in a terrible relationship and they'll have a short-lived, volatile and confusing affair (often one that leaves some bumps and bruises to their sensitive relationship egos).

It is likely that Mr Scorpio will be the individual who holds things back and internalises his feelings; and it will be Ms Sagittarius who will be pretty much an open book. It comes naturally to this outgoing gal of the zodiac to express almost everything outwardly, sometimes even those things that shouldn't be expressed! Both also have different opinions, goals and expectations, too. He values tradition, while she breaks the rules. He doesn't like to play games he can't win, while she just loves to play and doesn't worry about the end result. With so many opposing ideologies, no wonder these two often find each other so fascinating. If the attraction between them is strong enough, when the love potion hits their charkras, they'll both feel like they've been launched on a rocket ship ride, one that transports them off to the galaxy of love.

As fate usually plays a major role in the way the Sagittarian woman and the Scorpio man's relationship unfolds, rest assured that if these two are meant to be together, nothing will be able to tear them apart. But, be warned; with fate playing out the cards of destiny in their direction, if they aren't meant to be together, nothing will keep them together!

The Sagittarian ruling planet is the fun-loving Jupiter, while the Scorpio's ruling planet is the deep-thinking and somewhat obsessive Pluto. Combine this cosmic alliance and you'll create a couple that will either share a lifetime party together, or drive each other into deep depression (or a combination of both). This relationship is certain to run hot and cold, and have extreme tugs and pulls of infatuation and resentment cycles. Consequently this couple will either feel 'over the moon' about each other, or alternatively 'not be able to stand the sight or sound of each other'. So to keep everything between them on a positive level, they'll need to carefully tiptoe around any potential relationship quicksand.

Where are they most likely to strike trouble? As Scorpio is the most possessive and jealous sign of the zodiac, in any relationship with a Scorpio the flow of loyalty and trust play a powerful role in deciding how this relationship will fare when facing the test of time. If one partner should break the other's heart (particularly through infidelity), there's no easy way out of the hell that the resultant heartache will create. Emotional blackmail, accusations and temper tantrums can spoil this union and often leads to ongoing arguments or even separation.

So if one of them should break the other's trust, even if they do successfully work through other relationship tests or upheavals, still the bitter taste of disappointment, treachery or disenchantment that has taken place, will remain as a thorn between them for a long time to come. As much as they may attempt to patch things up and work out solutions to past problems, any break of trust can cause their relationship to rot at its core and eventually crumble into unhealthy decay. That's why if this couple is really devoted to making their relationship a success, it is imperative that they don't do anything to rock the relationship boat. There's often no second chance where these two are concerned. If they mess up, even if they remain together, they'll torture each other for years to come.

Sex will play a key role in their exchange and maintaining the ongoing attraction and force of their sexual passions will be extremely important to how they deal with the other areas of life. It is very likely that they will have incredible sexual chemistry between them and this will create a strong connection. They'll also be a mental and emotional challenge for each other; the kind of challenge that keeps them on their toes and forces them to learn and grow from their experiences with each other.

They'll constantly surprise each other with their opinions, plans, desires or worries, and this surprise will erupt because Ms Sagittarius and Mr Scorpio tend to have different ideas or ways of handling things. This difference in personal preferences or character traits will either entertain them or make them feel misunderstood. However, if this couple can create a sense of humour about their differences and see how they can sometimes be exactly opposite, they can share lots of laughs about them. Unfortunately, if a sense of humour is missing, their relationship will be repeatedly crashing against Heartbreak Rock before too long.

SCORPIO—CAPRICORN relationship

The *'Give me your heart and I'll give you mine back'* relationship

STAR SCORPIO–CAPRICORN COUPLE
Lara Feltham and Pat Rafter

Surprise, surprise! Though this couple may come from very different worlds astrologically, many happy marriages are forged between the Scorpio and Capricorn signs. Why do they often suit each other to a relationship 'T'? Because this zodiac combination still have loads in common. Scorpio is the fierce defender of its own personal space, armed with the big Scorpion sting to deal out its vengeance. Whereas the Capricorn is the Mountain Goat, the high-climbing, hard-hoofed achiever who's happy to climb to the top alone if others can't match their stride. This ability to be highly independent allows this duo a unique blend of independent togetherness. The ability to be strong whether as a single person or in a close relationship can help them become a great team. Unfortunately, relationship paradise is seldom perfect, especially as both these signs are extremely strong-willed. So they'll need loads of diplomacy and give-and-take in this relationship to make this match a happy-ever-after one.

Scorpio woman — Capricorn man

 The *'It's a strange day for falling in love'* relationship

When the Scorpio gal and the Capricorn guy merge their astro-energies together and fall in love, unexpected changes suddenly occur in their lives, and these changes overflow into the lives of those around them. Sometimes their union or decision to be together influences the world at large as well. That's why there's something very fateful about this combination; and when they merge they often become leaders, trendsetters or examples to others in some form or fashion. If the relationship chemistry mix between them is a sexual attraction, nothing is likely to stop them from being together if that's what they want.

These two are not 'game players'. Although they are usually highly responsible people, if the power flow between them is strong enough, they'll break all their own taboos and do things they had never thought possible to be together. If, for example, once their initial romancing, mating and dating days are over, and they commit to each other, usually they commit for life. Having said that, if they don't make it through the long-term tests that all relationships face, their break-up is likely to be an extremely nasty, mean-spirited experience for both of them.

More often than not, if these two sort out their initial infatuations and resolve their possible resentments with each other, they settle into a great team, both usually appreciating what the other offers. These two have been looking for 'Mr or Ms Right' for a major part of their lives, so if they find someone who measures up to their high relationship expectations, they usually feel a sense of 'coming home' or 'completion'. They've probably had enough heartache in the past, they don't want to go through it all again. So if the magic is working between them, they are both wise enough to respect that this is a special feeling or opportunity that is being offered to them.

If either Ms Scorpio or Mr Capricorn makes a commitment, they usually don't change their minds. These two very serious-minded individuals have a highly developed stubborn streak (and a somewhat controlling outlook). Consequently they hate to make errors and will go to great lengths to avoid change. While they will search for the 'right' or 'perfect' partner more diligently than most other signs of the zodiac, once they have made their choice or selection, come hell or high water, they'll often tolerate extremes of relationship stress or pressure, rather than admit defeat and get divorced. Even if their relationship puts them through some rough patches, they'll usually work hard at repairing any potential rifts.

Now once they have found each other, it is likely that they will unleash some highly passionate sexual bliss at the same time, which will help them quickly realise that they are well suited. Sexual togetherness is often a tremendous power that these two share between them. Sex helps these two overcome a lot of problems, but if they go through sexual problems, often their relationship suffers tremendously in other areas.

Both Ms Scorpio and Mr Capricorn are very determined, willful individuals, so consequently dealing with control issues is where this couple will face the majority of their relationship problems. Both of them are control junkies, and they can become obsessed about getting things to go their way. Neither likes to budge an inch and that can mean they often end up sulking or disillusioned with each other. This willful, stubborn side to both their characters can naturally, if not monitored, lead to explosive consequences, or build invisible, impenetrable emotional brick walls of negative energy between them.

If they realise they both have a powerful subliminal desire to run the relationship fort, and that they have found an equally 'controlling person' in each other, then with some sensitive discussion they may be able to avoid fireworks. Both of them are very strong individuals, so it's well worth their while, after the honeymoon is over, to sit down and organise which of them is best to 'control' various areas of their joint affairs. If they do this they will quickly realise they have special skills that can be used to benefit the relationship and each other; that is, possibly he controls the money, she controls the home, or vice versa. If they can work this out, then their relationship can turn out to be a wonderfully productive union and the expression that 'behind every great man/woman is a great man or great woman' often holds true with this zodiac couple.

If there are no 'bad feelings or grudges' in effect to undermine their close connection, when Ms Scorpio sexually clicks with Mr Capricorn their love-making could put the karma sutra to shame. Beyond their lusty lovemaking connection, the other benefit they can provide each other in abundance is a total sense of security. If they realise their value to each other, they will be very devoted. Before this occurs they may face tests of loyalty early in their relationship. But if they pass these tests, build a home, start a family, construct an empire or initiate a special union together, it will take something or someone quite powerful to interfere with their universe to unravel this connection. This couple both appreciate strength and look down on weakness, so they tend to be prepared to fight for what they want, rather than surrender it easily. And they will fight for love and each other if they know that in each other they've met their perfect lifetime match.

Scorpio man — Capricorn woman

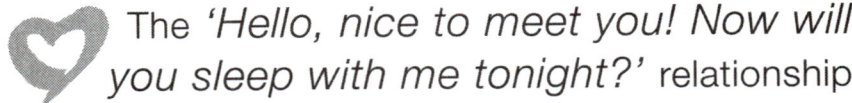 The *'Hello, nice to meet you! Now will you sleep with me tonight?'* relationship

If there are two signs of the zodiac with a talent for bringing out the best in each other sexually, it's the highly passionate Goat gal and the ultra-sexy Scorpion guy. When this couple's sexual energies ignite, their sexual connection and erotic compatibility often makes them both go 'weak at the knees'. When the chemistry is truly sizzling these two will not only have a wild time at the OK-sexual corral for a long time ahead, but also possibly be worthy of an entry in the *Guinness Book of Records* for maintaining a sexual marathon. When the Goat gal and the Scorpion guy team up, their sexual antics often become the icing on their relationship cake. But that doesn't mean that their sexual exchanges are all they have in common or can look forward to in their time together. To their mutual benefit, there's probably much more going on between them than sexual passion, because the Capricorn woman and the Scorpio man usually have a great deal more in common both in and out of the bedroom.

On many diverse astro-levels of operation the Capricorn woman and the Scorpio man have strong connections. If they could they would both love to run the world, be fabulously rich, make a difference; and if they are ambitious and hardworking enough they often do, even if this 'rule the world' side of their characters only applies to their own sphere of worldly power. They both put a great deal of stock in reputation, appearance and living up to their own expectations. Consequently the areas where they are both super sensitive and easily unsettled, or have problems between themselves, is any area where their reputations, loyalties, trust, money or possessions are involved or are negatively affected (all things that they value highly).

Money matters in particular, can quickly come between them, as they both have a strong love and respect for financial security and the power that it provides. Often they become very good business partners as well as romantic partners. Whether they use their compatible exchange in the boardroom making deals, in the bedroom making love, or to expand in other areas, if these two individuals join forces, they are usually a very competitive, successful and hardworking couple. One of the things that generally assures their success is that neither of them have any desire to accept failure — in fact 'failure' is frequently a word that neither of them will accept in their vocabulary.

Now the successful expression of their highest potential noted above is hugely dependent upon their individual maturity and the real soul power generated by their connection. Obviously not all Capricorn gals and Scorpio guys are going to be instantly hooked up to each other in a way that assures a powerhouse of combined energies. There are many areas where this relationship can run aground. Sometimes the Capricorn gal is too controlling for the very suspicious Scorpio guy, or he's going to be far too controlling for her. They both excel at playing the same relationship games, so frequently they have met their 'match' in each other in more ways than one!

After all, Ms Capricorn is really one of the most powerful gals of the zodiac, although she is frequently cleverly disguised in a most feminine, soft-sell package; and Mr Scorpio is one of the most powerful guys of the zodiac, cleverly disguised in a soft-sell package, too. With undercurrents often operating between them, there are many times when this couple teams up that someone is likely to be 'fooling with the other'. And, should these two ever decide to play romantic games with each other's affections, they can create relationship havoc. Neither Ms Capricorn nor Mr Scorpio take kindly to romantic games let alone (eek!) the dismal curse of rejection! Both of them are very self-protective. Should they feel the other person is taking any kind of advantage, or not being completely connected to them — as much as they can merge together into a terrific team — this couple has the potential to become quickly disconnected (or even enemies) if the power flow between them turns negative.

SCORPIO—AQUARIUS relationship

The *'I can't get you out of my thoughts'* relationship

STAR SCORPIO–AQUARIUS COUPLE
Julia Roberts and Daniel Moder

Cupid, Eros, Venus, the Love Gods and Goddesses: whatever force it is that hands out those love-magic pills, those invisible love pills that intoxicate us like an intangible Love Potion No 9, love making a Scorpio and an Aquarius their targets. These purveyors of romantic notions get up to some special emotional, sexual and romantic hijinks when they romantically team up a Scorpio with an Aquarian. When the invisible (angelic) love brokers who hover in the Universe above us decide to bring a Scorpio and an Aquarius together, they probably sit around stirring a big, boiling, romantic relationship pot, mumbling words like, 'Hubble, bubble, toil and trouble'.

In the many different ways of looking at these two signs, put them together and there is strange ingredients and potent magic at work! No matter how well-suited they may be, over the longer term of their relationship this couple will sooner or later discover that they have plenty of relationship pluses going for them, as well as plenty of relationship minuses. One thing this relationship is destined to do is put this couple through the greatest test of all — the test of truly learning the meaning of loving each other 'unconditionally'.

Scorpio woman—Aquarius man

 The *'You can be unsafe here with me'* relationship

Ms Scorpio and Mr Aquarius both share something major in common. Deep down in the depths of their secret selves (in places no other mortal being close or distant to them may even fathom exists within them), they are both desperate to be loved. Often they feel they are born sad because they are born with a lonely heart. No two signs of the zodiac can feel as separated or detached from the world around them than Ms Scorpio and Mr Aquarius. Consequently both of them often feel envious of those other signs of the zodiac, which seem to easily slip in and out of relationships. For both Ms Scorpio and Mr Aquarius relationships are nothing light and breezy, and usually when they fall in love, they fall strongly in love. They don't like to do anything half-heartedly and that's why sometimes they prefer to be alone, than be with someone who isn't right for them.

When Cupid, fate and fortune decree that this couple team up, their lives will become extremely interesting on all kinds of levels. Should they decide to make a long-term commitment to each other, watch out! This combination, while often greatly suited to each other, is still likely to create a relationship exchange that turns out to be highly volatile. In propelling Ms Scorpio into a relationship with Mr Aquarius where both people in this relationship are born under a fixed sign (which, in zodiac language, means they only have one way of doing things — their way), the universal forces are attempting to create a masterpiece of a relationship. This union is either going to work wonderfully or turn into a cosmic free-for-all.

Whatever occurs between these two, even if it is a romance made in heaven, their journey through life together isn't likely to be a walk in the cosmic park. They are going to have their work cut out for them. This couple is comprised of two very stubborn, strong-willed people, who hold fixed opinions and who certainly don't like to have to tolerate or go along with anyone who doesn't agree with them. They are not necessarily team players; they like to run their own ships, consequently they usually prefer to have easy-going, affable, people as partners, so that they can call the shots. That's why it's so surprising to discover that these two zodiac people often end up with the exact opposite of the easy-peasy partner! Consciously or unconsciously they opt for someone who challenges them and puts them to the test and they'll have their challenges one on top of another when Ms Scorpio teams up with Mr Aquarius.

Although each of them may date, flirt and generally shop around for a nice supportive, easy-going partner, they eventually find the possibility of being with Mr or Ms 'Nice' is totally boring. They discover that to achieve a sense of self-worth, or living up to life's challenges, it's better for them to actually have someone to keep them close to the relationship edge. If they marry or become permanent partners with their Ms or Mr Nice, even if their relationship has the outer appearance of moving along merrily, they can soon become bored to tears and start to suffer from health, emotional or mood swing problems.

When Ms Scorpio finds the right Mr Aquarius, she often finds her kindred spirit. He can mix and match it up with her on the deepest emotional levels better than most. While she can be the master of hidden control, so can he. No other sign of the zodiac can sulk as completely or efficiently as her, or withdraw their emotions like an inverse slingshot if they felt they've been treated unfairly. He can give this powerful gal of the zodiac (especially on unspoken levels) a good run for her money, and sometimes that sense of never really knowing what the other is capable of, is the spark that keeps this relationship afire.

So what do they find *sooo* attractive about each other? Mostly each other's unique form of vulnerability carefully clothed in independence and strong will. And what will provide the biggest obstacle to their ongoing romantic attraction is surviving each other's vulnerability, independence and strong will. Consequently, the very qualities they admire most in each other are likely to be the things that push their buttons the most; or may bring their relationship undone.

The psychological magic ingredients that work wonders for the Ms Scorpio–Mr Aquarius couple, who know intuitively as they embark upon it that they are setting themselves something of a relationship mission impossible, are love, trust and commitment. If they merge and blend their many mind-powers together, instead of using their wills against each other, they can turn the world upside down, dance on it and get whatever they want. But if they begin to play powerful mind games with each other, prepare to scramble for shelter as there will be tough times ahead for one and all.

Scorpio man—Aquarius woman

 The *'You're a total mystery to me'* relationship

This should prove to be a most enlightening, informative and educational relationship because two very powerful individuals are teaming up with this zodiac combination. Rather than a smooth-sailing affair, it will be a meeting of two extremely powerful forces. These two actually have much more in common than first appearances reveal (especially on personality levels). Mr Scorpio has a very fixed mind, a strong will and a determined attitude about what he wants, how he wants it and when he wants it. Ms Aquarius has pretty much the same components of strong will and fixed attitudes to life within her too, so when this couple decides to do the romantic fandango together, they often come up with some unusual romantic dance steps.

Who is going to adjust to their partner's rhythm, beat or step is what will keep this couple on their toes for many years, as there's definitely going to be some consistent power struggles going on before these two manage to reach ongoing levels of romantic, harmonic bliss. What makes the process of learning to dance to each other's tunes easier, depends whether or not they dance well together 'horizontally' in the bedroom. If they've got the right sexual rhythm, there's not going to be too many obstacles or problems they will face that they can't overcome. But if their bedroom dancing is out of step, there could be some major problems ahead of this very self-willed and strong-opinionated couple.

As a team, if they are connected by their heartstrings, they are likely to be unbeatable. They can withstand and beat any competition or drama that surrounds them because they both have strong identities and strong survival instincts. Mr Scorpio is probably going to be easily swayed by the cute appeal of Ms Aquarius. Especially if she's clever enough to ensure that when she wants something, she lays a trail so that he thinks he has come up with the idea (or plan, or arrangement she has in mind) all by himself. Ms Aquarius is quite a smart girl. Her brain is very adept at coming up with concepts, solutions or ways of presenting situations to others, and she can usually put this quick-witted aspect of her personality to good use, when it comes to getting Mr Scorpio to see things 'her way'.

Mr Scorpio wants to be wrapped around his romantic partner's finger. He loves to be seduced and cajoled by the one he loves, but he's also a proud individual who demands respect and high regard. He naturally wants to be a Lord and Master type, even though he sometimes plays the sexual slave when the moment is appropriate. So depending upon time, place, mood and occasion, there's going to be lots of role-reversals going on between these two. One day he'll be the boss, she the next, but as long as they don't admit to each other that this is the way it is — and he's always given the appearance of being Lord of the Manor — peace, harmony and romantic bliss should reign.

So there's definitely some rules of astrological etiquette to be followed when this couple team up. She (Ms Aquarius) needs to be prepared to go out of her way to seem like she is demure, cute and super soft, even when she's actually much more persuasive and self-directed than is proper for any gal married to the most powerful man of the zodiac, Mr Scorpio. She'll get exactly what she wants, by appearing not to want it too much at all, and thus avoid many a battle of will, simply by being smart enough to skirt around them before a stand is taken by either party.

What's wonderful about this zodiac couple is, that if they can work out a mutually harmonic relationship exchange, they can be the best of lovers, friends, parents and playmates. Their journey through life will be an ongoing adventure and a thing of great joy and fulfillment. But before they reach that level of 'completing' each other's lives, naturally they'll have some sorting out to do when it comes to trusting each other, reaching the right level of attentiveness to each other, balancing out their mutual finances and organising their family affairs. These everyday type affairs could turn out to be sensitive areas for them both because they may have widely different opinions on certain aspects of them, and they need to reach many wide and unusual compromises. At least, once they have found the right balance between them, they should be able to make their relationship withstand the difficult test of time. For once the Scorpio man and the Aquarian woman commit, it is usually (like the black swan, which only mates with one mate in its lifetime) a zodiac match that lasts forever and is not one that is easily put asunder.

SCORPIO—PISCES relationship

The *'As long as we don't get married, I truly think we may be the perfect couple!'* relationship

STAR SCORPIO–PISCES COUPLE
Goldie Hawn and Kurt Russell

'Can't live with you, can't live without you' type attractions and volatile sexual chemistry are created when a Scorpio and Pisces fall in love. When the love dust hits their eyes they can be jet-propelled on a heady and intoxicating love-flight direct to cloud nine. Strong, sexual passion and romantic, emotional content are stirred up when Cupid's arrow hits the hearts of this duo. In terms of romantic relationships, these two signs are highly compatible and consequently it is quite natural that they often find themselves attracted to each other. Pisces Elizabeth Taylor married Richard Burton (Scorpio) twice, and the tugs and pulls of emotion and attraction between these two signs are often highly charged and quite volatile (as Liz and Richard discovered). And Goldie Hawn (Scorpio) has been a long-time partner of Kurt Russell (Pisces), and they seemed to have successfully endured many tests and challenges to their relationship. (Probably because Goldie is the Scorpio the gal with the sting, not the Pisces, the one that floats along with the breeze.)

The Scorpio often provides a secure emotional balance for the more highly charged-up Pisces who tends to be more changeable and flighty than the steadfast Scorpio. Where Pisces is easily distracted or waylaid, the Scorpio stays on course and is much more strong-willed and determined. Together, this duo can make a terrific relationship team, but because they share a highly volatile emotional nature there will probably be many times that their relationship will be put to hard test. One of the greatest tests they are likely to face over time will come from maintaining fidelity. Their passions often run their lives and sometimes if they get out of step with each other 'the grass looks greener elsewhere', and they will wander away from each other often at an extremely high price in the longer term.

Scorpio woman—Pisces man

 The *'Met him on Monday and married him on Sunday'* relationship

Talk about a romantic match forged in the most powerful domains of the realms of the zodiac — that's the Scorpio woman and the Pisces man. This couple is so highly connected to each other in astro-terms, if their stars should become lovers' stars, they'll discover they are zoomed into the land of romance at a rapid speed. They'll soon discover that within their powerful connection they experience all the cycles of love and hate, and everything else in between before this love exchange is through (if indeed it ever is through!) Nothing will be commonplace or ordinary about their relationship, and if it withstands the test of early days, this same extra-ordinary quality or experience that flows between them will continue in the way they live out their lives together.

Why is this relationship such a potent one? After all Ms Scorpio's ruling planet is the awesome Pluto, the most powerful of all planets in the zodiac realms, which means that even if she's cute, sweet and appears 'Ms Light and Breezy Easy-Going', she is still a zodiac force to be reckoned with. She's a zodiac gal with a powerful punch and being the Scorpio she is the one with the hidden sting, which she can yield at will! Her ruler, Pluto in mythology is the God of the Underworld, the God who operates on subterranean levels. Operating from the depths of her subconscious, she's no ordinary zodiac lass, she's a high-powered, competitive and strong-willed individual. She doesn't like to mess around and prefers to cut straight to the chase.

Now Mr Pisces however, doesn't like to be confined (particularly emotionally). He likes his freedom, and if he wants to roam or play games, he is certainly dating or married to the wrong gal. He's mercurial in nature because the ever-changing planetary force Neptune rules him. And Neptune is the planet that governs our oceans and controls the swirling hidden life and energy ebb and flow that exist beneath the ocean's waves. So what's going on in his life is often hidden from view or under the surface. And if there's one lass of the zodiac who is clever enough to find out what he is thinking, dreaming about or planning, it's Ms Scorpio. So he'll need to be ready to deal with her if he wants to keep the love fires burning in her eyes where he is concerned.

If he plays romantic games (and Mr Pisces often does), he will create doubts, fears and even distrust which will affect both of them; feelings that often would need careful observation to avoid them from becoming too overwhelming. So he'll need to play straight with her, or end up paying the consequences — big time! It isn't going to be easy for this couple to fool each other either, for any length of time anyway. Whether they are aware of it or not, there is a strong psychic interaction between them. If Ms Scorpio is happy, it can help Mr Pisces become happy too. But if Ms Scorpio is depressed or displeased, her lack of enthusiasm will quickly 'bring down' her Piscean partner's mood.

It's hard for these two to be separate individuals from each other because of the powerful psychic unconscious links that operate between them. As there are such powerful connections between them, the secretive Scorpio woman or Pisces man may sometimes find this sense of always being 'connected to someone else' unsettling. So though this Scorpio–Pisces connection is a powerful one, in certain cases this link between them can cause difficulties or a sense of loss of 'self-will', rather than help the relationship evolve.

In most cases, the fact that they are so aligned with each other opens up all kinds of windows of opportunity. They can become true companions if they reach and maintain high levels of trust and compassion between them which give them a true sense of belonging to each other. Because they're so attuned, if things go wrong between them it can often lead to intense internal suffering; the kind that breaks hearts and bring on legal problems and general disharmony. Consequently the Scorpio woman and the Pisces man need to treat each other with high regard and consideration. If they mess up, they'll mess up big time and the beautiful times they might otherwise share together can turn instead into tearful, breaky heart times.

Scorpio man—Pisces woman

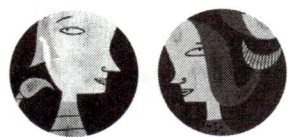

 The *'Just like Romeo and Juliet!'* relationship

When the most sexy, intense and passionate guy of the zodiac, Mr Scorpio, falls in love with the most romantic, emotionally highly-charged and changeable gal of the zodiac, Ms Pisces, the romantic angels begin to sing as a heavenly choir. There's invisible music in the air around them and something very special about the Mr Scorpio and Ms Pisces romance; and it is not surprising to sometimes hear others around them make the comment that they are 'meant for each other'. Certainly this astro-combination is a fantastic one for falling in love, but keeping the love light shining brightly and sustaining their initial passion may not prove to be so easy. Nevertheless whether this relationship exists for either the short term or the longer term, it is definitely likely to be an affair to remember. If this couple can overcome his possessiveness and her dramatic emotional behaviour, astrologically, the Scorpio man and the Pisces woman have what it takes to make a terrific lifetime team together.

She's super seductive and he's the sexual sign of the zodiac, so he's easily swayed by the flutter of her elegant long eyelashes. While other women of the zodiac often meet their match in Mr Scorpio and he runs the romantic show, Ms Pisces can wrap Mr Scorpio around her little finger if she really wants to. And even when he's playing tough guy and making rules and regulations about family, finances or even social plans she is making, she knows she can charm him around to her way of thinking — it's just a matter of time! He adores her and he wants to see her happy, so he'll go out of his way and make some huge sacrifices to ensure she gets a smooth ride through life. That is, unless she somehow breaks trust with him and this couple slide into unhappy circumstances where they are operating out of integrity with each other. When trust is broken between these two, it can mean they become warring companions rather than loving ones.

Feelings and sensitivity run super deep between this couple and therefore a small error of judgment, a casual word spoken out of place, a moment's indiscretion or hint of infidelity can tear them apart and break their bonds quicker than a wink of an eye. Nobody can break their partner's heart as successfully as Mr Scorpio and Ms Pisces can do to each other. They can really get into and under each other's skin and there will be times when they will sense each other's feelings, desires, passions and lies through the pores of their skin. It's hard for either of them to hide things from each other, and because of their psychic connection, sometimes there can be too much intensity between them to really make being together always comfortable. Their open-radar type connection can overwhelm them, and they may need to set up some boundaries between them or seek out some light relief at times to stop that constant connection from overshadowing their true individual expression of life.

When they want a break from each other they may go about it in many ways. They may seek romantic dalliances with other people, or find a hobby or work role that keeps them occupied and at an emotional distance (if not distance of space) from each other. But of course, any need to have 'space' from each other will only arise when they have exhausted themselves of each other's delight in the bedroom, spent too much time together, and generally overindulged in their romantic explorations of each other. It's like they say 'that too much of a good thing is bad for you'. In the case of Mr Scorpio and Ms Pisces sometimes they fall prey to this problem. The trouble with the Scorpio man and the Pisces woman is that they want their first relationship magic to miraculously continue long after the 'honeymoon period' has elapsed. And this huge expectation naturally places a great test on both of them because in the everyday world, how do you constantly manage to be connected at the heart and hip and still get something else done. It is setting any relationship up for disaster to hold this kind of expectation in the first place.

So when they've run the gamut of emotions, sex and romantic exchange, Mr Scorpio often ends up working late at night and Ms Pisces ends up spending more time with family members or with gal pals. They do this simply to survive in the outside world and create some sort of independent existence from each other. If they don't manage to find some private expression of themselves, they can burn out a wonderful relationship super quickly, simply because they expect every moment they share together to be intense, passionate and romantic. This is the cosmic couple of the zodiac, the prince and princess of love and romantic joining forces, but not all fairy tales are guaranteed to have a happy ending. Sometimes it takes a whole lotta love for this couple to actually make the distance, but if they do, it's well worth it.

sagittarius sagittarius sagittarius sagittarius
sagittarius sagittarius sagittarius sagittarius
sagittarius sagittarius sagittarius sagittarius
sagittarius sagittarius sagittarius sagittarius
sagittarius sagittarius sagittarius sagittarius
sagittarius sagittarius sagittarius sagittarius
sagittarius sagittarius sagittarius sagittarius
sagittarius sagittarius sagittarius sagittarius
sagittarius sagittarius sagittarius sagittarius

sagittarius sagittarius sagittarius sagittarius
sagittarius sagittarius sagittarius sagittarius
sagittarius sagittarius sagittarius sagittarius
sagittarius sagittarius sagittarius sagittarius
sagittarius sagittarius sagittarius sagittarius
sagittarius sagittarius sagittarius sagittarius
sagittarius sagittarius sagittarius sagittarius
sagittarius sagittarius sagittarius sagittarius
sagittarius sagittarius sagittarius sagittarius

SAGITTARIUS

[23 november – 21 december]

romantic pursuit: playful and friendly

romantic vibration: flirtatious

secret love desire: to share a lifetime adventure

with the one they love

element: fire

planetary ruler: jupiter

symbol: the archer

quality: mutable (= flexibility)

colours: light blues and yellow

gem: turquoise and diamonds

best companions: aries and leo

strongest virtues: adventurous, fearless

approach to love and life and a wonderfully

positive attitude to life

traits to improve: stubbornness, wilfulness,

thinking that you know everything

deepest desire: to do what you love

Sagittarius celebrities

Alyssa Milano, Amy Grant, Anna Nicole Smith, Ben Stiller, Benjamin Bratt, Bette Midler, Billy Connolly, Billy Idol, Boris Becker, Brad Pitt, Brendan Fraser, Britney Spears, Chris Evert, Christina Aguilera, Christina Applegate, Daryl Hannah, Deborah Hutton, Diane Ladd, Don Johnson, Ed Harris, Frank Sinatra, Gary Hart, Georgie Parker, Gianni Versace, Jane Austen, Jane Fonda, Jeff Bridges, Jim Morrison, Jimi Hendrix, John F. Kennedy Jnr, Judd Nelson, Katarina Witt, Katie Holmes, Keifer Sutherland, Kenneth Branagh, Kerry Packer, Kim Basinger, Kirk Douglas, Maggie Tabberer, Milla Jonovich, Muriel Hemingway, Marisa Tomei, Miranda Otto, Monica Seles, Ozzy Osbourne, Pamela Stephenson, Ray Martin, Rebecca Gibney, Rita Wilson, Sinead O'Connor, Steven Spielberg, Susan Dey, Teri Hatcher, Tina Turner, Tyra Banks, Walt Disney, Winston Churchill, Woody Allen

SAGITTARIUS — SAGITTARIUS relationship

The *'Prepare for some crazy romantic confusion ahead'* relationship

STAR SAGITTARIUS–SAGITTARIUS COUPLE
Billy Connolly and Pamela Stephenson

Put two feisty Sagittarians together and you have the makings of a 'twin-flame' relationship. They'll either blaze brightly together, or burn each other out quickly. If they fall in love and marry, this often indicates that a karmic connection exists between them and they were destined or meant to be together. Though there can be some intensity between them, too. Whether they are twin-flames or not, because they have the power to ignite each other's passions if the going gets too intense between them, eventually they'll burn each other out emotionally, financially, physically or psychologically.

If love magic is strong between them, the Sagittarius–Sagittarius couple often successfully zoom into the love zones of life. United by their outgoing, friendly and cheerful dispositions, if they are truly connected by their heartstrings, the versatile and multi-talented Sagittarian couple can move through life sharing a lifetime party together. However, this 'let's party' aspect of their characters either gives them a fantastic life, or leads to loads of trouble, but thankfully usually the former applies.

Being born under the lucky sign, good fortune naturally smiles on them, and this natural ability to tap into good fortune often helps these two bounce back from any relationship adversity that they face. When the right Mr and Ms Sagittarius align their lives together, they can possess a combination of natural savvy and child-like spirit that makes them the most fascinating (and probably enthusiastic) couple in the zodiac neighbourhood.

Sagittarius woman—Sagittarian man

 The *'Romantic up, up and then down, down'* relationship

One thing's for sure, when Mr Sagittarius and Ms Sagittarius meet, they generally instinctively feel in tune with each other. Things are *big*! On their first dinner date, they indulge their big, healthy appetites, talk about their big, exciting plans for the future and most likely run up a big bar bill. They'll laugh big and heartily, and tell each other stories of their latest big adventure in some big exotic country. If, the Sagittarian couple happen to fall in love with each other's big heart, they'll have a big wedding, share a big, roomy house, raise a big brood of children and have a dog called Mad Max. They just can't help it! Ruled by abundant Jupiter, Archers simply do things in a 'big way'.

The wonderful thing about a Sag–Sag love match is their combined positive attitude to life. This natural optimism allows the Sag couple to take on projects together (that might faze others), such as buying a house, raising children or backpacking around the world for a year. Life is an adventure for them. Sagittarians also tend to be very lucky people and their combined forces are likely to strike good luck in the lottery, pokies, horse races, bingo or the local chook raffle! Where work is concerned, both understand the philosophy that if you simply 'do what you love', life will be much more enjoyable. Together, they can turn favourite hobbies into successful businesses. A Sagittarian friend of mine and her Archer husband turned a much-loved pastime (interior decorating) into a successful business, both leaving behind careers with which they had become disenchanted. The Sagittarian couple will also indulge together one of their biggest passions: travel.

The symbol of Sagittarius is the Centaur: half human and half horse. This is why Sagittarian lovers go through life in duality: changing back and forth from happy/sad; wise/irresponsible; serious/playful; couch potato/super-active. The nice thing about a double Archer love match is that when one Sag is feeling down, upset or deflated, the other will turn into an animated clown, telling jokes and grinning widely to cheer the other one up! Thankfully, more often than not Sagittarians are cheerful, happy-go-lucky souls who know instinctively how to 'suck the juice' out of life.

Sporty and active, they are constantly 'on the go', which means they'll have to coordinate their busy schedules if they want to see each other! After work both Mr and Ms Sag will have organised a game of tennis or an aerobics session or maybe a French or philosophy class at the local evening college. Some weekends you'll find them at the pub talking animatedly to friends, other times playing scrabble at home or bushwalking in the mountains. Sex between these two fire-sign adventurers is likely to be explosive. They are highly in tune with each other's sexual needs and desires.

Although Sagittarians are physically active, graceful and strong, they are often clumsy when it comes to expressing their softer, emotional sides. The King and Queen of Tactlessness are likely to make many an embarrassing blunder as they go through life arm in arm! Imagine two Archers, shooting their pointed arrows of truth into each other and you can see how fire starts. Both believe their *truth* is the *only* truth. At times stubborn and unmoving, they will need to learn to give a little, or simply learn how to duck the arrows! Luckily Sagittarians are not overly sensitive souls, they can take harsh words and they're quick to forgive. Both tend to turn the other cheek quickly after arguments as they prefer to get on with life rather than hold grudges or bad feelings, so basically Mr and Ms Sagittarius will live harmoniously together. They can frankly admit they've been wrong, but more often than not they'll show they're sorry with actions, rather than words.

If there is one key ingredient missing in this love match, it's the lack of really romantic romance. Sagittarians are big-hearted, affectionate and generous, but not the sign most known for wildly romantic gestures. Sagittarian men have a tendency to treat their girlfriends or wives as 'one of the boys'. It's not that he's not crazy about her. It's simply that he shows his love in practical ways, like fixing her leaking washing machine, or tuning her car, rather than spoiling her with flowers, champagne and chocolates. Though Ms Sagittarius is the kind of woman comfortable in evening *or* hiking wear, she is likely to get a little weary of his lack of romantic touches. But the Sagittarian woman has strong ideas about herself, her relationship and the world around her. She's not shy about telling her Sag guy what it is she wants, needs and desires. They'll laugh about it heartily, make passionate love and continue through life, hand in hand, under Jupiter's broad smile.

SAGITTARIUS—CAPRICORN relationship

The *'I wonder how this is going to end up?'* relationship

STAR SAGITTARIUS–CAPRICORN COUPLE
John F. Kennedy Jnr and Carolyn Bessette-Kennedy

Heeeelllo! Did somebody care to warn the sensible and sure-footed Capricorn Mountain Goat that the Sagittarian Archer is the feisty, unpredictable life of the party? And did anybody think to advise 'live-for-the-moment' Sagittarius that Capricorns have a tendency to cling to the past and stick to tried-and-tested methods? I don't think so. These two wander into a relationship together all bright-eyed and bushy-tailed, only to frequently leave it with their eyes glazed over and dragging their weary bedraggled tails behind them.

What goes wrong? Plenty usually. Well, when it comes down to the nitty gritty, Sagittarians are optimists, while Capricorns are pessimists. Sagittarians love to dare to be different. Capricorns like to avoid any kind of change or adventure that puts them out of their safety zone. This chalk-and-cheese relationship certainly has its challenges. Though many Capricorn–Sagittarius unions tend to sizzle and burn in the early stages of the relationship, this is not always the case. Sometimes these two just seem to fit together like two good, solid silver spoons. There's an undeniable attraction when such different creatures from the zodiac are brought together in the name of love and/or lust. They are definitely going to be great insightful teachers to each other. However, this is likely to be a relationship where one partner or both will suffer from either serious boredom or burnout sooner or later. Naturally, there are always exceptions to any situation and sometimes a Sagittarian and a Capricorn just might make it through the night into the next day, and the next day and the next; and it all turns out perfectly wonderful after all.

Sagittarius woman — Capricorn man

 The *'If you don't wanna have fun, don't hang around with me'* relationship

If you are one half of a Ms Sagittarius–Mr Capricorn love match you might sometimes feel that the Gods must be crazy. How on earth did you end up with this person who's so clearly from another zodiac planet? Yes, it's true. The Archer gal comes from fun-lovin' Jupiter, while her Mountain Goat guy hails from the serious planet of Saturn. You're up against many personality differences in this romantic match, but no matter if it's a short and steamy love affair or a lifetime marriage, keep in mind that patience, understanding and acceptance are needed in big doses in this love mix.

The Capricorn man is often a born organiser and 'neat freak'. Just imagine this scenario; while his Sag gal sits on the sofa, munching on a sandwich and watching a TV travel documentary or sports show, Mr Capricorn is propping up the sofa cushions, tidying up the magazine rack and frowning at the crumbs she's spilling everywhere. Yep, at times it seems like an episode of *The Odd Couple* in the Archer gal–Goat guy household.

Still, this couple *can* learn how to find middle ground. The Capricorn man provides stability for the roaming Archer gal, who really does benefit from the security and reliability he gives her. He's an old-fashioned gentleman who treats her with love and respect, though it takes Ms Sag a while to get used to his lack of public displays of affection. The Sagittarius gal is spontaneous and loves to give impulsive bear hugs and big kisses. Mr Capricorn on the other hand, isn't the type to kiss and canoodle in public (he cares very much about 'what people think'). Although he doesn't wear his heart on his sleeve, she knows deep down that he adores her because he's emotionally mature and isn't into game-playing. This will be a welcome surprise for many an Archer gal who's sick and tired of clingy, insecure or boyish men.

While the Capricorn guy is not a classic Casanova, he has the ability to give his Sagittarian gal a surprisingly shy and sexy look that says it all. Behind closed doors the earthy Capricorn man is sensual and often downright kinky. She too, is a sexual adventurer who loves to let her hair down. When they first meet there is an undeniable curiosity that creates high passion, though for the magic to continue into the future there needs to be plenty of patience (her) and imagination (him).

Outside of the bedroom, however, Ms Sagittarius gets frustrated with her Capricorn guy's cautious nature. *'How do you know you don't like Cambodian cuisine?'*, she'll say, exasperated, *'you've never tried it before.'* But whether he's trying a new cuisine or experimenting with a different hairstyle, Mr Capricorn is conservative by nature. He prefers tastes, feelings, sensations and ideas that are tried and tested. Since he was a young boy his parents taught him good manners *and* to take the sure and steady path (though as he gets older, the Capricorn man starts to loosen up).

Ms Sagittarius, on the other hand, was more likely encouraged by her parents to take the 'road less travelled'. Many adventurous and independent Sagittarian gals leave the family nest at a young age, and they might even make fun of Capricorn lover's attachment to his mother. I have a Sagittarian girlfriend who scoffs at how her forty-year-old Capricorn partner still takes home his dirty washing to his mother's house on weekends! (Though she is happy there is one less household chore to do!)

One of the main points of conflict in this cosmic duo is their attitude to money. He believes in saving it, while she is more adept at spending or gambling it! Ms Sagittarius is known for her excesses: she's famous for her shopping sprees, and this is one stargal who can drink the guys under the table if she's in the mood! Mr Capricorn, conversely, was born with a deep sense of self-restriction. It's likely that his Sagittarius gal thinks that saving for a rainy day is only for nerds! Especially where married or de facto couples are concerned, it will take a while for them to meet halfway in the money and finance side of their shared life. When they do, chances are they'll discover the world's perfect balance between saving and spending. A small step for mankind but a big step for Ms Sagittarius and Mr Capricorn!

Sagittarius man—Capricorn woman

 The *'You can take my patience away, but not my love'* relationship

At first glance, it might seem that Mr Sagittarius wears the pants in this relationship, but more than likely it's practical Ms Capricorn who leads the way. Dressed to go out for dinner with her Sagittarian man, the Capricorn lady is classy, feminine and immaculately groomed. Standing by the front door with her keys in her hand, she glances at her watch. Suddenly, Mr Sagittarius bounds out of the bedroom, flicking his still wet hair out of his eyes. He's wearing baggy pants, sports shoes and a shirt with a stain on the cuff. She'll spot the stain and ask him to go change the shirt. The Sag man stands his ground, emphatically stating that she should accept him for who he is and not for what he's wearing. She smiles her shy, entrancing Capricorn smile. His heart melts and he returns to the bedroom to change his shirt and dry his hair.

For all their differences, there's a strong lustful attraction here. Their relationship is multi-faceted in the span of the unusual and unique connections that it forges between them. It is also a relationship where deep life lessons can be learned from each other; and when it works, it's fabulous! There's a sense of excitement about discovering someone who keeps them on their toes. Each has qualities that appeal to the other. She deeply admires his spirit of adventure and his individualism, while he respects her self-discipline and the fact that she knows exactly where she's going in life. Just think of the dynamic that existed between charismatic Sagittarian John F. Kennedy Jnr and his elegant Capricorn wife Carolyn Bessette-Kennedy. Now they certainly had a true spark between them, but one that seemed to sometimes burn too brightly and had the intensity to injure, disrupt and singe them both. The Sagittarian guy and Capricorn gal have to remember constantly that they come from very different zodiac backgrounds. This sometimes makes them very foreign and distant in some ways to each other, but true love speaks all languages and bridges many gaps.

The Capricorn gal has a tender heart (much more tender than it appears from outside observation) and she often shields her emotions beneath a crack-free, tough-styled veneer. Only when she's deeply in love and trusting of her lover can she readily share her feelings. But with Mr Sagittarius, she's dealing with a guy who, when trying to make things better, has a tendency to trip over his feet in the process! He has a tendency to blurt out whatever he is thinking and then suffer the consequences later.

Though not terribly romantic in gestures (the Sagittarian man rarely brings home flowers unless he is prompted), he *is* a romantic figure to her. The Archer man is dashing, brave and he's an adventurer, and Ms Capricorn admires his tendency to play big and take risks. Throughout her life she's learned that the well-trodden path to the top of the mountain is the trail that all good Mountain Maids should follow. Her Sag guy, however, is an expert at forging his own path. He'll take the hardest route, throwing his rope to a high ledge and hoist himself up. At times, he'll even climb with no rope at all in a 'look mum, no hands!' kind of style! He thrives on risk, whereas she avoids it at all cost.

Ruled by Saturn, the planet of life lessons, Ms Capricorn is wise beyond her years, whereas Mr Sagittarius, governed by jovial Jupiter, is at times a big kid. She'll be annoyed when he ignores her Saturnine wisdom, and goes out to do exactly what she warns him NOT to do. If he falls flat on his face and returns heartbroken, she won't give him the 'I told you so' lecture, but will heal the hurt with her loving tenderness and wisdom.

More than anything, Mr Sagittarius admires his Cap gal's self-discipline, organised manner and consistency. She's organised with her time too, whereas he can become so engrossed in a book, project, job or study program, that he completely loses track of time! He falls in love with the enchanting, feminine Ms Capricorn and he loves that she listens quietly to his grandiose plans and projects. He's a man with lofty goals who is curious about the world around him. Philosophical, and himself a great teacher, they find an intellectual rapport immediately; and both share a mutual dedication to their respective goals.

They are polar opposites though when it comes to money matters. She saves it, he spends it, and most frustrating of all for Ms Capricorn, is that he spends it on what she calls 'expensive toys'. Her Sag guys loves climbing, skiing, sailing, diving, you name the sport and he's got the equipment. (He also adores the latest Play Station games, television and stereo equipment.)

Mr Sagittarius shows his Mountain maid how to have faith and believe that everything will turn out all right in the end. He'll get her out of her comfort zone, take her travelling and show her that life is meant for living. Though Mr Sagittarius is known to be one of the more romantically promiscuous male signs, when he falls deeply in love he's capable of loyalty and devotion. With a Capricorn gal by his side, he'll find all he ever wanted, and more.

SAGITTARIUS—AQUARIUS relationship

The *'What on earth are we doing together?'* relationship

STAR SAGITTARIUS–AQUARIUS COUPLE
Brad Pitt and Jennifer Aniston

When the zodiac's two most independent and feisty freedom lovers match up in the game of love, it's often a case of catch me if you can. It's an interesting dynamic that occurs in this relationship. Destiny often forces them to spend periods of time apart, during which time they'll declare their undying love for each other on long telephone calls, followed by intense periods together when they wish they were somewhere else! There's a fine line between 'being' together and 'suffocating' each other. Both these star signs need space and freedom, yet they realise deep down that the other could very well be 'The One'.

One difference in their *modus operandi* is that Sagittarius is a 'mutable' sign and Aquarius a 'fixed' sign. That means that Archers are communicators and quite flexible to change, while the Water Bearers can be impatient, stubborn and unmoving in their point of view. Luckily, the Archer's blunt arrows of truth don't seem to wound the Water Bearer as they do other signs. The Aquarian likes the truth and actually appreciates Sag's tactless way of operating! Though they do have their differences, this couple is more likely to experience together the dizzy heights of relationship bliss rather than the dreary lows of coupledom hell.

Sagittarius woman — Aquarius man

 The *'Let's cross our fingers and hope for the best'* relationship

Uranus, the ruling planet of Aquarius, governs electricity, technology and scientific breakthroughs. When Ms Sagittarius meets the Aquarian man there's definitely a buzz in the air; and when the lightning bolts hit her, the Sag gal is going to be knocked off her feet. Mr Aquarian's unpredictability excites her (though she might not initially admit this!) and she *loves* the fact that he's constantly surprising her.

He is *different* and thank goodness for that, because the Sagittarius maiden has a short boredom threshold. She's the kind of woman who doesn't *need* a man to make her happy. She doesn't mind being single *and* she has plenty of friends to keep her company when she is on her own. The fiery and passionate Sag is also likely to have one-night stands or steamy affairs if she doesn't have a serious relationship. So, as you can see, it takes a *very* special guy to make Ms Sagittarius commit to a serious relationship.

But when the cosmic cowgirl and the outer space Superman get together in the game of love and romance their relationship is anything but 'serious'. *Anything* is possible when jovial Ms Sag meets eccentric Mr Aquarius. Both love to have fun and break the rules and they refuse to conform. In any case, trying to 'fit in' is not a good idea for the Aquarian guy. It can make him feel physically sick, depressed or cause other kinds of problems for him.

On their first date, he is more likely to take her to an amusement park than a sophisticated restaurant. He'll take her on the most futuristic and thrilling ride and then, when they come back down to earth, he'll buy her fairy floss and lead her towards the laughing clowns. She won't know whether her heart is jumping from the thrill of the ride or the excitement of being with him. It's more likely the latter!

The Aquarian man not only *acts* differently, he also *looks* unique. His facial features are usually aquiline and there's something different about his eyes (they may be unusually coloured or he could be ever so slightly cross-eyed). If he's not working in the corporate sector, Mr Aquarius might be inclined to wear dyed jeans or shave off all his hair. With partner-in-crime Ms Sagittarius by his side, she's probably the one who'll shave it for him! Both these crazy individuals have a healthy disrespect for the establishment.

There's something completely honest and natural about the Sagittarian woman that makes her Aquarian guy go weak at the knees. There is nothing pretentious about her (and he hates nothing more than a woman who can't be herself). She's usually a natural beauty, with little fondness for make-up, designer clothes, or flashy jewellery. Ohhh yes — his friends *adore* her, and whether he admits it or not, his friends hold a great deal of influence over him. Ms Sagittarius likes simple pleasures; like walking her dog, meeting friends for brunch, reading a good book or going on a camping trip. She *loves* to travel, she's philosophical and has a great sense of humour.

Sexually, this couple ignite the Aquarian imagination and the Sagittarian passion. Though Mr Aquarius is not a 'highly charged' sexual being, when he *is* in the mood for sex he's creative, inventive and very erotic. Like most air signs, he responds well to sexy bed-time talk and the occasional pornographic movie or magazine. Air signs live on such a mental plane that they often need a sexy 'idea' planted in their head in order to feel turned on. Ms Sagittarius on the other hand is a fire sign, so she's a raunchy and passionate lover who needs few suggestions to get her fired up for sex. They're also very compatible in bed because they consider the other to be a friend as well as a lover. They know how to laugh about sex and talk about their desires and *that's* a very healthy thing for these two.

But as much as the Sag gal adores her Aquarian boyfriend / lover / defacto / husband (and she may use one *or* many of these terms), there are times when he drives her insane. She'll get temporarily infuriated, especially when he absent-mindedly forgets they have a date, that it's her birthday, or that they were going to visit her sick grandmother in hospital. Look out Aquarius! Because when Ms Sagittarius gets mad — she gets *really* mad. Fire signs are, by nature, quick to anger and she'll fire her Archer's stinging arrows of truth in his general direction. Thankfully, she's also just as quick to calm down and she's not the kind of girl to hold a grudge. Though Mr Aquarius may be a little left-of-centre, he can be surprisingly stubborn at times. He is a fixed sign, which means that when he makes up his mind about something, she'll have to move heaven and earth to get him to change his ideas.

The wonderful thing about this couple is that they share a mutual love of excitement and novelty, and they will share all kinds of adventures and travels. If they decide to live together there's a strong possibility that they won't get married. Though it is unlikely this cosmic couple will marry, if they do commit to a long-term relationship, they will probably remain as de factos for many years, choosing to invest money in property or shares rather than spending it on a lavish wedding. They may even start a business venture together. Their house will most likely be big (her planet Jupiter rules 'expansiveness') and full of *his* strange collections of things. Whatever occurs in this relationship, it will never be dull and that's the secret that Mr Aquarius and Ms Sagittarius share. Now, if they could just put it in a bottle and sell it.

Sagittarius man — Aquarius woman

 The *'Yikes! I'm travelling down the icky romance road again'* relationship

It won't take long for Mr Sagittarius to realise that his Aquarian gal is . . . well . . . *different*. And it's not just the way she acts; it's the way she looks, talks, thinks, dresses and generally behaves. Ms Aquarius was born under the futuristic planet of Uranus and everything she does is unique. The Aquarian woman is a non-conformist, who can be downright shocking at times. She's a dazzling gal who marches to the beat of her own drum and there's something *about* her that impacts people wherever she goes. So, when Mr Sagittarius enters her sphere of enchantment, he is *impacted* in a major, major way. Their first meeting is usually completely out-of-the-ordinary. She might meet him on a train on her way to the Young Inventors Annual Conference; knock on his door to sell him the new, can't-live-without-it household product; or she might even strike up a conversation with him on a hiking trip in the mountains.

No matter how they meet, her eccentricity and unconventional behaviour is likely to delight, rather than annoy him. In fact, dating an Aquarian woman is a challenge for most men, as they simply don't know what to expect next. She's intelligent, contradictory and unique. In fact, this is what the Archer loves about his Water-Bearing gal. She is always surprising him, and thankfully he is a man who abhors routine.

Ms Aquarius is a gal who takes chances and she takes a big chance on Mr Sagittarius (particularly as he has a reputation for being a heartbreaker). The first things she noticed about him are his wise and worldly attitude, and his strong, muscular thighs. Yes, I *did* say thighs. Most Sag men have very muscular thighs, after all his astrological symbol *is* the half-man half-beast Centaur. Though apart from lusting after his thighs (and other muscular parts of his body), it's unlikely that Ms Aquarius will take their relationship too seriously — at least at first.

Some unions between an Aquarian woman and a Sagittarian man remain in the 'short-lived-but-very-passionate' relationship basket. If they stick it out, these two will find they actually have a lot in common and the sufficient compatibility to make a lifelong partnership. Just look at husband and wife team, Sagittarian Brad Pitt and Aquarian Jennifer Aniston. Both are typical of their sign. Heart-throb Pitt has the loveable and magnetic Sag charm and Aniston has that special offbeat Aquarian star-quality that you can't quite put your finger on.

The forward-thinking Aquarian woman is ahead of her time (just look at her clothes, hairstyle, car, apartment, choice of movies, books etc). She's all for love and sisterhood and many Water Bearer ladies are feminists, political activists, environmentalists or revolutionaries of some kind. She's concerned with the welfare of humanity and the future of mankind. The typical Aquarian gal does not sit back lazily and let the world go by. She's an active part of it, and if necessary she'll try and change it! The Sagittarian guy, similarly a visionary but maybe not quite a radical, admires her spunk and get-up-and-go. She's intelligent, interesting and passionate.

Although she has a large circle of friends, the Aquarian woman can be a bit of a Lone Ranger, who appreciates time on her own. Thankfully, words such as 'space' and 'freedom' also pop up frequently in her Sag guy's vocabulary. So, when Ms Aquarius decides to go away for the weekend with a bunch of girlfriends, Mr Sagittarius won't feel insulted. Neither will the Aquarian woman worry too much if her Sag guy decides to go travelling around Europe for two months with little more than a backpack. It could be a case of absence making the heart grow fonder in this relationship.

Though they might not actually *see* each other often, the time they spend together is wonderful. The truth is, Mr Sag and Ms Aquarius have a lot in common. Both are humanitarians, they have lots of friends, full social calendars and a true *interest* in what makes people tick. They also like spending time in the great outdoors and might share a love of travelling, sport and keeping healthy.

Of course there are times when they will knock heads. Fire-ruled Sagittarius is often a little overly passionate and volatile and sometimes the air-ruled Aquarian gal will whip him up into a frenzy, fanning his fiery nature into flames, but basically the two enjoy a relationship based on friendship and respect. She's the type of woman who likes to be 'one of the boys', so she'll be equally happily joining a mates' night out or doing her own thing at home.

The wonderful thing between these two, is that they love the things about each other that usually offend, annoy or confuse other signs. Mr Sag loves his Aquarian gal's eccentricity and unpredictability, while Ms Aquarius has no problems with her Sag guy's love of freedom and forthright bluntness. In fact, Ms Aquarius is one of the few women in the zodiac who's not offended by her Sag guy's habit of putting his foot in his mouth! She'll laugh, agree or roll her eyes heavenward, but rarely will she be deeply hurt or offended! What might drive him crazy is her penchant for changing her mind (in typical air-sign fashion), or absent-mindedly forgetting to do something she promised him she'd do.

Though there is a fierce attraction between the two when it comes to the crunch, Ms Aquarius and Mr Sagittarius are wonderful friends. Even if their romantic relationship fizzles, you can bet that they will remain buddies. One thing they need to make sure they do is to allocate time in their busy schedules for each other. If they don't make an effort to inject romance into their relationship (and neither are 'flowers and candles' type of lovers), it's likely that the passionate flame that brought them together initially will be snuffed out. Mmmm, but with a Sag Stud like Brad Pitt in the romantic formula, I would find that hard to believe.

SAGITTARIUS—PISCES relationship

The *'We will smile even when it hurts'* relationship

STAR SAGITTARIUS–PISCES COUPLE
Milla Jonovich and Luc Besson

Are you a Sagittarius looking for a highly challenging love affair? Or perhaps you're a Pisces with a penchant for tense romantic relationships? Then look no further. This is the perfect love match for you! Seriously, if you're one half of a Sagittarius–Pisces romantic union, you will understand when I say that 'this relationship wasn't meant to be easy'.

Although Sagittarius and Pisces are not the most compatible duo under the zodiac, it is true that their relationship has an element of 'destiny' to it. The Archer and Fish learn important life lessons next to each other, and whether their union is short and passionate, or long and loving, it is sure to impact greatly them both.

Sagittarius woman — Pisces man

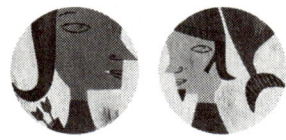

 The *'C'mon, take a chance on me'* relationship

To outsiders the Sagittarius woman and Pisces man often look like the 'Odd Couple', but these zodiac lovers have more in common than meets the eye. Both are tolerant and compassionate. They are idealists, but their relationship can be tense due to their different attitudes to the concept of 'truth'. The Archer gal's kind of honesty consists of the brutal in-your-face variety that can wound deeply. Sensitive Mr Pisces prefers to protect people's feelings, even if it means slinking around, weaving or stretching the truth in some way.

Given the strong astrological influences, tension arises due to their different personalities but at the same time it creates an attraction that's spellbinding. If these two star-crossed lovers expect to create serenity together they will have to cool it when the tension begins to mount. That means *choosing their battles*, knowing when to give in, and knowing when to insist on having it their own way. It also means accepting each other for *who* and *how* they are. In most cases it's the Sagittarius woman who will insist on having things her way. The Pisces man is non-confrontational by nature, preferring peace to sparring with his partner. Mr Pisces is a lover, not a fighter and he'll woo his Sag love with poetry, flowers and champagne. The Pisces man is renowned in the zodiac for being a wonderful lover. Sensitive, romantic and sensual, he'll read his Sag gal's mind, knowing instinctively if she wants tender and romantic lovemaking or wild and passionate sex. She loves adventurous sex and together they'll find a healthy combination of love, romance and passion.

While there's affinity in the bedroom, it's Mr Pisces career arena that often causes friction between the two of them. Ruled by the changeable and elusive element of water, Mr Pisces is constantly intrigued by life's multiple choices. He's a dreamer who lives in his imagination, intuition and dreams. He'll change track mid-career and ditch law in favour of becoming an artist, or perhaps swap his job as a professional landscaper to a writer. The truth is, this is a man of many talents and the Sag gal had better get used to his changeability. Though at first she might find it charming (especially if his change in career involves travel, her favourite pastime!) sooner or later she's likely to let him know, not so tactfully, to get his act together. You see, the Sagittarian woman knows what she wants in life and she designs a plan to go out and get it.

Unfortunately, she expects him to be the same and the fiery Sagittarius tongue can cut him down in a heartbeat. She's impulsive and outspoken and her comments can easily wound his sensitive soul. If these two plan to live happily ever after, the Archer gal needs to learn to soften her tough Sagittarian approach, *or* risk losing her Neptune man, who will disappear downstream with one fluid impulse of his Fish tail. He in turn needs to learn not to take her comments so personally. In this love match, the Queen of Self-Will versus the King of Self-Pity can become their own biggest enemies.

Although many Pisces men make several career changes, they're not the type to jump from girl to girl. When in love, they remain constant, supportive and true. This is where the Sagittarius gal finds a true supporter in her Pisces guy. He has an open mind and a compassionate and patient nature. She feels completely at ease telling him her innermost feelings, as well as sharing her goals and visions. No matter how outrageous they seem he'll listen to her every word without judging or trying to 'fix' her problem.

The Sagittarius woman is intelligent and curious, and she'll constantly catch herself pondering, questioning and trying to work out *why* he is the way he is. In the end, she should give up and just enjoy being with a special otherworldly creature such as Mr Pisces. He in turn should realise she really does love him; it's simply that her astrological make up doesn't include tact or high sensitivity.

Though their personalities may clash, there's room for success here. Both Sagittarius and Pisces are open-minded and have friends from all ages and backgrounds. This makes for a vibrant social life together (and wonderful dinner parties!) though it's Mr Pisces who periodically craves moments of solitude. On these occasions he'll take off on a solitary walk along the beach, hole up in his studio painting or drawing, or perhaps escape on his own to watch a movie. The empathetic Pisces man absorbs so much from people in everyday life (just note how people tend to pour out their hearts to him) that he needs to disconnect at times to recharge. The Sag gal understands his need for space and luckily she's a gal who values her own freedom. Neither is particularly jealous or possessive. When married, they have a jovial, creative if not slightly 'eccentric' household. Both love children and their offspring will no doubt grow up to be fascinating individuals in their own right, following family tradition.

Sagittarius man—Pisces woman

 The *'Tell me, which love zone are you from?'* relationship

Expect a fairy-tale romance when Ms Pisces and Mr Sagittarius meet. There's a strong physical attraction between the sweet and feminine Pisces woman and the brave and masculine Sagittarius guy. He's the kind of courageous Prince Charming she's been waiting for to free her from imprisonment in the Castle Tower. Meanwhile, he instinctively feels that he could love and protect the beautiful Pisces princess forever. But like any story-book romance, there are challenges ahead for this astro-couple. Though the attraction is strong, fire-ruled Mr Sag and water-babe Ms Pisces are essentially from different worlds.

Neptune is the ruling planet of Pisces, and in ancient Greek mythology Neptune ruled the hidden unseen depths of the ocean. The ocean is a world within worlds, and Pisces are otherworldly beings whose emotions can change like the oceans, from turbulent to calm and back again in a matter of hours. Ms Pisces is unique, artistic and creative.

Trailblazing Mr Sagittarius, on the other hand, is ruled by jovial Jupiter, in Greek mythology the ruler of all the Gods, and the governor of abundance, gift giving and the good life. Mr Sag is often the life of the party, or if not he's the one throwing the party! The Sagittarius guy is also like his symbol the Archer; he's straightforward and direct, but it's often his 'straight-shooting' arrows that harm his sensitive Pisces maiden. His *faux pas* in the diplomacy department will wound her (harsh words make her wilt like a flower), and in effect his strong 'fire' will slowly start to dehydrate her 'water'.

The Pisces woman needs gentleness. Her Archer guy's heart is in the right place (he merely wants to help and guide her), but Mr Sag needs to learn that his Pisces lover has a different *modus operandi*. And truth be known, she could live quite happily without him thank you very much. Though Ms Pisces may sometimes appear delicate this gal *can* stand on her own two feet. Just look at capable Pisces women such as Cindy Crawford, Chelsea Clinton, Liza Minnelli and Jennifer Love Hewitt.

Though the Pisces gal is emotional, she can be cool at times when it comes to showing her feelings and passion. The fire-ruled Sag guy has big desires and a big way of showing them. Tenderness and a sweet touch is what appeals to this gal in the bedroom and the robust, passionate Sag lover needs to learn to show his love and affection outside of the bedroom, too. Feeling loved, adored and cared for is the biggest turn-on for this woman.

Despite his verbal clumsiness and brusqueness, she can't help but adore him. He has a big heart, a positive outlook on life, and a wonderful spirit of adventure. But if Mr Sagittarius has cold feet at any time (and many Archer men are commitment-phobic), the Pisces woman is sure to know about it. She has a sixth sense when it comes to picking up on people's feelings, and she'll draw him out to talk about any doubts he might have. She has such an empathetic way of putting herself in other people's shoes that he will fall in love with her again and again and again.

The Pisces gal is also a fabulous listener who truly is interested in what her Sag guy has to say. Just as well, because Archer men enjoy nothing more than talking to someone who pays one hundred per cent attention to what they say. If he's the quiet Sagittarius type (and yes, they do exist), she'll be able to get him talking about his goals, dreams and desires at the drop of a hat.

Both of these people are idealists who are searching for a true, pure and honest expression in life and this is what they admire most in each other. They both have a real interest in other people and what makes them tick. Mr Sagittarius is often found working as a teacher, or in the areas of philosophy, religion or law. His Pisces maiden is a humanitarian with a passion for protecting the rights of animals, older people or children. She's a champion fighter for the underprivileged. In fact, Mr Sagittarius and Ms Pisces often meet through their work or humanitarian interests and many times their mutual friends introduce them to each other saying, *'I just know you two will click!'*

If these two cosmic lovebirds accept each other for who they *are* instead of what they *are not*, then their fairy-tale romance will be one of the 'happy-ever-after' kind.

capricorn capricorn capricorn capricorn
capricorn capricorn capricorn capricorn
capricorn capricorn capricorn capricorn
capricorn capricorn capricorn capricorn
capricorn capricorn capricorn capricorn
capricorn capricorn capricorn capricorn
capricorn capricorn capricorn capricorn
capricorn capricorn capricorn capricorn
capricorn capricorn capricorn capricorn

capricorn capricorn capricorn capricorn
capricorn capricorn capricorn capricorn
capricorn capricorn capricorn capricorn
capricorn capricorn capricorn capricorn
capricorn capricorn capricorn capricorn
capricorn capricorn capricorn capricorn
capricorn capricorn capricorn capricorn
capricorn capricorn capricorn capricorn
capricorn capricorn capricorn capricorn

CAPRICORN

[22 december – 20 january]

romantic pursuit: careful and conservative

romantic vibration: lusty and controlling

secret love desire: to strike gold in their lover,

partner and social success, thereby upgrading their own

personal and professional circumstances

element: earth

planetary ruler: saturn

symbol: the goat

quality: cardinal (= activity)

colours: greens and golds

gem: white onyx and moonstone

best companions: taurus and virgo

strongest virtues: your disciplined approach,

organisational skills, and consistency

traits to improve: clinging to the past, inability

to forgive others, taking life too seriously

deepest desire: not to miss

out on a moment of life's magic

Capricorn celebrities

Annie Lennox, Anthony Hopkins, Aristotle Onassis, Ava Gardner, Carolyn Bessette-Kennedy, Cary Grant, Christy Turlington, Cuba Gooding Jr, David Bowie, David Lynch, Denzel Washington, Diane Keaton, Diane Sawyer, Dolly Parton, Donna Summer, Eartha Kitt, Elvis Presley, Faye Dunaway, George Foreman, Harry M. Miller, Helena Christensen, Jack Jones, Jared Leto, Jim Bakker, Jim Carrey, John Denver, John Voight, Jude Law, Julia Louis-Dreyfus, Kate Moss, Kevin Costner, Kid Rock, Kirstie Alley, Linda Kozlowski, Marianne Faithfull, Marilyn Manson, Marlene Dietrich, Marquis de Sade, Mel Gibson, Michael Crawford, Muhammad Ali, Nicholas Cage, Pat Benatar, Pat Rafter, Paul Keating, Ralph Fiennes, Ricky Martin, Rod Stewart, Rowan Atkinson, Rudyard Kipling, Sade, Sarah Polley, Shirley Bassey, Sissy Spacek, Ted Danson, Tiger Woods, Tippi Hedren, Tracey Ullman, Val Kilmer

CAPRICORN—CAPRICORN relationship

The *'This romance could carry us away to some crazy places'* relationship

STAR CAPRICORN–CAPRICORN COUPLE
Victoria Principal and Desi Arnaz Jnr

This relationship sometimes fails to *even* happen, as Capricorns are so timid and cautious when it comes to taking chances with love and romance. Luckily, when *one* of them finally makes the first move, it can be the beginning of a beautiful, loyal, long-lasting and stable relationship. These two want the same things and that's a great start in any relationship. Born under an earth sign, they are dependable, quiet and goal-orientated; and when two Goats team up for a romance, affair or marriage, they are comforted by the thought that their partner thinks along the same lines as they do. Their connection is earthy, sensual and comfortable and their goals and values in life merge together quite naturally. They also make wonderful organisers, so two of them together can become high achievers. One of Capricorn's greatest strengths is the ability to keep a goal in focus until they achieve it, no matter how long it takes. These superb organisers have a talent for seeing the big picture, while taking little steps every day to make their dreams come true.

When an earth sign links up with another earth sign, as is the case with two Capricorns, they have the ability to build their relationship into a high mountain of strength and faith. Alternatively, if there's no give-and-take it can become a dry desert *or,* if they're angered, a violent volcanic eruption! Much depends on the willingness of each couple to give and take. As both are cardinal signs (they are born leaders) they may argue about who 'goes first' in everything they do! The wonderful thing about this couple is that as they grow older they also grow younger. When they are young their romance is often marked with a serious and gruff tone. As they grow old together they tend to kick up their heels, relax and have more fun. This is when the fun-loving Mountain Goats show their real colours and frolic through the wildflowers, letting the other lead the way and just being happy to be alive.

Capricorn woman — Capricorn man

 The *'You go climb every mountain . . . and I'll see you later'* relationship

Okay, so our two star-crossed Cappy lovers have met, they've manoeuvred their way around the issues of love and need (which to a Goat sound suspiciously like some form of inherent weakness), and they've decided (or perhaps *agreed* is a better word) that there is a mutual level of feeling between them. What now? Well, there are certain rules, regulations and other formalities to attend to, not the least of which is whether our respective Goat couple's *families* will get along with one another. Sounds quite mad, doesn't it? Most people couldn't give a hoot if *her* cousin Johnny can't stand to be in the same room as *his* Aunt Edna. But, Capricorn guys and gals are *not* most people. They are a law unto themselves in many instances, which is what happens when you're ruled by serious planet Saturn. And where there is law, well, there are people to uphold it, and that's where Mr and Ms Capricorn enter the picture! Family values are vitally important in this earth-sign combination and if Goat guy's and Goat gal's parents, brothers, sisters, aunts, uncles, cousins, nieces and nephews don't all get along famously, there's bound to be trouble in paradise.

So, assuming we've made it through the 'family test', what can one expect from a pair of Cappy lovers? To begin with, there is a strong bond here of trust and respect. Reliability and maintaining a successful image are important matters to this earthy couple and in many ways their dreams have been answered in this union. Not only does one completely understand what motivates and drives the other, they are also one of the few couples capable of upholding a successful working partnership as well. (So a sense of responsibility is strong, and there are certainly no upsets if one, or both have to stay back at the office to finish an important job with an urgent deadline!)

Now one would think that any couple this serious or responsible would have to be a no-show in the bedroom, right? Wrong! Don't make the mistake of judging a book by its cover. If you look hard enough, this pair isn't the technical manual you'd expect — the *Karma Sutra* would be more fitting to their unabandoned style of lovemaking. Though it may not be apparent on the surface, you can rest assured that the embers of hot and passionate love are smouldering just below the surface, waiting to be ignited. In short, these two are hot in the cot (kinky comes to mind!). The discovery that they can open the floodgates on their often pent-up emotions when in the company of one another, paves the way for some fulfilling (and exciting) sex. When they do get going — well, put it this way, the answering machine will definitely be *on*!

Once they have declared their undying love for one another (albeit, *very* unassumingly), exchanged bank account details, checked out the other's plush homes and luxury cars, and everything meets the expectation of quality and wealth, then down the aisle our happy couple will march. For all intents and purposes (one *must* have purpose), this is a match made in heaven — Cap man and Cap woman love their families, their possessions, their bank accounts and their careers. What else could there possibly be?

Variety of course! These two mountain climbers need to keep in mind that all work and no play can make them two very boring old Goats. Serious as they are, one or the other needs to take the time to inject a little fun and excitement (outside of the bedroom) into their daily lives. Otherwise, twenty years down the beaten Goat-track, one or both of our Rocky Mountain High lovers may realise that the double-whammy of Saturnine caution and restraint has done nothing other than bury their dreams underneath tonnes of practical, no-nonsense *rubble*.

So, while one of the main focuses in this relationship is getting down to the serious business of *business*, this can be a very happy and solid union, and one that has more than an even chance of going the distance. As long as this Capricorn couple doesn't forget that the magic ingredient to any fulfilling relationship is *fun* (even a Goat needs to venture into greener pastures every now and then), then this love affair is definitely one worth the risk.

CAPRICORN—AQUARIUS relationship

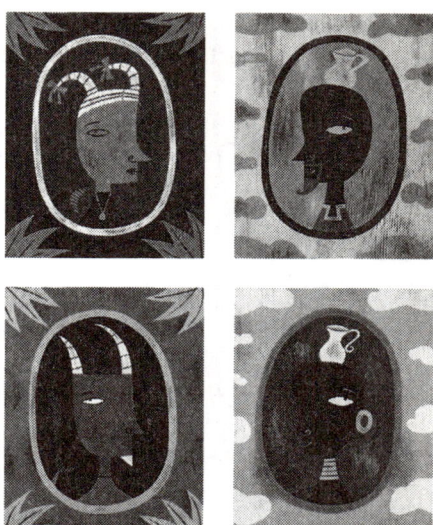

The *'I see your true colours and they clash with mine'* relationship

STAR CAPRICORN–AQUARIUS COUPLE
Nicholas Cage and Lisa Marie Presley

The Water Bearer was born to break traditions, yet the Goat is on earth this time around to uphold them! This is just about as tough as it gets. Alternative Aquarius and conventional Capricorn are from such different planets that they sometimes need an interpreter to translate the other's language! Aquarius wants to change things and Capricorn wants to keep things as they are. Whether this relationship makes it or breaks it depends on how tolerant the Goat is of the Water Bearer's eccentricities and how much Aquarius is willing to put up with Capricorn's stern and serious ways.

Nevertheless, both signs get the feeling they could learn from each other. They share honesty and integrity in life. This bond is more important than they realise and if trust and faith is broken in this relationship, they may as well part ways. At times Capricorn's hang-ups regarding duty, tradition and responsibility make Aquarius roll his or her eyes up to heaven. There are also times when Aquarius' rebellious nature and love of shock tactics make Capricorn shake his or her head in disapproval. Other days, Capricorn's TLC makes the heart of head-ruled

Aquarius melt. That's when Capricorn is inspired to move mountains by the contagious love of life that Aquarius brings. When they put aside their differences and love each other for the good qualities, the Goat and Water Bearer prove that opposites *do* attract and they *can* find lasting happiness in each other's arms.

Capricorn woman — Aquarius man

 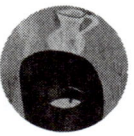

 The *'Tell me, that our love isn't true, and I'll never speak to you again'* relationship

Sometimes the Aquarian man is just too over-the-top and unpredictable for Ms Capricorn. She is a woman who likes to uphold tradition, convention and the status quo, whereas his goal in this lifetime is to break with them! The Capricorn woman is concerned about what other people think and she can become slightly obsessed about her position in society. She takes great care of her personal appearance and she's likely to spend a reasonable amount of money on elegant clothes, well-made shoes and the best beauty and hair-care products she can afford to buy. Mr Aquarius, on the other hand, often has a distinct dishevelled look about him and he may or may not like to wear shoes at all! At best, he personifies 'smart casual' but more typically he dresses in an eccentric, individual way. His Capricorn gal often has the habit of tucking in the label at the back of his shirt, straightening the knot of his tie (if he in fact bothers to wear one), or suggesting he throw out his Hawaiian shirt and go shopping for a classic pinstripe style instead. So it's not unusual that their stark differences in appearance extend to major differences in personality!

In fact, the uniqueness of Mr Aquarius is magnified and viewed as downright strangeness through the eyes of the sedate and proper Capricorn gal. He's unconventional in everything he does, and he doesn't care what people think about him. In life the Aquarian man marches to the beat of his own drum. He's fun, friendly, intelligent (bordering on genius), outspoken and completely unique. There's something about his honesty and integrity that attracts her and the fact that she doesn't know what he's going to do next sends a shiver of excitement down her spine. You see, most Capricorn women would love to break free of the severity and seriousness of their ruling planet, Saturn. Many would adore being more spontaneous but Saturn gives them a sense of responsibility and self-discipline that makes them hold back. She secretly looks up to her guy's ability to live day by day. Of course, Saturn's influence gives the Capricorn gal wonderful qualities too. She's dependable, trustworthy, goal-orientated and able to turn her dreams into reality with hard work and persistence. Most Capricorn gals have a wonderful sense of humor and fun-loving attitude to life, but her friendliness can be punctuated with spells of gloominess, guilt and depression. Thankfully, Mr Aquarius doesn't take it personally when she falls into her occasional brooding bouts of melancholy. He's patient and will be there for her when she snaps out of it and returns to her lovely, sweet self again.

Funnily enough, though her conventional behaviour makes him yawn at times, Mr Aquarius would love to have a bit more of her self-discipline and focus. He's a very inspired man, but he also spends a lot of time in life feeling confused and torn in different directions. Being around his Capricorn gal helps him to be less erratic and she is one of the most supportive women in the zodiac, *and* she's clever. In fact, when unpredictable Mr Super Cool Aquarius arrives in her life (usually by complete surprise) she senses a prince in disguise. What she admires about him is his honesty, and if he's loyal she can forgive him his loud shirts and knack for shocking people. She is patient and figures with time she'll be able to smooth out his rough edges! Tensions in this relationship occur because Ms Capricorn wants to lead (she's a go-ahead cardinal sign), and Mr Aquarius is not the kind of guy to obediently follow. He's independent and a stubborn 'fixed' sign with very firm views on life. He values freedom, his friends and partner (and sometimes in that order!)

Thankfully, the Capricorn maiden is typically an unobtrusive kind of gal, who's patient, tranquil, supportive and non-demanding. Both have days where they switch off their emotions and can be distant and detached, but normally it's a relationship full of fun, affection and respect. Level-headed Ms Capricorn sometimes calls her Water Bearer guy a dreamer, but he's actually quite logical and analytical. The Aquarian man possesses a unique combination of practicality *and* vision. He's an inspired thinker and she won't always be able to follow his line of logic. Uranus, the planet of 'genius', rules Aquarians and many famous, brilliant scientists (like Thomas Edison), writers (Charles Dickens), and composers (Mozart), are born under this sign. Being different is what Mr Aquarius is all about, and if his Capricorn gal is the type who can't accept being in an unpredictable relationship, then it is unlikely to last.

The Aquarian man doesn't follow protocol and she can't expect to change that. He, too, needs to be flexible and adaptable in order to cope with his Capricorn woman's mood swings and need for acceptance by other people (particularly her family). He needs to understand that emotional and financial security make her feel safe, which is why she desires a healthy bank balance, a husband, children, a good career and a home in order to feel that she's 'made it' in life. Mr Aquarius, on the other hand, could quite happily live with her in a cosy caravan with few possessions, plenty of freedom and a diverse range of friends from all walks of life. Nevertheless, after he experiences love with the Capricorn woman, he won't find it easy to leave her. She's an earthy, affectionate and tender lover and she is one of the most loyal and caring women in the zodiac. One thing is for certain, this couple appreciates each other's honesty and that forms the basis of a solid relationship. Mr Aquarius is a seeker of truth and many times he finds the wisdom he's looking for by his Capricorn gal's side. When they accept each other for *who* they are, instead of who they're *not*, then the Goat and the Water Bearer can live happily ever after.

Capricorn man — Aquarius woman

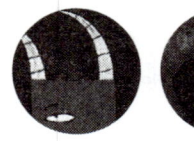 

 The *'It's the wild season for romance'* relationship

When Mr Capricorn meets Ms Aquarius he may come to the conclusion that she's somewhat crazy. Alternatively, he may decide that she's a genius. Either way, he's probably right. The ruling planet of Aquarius is Uranus, and this planet governs both genius thinking and insane behaviour. One thing's for sure, the Aquarian gal is unique: she's brilliant, spontaneous, innovative, eccentric, outspoken and honest. From her individual beauty to the eccentric or unique clothes she wears, this gal is different. Even if she does look and dress conservatively, you can bet that her individuality shines through in other ways. You can see the Aquarian individuality in outspoken TV personality Oprah Winfrey, kooky actress Geena Davis, rebellious Princess Stefanie of Monaco, and the *different* beauty of actress Jennifer Aniston.

There's an electrical, unpredictable vibe about the Aquarian woman that can initially make the Capricorn guy nervous. Saturn, the planet of restriction, discipline, wisdom and consistency, rules him, so he likes to be in control of his life, *especially* where his sensitive heart is concerned! This certainly doesn't mean that he's boring or dull. Many Capricorn men have a sly or dry sense of humour, and others (like comics Jim Carrey and Rowan Atkinson) have a wonderful sense of the ridiculous, but at his very core the Capricorn man takes life seriously. So when the impulsive Aquarian gal enters his life, no wonder he feels uneasy. It's probably because he will never *ever* really *know* her, and just when he thinks he does, she will completely surprise him. That's because the Aquarian gal doesn't know what's going to happen next. Nevertheless, the Capricorn man finds himself magnetically attracted to her and when he decides to take the plunge and initiate a romance he woos his woman in an old-fashioned, romantic way including flowers, chocolates and candle-lit dinners. When they do consummate their relationship you can be sure that Ms Aquarius makes the first move. Sex between this couple combines his earthiness and sensuality and her element of surprise and inventiveness. At times, they find themselves out of sync when it comes to lovemaking, that is, he takes longer to get in the mood, and she needs loads of variety; but as Mr Capricorn says with a grin, *'practice makes perfect'*.

There will be days when she is simply too outrageous for his conventional standards, and other times she thinks he's too dull, drab and disciplined for words! Many Aquarian woman–Capricorn man couples just don't make it because they can't cope with the tension their differences bring. However, understanding what makes the other tick can relieve most of their tensions. One of the first things the Water Bearer gal has to learn about her Capricorn guy is his closeness to his family. He feels a strong obligation towards them and he'll do just about anything to help them. Ms Aquarius admires his innate sense of duty, but on the other hand she's outspoken if she feels his family is taking advantage of him. For example, she won't hesitate to tell him he's crazy to lend money to his brother who has a gambling problem, or that his mother has a way of using emotional blackmail to get what she wants. Look out Ms Aquarius! Criticising his family is akin to taking the Lord's name in vain and if she loves him, putting up with his family is part and parcel of the deal. Similarly, he will need to understand her devotion to her friends. In fact, if Mr Capricorn is set on romancing the Aquarian gal he had better make friends with *her* friends. Ms Aquarius is incredibly loyal to her buddies and in most cases she's closer to them than her own family!

When *his* family and *her* friends are out of the picture, this couple *can* have a wonderful relationship together. The key to success in this relationship is celebrating their differences, instead of trying to change each other. There are many Water Bearer gals and Goat guys who learn from each other and have fabulous relationships. Happily married Hollywood actors Ted Danson and Mary Steinbergan show that the Capricorn–Aquarian equation can be a wonderful success. As Capricorn men are wont to do, Danson has brought a sense of stability into Steinbergan's chaotic and colourful Aquarian life. She, on the other hand, puts the zippity-doo-dah into his existence.

The Aquarian woman injects much needed fun and frivolity into her Capricorn guy's life. She teaches him that life is for living and that he shouldn't worry what other people think about him. Though he's a persistent, determined and ambitious man, he can easily get stuck in ruts and routines. With the Aquarian woman by his side, he learns that there's no such thing as the word 'impossible'. The good news is, as Capricorns get older they tend to enter a more relaxed, fun-loving period (almost like a reverse childhood), and this is when they start to let their hair down. He begins to take himself, and life, less seriously and as a result there are less tensions with his Aquarian woman.

To his credit, the Capricorn man can also be the best thing that ever happened to his Aquarian woman. He's the most practical guy in the zodiac, who is able to help her turn her inventive ideas, inspiring thoughts and hunches into reality. He shows he loves her by helping her in practical ways. He's loyal, devoted and protective of her, and even though she's unconventional she really is seeking a reliable, stable relationship. If things become serious he'll start planning (slowly but surely) for the future and wedding bells are sure to ring. The Capricorn man is a firm believer in the institution of marriage and he wants to do things 'the right way'. Ms Aquarius is typically *not* a big fan of marriage until she meets the man she is destined to marry! But she had better realise that her Capricorn husband-to-be leans towards conventional male–female roles, and while he's happy for his *girlfriend* to have her own career and a social life that excludes him, that can often change when they marry. This is an issue they need to talk about *before* exchanging vows, as Ms Aquarius is seldom happy spending her married life raising children and looking after the house. Aquarian women are born under the mental 'air' element and they need to stay active physically and mentally.

When it comes to the crunch, this can be a wonderful relationship and the longer they're *together* the more they become like each other! With his calming influence, Ms Aquarius becomes more stable and settled, and courtesy of his Aquarian gal, Mr Capricorn loosens up in life and starts to have more fun.

CAPRICORN—PISCES relationship

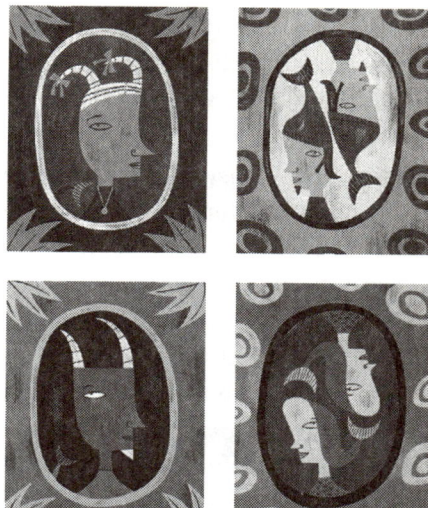

The *'You were amazing . . . I am amazing. We both did amazing things to each other, but that's enough'* relationship

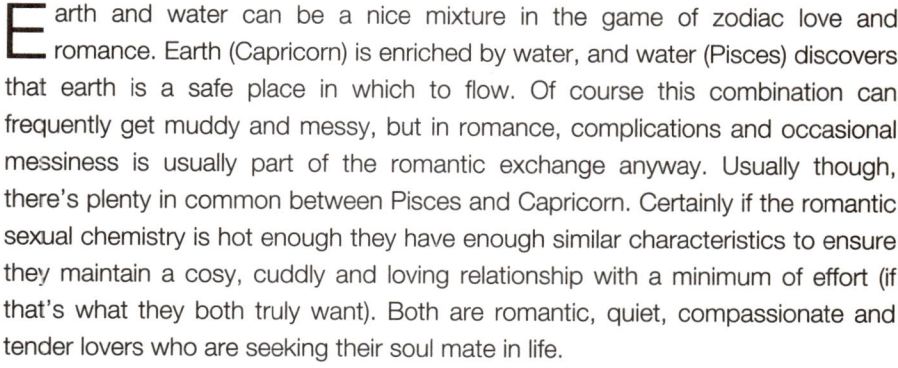

STAR CAPRICORN–PISCES COUPLE
Larry Fortensky and Liz Taylor

Earth and water can be a nice mixture in the game of zodiac love and romance. Earth (Capricorn) is enriched by water, and water (Pisces) discovers that earth is a safe place in which to flow. Of course this combination can frequently get muddy and messy, but in romance, complications and occasional messiness is usually part of the romantic exchange anyway. Usually though, there's plenty in common between Pisces and Capricorn. Certainly if the romantic sexual chemistry is hot enough they have enough similar characteristics to ensure they maintain a cosy, cuddly and loving relationship with a minimum of effort (if that's what they both truly want). Both are romantic, quiet, compassionate and tender lovers who are seeking their soul mate in life.

Although they believe in love *and* in each other, there are tensions along the way, and sometimes this relationship can suffer from burnout or boredom (an overdose of either or both). The one most likely to burnout is Pisces. The Fish doesn't like to be pressured or tested. Pisces hails from the rulership of the mysterious, elusive planet Neptune, ruler of the ocean, magic, dreams, spirituality and the unseen. This makes Pisces an otherworldly person with high intuition, creativity and an almost psychic ability to tune in to what other people are feeling. Capricorn, on the other hand, is a salt-of-the-earth sign ruled by Saturn, the planet of wisdom, reality, discipline and restriction. Though many Capricorns have an innate sense of 'knowing' (and can be quite wise), they are more practical souls who tend to believe only what they see. Sometimes when *super sensitive* Pisces and *insensitive* Capricorn get together they end up wounding and hurting each other, and Capricorn can be a little too demanding. Consequently, Capricorn is likely to become bored with Pisces (after the initial romantic passion has diminished).

Although they may experience highs and lows (or burnout or boredom), if it is in their stars for this couple to be together, then things have a way of working out and they teach each other great life lessons. Capricorns help Pisces get their thoughts, goals and responsibilities in order and make sense of life's confusion. Similarly, Pisces teach Capricorns to be less strict and stern on themselves and to give them the confidence to live their dreams, once in a while.

Capricorn woman — Pisces man

 The *'You are my wonder . . . my surprise . . . my biggest romantic test'* relationship

A Capricorn woman who knows exactly what she wants can be a powerful, awesome, force, something like a heat-seeking missile. She can tune into things and move on them with uncanny accuracy. Being a woman who usually gets what she wants, the Capricorn gal can often find the Pisces man a frustrating conquest. If she desires him to notice her, it's not that he's a difficult Fish to hook, but attracting his attention or getting him sometimes is far easier than keeping him. The big question is whether Goat gal can keep him dangling on the line long enough to reel him in. If she does, he's likely to be the lucky one, because he'll do very well in her company. She can give him focus and options he would seldom find without her. Being a Fish, Mr Pisces sometimes tends to swim around in circles, without really getting anywhere fast. Once Ms Capricorn appears in his life, he's likely to suddenly discover he's got sufficient jet-power to move him into new oceans of experiences. Ms Capricorn is a gal who can provide him with sufficient powerful structure in his life. She'll even be the wind beneath his Fish-wings if he'll let her, and he can be her Knight in Shining Armour if he can fulfil her many high expectations of what this 'knightly' role demands.

However, before they become the power couple of the future, like all good relationship beginnings, they are going to have to work out a thing or two before they can settle down into romantic bliss. For a start, Pisces man needs to be comfortable with the notion that he may occasionally need to play second fiddle to his gorgeous Goat love's social, business or family affairs. In any Capricorn gal's life there is a strong sense of responsibility and duty where financial security, social status and her parents and siblings are concerned. Even if she's a Goat without a traditional family unit or a job, you can rest assured she'll be a part of some kind of 'clan', have a major project she's tackling or be caught up in some kind of study or negotiation exchange. Initially, Mr Pisces will secretly enjoy the novelty of what Ms Capricorn brings into his world. She expands his horizons. He senses that this gal operates with an eye on the future. She offers a close-knit unity, and she represents the very things he desires most: stability and emotional security. But once their honeymoon phase is over and the once-charming notion of 'togetherness' begins to infringe upon his personal freedom, the Pisces man might begin to disappear quickly and quietly back to the peaceful watery depths from which he came. Ms Capricorn can make him feel like he should be busy all the time, or guilty that he isn't achieving more! When he stops coming home or starts making excuses one after the other for being absent, that's when Ms Capricorn had better start making things very attractive for him at home again.

Being an organised gal who loves to plan (given that he's the zodiac's most dedicated daydreamer), certainly Ms Capricorn needs to 'go easy' on her Pisces white knight. She needs to help him live his fantasies, not talk him out of them. Life is an adventure to the Piscean man and he loves the fantasy that comes along with living out his very own fairy tale. He's the director and producer of his life, making sure it is the most entertaining escapade of all time, complete with leading lady and a love affair to remember. This of course, is where things get tricky. Miss keep-both-feet-planted-firmly-in-reality Capricorn, may find his world of make-believe a little unrealistic, foolish and short term in its vision, and at times she'll say so. Her tell-it-like-it-is attitude may be direct and intended as constructive, but to her Pisces man, she may as well have cut his heart *out*. So

Ms Capricorn needs to learn to say nothing, rather than risk saying the wrong thing! The same goes for him. Mr Pisces also needs to watch his criticisms of his Capricorn stargal because sensitivity and diplomacy (whether they have it or not) can make or break this couple.

Unrestricted freedom, a respect for privacy and a reverence for unconditional love are paramount if Ms Capricorn wishes to continue merrily along the yellow brick road to relationship heaven, arm in arm with her Pisces lover man. He needs to be on his very best, most loyal and dependable behaviour as well. Hard as it may be for her to relinquish her powers of control (and Ms Capricorn loves to be in control), Ms Goat gal will be richly rewarded for her sacrifice. If she softens her approach and tunes into her feminine wiles, she has much to gain. He also needs to be consistent (something he often fails to achieve), and show he's made of long-term relationship stuff, as much as short term.

At least if they do pass the initial romantic tests, they can keep each other smiling. Such tender loving care can flow so freely from the Pisces man, as to almost take the Capricorn gal's breath away. Although this guy of the zodiac has been known to have a short-term attention span where relationships are concerned, if Miss Capricorn cherishes her Fishy beau's romantic sentiments and returns them to him so he feels safe and secure in her arms, his heart will be hers to keep. He too needs to ensure she's feeling secure, otherwise she'll start subtly shopping for her white knight elsewhere. But, the day that Capricorn gal attempts to rein in her Pisces guy, or decides she is far too busy to make time for him and for their romance, is the day the love-bubble bursts. You can quite literally see a Piscean man's heart break, however Ms Capricorn will only ever see it happen once. Frequently if he loses faith in her, Mr Pisces won't hang around long enough to be hurt a second time. The day Mr Pisces wanders in his loyalties, Ms Capricorn will build-up strong resentments and distrust against him that may be nigh impossible to remove.

Pisces man and Capricorn woman are certainly not carved from the same zodiac materials. Although they often complement each other, there are distinct differences that, unless acknowledged, can lead to problems further down the love track. Everything about Ms Capricorn's life is structured, boundaried and *formal*. By stark comparison, Pisces man is the epitome of *casual*. Tradition and custom have little place in his castle of dreams, but it is in this realm that Pisces man can really work his magic. He teaches his Capricorn sweetheart to relax and have fun; he makes her laugh, both at herself, and at the dismal things happening in the world around them. He gives her some dreams to dream, she gives him some foundation to build his dream. If he takes care enough of her, in return,

Ms Capricorn will ensure her Pisces lover remains grounded long enough, so as not to fly off with the birds to Never-Never Land. She will endeavour to give him a greater sense of purpose in life and the opportunity to be motivated, positive and productive. And if she gives him her love, she will give it completely.

In order for this love affair to withstand the test of time, the Goat gal needs to loosen her iron grip on reality, becoming less cautious and more willing to take risks on both herself and her Piscean partner. He needs to be committed and dedicated to this union too. Once her Fishy beau realises he has it all — the love he so desires, along with the trust and freedom paramount to his personal and emotional survival — he will give his heart away to her forever; and if he's proven himself to her, she will do the same in return.

Capricorn man—Pisces woman

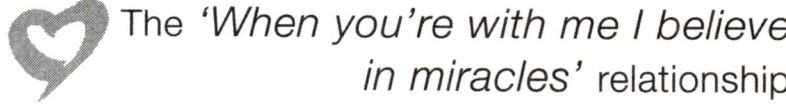 The *'When you're with me I believe in miracles'* relationship

Ms Pisces is a romantic woman and since she was a little girl she's dreamed about being rescued by her Knight in Shining Armour. The truth is, this gal often locks like a fairy tale princess; she is lovely in a feminine, enchanting and sweet way. Her eyes are normally big and dreamy and she often has silky hair, a soft voice and very feminine curves. Elizabeth Taylor, Drew Barrymore, Cindy Crawford and Vanessa Williams, all epitomise the graceful Pisces woman. So when her charming and gallant Capricorn man arrives on the scene, it's no wonder she often feels like a damsel in distress! You see, there is something positively masculine, sexy and heroic about him and he can make women go weak at the knees. It's no wonder Capricorn actors Mel Gibson, Kevin Costner, Denzel Washington and the late Humphrey Bogart, have had such success playing the chivalrous-hero type in movies, it just comes naturally to them.

Even though he's a dauntless and determined hero, the Pisces gal gets the feeling (*and* she can be quite psychic) that there is more to her Capricorn man than meets the eye. He's a tender man who can fear giving his heart away. He wants people to like and respect him, and he wants to do the right thing in life. Ms Pisces (being a dual sign) understands him and appreciates his tenderness and sense of duty in life. Though once she gets to know him better, the Pisces woman can be taken aback by his sternness, negativity and seriousness. She's an inspired thinker who often comes up with creative ideas that might not always seem practical. But that's part and package of her beauty. The Pisces woman is not bound by the rules that other people follow. She's entitled to dream and many times she does make her dreams come true. The Capricorn man has the ability to burst her bubble with a few words. He has his feet firmly planted on terra firma and she can often have her head up in the clouds.

Mr Capricorn is extremely practical and as he's very direct, he can sometimes insensitively label her behaviour, ideas or thoughts as 'immature' or 'ridiculous'. Though he might be right at times, he had better learn that taking away the wind from underneath his Pisces gal's wings will only lead to trouble. His sternness and disapproval can cut her like a knife. Ms Pisces is a sensitive woman (and often insecure), and she won't stay around long if he keeps raining on her parade. Of course, there are times that his organisational skills, discipline and determination serve her well. He is not a man who suffers fools, liars and procrastinators well and the Pisces woman is definitely the *latter!* She has the ability to put off everything, from her work and creative projects to making overdue phone calls and paying bills, with the simple phrase 'I'll do it tomorrow'. Mr Capricorn, however, loathes procrastination and he can help her not only *make* goals, but *achieve* them as well.

Thankfully, the Pisces woman is understanding, tolerant and adaptable, and if she loves her Capricorn guy she's usually willing to put up with his occasional inflexibility, harshness and domineering attitude! It takes patience to bring Mr Capricorn around to someone else's point of view, but Ms Pisces manages to do it with her compassion, good listening skills, tolerance and charm. She tends to work magic on him, and perhaps more than any other woman in the zodiac she has the ability to get her Goat guy to change his mind. The relaxed dreaminess of Ms Pisces makes the Capricorn man (who is prone to feeling tense, gloomy and negative) feel surprisingly loose and tranquil. With Ms Pisces by his side he's also more likely to break free from the serious strictness of ruling planet Saturn and kick up his heels.

She loves him because he is one of the most dependable, protective, caring, loyal and kindest men in the zodiac. Emotional security is important to Ms Pisces, and in the calm presence of her Capricorn guy, Ms Pisces feels snugly secure. His stability calms her restless spirit and she admires the way he expects so much of himself. The differences in their ambitions are not usually a problem. If they marry,

Ms Pisces is often quite content to raise their children, take care of their home and give him the support he needs. That's not to say that married Piscean women won't have successful careers, it's simply that her maternal instincts and love of creating a cosy nest for her family often override any aggressive career ambitions. Some Capricorn men are old-fashioned and prefer to be the 'sole provider' for their wife and family, but each Capricorn–Pisces couple will need to work out the best arrangement for themselves.

Though sometimes their relationship is marked by her super-sensitivity and his periods of glumness, Ms Pisces and Mr Capricorn find plenty of time to laugh. She, in particular, will constantly come up with funny ways to draw and tease him out of his periodic depressions. Ms Pisces has the ability to paint a picture of a funny story or scenario that will have him rolling on the floor in fits of laughter. Some Capricorn men can have a very dry sense of humour, while others are just plain wacky. Laughter, affection and romance mark their relationship and they tend to tell each other 'I love you' very often. Both are romantics at heart and Mr Capricorn is a true gentleman (just the kind of Knight in Shining Armour she was hoping for!), who'll spoil her with romantic dinners and special gifts marking their anniversary or her birthday. Both are close to their families and prefer quiet nights at home with a few friends than painting the town red. Crowds make them feel nervous.

Sex is an enriching and a profound experience for Capricorn and Pisces, as both believe that sex can't be separated from love. Their lovemaking is tender and emotional, and as there's plenty of trust in their relationship they are able to awaken new and unexplored sexual desires within each other. There will be times, particularly if they marry, where their desires will ebb and flow, but like any couple they need to be sure they make time for each other and to communicate what's going on. The Capricorn man carries his stress in his back and shoulders and he will adore her sensual massages as a prelude to sex. Like all earth signs it can take him longer to 'get in the mood' than water-ruled Ms Pisces. But there's a nice sense of cooperation and compatibility between Capricorn and Pisces as these two astro-lovebirds think along the same lines. The more they are together, the more they actually take on qualities of the other. Funnily enough, Mr Capricorn becomes more of a dreamer and Ms Pisces will start taking an interest in the stock market and managing their money.

aquarius aquarius aquarius aquarius
aquarius aquarius aquarius aquarius
        aquarius aquarius aquarius aquarius
    aquarius aquarius aquarius aquarius
aquarius aquarius aquarius aquarius
        aquarius aquarius aquarius aquarius
    aquarius aquarius aquarius aquarius
aquarius aquarius aquarius aquarius
        aquarius aquarius aquarius aquarius

    aquarius aquarius aquarius aquarius
aquarius aquarius aquarius aquarius
        aquarius aquarius aquarius aquarius
    aquarius aquarius aquarius aquarius
aquarius aquarius aquarius aquarius
        aquarius aquarius aquarius aquarius
    aquarius aquarius aquarius aquarius
aquarius aquarius aquarius aquarius
        aquarius aquarius aquarius aquarius

AQUARIUS

[21 january – 19 february]

romantic pursuit: extremely cautious

romantic vibration: difficult to fathom

secret love desire: to be closely intimate with their

lover, but have their own space for quality time

element: air

planetary ruler: uranus

symbol: the water-bearer

quality: fixed (= stability)

colours: electric blues and violet

gem: sapphires and opals

best companions: gemini and libra

strongest virtues: reliability, artistic talents

and bright vision of the future

traits to improve: emotional detachment, fear

of rejection, lack of appreciation for themselves

deepest desire: sharing their

lives with the right people

Aquarius celebrities

Alan Alda, Andrew Peacock, Anthony Lapaglia, Athina Onassis, Barbara Hershey, Benny Hill, Boris Spassky, Boris Yeltsin, Bridget Fonda, Burt Reynolds, Cathy Freeman, Charles Dickens, Christie Brinkley, Cybill Shepherd, Ellen DeGeneres, Emma Lee Bunton (Baby Spice), Farrah Fawcett, Geena Davis, Gene Hackman, Greg Norman, Heather Graham, Jane Seymour, Jennifer Aniston, Jennifer Jason Leigh, Jimeoin, John Belushi, John McEnroe, John Travolta, Linda Blair, Lisa Marie Presley, Matt Dillon, Mia Farrow, Michael Hutchence, Minnie Driver, Molly Meldrum, Morgan Fairchild, Mozart, Natalie Imbruglia, Natassia Kinski, Neil Diamond, Oprah Winfrey, Oscar De La Hoya, Paul Newman, Phil Collins, Placido Domingo, Prince Andrew, Princess Caroline of Monaco, Princess Stefanie of Monaco, Rene Russo, Ronald Reagan, Sheryl Crow, Sigrid Thornton, Stockard Channing, Tom Selleck, Vanessa Redgrave

AQUARIUS—AQUARIUS relationship

The *'I can give you everything but . . . myself'* relationship

STAR AQUARIUS–AQUARIUS COUPLE
Minnie Driver and Josh Brolin

This couple is born under the sign that has the reputation for being 'The Lone Rangers of the Zodiac'. Aquarians love their own company and because they have a need for occasional solitude, the two of them together could suit each other very well. They possibly realise the value of allowing each other some creative thinking space. But if they expect their partner to play the role of a constant, tuned-in companion, then this relationship could turn into a big disappointment — eventually.

Unlike other zodiac pairings, the Aquarius–Aquarius partnership, is in a league all of its own. Whether the partners want something different or not, they'll get it. This is one love match that keeps everyone guessing, including the zodiac's most unusual lovers themselves. Not that they seem to mind though. In each other, our Aquarian lovers hope that at last they have found at least one other soul in the Universe who actually sometimes *understands them*. Though they may find that holding this expectation of 'total understanding' has them barking up the wrong relationship tree.

For a multitude of reasons the road to romantic heaven is destined to be a bumpy, unpredictable ride for these two. So if you're an Aquarian who is in love with another Aquarian you are going to need to open up your romantic boundaries to let love in. That won't be too difficult if the magic of love is the real honest link between you two. And if you're prepared to go with the relationship flow, you're about to learn a great deal, both positive and negative, about love, yourself and others and what relationships are about (for both better and worse).

But be warned! To be successful, an Aquarius–Aquarius relationship has to operate from a deeper level of love, commitment and understanding than most relationships. It requires them to learn to love each other unconditionally. When and if you do manage to master this, then you'll find yourself both soaring off to love wonderland. If you don't manage to love each other unconditionally, you probably won't be around each other for very long; because you'll realise you just don't have enough interest in each other to keep things sizzling.

Aquarius woman — Aquarius man

 The *'You can fly anywhere you want with me at anytime'* relationship

This star coupling is kinda reminiscent of the Space Captain meeting one of Charlie's Angels. They are both interesting and unique individuals, but you somehow wonder what they are attracted to in each other — and you kinda guess it has to be sex and adventure! Certainly it's going to be a strange combination of male–female energies, and a very interesting one with an outcome that can't be predicted. When two individual's born under the same zodiac sign are attracted to each other there's special love-magic in the air; but with the Aquarian couple there's a neat twist to this magic.

As much as same-sign pairings sometimes provide a potential relationship bonus, they also often come at a price. In the case of the Aquarians joining up to create a relationship it can be just a bit too crazy or weird for both of them to handle over the long term. Where most same-sign couples can easily fall into step with each other better than most, this often doesn't happen for the Aquarian duo. Falling into step could be tough, as they both march to the beat of their own private drums; so let's hope their individual drums are beating at a similar rhythm or this could be a very discordant, out-of-step affair. And in the case of the Aquarius couple they are in a zodiac league of their own as they are truly unusual characters in their own right. By putting two Aquarians together you have one of the most unique, unusual relationship couples of the zodiac. While they may sometimes be bored with each other, outsiders are seldom likely to be bored observing them together or following their antics.

Nobody totally will ever understand what makes this couple tick (even the couple themselves). They are attractive, funny, very serious and also sometimes quite distant (from the world and from each other) and they usually say and do the last things most people would think imaginable. But who cares what makes them tick, *really?* Not our two airy-fairy, Uranian-ruled lovers. They are together, that's what matters to them and they are together to give it a shot. As many of them will tell you when they get married, *'If it doesn't work, well we'll just get a divorce!'* If ever a movie were made about two Aquarian lovers, it would be called 'A Strange Love Affair to Remember'. Even if these two do fall madly, deeply and truly in love and open up their hearts completely to each other (which doesn't happen very often for this sign anyway), it could take time for them to share their real feelings or needs with each other. This sign tends to live a lot in their own inner universe, the universe that exists between their ears, and because they think something in their mind, they often think they have said it out in the open (when they haven't). That's why they often leave unsaid the very things that need to be expressed to smooth over troubled waters or misunderstandings or to share special feelings.

Even if they can't always communicate well verbally, often they can be very connected on the invisible levels of communication. Like a set of identical twins, the Aquarian couple often possess an amazing ability to read each other's mind, or to finish the other's sentence for them. They frequently look a little alike or dress in a similar fashion too, though not always by choice, mind you. It's just that no one else on the planet seems to possess the same *curious* taste in clothes, or the ability to wear items that the rest of us would either give to charity or turn into nice cushion covers. That said though, they sure know how to stand out in a crowd; just think of Aquarians Yoko Ono, Princess Stefanie of Monaco, who actually ran off with a guy from the circus (how Aquarian is that?); and comedians, Ellen DeGeneres, John Belushi and Benny Hill.

However, with their uniqueness and differences, the Aquarian couple can find each other quite fascinating. They are likely to be bonded by their interest in rescuing stray animals, worrying over the starving children in Africa, or the oppression of the high rollers of society over the downtrodden people. This is a very humanitarian sign, so often this couple work well together for many different causes that inspire them.

Aquarius is also known as the sign of *geniuses*. Yep, Mr and Ms Aquarius belong to that select group of truly inventive, groundbreaking folk (Thomas Edison comes to mind) who think abstract thoughts and make the impossible seem quite within our reach. They might be experts at fathoming out riddles, doing crosswords, or one or both of them might even belong to Mensa or some other very important group. Knowing this sign's ability to be extremely intelligent, it's little wonder you find so many of them being honoured in the American Science Hall of Fame. On the other hand, statistics reveal that this sign is also to be found residing in mental institutions, so that shows how they can be extremely quirky, merging both genius and eccentricity, as a couple. Two of them together can come up with astounding concepts, dreams, ideas and projects.

Now one of the issues that might come between them is stubbornness. These airy souls can be quite immovable once they've made up their minds about something. Aquarius is a 'fixed' sign, which means, just that. In complete contradiction to their shock tactics, surprise-loving nature and belief in change, Aquarius guy and gal can be totally unbending at times especially where the cause for concern is themselves. By their own far-out reasoning, diversity is good, except when it directly involves their own lives.

It might be something fairly *simple* that causes discontent between these two zany lovers but it will never be *ordinary.* Not in the way you or I imagine (but then, 'ordinary' to us is not the same to any Water Bearer). It may be that Aquarius gal insists on cooking dinner every Friday night even though she has never once, put together anything that wasn't a disaster. In fact, it matters not that both are forced to order take-out as a result each week it's just that she does things her own way. Or perhaps her Aquarian beau has taken to wearing a scarf and beanie to bed, even in the middle of summer. No amount of coaxing, cajoling or downright intimidation will put an end to this bedtime fetish, not until *he's* good and ready, anyway. In true Trekkie style, 'resistance is futile' when facing-off against the fixed Aquarian resolve.

Like most aspects of their lives, sex between the Aquarian couple is bound to be a little on the *avant-garde* side. That is, almost nothing is out of the question or taboo when these two ignite between the sheets. Mr Aquarius and his like-minded zodiac gal are more prone to experiment with some wild and unusual sex, (gizmos, gadgets, books or ideas), even if simply to find out just what's so fascinating to others and to discover if 'hanging from the chandeliers' type sex turns them on or not. They can be irregular lovers who tend to run hot and cold, and naturally it greatly helps their sex life if they both run hot and cold in the same phases, otherwise someone is likely to end up going to bed in a cranky mood!

These two expect a lot from their partner. I know one Aquarian guy who insisted he and his wife take turns each Tuesday night to surprise the other with a home-cooked meal from another country, complete with traditional costume from the nation of choice — try doing that in a conventional relationship! It would only possibly work well in the highly inventive and creative Aquarian–Aquarian household (I'd imagine anyway).

In each other, Mr and Ms Aquarius generally have a better chance than most at finding that elusive (yet ever-so interesting and uplifting) love success that offers something unique. Will this couple live happily ever after? Who knows? But they are likely to have some interesting, challenging and unusually inspiring times, finding out.

AQUARIUS—PISCES relationship

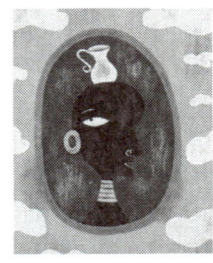 

The *'Let's go out and find us some stray animals to take care of'* relationship

STAR AQUARIUS–PISCES COUPLE
Natalie Imbruglia and Daniel Johns

When an Aquarian Water Bearer and a Pisces Fish join forces, a very intense aura of brightly-coloured lights, like a psychic rainbow suddenly exists between, and around them. And, if you're patient enough, you may catch a glimpse of it or witness some rather extraordinary magic when these two get together. Aquarians are, by nature, quite visionary, unique characters. They have the ability to imagine concepts and ideas that are way beyond the scope of most people. Pisces too, have a similar ability to contemplate the great, unsolved mysteries of the Universe (though their imaginings are more likely to be soft, dreamy illusions of wonderment, rather than abstract revelations.)

Put these two voyagers of the mind together, and you might discover you have a mutual admiration love society, all rolled up into a love affair greater than any amount of wishful thinking could ever conjure up. But that's only if there's magic between them. If they are operating on everyday levels, then this relationship possibly won't expand much farther than a couple of dates!

Aquarius woman—Pisces man

The *'Wanna come with me, on a magic carpet ride?'* relationship

When Ms Aquarius, Queen of The Extra-Ordinary meets Mr Pisces, King of the Realm of Dreams, no wonder there's an unusual sense of willful enchantment (and often abundant confusion) in the air. She's no doubt one of the strangest but most alluring, feminine gals he's ever come across, yet there's something about the way she moves that makes him take a closer look to check her out again. And, he is undeniably one of the most *interesting, charming and creative* individuals she's ever encountered anywhere (and believe me, she's met a *lot* of people!) Pisces man doesn't even mind that his Aquarian lady is a little left-of-centre either. He's so patient and downright accepting of other people's *idiosyncrasies* that no matter what colour she decides to dye her hair *this* week, it's okay in his books. No, it doesn't matter at all that she's unconventional, unpredictable and heck, totally off the planet. He can readily accept this as just part of the big plan (God's or whoever else he puts his faith in).

To her credit, Ms Aquarius won't poke fun at her sweetie's softer side or dismiss his emotions as something only other women (and out-of-the-closet men) experience. Truth be known, the mere fact that he possesses and displays a gamut of feelings is one of the many things that intrigues her about this mysterious man. But oh, there are other things as well. He has a level of tolerance only a Taurus Bull could rival and an open-mindedness to put a Sagittarian to shame. And when you're dealing with a woman as complicated and intricate as Ms Aquarius, you need all those virtues and more if you're going to make it safely down the relationship road with your sanity intact. But, more than anything, the Pisces man has seen it all — literally. Mr Fish has ridden the Karmic Ferris wheel non-stop through his many incarnations and there is little that will surprise or shock this cool, calm and collected Merman. He understands human nature like no-one else, and no-one else defies human nature as much as his Aquarian mate.

Magic does happen, and it's quite evident when Aquarius gal teams up with her Pisces guy. He dreams the dream, while she has the brilliance and visionary talent to make the dream a reality. She's ruled by Uranus, planet of revelation, shock tactics and surprise antics. He's ruled by Neptune, planet of alternate states, enchantment and wishful thinking. It's easy to see why this combination of air and water produces such a 'misty' effect. It's only when the mist turns to fog that this pair of lovers need to take care they don't bump into anything that might upset the apple cart of their romance.

Ms Aquarius in particular does need to remind herself on occasion that her Pisces boy is, and always will be, emotionally dependent on her. If her Pisces guy is one of those more emotional Fish men who wear their hearts on their sleeves (some, but thankfully few, Pisces men are quite the opposite, angry, embittered souls), it can sometimes get a little worn out, or slightly damaged if Aquarius gal forgets to mind her romantic manners. Unfortunately, when emotional warmth was being handed out, most Aquarians were off somewhere else unlocking the secrets to the Universe. It's not that they *don't* feel or anything, it's just that they're still trying to discover precisely how it all works, and whether they need to become actively involved in its development. So occasionally Ms Aquarius does tend to act more with a tough love approach than a gentle one; but this kind of rough edge to her can keep Mr Pisces dangling more intensely on her arm simply as she keeps him guessing at what she is capable of next. However, if Mr Pisces is a jack-the-lad type, he can also spin her heart around in cartwheels and sometimes cause her to have some sleepless nights worrying about where and who he is.

In truth, this pair of lovers, however different they may seem at first, share many similarities which make them fit together quite nicely when they make the effort. Though if you ask Ms Aquarius, it's the little distinctions between the two of them which make the relationship so remarkable (to her, at least!) Just as well her Pisces man is so darned *understanding!*

Aquarius man—Pisces woman

The *'I dreamed about you and knew I loved you even before I met you'* relationship

If you have a fertile enough imagination to conjure up a picture of Alice Through the Looking Glass, falling in love with the Lone Ranger and then going charging off around with him on his horse Tonto, then you could possibly catch a glimpse of what a romance between these two different, but also unique, zodiac personalities might be like together. Although one might think Alice would be looking for more attention and fantasy treatment than what the Lone Ranger possibly has the time or the notion to provide her ('cos he's such a busy guy); she's prepared to wait at home for him when he has things to do, 'cos he's worth it. And you can't stop the love planet Venus from making people fall in love, even the most unlikely of couples, as in this case.

Indeed, there are some things in life that are just *meant to be*, especially when it comes to falling in love. And if you believe in fate, destiny and true love, then you may believe that though they may be poles apart in their desires, hopes and wishes, if the planets and stars decree it then a long-lasting union between this zany Aquarian son of Uranus and this intuitive, dreamy fantasy Pisces daughter of Neptune could actually be meant for each other. But, only if they have some help from above, because unless there are some super powers aiding and abetting them they possibly just won't make it too long past the honeymoon phase.

As opposites so dynamically attract, imagine, the two of them eyes locked across a crowded room. He's usually someone who stands out for sometimes all the right and bizarre reasons. And if he's her starman (because she's so intuitive), she possibly trembles at the sight of him and knows — just knows — that this is *the one.* He's also got a psychic kind of mental radar that can bleep all kinds of romantic Morse code messages into his consciousness. His ears may prick up, his eyes may widen and his brain may suddenly go into a scramble. It's likely that he has an inkling that this gal is kinda *different* and straight away, he realises he must get to know her a little better. Well having established that fact, what does he do? As she has somehow subliminally got under his skin, then, he completely ignores her the rest of the evening. He avoids her. And because she felt psychically *sooo* connected to him, his behaviour of abruptness now makes her feel abandoned. Faced with his emotional stonewall or indifference and avoidance, it is very possible that she leaves; and if she's a real Pisces Mermaid gal with super sensitive feelings, she'll leave with tears streaming down her face. *How could anyone be so horrible?* she silently asks herself. *Where'd she go?* he wonders in between games of Twenty Questions and mathematical equations. As usual these two have hit each other's romantic bull's-eye but failed to communicate sufficiently to make the hit a successful one.

Okay. So not all good things romantically manage to get off to the flying start we'd like. But if you want something or someone badly enough (like these two might want each other if Venus is spreading the love bug through their veins), then you're bound to make your way past the obstacles and onto the true path of happiness. There could be some to-ing and fro-ing ahead. Mr Aquarius can't help that he doesn't quite know how to act around this gorgeous, vulnerable dreamboat who's caught his eye. He has to do his calculations first, to see how things might pan out. Once he's certain that the risk factor is low, and that there are several possibilities (all of them interesting), he may even surprise her with a 'Hi' at their next chance meeting (which almost startles her so that she jumps). She, by comparison, has already cried herself to sleep several times since their first meeting and wonders if they have any chance of a life together and if she is going insane, because she truly picked up that that guy kinda liked her and if he hadn't acted so weirdly, she would have been in his arms and into his heart in a matter of moments. In true Hollywood style, he had her (well and truly) at *hello.*

Once Ms Pisces cottons on to the fact that Mr Aquarius' apparent lack of interest means he is, in fact, wildly infatuated with her and trembling at the enormity of his feelings, then this relationship can finally start moving along at a respectable pace. Deep down, because Ms Pisces Princess is a highly psychic sign, she eventually (after her insecurities about herself are pacified) understands his motivations and actions better than he does, and realises his indifferent attitude is more a case of love fear than anything else. In fact, if anyone is more accepting of another person's peculiarities or foibles (because they have enough of these themselves), it's a Pisces and more importantly, a Pisces woman. She's kind-hearted and she truly believes and even appreciates that it takes all kinds to make the world go round. Once they've got over the initial panic attack involved in having feelings that are more intense than comfortable, then the Pisces gal will respect her
Aquarian guy's individuality and expects his quirky behaviour as surely as she

expects the sun to rise each morning. And he'll deal well with her ability to see and sense those special things about him that nobody else ever notices.

So, although she's not the usual type of gal he has been attracted to in the past, and she is ultra-feminine, intelligent and oh-so confusing, the Aquarian male may have finally met his match in this woman. He finds her fascinating. She can listen attentively to his original outlook, far-out concepts, crazy ideas and madcap notions, all without losing her marbles in the bargain. You can almost hear her Aquarian mate cheering loudly at how correct his initial calculations proved. He can't believe he's found a living, loving, receptive sounding-board with which to bounce off his theories and abstract thoughts. This is the girl of his dreams (or should that be deductive reasoning?)

Behind closed doors, this couple are so in-tune with each other sexually, it's scary. Especially when you consider that sex to an Aquarian male, for the most part, is just another one of life's mysteries waiting to be solved. Usually, once he's done a bit of research into the matter, Mr Aquarius changes the sheets and goes right back to sleeping (something he understands totally). Not so with his Piscean mistress. She teaches him all the passion, romance and deep physical commitment a Neptune-born seductress can, and he learns that not all mysteries in life *should* be solved, they should continue to be researched indefinitely. He ends up eventually becoming her star pupil in the bedroom.

So with the stars, planets and all the Universe around us, no wonder life is full of both big and small surprises; none more so than the attraction between these two star-crossed lovers. A mutual understanding and respect for each other's uniqueness is what makes this love affair a match made in heaven (or turns it into an emotional battle ground). There's plenty of potential for ever-lasting happiness if this fling becomes *the real thing*.

pisces pisces pisces pisces pisces pisces
pisces pisces pisces pisces pisces pisces
pisces pisces pisces pisces pisces pisces
pisces pisces pisces pisces pisces pisces
pisces pisces pisces pisces pisces pisces
pisces pisces pisces pisces pisces pisces
pisces pisces pisces pisces pisces pisces
pisces pisces pisces pisces pisces pisces
pisces pisces pisces pisces pisces pisces

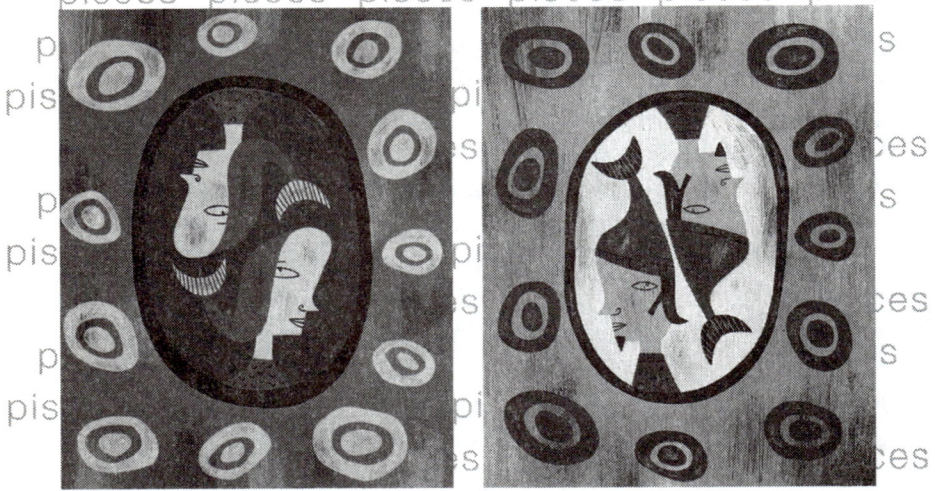

pisces pisces pisces pisces pisces pisces
pisces pisces pisces pisces pisces pisces
pisces pisces pisces pisces pisces pisces
pisces pisces pisces pisces pisces pisces
pisces pisces pisces pisces pisces pisces
pisces pisces pisces pisces pisces pisces
pisces pisces pisces pisces pisces pisces
pisces pisces pisces pisces pisces pisces
pisces pisces pisces pisces pisces pisces

PISCES

[20 february – 20 march]

romantic pursuit: zigzagging all over the place

romantic vibration: over-reactive and sensitive

secret love desire: to sail away with their lover to an

enchanted land where they continue to live happily ever after

element: water

planetary ruler: neptune

symbol: the fish

quality: mutable (= flexibility)

colours: greens and deep blues

gem: chrysolite and moonstone

best companions: cancer and scorpio

strongest virtues: intuition, adaptability and

creative approach to life

traits to improve: self-indulgence,

over-sensitive responses and lack of

faith in the future

deepest desire: to meet your true soul mate

Pisces celebrities

Aidan Quinn, Albert Einstein, Andrew Shue, Billy Crystal, Billy Zane,

Bruce Willis, Cameron Daddo, Chelsea Clinton, Chuck Norris, Cindy

Crawford, Dana Delaney, Daniel Johns, Drew Barrymore, Edward (Ted)

Kennedy, Elizabeth Taylor, Freddie Prinze Jr, George Harrison, Glenn

Close, Holly Hunter, Ivan Lendl, Ivana Trump, Jennifer Love Hewitt, Jerry

Lewis, Joanne Woodward, Jon Bon Jovi, Kurt Cobain, Kurt Russell,

Lleyton Hewitt, Liza Minnelli, Lynn Redgrave, Michael Bolton, Michael

Caine, Michael Chang, Mikhail Gorbachev, Nat 'King' Cole, Niki Taylor,

Nina Simone, Patsy Kensit, Peter Fonda, Prince Albert of Monaco,

Prince Edward, Queen Latifah, Quincy Jones, Rob Lowe, Robert

Altman, Ron Howard, Rove McManus, Rupert Murdoch, Shaquille

O'Neal, Sharon Stone, Sidney Poitier, Spike Lee, Téa Leonie, Thomas

Enqvist, Tom Arnold, Tony Robbins, Vanessa Williams, Willam Hurt

PISCES—PISCES relationship

The *'When we fall in love it will be just like a fairy tale'* relationship

STAR PISCES–PISCES COUPLE
Cindy Crawford and Randy Gerber

Once upon a time, on a far off planet called Earth there lived a beautiful princess. She was all alone and very sad, because she longed for true love to come her way. One day, she was sitting brushing her beautiful, long, golden hair and along came a gorgeous, breathtakingly handsome prince! At first glance, they instantly fell in love. Then they got married, produced a wonderful family of equally beautiful children that looked just like them, got a beautiful pussy cat called Isadora and a cute and cuddly puppy dog called Sam, and everyone lived happily ever after . . .

Sounds like the perfect romantic fairy tale, doesn't it? Well for you and I it might be a fairy tale but almost every Pisces princess has this fairy tale (or something pretty close to it) invisibly engraved upon her heart. Yes, subliminally she expects the fairy-tale romance to come true, maybe not for everybody else, but for her. Consequently wherever she goes and whatever she does as she goes through life, she expects this romantic fairy tale to unfold. Little wonder throughout the course of her life, especially as she passes through her teenage years and her prince hasn't arrived, followed by her twenties, thirties, and then by her forties she gets seriously worried.

When faced with the disappointment and disillusionment of everyday romance, she can become negative and even cynical where relationships are concerned. Although nowhere near as unrealistic, often her male Pisces counterpart tends to view romance with almost equally rose-coloured glasses (if not quite so outrageously as she) and after he suffers several relationship setbacks, and his own gorgeous princess seems to have missed him in this lifetime, he often ends up disillusioned too.

So considering the unrealistic fantasy expectations that naturally come as part of the Pisces duo's outlook, no wonder those born under this sign often have their hearts broken and spend a great deal of their lives trying to mend them again. So when a Pisces is romantically linked to another Pisces, their love connection is likely to be an intense and very heady experience. It can work wonders for them or turn into a double relationship heartbreak dilemma, dependent upon whether they are truly suited, in the same phase of evolution or ready for each other. But on a basic level, at least they want the same thing from each other (a total fantasy) and together, if the love stars favour them, they might just be lucky enough to create it.

At least these two have the opportunity to experience a depth of love emotion that churns up their souls and sets them apart from the rest of the zodiac. Certainly handled carefully and with a whole lot of romantic luck, this zodiac union has the potential to be a fairy-tale romance. And if they remain calm under pressure, are not too highly strung and over-reactive to the small stuff, then their romantic desires and needs may help them rise above some relationship adversity. However, the truth is that usually fairy tales are wonderful stories you read to children to send them to sleep at night, not something that you set your heart's compass towards living out in real life. But occasionally, fairy tales do come true and indeed they may for this couple. But there are definite potential relationship pitfalls ahead, and a great need for both the Pisces prince and princess to take it nice and easy when romantically aligning themselves with any individual of any sign, yes, even their own.

Pisces woman — Pisces man

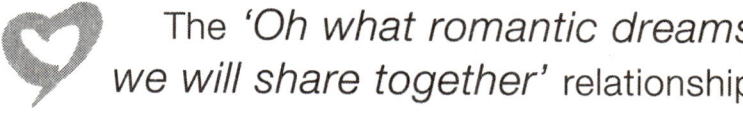

The *'Oh what romantic dreams we will share together'* relationship

When two individuals born under the same zodiac sign are attracted to each other there's special love-magic in the air. Nevertheless, just as much as same-sign pairings sometimes provide a potential relationship bonus, they also often come at a price. Naturally a same-sign couple have plenty in common and can sometimes understand and communicate with each other better than most. In some instances, however, the double-whammy of cosmic influences can spell disaster for even the most well-intentioned lovers. In the case of the Pisces couple though, there appears to be a greater chance for success in their romantic pursuits, so long as both are aware of the dangers that come with wearing the title of Fantasy King and Queen of the zodiac.

It's fair to say too, that there's a bit of neediness, dependency and romantic soppiness running around when two water signs join forces and this Pisces–Pisces match is certainly no exception. You've all heard about being swept away by a flood of emotion. Well, in this instance, keeping one's head above water can be an ongoing challenge. It's sink or swim, do or die, on many levels for the Mermaid and her Merman as to whether this pairing can stand up to the all-too-real test of time. One thing's for certain, there'll never be any lack of romantic intention between these two. Surprise candle-lit dinners, special treats, poetry and heartfelt messages left on answering machines are just some of the earthly delights awaiting the Pisces couple.

Pisces are born 'givers' and will go to almost any length to accommodate the wishes of others no matter how great the sacrifice on their part. But when there's real love involved, Mr and Ms Pisces will bask in the delight their efforts bring. But they also expect a great deal from their partners and if they give abundantly, they also expect a great deal back! Any shortfalls or disappointments that arise in the love exchanges that take place between them are quickly noted, remembered and brought up when arguments arise between them.

The dating phase of their relationship is often dramatic but extremely passionate and romantic. During the love-struck stage of the relationship, an amazing thing takes place. This couple somehow manage to leave the rest of the world behind, transcending into a world of deep, physical intimacy that leave most other couples for dust. While their love-making efforts may not appear as wildly passionate or experimental as some, this couple share a heart and body closeness that goes way beyond plain, old sex. A Pisces in love is probably the most generous lover of all.

Now being generous with caresses, kisses and cuddles is one thing, but when it comes to being generous or understanding in other areas, often the Pisces couple faces problems. Setting down 'fair exchange' between them on all kinds of levels often falls short of the mark for somebody. The Pisces man may be less generous with the quality time he spends with his true love than she expects him to be. Or she may not be as conscientious about the way she handles the couple's finances as he expects her to be. There's certain to be some emotional buttons being pushed between these two before too long; because just as much as they can get into each other's skin, they can also get under it and annoy each other.

Regardless of who brings home the bacon, most Pisceans unfortunately find the money they do accumulate slips through their fingers before they've had a chance to do anything sensible with it. When planning to make a nest together, this couple should set some definite ground rules and employ the assistance of a professional to help keep their finances in order; and dealing with money issues is often something that brings enormous rifts between them if they don't see eye to eye in this area of life.

In the home too, unless one of the partners is a neat freak (which occasionally does happen), you may also witness the less endearing qualities of this dreamy duo! Both would have decided early in life (and probably well before they got together) that chores such as dusting, vacuuming, mowing the lawn and scrubbing the shower were not for them. No sir-ee! If there's one thing many a Pisces hates to do it's housework. Even the few who will opt to pick up a can of Mr Sheen on the odd occasion are notorious for cutting corners and not doing the job properly wherever possible. Thankfully, as neither is inclined to worry about making (or leaving) a mess, this generally doesn't cause too much friction between these lovers (most of the time!) Ignorance is bliss and by a Pisces' reasoning, if you ignore the clutter around you, then it really isn't there. I'm sure somewhere there are a load of Piscean couples with very busy housemaids!

There's a lot more depth to the dual Pisces combination than in most relationships but not without its own set of unique problems. While everyone likes a happy-ever-after ending to a fairy tale, there are sometimes more than a few alternative endings for this pair of Pisces. As with the positive side to any match there's bound to be an equal amount of negative possibilities. There is a doubling of Piscean insecurities, jealousies and anxieties; a tendency towards idleness; lack of motivation; daydreaming; and a distinct separation from reality (which can sometime lead down the path of destruction to alcohol and drug dependency, just look at Pisceans Liz Taylor, Drew Barrymore and Kurt Cobain). Indeed in this relationship, it's quite possible for one or both partners to become almost 'addicted' to the other (remember Glenn Close in the movie *Fatal Attraction*?) Well, maybe that's a little extreme as most Pisces guys and gals are soft, compassionate souls. Just the same, to have one's love or affection unrequited or denied is like poison running through the veins of Mr or Ms Fish.

If these two can embark together on a path towards unconditional love, which means leaving each other a lot of emotional freedom to express who they truly are rather than constantly attempting to keep the other person happy at their own expense, this can be a magical love union. And so long as the Pisces twosome are content to swim freely with the tide, rather than fighting against the current and each other, there are plenty of long-term, wonderful partnership possibilities when these two pair up.

ABOUT ATHENA STARWOMAN

Athena Starwoman began learning to read the stars before she could sing the ABC. Her grandmother, also known as 'Starwoman', taught her the names of the constellations in the zodiac and by the time she was in first grade, Athena was already an adept astrologer.

Athena is today's leading international astrologer. As well as writing for magazines worldwide, in Australia, Athena's horoscopes appear regularly in *Australian Women's Weekly*. Her first book (published by HarperCollins and co-authored with Deborah Gray), *How to Turn Your Ex-Boyfriend into a Toad*, is an international bestseller and has been translated into six languages. Athena's latest book, *Zodiac*, a comprehensive astrology guide for the new millennium (also published by HarperCollins), has been reprinted several times.

You can connect with Athena at www.starwoman.com to get the latest and most up-to-date information about her and the astrological outlook.

[ASTROLOGY]

You can also hear Athena Starwoman's recorded weekly astrological updates for your sign by calling 1–900–957–014 for a cost of $1.05 per minute including GST (mobiles and payphones extra).

[PSYCHIC READINGS]

You can also have a personal one-on-one consultation with one of Athena's highly qualified psychics by calling Athena's Psychics on 1–902–220–265. Cost of these calls to a live psychic is $5.45 per minute including GST (mobiles and payphones extra).

[PERSONAL HOROSCOPES]

If you would like Athena to do your personal horoscope, please send A$95.00 (includes GST), along with your date, time and place of birth to Athena Starwoman at the address below.

[RELATIONSHIP (SOUL MATE) HOROSCOPES]

If you would like to find out whether or not you've found your true love and soul mate in a relationship, Athena can draw up your special relationship (soul mate) horoscope. Cost for the horoscope is $95.00 (includes GST). Please send your payment and order to the address below, along with the following information for BOTH you and your partner in order for Athena to draw up your relationship horoscope:

> your full names
> dates of birth (written in full)
> places of birth: the town, city, country (if you were born in a small place, please give the nearest major town so that Athena can locate the latitude and longitude)
> your mailing address to which the horoscopes shall be returned to you, as well as your phone number and email address in case further information is required to fulfil your order

Your Personal Horoscope or Relationship Horoscope shall be sent to you within approximately three weeks of receipt of your order. Please send payment, order and details to:

Athena Starwoman
PO Box 343, Main Beach QLD 4217
Australia

ZODIAC

Your astrology guide for the new millennium

Drawing on 40 years of astrological experience, Athena Starwoman's *Zodiac* offers a fresh 'new millennium' perspective on each star sign, from babyhood on. Athena examines the key areas of life (relationships, social connections, career, finances, health, mental outlook and spirituality) to describe each sign's unique characteristics for men and women. Gain a better understanding of yourself and others.

ISBN: 0 7322 6781 1